THE MAKING OF EASTERN EUROPE

Also by Philip Longworth

ALEXIS, TSAR OF ALL RUSSIA

THE ART OF VICTORY

THE COSSACKS

THE RISE AND FALL OF VENICE

THE THREE EMPRESSES

THE UNENDING VIGIL

The Making of Eastern Europe

From Prehistory to Postcommunism

Philip Longworth
Professor of History
McGill University, Montreal, Canada

Second Edition

St. Martin's Press
New York

THE MAKING OF EASTERN EUROPE

For information, address:

St. Martin's Press, Scholarly and Reference Division,
175 Fifth Avenue, New York, N.Y. 10010

First published in the United States of America in 1992
Reprinted 1993, 1994 (with corrections and new preface)
Second edition 1997

This book is printed on paper suitable for recycling and made from fully managed and sustained forest sources.

Printed in Great Britain

ISBN 0-312-17444-6
ISBN 0-312-17445-4

Library of Congress Cataloging-in-Publication Data
Longworth, Philip, 1933–
The making of Eastern Europe : from prehistory to postcommunism / Philip Longworth. — 2nd ed.
p. cm.
Includes bibliographical references and index.
ISBN 0-312-17444-6. — ISBN 0-312-17445-4 (pbk.)
1. Europe, Eastern—History. I. Title.
DJK38.L66 1997
947—dc21 97-1346
CIP

[redacted]

To Ruth, happy companion who shared most of the joys and travails of the journey

Contents

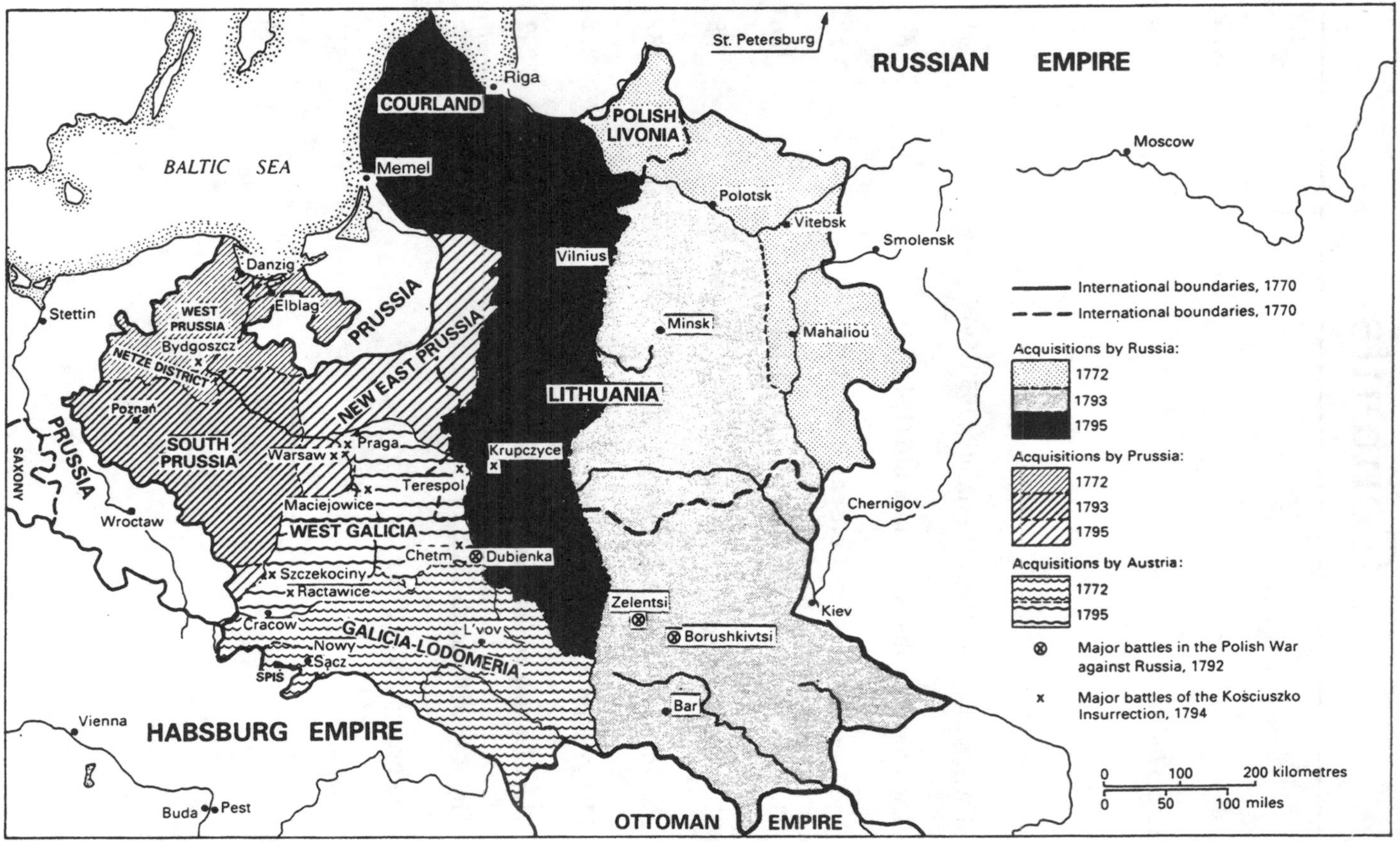

The partition of Poland, 1772–95

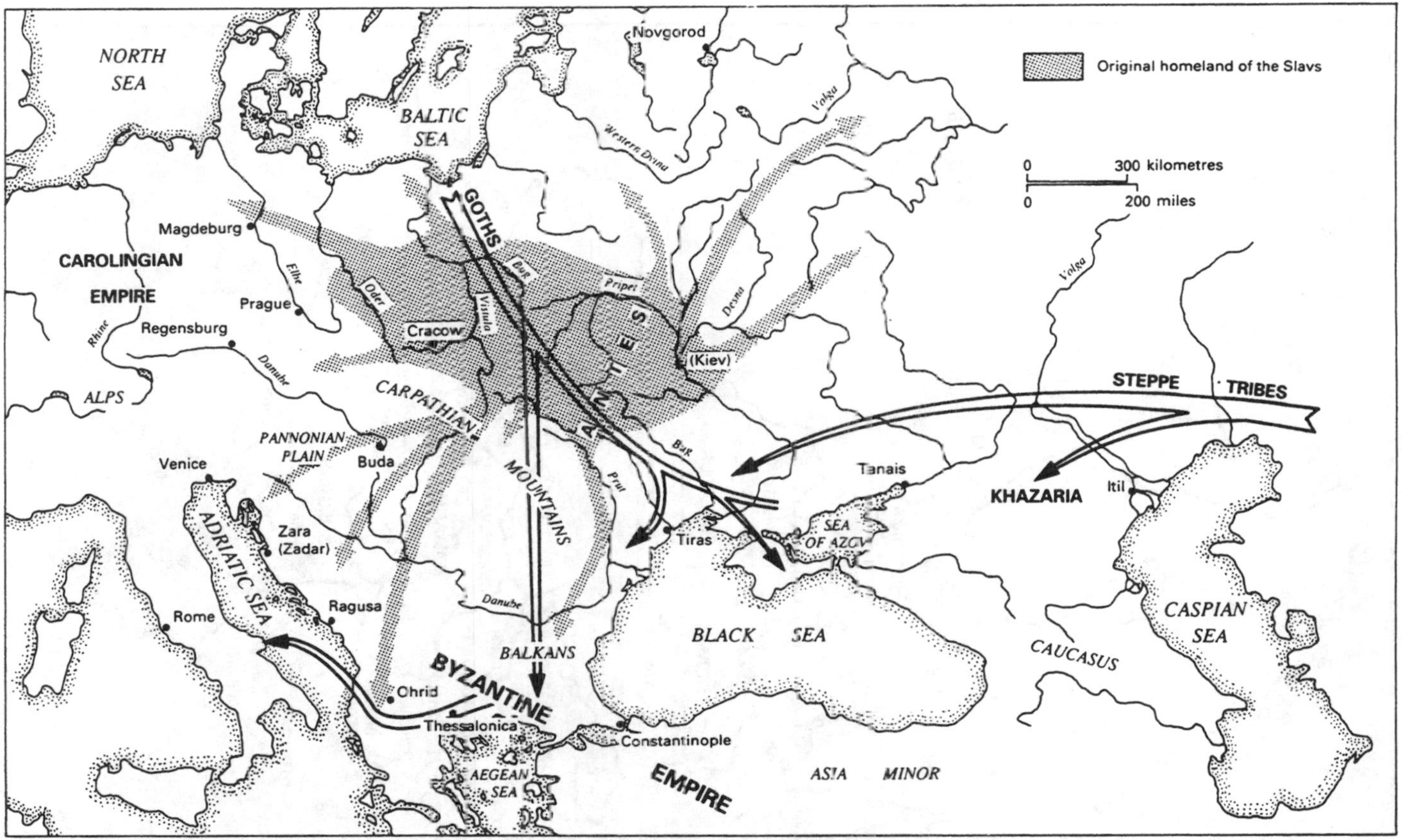

Eastern Europe, AD 250–800

Russia and Eastern Europe, 1994

Preface to the Second Edition

This edition allows me to update the book with a new introduction and an extra chapter analysing the collapse of Communism and the advent of post-communism. The opportunity has also been seized to correct several mistakes and take account of recent findings (on such diverse matters as the Hungarian revolution of 1956 and the death of 'good' King Wenceslas).

The first edition met with an unexpectedly generous reception – unexpected because the book broke conventions in the writing of history, and because it challenged widely-held assumptions about Eastern Europe and its fate. It was not gratuitously controversial however, and the combating of widespread, and serious, misconceptions about an important part of the world was not its only purpose.

At a time when many bookshops give more space to the occult than to history; when deconstructionists among historians have been trivializing their craft, and when most history taught in schools is confined to the recent past, there is a need to assert the fact that history can serve useful purposes other than to promote national pride and to legitimate causes. *The Making of Eastern Europe* was intended as a modest contribution towards this end, to assert the value of historical enquiry, to demonstrate history's contemporary relevance.

A good understanding of the roots of problems can make an important contribution towards their solution or containment; an understanding of how the past has shaped institutions, mentalities and traditions can have political value in helping to define the limits of the possible; and what happened (or failed to happen) in the distant, as well as in the recent, past can be helpful in managing the present. But, recognizing that historical understandings are refined by exchanges of opinion, I also hoped that the book would stimulate argument; and it has done so.

Not all critics agreed with my methods and my findings. Some were disturbed by the anti-chronological method (though others were intrigued by it). I retain it for my original reasons: it allows readers with little knowledge of Eastern Europe to acclimatize themselves gradually to the world of unfamiliar peoples, institutions and mores. Furthermore a chronological format would have lacked rationale. Histories which cannot claim to be comprehensive should be explicit about their assumptions and their purposes; and about what is regarded as relevant. In this case the historical agenda was dictated by the historical enquiry; and since this was a search for the roots of a complex series of problems it had to proceed from the present into the past.

The book has been characterized as a personal view.[1] In a sense all histories are. It is a view, however, which takes account of other views, and of evidence. I have not diverged lightly from conclusions that others have come to. This said, evidence can sometimes bear alternative interpretations, and percipient critics have drawn attention to matters I neglected and issues I had not considered. As a result I have sometimes changed my mind.

A case in point was the scant attention I paid to the First World War.[2] Although it was the consequences of the war, not the details of campaigns that were important to the argument, I am now inclined to attribute more significance to that war and to the civil wars which followed, not least in stamping a mentality of total war on the Bolsheviks. This makes it easier to explain their ruthless treatment of dissidents, their mobilization of opinion through propaganda, their organization of the economy, and their furious assaults on economic and agrarian problems.

Three other points of substance raised by critics touch on important issues and call for comment. They concern obstacles to the creation of a 'civil society'; serfdom; and legal formation.

Alexandru Dutu has suggested[3] that the bourgeoisie was perhaps even more to blame than the nobility for the failure to develop a 'civil society'; and that a disinclination to engage in the political process encouraged low standards in public life and the rise of mediocrity. The bourgeoisie was small, of course, and often alienated from the masses (though it contributed to this alienation); and difficulties in communication also played a part. But the question is worth pursuing further because it bears on current prospects of developing a workable participatory democracy in Eastern European countries.

The second issue of substance was raised by Antoni Maczak[4] who challenges my rejection of the 'second serfdom' (see note 13 of Chapter 8). I am still inclined to follow the argument of the late David Prodan, the great authority on serfdom in Romania and Transylvania, on the matter; and other critics have endorsed my opinion. Nevertheless Professor Maczak's evidence cannot be ignored. Our divergent views may yet be reconciled in a formula that takes account of local variations and differences of legal understanding. Meanwhile they demonstrate the fact that historical conclusions are rarely cut and dried.

Jan Havranek[5] has taken me to task on another matter affecting 'civil society': regional differences in legal development. The question involves the geographical limits of Roman Law and of the Byzantine legal tradition in which the wishes of the state are paramount. His view reinforces the distinction between East-Central Europe and the remainder of the region, and I accept much of his argument. But he has not persuaded me on all counts. Roman Law, whose influence was greater to the east than to the west of the Rhine, also accorded wide authority to rulers and less legal space to individuals;[6] and in most areas to the north of Hungary the Church was effectively subordinated to the local secular authority. In any case I did not mean to give the impression that legal traditions alone explained the absence of a 'civil society'. Social developments and intellectual fashions were also relevant; and in these respects the situation prevailing in East-Central Europe was broadly similar to that in the rest of Eastern Europe.

I am indebted to these and other friendly critics, colleagues and students, both in Eastern Europe and the West, for widening the discussion and pointing out errors; to the Social Science Research Council and McGill University for support enabling me to spend several months in Eastern Europe in 1986–8, to re-visit four countries of the region in 1993 and 1994; and to others, notably Constantin Giurescu, Miroslav Hroch, Zbigniew Landauer, Emil Niederhauser and Jerzy Topolski for information and advice. The shortcomings of the book, however, are my own responsibility; and, as before, my greatest debt is to my wife, Ruth.

PHILIP LONGWORTH

December 1996

REFERENCES

1. Robin Okey, *The Slavonic & East European Review*, vol. 73 (1995), pp. 131–2.
2. Raymond Pearson, *Irish Slavonic Studies*, pp. 149–50.
3. Alexandru Dutu, *Sud-estul in contextul European*, Buletin II, Romanian Academy, Institute of South-Eastern Studies, Bucharest 1994, pp. 9–11.
4. Antoni Maczak, *The American Historical Review*, vol. 98, no. 4 (1993), pp. 1288–9.
5. Jan Havranek, *Journal of Modern History*, vol. 67, no. 4 (1995), pp. 979–82.
6. See M. Rady in M. Fulbrooke, ed., *National Histories and European History* (Boulder, 1993), pp. 163–82.

Introduction

This is not as we were formerly told.

Edmund Blunden, *Report on Experience*

In 1989, the bicentenary year of the French Revolution, another *ancien régime* began to crumble. With an exhilarating rapidity and amid great rejoicing, the Soviet empire in Eastern Europe began to collapse. The two Germanies were soon reunited, and within two years the Soviet Union itself disintegrated. So did Yugoslavia. And then the Czechs and Slovaks broke their union and went their separate ways. Communism had been vanquished; an ideological system which had held half Europe in thrall for decades suddenly dissolved. Frontiers were opened; controls and censorship removed; the captive nations freed. It was exciting, unexpected, almost miraculous.

In both the east and the west the transformation was greeted with delight and pundits predicted a rosy future for the region. A few experts raised doubts about the great change. The Communist Bloc countries, some thought, had done better than most others in the world in terms of 'agricultural growth, the elimination of poverty and the creation of human capital'; and overall much better 'than their popular image would suggest'.[1] But such voices were drowned out by the chorus of rejoicing: an oppressive system had been vanquished. A deformed economic system had demonstrated its failure. Democracy would now empower the people; civil society would be swiftly restored; participation in the world economy would bring prosperity to millions, enabling them to live normal lives; and a new, benign world order, presided over by the USA, would henceforth ensure universal security.

It did not work out in quite that way. The seven lean years which followed the revolution showed these expectations to have been wrong on almost every count. So far from bringing security, the world became more dangerous: vicious civil wars broke out in a region that had been at peace for decades. The price of liberty turned out to be increased lawlessness and the rise of mafias;[2] and the expected economic miracle failed to materialize. The advent of a market economy brought prosperity to a few, but poverty to millions. The expected flood of Western aid turned out to be a trickle. More money probably left the region than entered it. And capitalism, as it transpired, could not work its wonders without capital.

The transition from the planned to the market economy involved the reduction of subsidies, the freeing of prices, and the privatization of industry and agriculture. The process was sometimes swift, as in Poland, sometimes fitful and incomplete, as in Russia, and sometimes, as in Bulgaria where successful collective farms were broken up into uneconomic units, injudicious. But it was everywhere difficult and always painful.

These problems of transition were exacerbated by the reorientation of Eastern Europe's commerce. The determination of the newly liberated Bloc countries to cut away every trammel of the Soviet Union led, in June 1991, to the dismantling of the Bloc's trading organization COMECON. This, together with the dissolution of the Soviet Union which followed soon afterwards, proved to be economically disastrous.

Enterprises throughout the region immediately lost assured markets for their products. Prompted by a sense that they were returning to the West, to which they naturally belonged, many countries expected the West to provide alternative markets for them. They were to be disappointed. The West did not want goods which were inferior nor produce which undercut its own. So production shrank. By the time the mistake was recognized it was too late.

When the dust began to settle the landscape looked bleak. By 1995 the countries nearest the West had begun to experience a modest economic upswing. Even so, that year Poland's economy generated less wealth (GDP) than it had done in 1989; Hungarian, Czech, Slovak and Romanian GDP was 14 per cent below the 1989 level, those of Bulgaria and Albania 25 per cent below, and in the Baltic States and Russia matters were even worse.[3] In 1996 the Russian economy was at last expected to grow again, for the first time since 1989[4] – but over a base which had been slashed by almost half. And some countries, like Ukraine, were continuing to grow ever poorer.[5]

As economies were dislocated and government incomes shrank, public services were disrupted, and medical care and welfare services declined. There were even some breakdowns in public health. Over most of the region psychosocial stress increased, the position of women declined,[6] and death rates soared. In 1995, by which time the economic situation was said to be improving, the United Nations Children's Fund reported:

> there is as yet no clear and general evidence that the welfare crisis that has been affecting the region … is approaching an end.[7]

Visitors from the west were often unaware of these costs, and gained an entirely positive impression of post-communist recovery. They stayed in comfortable hotels, ate in good restaurants, and saw busy streets and shops well stocked with luxuries and Western goods. All this seemed to indicate general prosperity. But appearances were often deceptive. The restaurants were full of foreigners, not natives; the goods in the shops were priced beyond most people's pockets, and many of the imported comestibles had passed their sell-by dates. The centres of capital cities were not like the depressed industrial towns and the privation was not very visible. Poverty tends to hide itself indoors.[8] But popular disillusionment with the fruits of liberation was increasing.

It found partial expression in increased migration. Although there was an inward flow of returning émigrés (some to help rebuild their countries, to reclaim family property, to retire or die – but also carpetbaggers and extremists barred by the old regime) the outward flow was much greater. Between 1987 and 1990 the westward movement of people from the region tripled to almost a million a year. By 1992 it doubled again.[9] In 1993 controls on the West's frontiers with Eastern Europe became more stringent and Germany revised its generous law governing the admission of refugees. The wall between east and west, erected by the Communists to prevent Eastern Europeans leaving, was now effectively re-erected by the West in order to keep them out. Discontent also found expression in the ballot box.

At first every difficulty had been attributed to the old regime; former Communist leaders, like Todor Zhivkov of Bulgaria and Ernst Honecker of East Germany were put on trial; and elsewhere former officials were removed from their posts and barred from seeking office. Sometimes, as in the Czech Republic, this process was referred to as 'lustration', a ritual cleansing. But there was little popular enthusiasm for revenge; and the credibility of those who attributed all the woes of the age to the Communist inheritance began to wane. The perception spread that some post-Communist leaders might be no better than their predecessors (indeed the Berisha regime in Albania seemed even more oppressive), and that the revolution had only served to exchange subjection to Moscow for rule by the International Monetary Fund.[10]

Anti-Communists were soon voted out of office everywhere except the Czech Republic. Even Lech Walesa, standard-bearer of the 'Solidarity' movement, lost the Presidency of Poland, though Vaclav Havel, once the personification of anti-Communist resistance, remained President of the Czech Republic, albeit as a complaisant figurehead. Yet though nostalgia for the certainties of the old order had been growing and former Communists were returned to power almost everywhere, there was no prospect of Communism returning with them. The economic cornerstone of Communism had been shattered. The land of lost content as some, to their surprise, were now coming to regard the old order, could not be resurrected.

On the other hand the public was becoming disenchanted not only with the post-Communist political leaders but, as declining turnouts at elections indicated, with the democratic process itself.[11] There was a retreat into privacy; and apathy became widespread. By 1995 freedom of expression, a luxury to savour five years before, had become commonplace. The revolution had produced a profusion of publications about everything and nothing but books had soon become difficult to sell, and writers, including former dissidents, lost the social cachet and political importance they had once enjoyed.[12] Only pornography retained an appeal.

It became clear, indeed, that the collapse of Communism entailed the disintegration of a moral order. This made it easier to confuse swindlers with entrepreneurs and freedom with licence. Respect for authority declined and corruption increased. The churches found it difficult to fill the moral gap; and when they asserted themselves, they became embroiled in public squabbles, as in Catholic Poland and Hungary, over education, abortion and the retrieval of property taken over by the state.

Malaise also afflicted the arts – not only because of the huge cutbacks in subsidies and inflation which threatened all kinds of artistic enterprises from opera to the circus, but, now that control by the authorities was broken, a moral uncertainty too. Critical standards lapsed; contempt for culture became more widespread. Now that anything was permitted, little seemed valuable.

Problems arose with education and in academe. The privatization in agriculture encouraged parents to withdraw children from school to help on the farm. Financial cutbacks led to the closure of schools for lack of heating, and to arrears in teachers' pay. Academics generally became impoverished. There were several positive developments: Marxism-Leninism was banished from the curriculum and attempts made to resurrect philosophy. But high standards had prevailed in several areas of research under the old regime, and these were threatened by the transition. Had it not been for the personal intervention of the capitalist millionaire George Soros, parts of the research establishment might have been destroyed entirely.

Most countries of the region managed to avoid violent civil strife despite the pain of the transition, but there was a violent flare-up in Moldova, bitter wars in the Caucasus and civil strife in Croatia and Bosnia. These conflicts were widely attributed to resurgent nationalism which offered itself as the most convenient ideological alternative to communism. Yet most Eastern Europeans were not extreme in their nationalism. The civil wars which broke out, and the atrocities associated with them, were precipitated by radicals from the fringes of society, and sponsored by political interest based abroad as well as within the countries concerned (See Chapter 1).

All the efforts of European diplomacy and intervention by the United Nations organization failed to bring the conflicts in Yugoslavia to an end. Eventually it was the United States which did so. Croatia regained Slavonia and the Dayton Accords promised peace to a divided Bosnia.

Nonetheless it was not the United States, but Germany, which emerged as the dominant economic power in both the Balkans and East-Central Europe.[13]

* * *

The collapse of the old Communist order suggests that Eastern Europe may have lost significance as a useful term in political geography. Poland, Hungary and the other countries between Germany and Russia are often viewed as parts of an enlarged Central Europe; and if NATO should extend its membership eastward this understanding would be reinforced. It would also conform to an earlier pattern when the old battle-line of the *antemurale christianitatis*, Christendom's first line of defence, guarded Catholic Europe against the schismatic Orthodox of Russia and the infidel Turks in the Balkans.[14]

Furthermore, particularists will insist that, since each of the region's constituent nations is visibly and audibly distinct, it is unreasonable to treat them as a unit. How can Poland be compared to Bulgaria, or Hungary to Russia? Would it not be more sensible to treat Europe as a zone of gradual change from the quintessential West, represented by Britain, France and the new engine of the European economy, Germany, to the quintessential East represented by Russia and the Balkans?

These objections have force, and the national differences are undeniable. But so are the features, and historical tendencies, that these countries share.[15] Though ideology and direction from Moscow no longer give coherence to the region, the legacy of Communism does. Its social engineering and the rigidities of planning left deep marks. So did its encouragement of expectations – for full employment and cradle-to-grave welfare. And the relative poverty of these countries, which makes them unacceptable candidates for membership of the European Union, also ties them together. Furthermore the historical formation of the region sets it apart from the West.

A division between Eastern and Western Europe existed in the time of Charlemagne. For the greater part of the last millennium the lands of Eastern Europe have been characterized by endemic shortage and poor development. The demography of the two Europes was distinct, their linguistic history largely different; and Eastern Europe has long been peripheral to the world economy. Its population's attachment to democracy has been both uncertain and of brief duration; its institutions were weaker than the West's, its legal formation less developed. Certain distinctive inclinations and habits of mind also arose: tendencies to bureaucracy and collectivism; stronger urges to national self-realization than to personal autonomy; a disposition to ideology. And love of poetry, idealism and cynicism are all more evident in Eastern Europe than in the West.

These historically formed traits and tendencies were explored in the first edition of this book;[16] but recent developments raise questions which demand a new enquiry. Why precisely did communism collapse? Why did its collapse take everyone (including those who thought it doomed) by surprise? Why were hopes of a successful transition to democracy and the free market so strong? Why did the aftermath prove so dangerous and disappointing? Why should the Soviet Union have disintegrated and Yugoslavia dissolved in chaotic civil wars? To understand these matters we must turn the clock back to the seventies when Communism seemed to be flourishing and the Soviet system was in its prime.

REFERENCES

1. Frances Steward, *The Times Literary Supplement*, 26 January 1990.
2. Including the smuggling out of nuclear materials and prostitutes to the West – see, for example, Stewart Tendler, *The Times*, London, 3 December 1994, p. 17.
3. *Financial Times Survey: Investing in Central and Eastern Europe*, 15 April 1996, p. ii. The 1995 figures are based chiefly on government estimates; those for 1996 are projections by the European Bank for Reconstruction and Development (hereafter EBRD).
4. Economist Intelligence Unit (hereafter EIU) *Country Report: Russia*, 1st quarter 1996, p. 7. In some other successor states to the USSR, however, the economies were expected to shrink – see EIU *Country Report: Ukraine*, 1st quarter 1996, p. 9.
5. There were discrepancies in performance explained by a number of factors: that some transitions, as in Hungary and Slovenia, had begun earlier (or, as in Albania, later) than others; the relative state of economic health beforehand (Poland's poor state before the transition flattered her achievement since); the levels of foreign, especially German, investment; and degrees of social stability and public tolerance. In general, transitions were much more difficult in large economies like Russia's than small ones like Hungary's. For a more detailed treatment, see Chapter 1.
6. See the essay by Gail Kligman in J. Millar and S. Wolchik, eds, *The Social Legacy of Communism* (Cambridge, 1994).
7. UNICEF Regional Monitoring Report No. 3: *Central and Eastern Europe in Transition: Public Policy and Social Conditions* (Florence, 1995), p. 1. For data on mortality see p. 12.
8. Personal observations in Warsaw, Lodz, Prague and elsewhere in 1993.
9. NATO Colloquium, *Economic Developments in Cooperation Partner Countries from a Sectoral Perspective*, Brussels 1993, pp. 79–105.
10. The IMF sometimes dictated changes in a broad range of domestic policies as conditions for its essential loans. For example, in Romania IMF conditions even extended to education.

11. See, for example, Slawomir Majman in *The Warsaw Voice*, No. 20, 16 May 1993, p. 8.
12. The revolutions produced a flood of publications. In Romania hundreds of periodicals appeared concerned with everything and nothing – from *Bun Ziva* [Hello!] 'the independent weekly for everybody' to a monthly 'journal of social and cultural commentary' published by the Young Heroes' Club; and from *Rebirth*, 'the Christian culture periodical of the Christian Democratic National Peasant Party', to an 'entertainment weekly' sponsored by the Association of Private Detectives.
13. See Joan Hoey, 'Germany's new drive eastwards', *Economies in Transition: Eastern Europe and the former Soviet Union: Regional Overview*, EIU London, 1st quarter 1996, pp. 5ff.
14. This was the conception of Oskar Halecki in his *Limits and Divisions of European History* (London, 1950) and *The Borderlands of Western Civilization* (New York, 1952). But these works are skewed by Russophobia, ignore the economic dimension, and present flawed arguments in respect of culture. Tomas Masaryk had earlier envisaged a 'Central Europe' stretching from Norway to Greece; and variations on these themes have been played by many scholars more recently (See, for example, the journal *Cross-Currents* [Ann Arbor], and the special issue of *Daedalus*, 1990). But there are problems with some of these visions, too – see my 'Selective Affinities', *The Times Literary Supplement*, No. 4512, 22 September 1989, pp. 1028 and 1038. Z.A.B. Zeman (*Pursued by a Bear*, London, 1989) sees these countries as vacillating between 'Eastern' and 'Central' according to whether Germany or Russia is the dominant power.
15. Remarks by the Polish scholar J. Jedlicki are suggestive here. See 'The Revolutions of 1989: The Unbearable Burden of History', *Problems of Communism*, July–August 1990, pp. 39–45.
16. See also the notable discussion of J. Szucz, 'The Three Historical Regions of Europe', *Acta Historica Scientiarum Hungaricae*, 29 (2–4) 1983 [1984]. Also R. Okey, *Eastern Europe 1740–1980* (London, 1982).

1
The Collapse and its Aftermath

Make the Revolution a parent of settlement, and not a nursery of future revolutions.

Edmund Burke

The distance separating the rich from other citizens is growing by the day.... The realm is divided into two classes: the greedy and insensitive, and murmuring malcontents.

Louis-Sebastien Mercier (1789)

Many reasons have been advanced for the collapse of Communism. It has been ascribed to America's achievement of military superiority over the Soviet Union through 'Star Wars'; and to the revolution in communications which made censorship impossible. It has been seen as a series of popular revolutions, as the triumph of nationalists and dissidents, as a victory for human rights activists and the Helsinki accords. It has also been attributed to the rise of a new generation, to an economic crisis, and to the errors of the last Soviet leader, Mikhail Gorbachev.

Not all of these explanations bear scrutiny. 'Star Wars' was not a perfect shield against Soviet nuclear missiles; the United States government was obviously astonished by its 'victory', and Western countries were almost as grateful as the Soviet Union for the 'peace dividend' it brought. Ideology played a part in the great change – though more through a decline in Communism's credibility than an attachment to Western values. Human rights issues may have been important in the Western world, but they made little impression on opinion in Eastern Europe. Nor does the evidence suggest that, though the crowds played a part in them and we expect tyrannies to be overthrown by the people, these were essentially popular revolutions. Furthermore, although some dissidents inherited the revolution, they did not make it. Indeed, shortly before the Revolution several leading spirits among them despaired of success in the foreseeable future.[1]

The causes of the greatest turn in recent history have, indeed, been widely misunderstood. Yet a rounded understanding of exactly what happened and why it happened is important, because of the light it throws on the disappointments of the post-Communist age and the problems confronting the region today.

So far from being simple the causes were several, complex and interconnected. The revolution derived in part from a sluggish response both to technological change, and to a growing generation gap. Individual decisions also contributed; so did changes in weather patterns; and at a deeper level it owed something to demographic developments (the chronic underpopulation of the USSR, overpopulation in Albania, and an aging population elsewhere). But above all, as with the French Revolution, it was a consequence of economic crisis[2] – perhaps a 'crisis of capitalism' which Marxists might have been expected to have noticed.

The crisis coincided with the collapse of authoritarian regimes in Spain, South Africa, Brazil and Chile; with an accommodation with private enterprise in China, and the state's withdrawal from involvement in the economy in India and elsewhere. And the West was affected by the crisis too. Unemployment rose; the gap between rich and poor widened, and, as business became globalized, governments everywhere found their ability to maintain income from taxation diminishing and with it their power to manage social problems. Privatization became a universal recourse, but most of the new rich displayed a rather poorer sense of social responsibility (*noblesse oblige*) than the privileged classes of the past.

Yet although the West also suffered from this uncomfortable transition, the effects on Eastern Europe proved more dramatic. This was surprising in so far as the Eastern Bloc economies had traditionally been insulated against world market forces. How then could they have been embroiled in such a dangerous capitalist crisis?

One root of the problem lay in a centralized planning system in which prices were unrelated to cost or demand. Intended, in part, as a bulwark against world market forces, it seemed to represent the realization of a dream born of the Enlightenment (see Chapter 6): man's mastery over the economy as over nature. But this was unrealistic. Since enterprises were not rewarded for profits nor penalized for losses, resources were used wastefully. And since quantity rather than quality of production was encouraged, stocks of inferior, unsaleable products grew. This is not to belie the fact that Soviet Bloc products (Russian watches, Czech cars, some Romanian wines) could be excellent, nor that cheap shoddy goods are better than no goods to the poor. But it trapped the region in an industrial time-warp while the developed world adapted and grew.

Then the sudden raising of crude oil prices by Arab countries in 1973 signalled the down-turn in the long economic cycle which the Soviet agrarian economist Nikolai Kondratiev had uncannily predicted half a century earlier. The impact on the Eastern Bloc economies was more indirect than direct. Awash with deposits from the oil states on which they had to earn interest, Western banks lent more freely, and Soviet Bloc states were among those encouraged to borrow large amounts. They did so as a means of renewing their industrial infrastructure,[3] though they did this by entrenching old technology based on steel, rather than developing new electronic and computer technology. The involvement with Western economies soon became closer and, as borrowing increased and interest rates rose, several countries got seriously into debt.

Political problems compounded the economic problem. In Poland successive governments, afraid of unpopularity, allowed incomes to outstrip production, and increased the country's indebtedness to maintain living standards. As a result, by the early eighties the excess of disposable incomes over available goods to buy with them had created a 'debt overhang' which promised serious inflation.[4] For similar reasons the Soviet government subsidized Poland and other satellites with cheap energy and credit.[5] Fortunately it had considerable resources of oil, whose value soared from $2.80 a barrel on the world market in 1972 to $14 a barrel in 1986.[6] However the Soviet Union seriously underpriced its oil, as it did other raw materials, within the COMECON trading area.

As a result, Czechoslovakia, for example, used twice as much energy and over twice as much steel as the United States or Britain to generate the same value of output.[7] Furthermore products were designed on the assumption that raw materials were cheap. Hence Soviet aircraft were built much heavier than others and required more powerful, fuel-guzzling engines – making them virtually unsaleable outside the Bloc. Besides, by 1975 the Soviet government was spending more rubles than it was taking in, and the deficit was becoming chronic.[8]

The Brezhnev regime brushed these problems aside – not just out of complacency, but because (like most experienced administrators) they thought it unwise to tinker with a system that had worked reasonably well for nearly half a century and address problems that might soon solve themselves. But Brezhnev's successor, Yuri Andropov, was alive to the fact that there were systemic problems, and commissioned a report on them from an Academy think-tank. It was critical of central planning and recommended drastic reforms.[9] But Andropov died before he could act on it, and under his successor, Chernenko, the direction of the Soviet Empire reverted to torpor. Only on Chernenko's death in 1985 when, for the first time and unimaginably, Soviet production fell, did troublesome reality have to be faced.

The new leader was Mikhail Gorbachev, a protégé of Andropov and a clever politician of considerable personal charm and mental flexibility. He favoured prompt action. Yet the 'basic directions' for the 12th Soviet Five-Year Plan published that November reflected a traditional approach: the 'speeding-up' (*uskorienie*) of production.[10] Oil, coal and steel production were to be jacked up by up to 10 per cent, electricity by 20 per cent, grain by 23 per cent and natural gas by 32 per cent. But then Gorbachev called for an overhaul of the centralized planning system itself.

He also followed Andropov in taking a moral approach to economic problems, fighting corruption, absenteeism and bad working habits. And he mounted a campaign against alcohol. This had the effect of slashing the government's taxation income at a time when expenditure on housing and health was rising. That year the deficit widened from 18 billion rubles to about 50 billion. And it continued to balloon, promoting inflation. Gorbachev had lost control of the financial situation.[11]

As we shall see, some of his political and administrative reforms also proved ill-advised. But Gorbachev was also unlucky. In April 1986 a reactor at the Chernobyl nuclear power station exploded. The disaster proved costly in economic as well as human and ecological terms. So did the fall of oil and gas prices on international markets. As a result, the Soviet Union's hard currency earnings from these exports fell to $11.6 billion in 1986 – little more than half of what they had been in 1984.[12] The Soviet Union net foreign debt that year was $10 billion. But within five years that debt was to grow more than six-fold.[13]

The ballooning budgetary deficit and the growing foreign debt precipitated a rethinking of military policy.[14] They also encouraged a re-examination of the Soviet commitment to underpin the unpopular regime in Poland and indeed to subsidize the other satellite states with cheap energy. Both directly and indirectly it was the Soviet Union's growing economic difficulties which laid the foundations of the dramatic changes which were soon to take place in Eastern Europe.

* * *

The first public expressions of the Soviet Union's new position on defence and towards the other countries of the Bloc came in the summer of 1989. But there had been movements towards liberalization before that. In the Soviet Union Gorbachev had promised to promote individual legal rights,[15] allowed a choice of candidates in local elections, and launched the policies of 'openness' (*glasnost'*) and 'reconstruction' (*perestroika*). Hungarian voters had been given a choice of candidates (though not of parties) since the 1985 elections, and a series of market-type reforms had been introduced. As a result Budapest had a thriving bond-market, Western investments were growing and, encouraged by Moscow, her foreign trade was coming to be priced in dollars. In Poland, too, there was increasing movement towards a free market economy, and towards democracy in politics.

Yet these reforms did not solve the problem of central planning. Nor could they change the prevailing, adverse, terms of trade. In Hungary (whose foreign debt per head of population was the highest in the region) output was faltering and inflation rising. In Poland there was serious inflation, welfare services were declining and there were food shortages.[16] Worse, the government lacked popular legitimacy. When opposition candidates were allowed to stand for the first time in the elections on 5 June 1989, the 'Solidarity' candidates defeated the Communists hands down. But the overture to the most dramatic phase in the Eastern European revolution was played in July 1989. The conductor was Mikhail Gorbachev.

In a speech to the Council of Europe on 6 July he confirmed that the Soviet Union was slashing military spending and starting to convert part of its military–industrial complex to peaceful purposes. His rationale was the so-called 'defensive doctrine of reasonable sufficiency'.[17] But if there was no point in maintaining so vast a military establishment based on 'overkill' in deterrence, what point was there in maintaining satellites in Eastern Europe at great cost?

An answer was suggested at a Warsaw Pact summit in Bucharest the same month. There Gorbachev acknowledged the right of every member to follow its own political line and emphasized the principle of non-interference in the affairs of other countries.[18] He was implicitly reversing the 'Brezhnev doctrine' invoked to justify the Soviet invasion of Czechoslovakia in 1968 (see Chapter 2); and refusing to rescue any more Communist regimes that might become unpopular. But of all the satellites only Poland and Hungary supported him.

Gorbachev also moved to break the Communist parties' political monopoly, abandoning the concept of their 'leading role'. He declared it 'impossible to decree the [Soviet] Party's authority' and warned that a 'dangerous discrepancy' would arise if the Party were to be less dynamic than the people.[19] And on 3 August he appointed the first-ever non-Communist to the USSR Council of Ministers.[20] On 19 August 'Solidarity' roundly defeated the Communists in Poland and five days later Tadeusz Mazowiecki took his seat as Poland's first non-Communist Prime Minister since the Second World War. But other Bloc governments stood out against the new line. This was an intriguing reversal of roles compared with former times. Moscow was now laying down a liberal policy and 'hard-line' satellite leaders were refusing to follow it. Notwithstanding the principle of non-interference, however, their disobedience would not go unpunished.

The first target turned out to be the East German regime of Ernst Honecker, but the approach was indirect. As elsewhere in the Bloc, deteriorating economic circumstances were causing discontent, and in May 1989 this found expression in widespread protests over electoral ballot-rigging. The government security service (Stasi) contained them, but then matters took a curious turn: increasing numbers of East Germans went on holiday to Hungary and then tried to cross to the West across the Austrian frontier.

The Hungarian government had opened part of its frontier with Austria on 2 May. Word of this spread. The East German government asked Hungary to stop its citizens leaving, but the request was rejected. The flow was controlled however, and by 1 July 25,000 East Germans were in nearby camps waiting to cross. Then, on 4 August, however, a crowd of East Germans occupied the West German embassy in Budapest. On 19 August about 600 East Germans moved towards a picnic that had been arranged on the Hungarian–Austrian frontier. The Hungarian frontier guards did not stop them. Three days later East Germans occupied the West German Embassy in Prague. On 11 September Hungary removed all restrictions on her frontiers and within four days over 20,000 East Germans had crossed over. By the end of September thousands were escaping to the West via Czechoslovakia and Poland too.

Pressed by the Czech and Polish governments to allow his citizens waiting in Prague and Warsaw to leave directly for the West from East German territory, Honecker agreed to their being moved out on closed trains which would pass through East German towns secretly at night. But the news leaked. On the night of 4 October crowds stormed Dresden station trying to board a 'freedom train'. These disorders were suppressed and, as thousands more East Germans voted with their feet, Honecker prepared to celebrate the fortieth anniversary of his German Democratic Republic.[21]

The circumstances of these curious events suggest collusion between the Hungarian and West German governments. But the critical factor in Honecker's impending downfall was the guest of honour at his anniversary celebrations – Mikhail Gorbachev. Gorbachev arrived in East Berlin on 7 October. The behaviour of the crowds that turned out to watch suggested that he was more popular than Honecker. And Gorbachev did not disguise his views: 'Life', he warned his host, 'punishes those who lag behind the times.' By the time he left, big demonstrations were under way in Leipzig as well as Berlin and Honecker knew that the Soviet troops stationed in his country would not help him.

Meanwhile his own colleagues were ganging up against him, and on the night of 17/18 October, having received an endorsement from the Soviet embassy, they voted unanimously to relieve him of his post. Egon Krenz became Party Secretary.[22] On 9 November, in confused circumstances, the frontier to the West was opened, and the notorious Berlin Wall, erected nearly thirty years before (see Chapter 2), dismantled. Chancellor Kohl of West Germany sensed an opportunity to promote what had been unthinkable for almost half a century: the reunification of the two Germanies. It was accomplished within a year.[23]

The day after Krenz allowed the East German frontier to be opened, the Bulgarian leader Todor Zhivkov was voted out of office by a majority of one in the Party Central Committee. His successor Petar Mladenov had only just returned from a meeting with Gorbachev in Moscow. Within a week the Bulgarian parliament had scrapped the law forbidding dissent. Only two leaders still stood out against Gorbachev and reform: Presidents Gustav Husak of Czechoslovakia and Nicolae Ceaucescu of Romania. Neither was to last much longer.

The critical turn in Czechoslovakia occurred on 17 November when police were seen to suppress a student demonstration with savagery, killing at least one protestor. This incident inspired a very much larger demonstration and the formation, next day, of an oppositionist umbrella organization, 'Civic Forum', headed by the celebrated dissident Vaclav Havel. Within a week there were changes in the government and Party leadership, which, on 28 November, surrendered its political monopoly.

The events in Prague resembled a popular revolution. But the crowd had been manipulated by the secret police in association with the KGB. Attempts had been made to get a protest under way near Wenceslas Square earlier in November and on at least one occasion a sizeable crowd had collected. Yet they seemed phlegmatic, showing little interest in the message of dissent. The economic situation was not as bad as elsewhere, and 'the only people interested in a revolution were the dissidents and the secret police'.[24]

And so the police resorted to theatre. It transpired that the death of a student from police brutality had been faked by an *agent provocateur*. This was an embarrassment to the democratic regime which succeeded the Communists. Having instituted a thorough inquiry into the 'Police Violence of November 17th', the Czech Parliament quietly wound it up many months later without issuing a final report.

The Ceaucescu regime lasted only a few weeks longer. The revolution was heralded on 16 December 1989 by demonstrations in the town of Timisoara, which had a substantial Hungarian minority, after a rumour spread that the police intended to arrest Pastor Laszlo Tokes, a civil rights activist. The affair escalated and sparked riots in several other Transylvanian towns. They were suppressed, and Ceaucescu left, as scheduled, on a visit to Iran. He returned on the 21st, and appeared on the balcony of Party headquarters to deliver his customary harangue to the gathered crowd outside.

This time, however, his audience soon turned from conventional applause to boos and catcalls. Ceaucescu and his wife were spirited away in a helicopter, then arrested at Tirgoviste and, with the revolution still in doubt, briskly tried and executed on the 25th. There had been firing in Bucharest, but now it died away.

Whether and to what extent the Romanian revolution was a product of conspiracy rather than spontaneous is a matter of dispute. There is evidence of previous conspiracies involving generals, and (as early as November 1988) of Gorbachev's sympathy for a movement to overthrow Ceaucescu. At a critical moment on the 21st, General Vasile Milea, ignoring Ceaucescu's instruction, had refused to order his troops to fire upon the crowd; and the military, elements of the security services and prominent civilians, including former ministers opposed to the regime, were quick to exploit the opportunity. A government of National Salvation assumed control. Its head, Ion Iliescu, was a personal friend of Gorbachev.[25]

With the fall of Ceaucescu the old order in the Soviet Bloc countries ended. Their Communist Parties surrendered their political monopoly and often changed their names; laws forbidding dissent were abolished and free elections were arranged. The available evidence is consistent with the view that Gorbachev hoped that reformist communists with experience of government would dominate the political scene, but allow former oppositionists a voice, perhaps even a share in power, an apprenticeship in office. If so, he was to be disappointed. The possibility of a gradual transition was almost everywhere swept aside by the revolutionary momentum.

In Poland the reservation of a substantial number of seats for the Communist Polish Workers' Party (PWP) did not prevent the advent of a government led by 'Solidarity' and Lech Walesa was elected to the Presidency. Although the Communists in Hungary had repudiated Communism the previous October, their new Socialist Party won less than 9 per cent of the vote in the general election of March/April 1990; in East Germany, in March, they won 16 per cent; and in Czechoslovakia in June a mere 40 of over 200 parliamentary seats. Only in Bulgaria, where they won 46.5 per cent of the popular vote, and Romania, where the National Salvation Front won 66 per cent in the May 1990 elections, did the reform Communists remain in power. But by then the Gorbachev regime itself was already on a slide towards disaster.

* * *

As we saw earlier, the Soviet Union's economic problems had contributed to the decision in 1989 to divest itself of empire. Yet the seriousness of the situation was to some extent hidden by a growth rate in 1988 of almost 5 per cent, the best for a decade, and by results that indicated that all the targets of the Five-Year Plan apart from agriculture were within range. Furthermore Gorbachev was riding high politically. In December 1987 he had struck a deal with the USA over nuclear missiles and was making progress towards cuts in conventional forces; he had removed the erratic opportunist, Boris Yeltsin, from the post of Party boss of Moscow, and been appointed President in October. But 1988 turned out to be his high point.

As the financial situation deteriorated Gorbachev became more radical politically, and a number of senior colleagues, notably Yegor Ligachev, who had counselled caution and retrenchment, began to desert him. The parliamentary elections of March 1989 went well for him, however, and in April he felt strong enough to remove his opponents from the Politburo. But with inflation creeping up to 20 per cent a year people began to hoard food as a hedge against price increases. A variety of goods became scarce, the distribution system began to break down, production faltered and the black economy grew. So did popular discontent.

Gorbachev's attempts at economic reform contributed to the problems. From 1987 he had encouraged the formation of private cooperatives, businesses and farms – but except in the Baltic republics and Georgia these were slow to take off. Ideological and bureaucratic objections were not the only impediments. State firms saw private concerns as a competitive threat; and ordinary people sometimes perceived them as inimical to their own interests. Furthermore Gorbachev's encouragement of devolution in economic decision-making led some line managers to doubt if every order from on high had to be obeyed; and the police became increasingly confused about what was or was not an economic crime. Deteriorating economic conditions also began to feed separatist movements in the USSR, as they were soon to do elsewhere; and in January 1990 tanks had to be sent to suppress an insurrection in Azerbaidjan.

As his problems multiplied, Gorbachev became more innovative administratively, and fitfully embraced a variety of reform schemes. He shifted his power base from the Central Committee to the Supreme Soviet and then to the Presidential Office; he merged departments and created super-ministries. Nor he did he neglect economic reform. In August 1990 he went so far as to back a 'shock therapy' plan to transform the Soviet Union into a free-market, privatized economy within 500 days. But then, fearing that this would compound the growing administrative and economic chaos his earlier reforms had done much to promote, he withdrew.

And if the economy was getting beyond control, so were political developments. Those who exploited the new freedom of speech to best advantage tended to be impractical idealists, unconstructive critics, and raw political opportunists, while the abolition of the Party's supremacy gave space in several constituent republics for nationalists bent on destroying the union.[26]

By the time the Party's political monopoly was abolished, in February 1990, the Soviet economy, so far from growing, had begun to shrink, and this encouraged the forces of separatism. In March the constituent republics of Lithuania and Georgia declared independence. In May Latvia did so, and in June Boris Yeltsin, the newly-elected president of the Russian (as opposed to the Soviet) parliament, pronounced the Russian Federal Republic to be sovereign. With the Union beset on every side there began a long series of negotiations between the competing governments. Eventually, however, Gorbachev recognized that he would have to use force to keep the Union together. He did so in January 1991 in Lithuania.

The Party leader in Lithuania, Brauzaskas, had tried to contain growing nationalist sentiment by accommodating it while seeking some compromise on powers with Moscow. But Brauzaskas was defeated at the polls by a political unknown, Vytautis Landsbergis, a musicologist specializing in the work of a little-known Lithuanian composer and a single-minded nationalist idealogue who believed that any political compromise represented moral corruption. He was representative of a type which the prevailing sentiment in many Soviet republics was bringing to the fore. Gorbachev recognized the danger.

So, from a different perspective, did President Bush of the United States. He sent his ambassador in Moscow to warn Gorbachev that the violent suppression of the Lithuanians, Latvians or Estonians would damage US–Soviet relations. In reply, Gorbachev asked the Ambassador to make Bush understand that 'we are on the brink of civil war. As president my main task is to prevent it'.[27] Troops were indeed sent in to seize strategic points, notably the television tower, in the Lithuanian capital Vilnius. But the operation was limited and clumsily executed. Its only fruits were 13 dead and a hardening of opinion against Moscow.

Two months later in a Union-wide referendum, an overwhelming majority of Soviet citizens voted to preserve the Union. Nevertheless the Lithuanian parliament voted to secede and enthusiasts paraded at the parliament building in national costume brandishing nationalist symbols and banners.[28]

During the spring and early summer of 1991 Gorbachev tried to negotiate a new union treaty with the constituent republics, but power was already flowing to the periphery, and competition between officials representing central and local authorities was increasing.[29] Only the Communist Party could resolve these tensions. But, deprived of its leading role, it was fast losing its authority and influence. Such were the circumstances in which 'hardliners' attempted a *coup d'état* in August 1991.

It was, ironically, the Party's tradition of obedience which had helped Gorbachev to survive so far. Senior colleagues who were sceptical of his policies, like Yegor Ligachev, had simply retired into obscurity. But there was now widespread conviction among governmental and army, as well as Party, leaders that the rot had to be stopped. Though widely represented as an attempt by the old *nomenklatura* to cling to privilege and power, it seems rather to have been intended to restore stability in the face of looming chaos.

But the operation was poorly planned, ill-coordinated, and indecisively implemented. President Gorbachev himself was placed under house arrest at his holiday villa in the Crimea, but the plotters were slow to seal off the parliament building and to prevent Boris Yeltsin from rallying the opposition. Photographs of him standing on a tank, visibly defending the democratic revolution, were to give a powerful boost to his bid for power.

The failed coup also gave Yeltsin the opportunity (illegally) to order the disbanding of the Party. It further undermined the public's faith in government; and encouraged nationalists to press for sovereignty rather than more autonomy. Latvia declared independence, and, asserting the authority of the Russian republic which he headed, Yeltsin rushed through an unconstitutional law confiscating Communist Party property. Returning to Moscow President Gorbachev felt compelled to resign as Party leader, but the initiator of the revolution had by then lost all credence. As the Primate of the Russian Orthodox Church, Patriarch Alexei, remarked in October 1991, his flock was 'losing faith both in the future and in their political leaders'.

Exploiting the vacuum, Yeltsin now delivered a final blow to Gorbachev's authority, challenging the legitimacy of the state itself, and wrecking the chances of renegotiating the Union. Despite Gorbachev's pleas (recalling Edmund Burke's warning not to destroy established institutions), the Communist Party was wrecked, and with his policies, like his authority, in ruins, Gorbachev resigned the Soviet Presidency with effect from 31 December 1991. Yeltsin anticipated his departure. He commandeered his Kremlin office before Gorbachev could remove his belongings and threw a party there. The Soviet Union had ceased to exist.

* * *

The last Communist regime in the region to crumble was that of Europe's poorest country, Albania, early in 1992. Albania had accepted no foreign investment since breaking with Communist China in the 1970s and maintained only minimal connections with the outside world. It was therefore less vulnerable than the others to world market forces. However, it faced a serious demographic crisis.

The population had almost trebled since the Second World War and by the 1990s demographic increase was 2 per cent greater than that of GDP.[30] So far from having an ageing population like Russia and some Western countries, the age structure was disproportionately young and the government had to create 76,000 new jobs a year to maintain full employment. To add to the regime's troubles, an unusual run of droughts in the later 1980s had damaged agricultural output and led to the felling of many trees which competed with essential crops for precious water.[31]

Ramiz Alia, Enver Hoxha's successor as party leader, knew systemic reforms were needed to fend off impending crisis. He ended the country's isolation and tried to encourage economic initiative, promote democracy and the rights of individuals under the law. But this was easier said than done. Enterprise had been discouraged for generations, and bureaucratization had created a general unwillingness to accept responsibility. The difficulties of moving from a planned to a free-initiative economy soon became apparent.

> Government departments [complained Alia] ... are hesitating to adapt themselves to the new reality and are finding it difficult to give up the methods of formal orders; on the other hand, the habit of waiting for orders from above is deeply implanted in enterprises.[32]

The new policies failed to stop the economic slide. Output which had fallen by 10 per cent in 1990 shrank by over 20 per cent in 1991. There were lay-offs, but those laid off still received 80 per cent of their salaries. A population conditioned to expect its welfare to be maintained had to be soothed. But with the state printing more and more money[33] the reckoning could not be long postponed.

In the elections of March 1991 the Communists won two-thirds of the seats. But in May there was a general strike. This led to the formation of a coalition government which pressed economic reform farther, freeing all prices except for basic foods, devaluing the currency, and restructuring the banking system. It also began to sell off state property and the humanitarian aid which had begun to trickle in. But it was still printing too much money, and finding it increasingly difficult to contain the country's rebellious youth.

The reforms themselves created confusion. In some localities there was chaos as crowds of unemployed people smashed communal property. Elsewhere infrastructures collapsed: 'telegraph poles... disappeared, the telephone does not work, newspapers and letters do not get through'.[34] Crowds of youths tried to break into foreign embassies and to rush onto ships leaving port. Some succeeded. Sixty thousand departed for Italy, a further 150,000 to Greece.[35] But it was not enough to relieve the rising pressure. In December 1991 a government of technocrats took over and, with elections approaching, the painful economic reforms were halted. Even so, in March 1992 the Democratic Party, led by Sali Berisha, was swept into office.

As elsewhere the great change encouraged popular expectations of instant solutions and a Western way of life. Yet nationalism had played no part in the Albanian revolution. Apart from some Greeks and Macedonians there were no significant minorities. However, there was a large irridenta across the frontier in Yugoslavia, and the Albanians of the Kosovo district in Serbia were to play a vital, albeit indirect, part in the downfall of Yugoslavia. It is to this that we should now turn.

* * *

The rate of demographic growth which made Albanians the youngest people in Europe was matched by the Albanian community across the frontier in Serbia where the number of Albanian-speakers in the autonomous Kosovo province had been multiplying much faster than the Serb-speaking population. They also became nationalistically assertive. This encouraged many Serbs to leave – which increased the disproportion between the two communities. Rising resentment among Serbs prompted the Serbian government to withdraw Kosovo's autonomy and to repress the Albanians. The temperature of conflict rose – and then Kosovo became the object of contention between the constituent republics of Yugoslavia, particularly Serbia and Slovenia. But there was a more sinister underlying cause of the coming conflagrations: the deteriorating economic situation, particularly since the early 1980s.

Like its Communist neighbours, Yugoslavia had suffered from adverse terms of trade, rising indebtedness, and from systemic economic problems which devolution of decision-making had failed to solve. But there was an additional disadvantage. During the booming 1960s West Germany had encouraged many Yugoslavs to work there, and the hard currency they sent home made a significant contribution to the Yugoslav economy. In the eighties most of these *Gastarbeiter* were no longer needed, however. Their return home led to both a sharp fall in Yugoslavia's hard-currency earnings and to a serious rise in unemployment.

Economic difficulties nourished social problems and fed political discontent which found expression in national animus. Serbs felt increasingly resentful of the more prosperous Croats and Slovenes to the north and of the Federation which had demanded sacrifices of them (not least over Kosovo), while Croats and Slovenes felt increasingly resentful of the poorer southerners whom they subsidized through taxation, and especially of Serbs whom they perceived as dominating federal institutions.[36]

In 1989 a Croat, Ante Markovic, became federal Prime Minister. Inflation was running at 800 per cent; the foreign debt had reached $20 billion, unemployment 20 per cent, and real incomes were 30 per cent less than they had been ten years earlier. Markovic introduced a series of tough economic measures which had some success. But his emergency plan called for greater sacrifices than people were prepared to make. Slovenes objected to the taxes they were required to pay; Bosnians regarded the plan as a sell-out to capitalism, and Montenegrins reacted to the proposal to bankrupt loss-making enterprises with consternation: four-fifths of their enterprises made losses. Furthermore, Markovic could not control the money supply. Banks in the constituent republics continued to issue credit. That year inflation reached 1,256 per cent.

Economic and political resentments now merged as opportunistic politicians channelled growing public anger into nationalist grooves. Slobodan Milosevic, Serbia's leader since 1987, exploited the Kosovo issue to whip up support; politicians in Slovenia and Croatia were equally cynical in exploiting nationalism, and since the southern republics were the poorest, and hence costliest, members of the federation, dissolution presented itself as an attractive prospect to the other partners. The Kosovo issue provided the excuse.

Wishing to raise support for their position over Kosovo, Serbs planned a rally in Slovenia. The Slovene authorities banned it. In retaliation, on 4 December 1989, Serbia imposed an embargo on Slovenia. Two months later the Slovene Communist Party broke away from the federal Party, its leader stating:

> My party is not on the side of separatism but for a Yugoslavia in which the status of the Slovenian representative is equal to that of a sovereign state.[37]

A few weeks later Slovenes elected a secessionist centre-right government, and on 25 June 1990 the new Slovene parliament unanimously supported a statement of intent to declare independence within a year. Tension rose and Federal Army (JNA) tanks took up positions at the Danube bridges and other strategic points.

Meanwhile in neighbouring Croatia a former general turned historian, Franjo Tudjman, had won the election of 27 April 1990 with the help of money from émigré Croats in Canada and Germany. They included some of the extreme right, among them Gojko Susak, a Toronto millionaire who subsequently became Croatia's Minister of War.[38] Tudjman's victory raised tensions among members of the Serb minority around Knin who feared another massacre such as the Ustasha had carried out in 1941, and Tudjman, though advised to do so, took no pains to reassure them. His adoption in the new Croatian flag of a symbol used by the pro-Nazi Ustasha in the Second World War positively alarmed them, as did the sacking of ethnic Serbs from the police force and from government jobs.

Most Croats were not rapidly anti-Serbian. Many still felt themselves to be Yugoslavs. But (as in Serbia) dissenting voices were silenced: and thugs sent to close down newspapers which failed to toe the nationalist line. A Tudjman spokesman raised the spectre of the past and gestured towards a dangerous future:

> We will expand Croatia [he said]. We are already expanding it into Bosnia-Hercegovina, because it is also a state of the Croatian people.[39]

In March 1991 the Yugoslav State Council, whose prestige was fast diminishing but which still disposed of a formidable army, decided, by a majority of one, not to take military action to prevent Croatia undermining the federation. Then in June 1991 both republics declared independence, and on the 27th tanks rolled into Slovenia and Croatia to reimpose federal authority. But the attempt was half-hearted. Few troops were committed, their morale was poor, and some units proved unreliable. The Slovenes on the other hand presented themselves as defenceless, though they were sufficiently well equipped to knock out tanks and shoot down helicopters. Milosevic of Serbia, no defender of the Federation, endorsed Slovenia's secession.[40] Nevertheless, the two Republics could not claim all the fruits of independence without diplomatic recognition, and this the international community refused to grant.

Meanwhile the curtain had been raised on a bloody conflict in Croatian Slavonia where communities of Serbs had been established for centuries. On 1 May 1991 Croat extremists, anxious to clear the area of Serbs while trying to present the Serbs as the aggressors, triggered a clash with local Serb forces which left several dead.[41] In July fighting between Serbs and Croats broke out again. Federal Army units separated them and a cease-fire was arranged. Then the European Union (EU) tried to mediate a general settlement.

This process proved to be both slow and frustrating. Many Croats and Serbs had become paranoiac in their fears and hatred of one another[42] and sporadic fighting continued. Nevertheless it was limited to a few localities; and the peacemakers had reason to believe they might succeed. By withholding recognition from Croatia until it guaranteed the rights of its minorities they put Tudjman under pressure to soften his line towards the Croatian Serbs. At the same time Milosovic was given to understand that if he went too far the EU might grant Croatia recognition anyway. But in December 1991 Germany broke ranks, declaring its intention to recognize both Croatia and Slovenia unilaterally and unconditionally. This act removed all restraints.

In recognizing Croatia and Slovenia Germany reneged on an agreement with its European partners, but she had compelling reasons. Germany had sizeable investments in both the break-away republics and wanted them (but not the rest of Yugoslavia) firmly within her sphere of influence. Moreover she was under growing political pressure from Slovenia's neighbour Austria, from her own Catholic constituency, including Croat émigrés, and from the Pope.

The excuse was provided by the Yugoslav army's alleged 'aggression' in bombarding Dubrovnik in violation of a cease-fire.[43] Other EU members and the United States could not allow Germany to be the only Western voice in Zagreb, so, reluctantly, they followed suit.

The focus in what remained of Yugoslavia now fell on the republic of Bosnia-Hercegovina. It was populated by Muslims, Serbs and Croats, none of whom constituted a majority. Hitherto they had all trusted the Yugoslav government to protect them. But the struggle in neighbouring Slavonia had been eroding trust between the communities. So had the apparent affinity between the local Serbs and the Yugoslav army, which had major bases in Bosnia. With the Bosnian Serbs determined to set up a state of their own, in October 1991 Bosnian president Alija Izetbegovic decided to seek independence. Both held referenda to legitimize their actions. In March 1992, in Lisbon, the leaders of all three ethnicities agreed to a Serb proposal to divide the republic into autonomous cantons. But then, sensing he could get a better deal, Izetbegovic reneged – and the Bosnian war began.[44]

Its peculiar viciousness was partly due to the fact that each ethno-religious group was a minority, so each felt vulnerable. It was their fear of one another that encouraged the preemptive strike and the deterrent massacre. Geographic and demographic circumstances also contributed: so far from each group being concentrated in a single area, there was a good deal of intermingling, so that each of the minorities had its own minorities, encouraging fears of 'the enemy in our midst'. Hence the 'ethnic cleansing' for which the war was to become notorious. Furthermore, most Muslims lived in cities while much of the country-side was predominately Serb.[45] This scatter of ethnic concentrations encouraged attempts to link them by driving corridors through the territories of others. It was a recipe for perpetual warfare.[46]

In circumstances of total struggle between communities, distinctions between combatants and non-combatants were blurred. Furthermore the sending of humanitarian aid and the intervention of UN peace-keeping forces prolonged rather than curtailed the struggle, giving sustenance and hope to losers and prolonging their resistance. The UN troops were intended to protect the innocent, but in this war there were innocents, and guilty, on all sides, and everything the peacekeepers did was perceived as helping or harming one of the belligerents. Hence the attempts made to manipulate them, to involve them in the propaganda war,[47] or to discredit them with false accusations of war crimes (the Canadian General Mackenzie was spuriously accused of rape).

The popular belief in the West that Serbs were the only ethnic cleansers is mistaken. If Milosevic could call on the services of extremists like Vojislav Seselj, Tudjman could call on the likes of Dobroslav Paraga. The band of cut-throats led by the notorious Arkan, a gaolbird wanted by Interpol for robbery and murder, indulged in ethnic cleansing for the Serbs; but a former protection racketeer 'Tuta' Naletalic headed a similar killing unit for the Croats; and the Muslims had their counterparts in Celo, a convicted rapist, and Juka, a former mobster.[48] The employment of Western mercenaries, especially by the Croats and Muslims who had fewer trained soldiers than the Serbs, sucked in social misfits and pathological killers from abroad. The war became a paradise for psychopaths and perverts.

The widespread, though misleading, impression that only the Serbs were guilty was deliberately induced. Ruder Finn Global Public Affairs, a Washington public relations firm, was retained for the purpose by both the Croat and the Muslim interest in 1991–2.[49] Their brilliant work roused public opinion against the Serbs and demonized their leaders. The public outcry eventually persuaded President Clinton to intervene on behalf of Izetbegovic's Bosnia. But the media reports were skewed. Sarajevo had the only television transmission dish in the country. Hence the concentration on Sarajevo to the exclusion of other points of conflict. The Muslim command exploited this fact, needling the Serbs into actions which outraged international opinion and helped turn the tables in the war.

It transpired that two notorious mortar bombs that killed dozens of Sarajevo civilians could not have been fired from Serb positions and may have been delivered by Bosnian government forces to deflect attention from their operations elsewhere and influence world opinion against the Serbs. The second explosion provided justification for US airstrikes on behalf of NATO against Serb positions carried out between 30 August and 15 September 1995.[50]

The United States ended the war in the only way possible, by joining one side against another. Its covert military aid enabled the Croatian forces to overrun Serb-occupied Krajina and evict its 200,000 Serbs,[51] and to make substantial advances together with Muslim forces in Bosnia. At the same time economic pressures and US air force strikes subdued the Bosnian Serbs. In November 1995 the Presidents of Bosnia, Croatia and Serbia were persuaded to sign a settlement. The USA agreed to take a leading role in policing it. An agreement was also signed permitting a gradual Croatian take-over of eastern Slavonia.[52]

By that time 3.5 million Yugoslavs had been displaced and Bosnia had contracted commercial debts of nearly $5 billion. However, a potentially more dangerous Balkan war was averted. The territory of the former Yugoslav Republic of Macedonia, an independent state since 1991, had long been in contention between Serbia, Bulgaria and Greece (see Chapter 5), and Greece now feared that the new Macedonia might claim the allegiance of the Grecized Slavs of northern Greece. United Nations troops were sent to patrol its frontiers, and the conflict became focused on the new state's right to its name. Mercifully that conflict was eventually settled.

* * *

The collapse of Communism had been unexpected but, as we saw in the Introduction to this book, the aftermath was hardly less surprising. The revolutions had been greeted with demonstrations of wild excitement and delight. From Ljubljana to Vilnius, from Prague to St Petersburg huge, joyful crowds surged into the streets. Expectations about a better future ran high. Now that Communism had been vanquished people could live 'normal' lives and grow richer in every way. A free market economy would raise their living standards; open frontiers would make all the good things of the Western world accessible; and democracy would encourage the development of a civil society. Yet all these expectations were soon proved false and the euphoria quickly evaporated.

So far from becoming richer most people became poorer. Western goods became available but few could afford them; so far from welcoming emigrants, as they had done, the West began to discourage them; those who profited most from the new freedom were crooks, asset-strippers and foreigners; civil society failed to develop, and democracy produced widespread disenchantment and tendencies to political instability. The first years of post-Communism proved bitterly disappointing. The promised gold turned out to be mere dross.

But what precisely happened? And why had it happened? Was the great transition mishandled? Were the expectations unreasonable? To answer these questions we need to survey the history of the post-Communist period – economic, social, moral and political.

The revolution marked the point at which even the soundest economies not already in difficulty began to falter. Statistics make hard reading, but only statistics can convey the scale of the hard and unexpected development. In Czechoslovakia in 1990, its first year of freedom, the generation of wealth (real GDP), which had hitherto been rising modestly, declined by 1.6 per cent. In Romania it fell by 5.6 per cent, and in Poland, where the Mazowiecki government had introduced radical measures of economic reform, by 11.6 per cent. So, far from recovering, the economic decline became steeper. In 1991 real GDP in Czechoslovakia fell by almost 14.7 per cent, in Romania by 12.9 per cent, and in Poland by a further 7 per cent. At the same time consumer prices soared – by 57.8 per cent in Czechoslovakia, 76.7 per cent in Poland and 174.5 per cent in Romania. From 1992 the Polish economy began to grow again, though at a very modest rate, and in 1993 consumption was

5 per cent less than it had been in 1989. In Hungary it was down 11 per cent, in Bulgaria 25 per cent, and in the former Czechoslovakia and Romania 30 per cent less than under Communism.[53]

In Russia, the Ukraine and other parts of the former Soviet Union the slump came later but was even more severe. Russian industrial production in 1995 was barely half of what it had been at the end of 1991. In Ukraine it dropped by over one-third in the first quarter of 1994 alone, and it continued to fall thereafter. In the first quarter of 1995, industry in Belarus produced less than 45 per cent of what it had done in 1990; in Moldova less than 40 per cent. At the same time inflation had soared. In Russia towards the end of 1995 consumer prices were more than 4,500 times higher than they had been when the Union collapsed at the end of 1991.[54]

Throughout the region a few made fortunes, often in the black economy, escaping taxation and hence any contribution towards the general good. More capital flowed out of the region than flowed in in the form of aid, loans and investment.[55] And population flowed out too, especially the young and the skilled. Soon after the Wall was dismantled the East German health service came near total collapse for lack of doctors and nurses. Most emigrants wanted to better themselves, but some sought refuge from war or from rising xenophobia. Long-established communities of ethnic Germans left Russia and Romania; many Jews also emigrated, and many gypsies tried to do so.

Eastern Europe was in the grip of a severe economic malaise. It was worse in the Baltic States than in those of East-Central Europe; worse in the Balkans than in the Baltics and worst of all in the rest of the former Soviet Union, where the value of the ruble had fallen to one ten-thousandth of its old value by the spring of 1994. Poland was hardest hit before the others and began to recover sooner, but the economy of every other country shrank over the period 1991–95, and every country experienced serious inflation.[56]

The malaise originated in a combination of factors already described: an unfavourable world economy, the imperfections of the planned economy, and unfortunate economic policies. But it was aggravated by dislocations caused by the abrupt disruption of the existing system, the collapse of trading arrangements, and the disintegration of multinational states. The problems of transition from the command to a free economy were addressed with great decisiveness in Poland where in January 1990 finance minister Leszek Balcerowicz introduced drastic policies to rein in galloping inflation, eliminate the huge savings 'overhang', and make the zloty a convertible currency. The programme was largely effective (though inflation soon returned) but the side-effects were painful.

Slashing government expenditure and forcing loss-making enterprises to close down restored faith in money and promoted business confidence, but had severe social consequences. Unemployment, virtually unknown under the old regime, rose to levels higher than in the West. In 1993 the annual rate was 12.9 per cent in Hungary, 16.4 per cent in Poland and 15.9 per cent in Bulgaria. The figures did not fall much thereafter. And even when employment levels remained high, incomes fell sharply. In the Czech Republic wages bought only 80 per cent in 1993 of what they had bought in 1989, in Bulgaria 74 per cent, and in Russia, Slovenia, Poland and Slovakia only 70 per cent. Between 1990 and 1993 individual consumption fell by 10 per cent in Hungary, Poland, the Czech Republic and Slovakia; by 29 per cent in Russia, and by 35 per cent or more in the Ukraine, Romania, Bulgaria and the Baltic states.[57]

The consequence was rising levels of poverty and distress. By 1992 almost 20 per cent of Czechs and Slovaks lived below the poverty line; over 40 per cent of Poles and over 50 per cent of Romanians. The figures for Russia and the Ukraine were little better and were soon to get worse.[58] Birth rates and life expectations fell, health became poorer and mortality increased. As a UNICEF programme director reported in August 1994,

> The ... health crisis burdening most Eastern European countries since 1989 is without precedent in ... peacetime .... It signals a societal crisis of unexpected proportions.[59]

All this was associated with the collapse of familiar institutions, with widespread anomie, psychological stress, and crime. Between 1989 and 1994 crime rates rose by more than 50 per cent in Poland and Russia, almost doubled in Hungary, Lithuania and Belarus, trebled in the Czech Republic and Slovakia, quadrupled in Bulgaria, and quintupled in Romania.[60]

In Romania falling incomes, endemic shortages and an inflation rate that eroded the value of savings encouraged faith in economic saviours – and scams. Hence the extraordinary success of Caritas, a pyramid savings scheme which attracted money from over two million people by the time it failed in the spring of 1994.[61] And if the Caritas phenomenon represented misplaced faith, the growth of crime reflected a collapse of a moral order. Freedom of expression reduced public interest in what the intellectuals had to say but encouraged the proliferation of pornography; and rather than a 'moral and spiritual revival of society' such as Vaclav Havel had hoped for,[62] there were surges in disorder and decadence. Confusion arose between enterprise and crime, and the police were often uncertain what did or did not constitute an offence.

By 1994–5 the economic outlook had at last begun to brighten, and the East-Central European countries were experiencing steady, if modest, growth again for the first time since before the revolution. In Romania, where GDP climbed about 7 per cent in 1995, unemployment dropped below 10 per cent and real wages rose 17 per cent over the 1994 figure.[63]

Yet in many other countries the decline of welfare continued. And meanwhile the economic collapse had rendered democratic politics unstable, encouraged a reaction against westernizing reforms, and promoted increasing nostalgia for the old regimes.

Political pluralism had at first been embraced with enthusiasm. Seven parties were returned to the Hungarian parliament in the elections of 1990; eighteen to the Romanian; 25 contested the 1992 elections in tiny Slovenia, and no fewer than a hundred the Polish election of October 1991. But something was lost in the process: 'Solidarity' and Civil Forum, so united under Communism, had split up into bickering factions as soon as Communism collapsed. And pluralism accentuated growing social divisions and promoted political instability. Bulgaria had four Prime Ministers between February 1990 and December 1991, Poland five between January 1991 and June 1992; and a poll carried out in June 1992 indicated that two-thirds of all Czechs had come to think that their country was too democratic.

In Russia the market reformers were routed at the parliamentary polls of 1995; in Hungary reformed Communists defeated the ruling Democratic Forum in the election of May 1994 and in February 1992 they gained 60 per cent of the vote in the very country whose nationalism had precipitated the break-up of the Soviet Union, Lithuania. In November 1995 Lech Walesa, hero of 'Solidarity', lost the Polish Presidency to a former Communist, Aleksander Kwasniewski; and in the Czech election of 1996 Vaclav Klaus lost his parliamentary majority, though not office.

Western experts considered a civil society to be essential to a sound democratic order, but it failed to flourish in the space left by the oppressive monopolistic state. Rather, a new kind of feudalism emerged as the weak sought the protection of the strong. Non-governmental organizations, like political parties, mushroomed (some encouraged by Western funding), but failed to engage significant constituencies or else promoted divisive ethnic agendas.[64] The dissident tradition of opposition to authority proved inimical to civil society; trade unions, though now free, declined in power, and the Churches failed to fill the gap. Indeed the influence of the Catholic Churches of Poland and Hungary diminished as they opposed abortion, attempted to regain former properties, and tried to control education.

The moral vacuum was exploited politically. Since the manna had not fallen from heaven someone had to be held responsible.[65] Usually it was an ethnic minority. In 1996 the Slovak government insisted on the use of Slovak for all official business, upsetting the large Hungarian minority. Estonia's minorities (almost 40 per cent of the population) were informed that they must speak Estonian if they wanted citizenship; Lithuania discriminated against its Polish minority, Latvia against its huge Russian population. Prominent former Communists were another favoured target.

In Czechoslovakia institutions were cleansed of Communist contamination through a 'lustration' law which barred certain categories of the old officialdom from holding office. The measure was of questionable democratic propriety and open to abuse. President Goncz of Hungary had referred a similar bill passed by the parliament in Budapest to the constitutional court, but though President Havel thought it wrong he felt obliged to endorse the will of parliament. In Albania former leaders were detained pending trials on questionable charges, and former East German leaders and border guards were tried for shooting escapees to the West although the victims had chosen to break the law of the land.[66]

The opportunity was also taken to rehabilitate elements which had hitherto been ostracized or suppressed under the old regime. Skinheads and youths in SS uniforms were allowed to parade through Leipzig and Halle singing 'Deutschland über alles';[67] the extreme right-wing Vatra Romaneasca won over 100,000 members in Romania; there were calls to rehabilitate Slovakia's wartime leader, executed for war crimes in 1947; and in Croatia President Tudjman planned a great gesture of 'reconciliation': re-burying the remains of executed Ustashi mass murderers (represented as victims of Communism and an 'historical wrong') alongside their Serb and Jewish victims on the site of the notorious Jasenovac concentration camp.[68]

Some new, avowedly democratic, political leaders retained power by questionable means. In Albania Sali Berisha had won the 1992 elections with the blatant help of the US whose diplomatic representatives accompanied his candidates round the country in specially-imported jeeps. He won again in 1996 though most opposition parties had withdrawn from the election in protest against alleged intimidation.[69] In Russia Boris Yeltsin took dictatorial powers in October 1993, sending tanks to crush the Russian parliament which opposed him.[70] Yet three years later (with the help of the populist General Lebed' and the media which gave his rivals no air time) he was reelected President with a comfortable majority, although the reform Communist candidate made an unexpectedly good showing.

The rising popularity of the reconstituted Communists aroused fears in the West. Yet, now that they had abandoned the party monopoly and the command economy was lost beyond recovery, Communism did not appear to stand for anything more sinister than a mixed economy, better social services, and law and order. The wasp had lost its sting.

* * *

In June 1996 it was decided to close the Gdansk shipyard which had given birth to 'Solidarity'. Its leader, Lech Walesa, having lost the Presidency, announced his return to his old job there as an electrician.

Now he was to lose his old job too. The turnabout, unimaginable seven years before, symbolized general disappointment with the fruits of revolution. Why, then, were the optimistic predictions confounded?

The most popular explanation has been the heavy legacy of Communism itself. But there were other reasons – not least the widespread and profound misunderstanding of why Communism had collapsed.

As we have seen, the revolution occurred during a global economic crisis, and the crisis persisted after the collapse. Indeed the economic difficulties were compounded by the political upheavals and market uncertainties. And since Western countries were themselves experiencing economic difficulties, only a fraction of the expected aid was forthcoming. As President Bush had told Gorbachev 'the pocket-book is empty'. There was no scheme like Marshall Aid which had revived the economies of Western Europe after the Second World War.[71] In its first year of operations a new European Bank for Reconstruction and Development spent more on its London offices than it dispensed on projects; and though the International Monetary Fund was more active its loans were often conditional on political, economic or even educational reforms.

A Russian economist had explained the perils of independence as the Soviet Union was breaking up in October 1991:

> No republic ... will survive ... without a rich and kind uncle ready to pay all of its accounts for at least ten to fifteen years. Is there such an uncle? They say that there is: America, the Common Market, Scandinavia, and, finally, their own diaspora dispersed throughout the world. Lies. There is no such uncle ... and no diaspora to pay annual subsidies ... to cover multibillion deficits from the unavoidable transition to world prices.... They will give money to a church, a hospital, and perhaps even for a university.... But supporting someone in this stormy world of ours ...? Come now, you must be joking.[72]

The warning was blithely disregarded. Hence the misery of the Ukraine, Lithuania and other successor states whose diasporas had insisted that independence would bring prosperity and general happiness. The opposite happened, but even outside the former USSR there was cause for despondency.

The lack of sufficient help from the West, the intrinsic difficulty of moving from planned to free-market economies, high inflation and foreign indebtedness were not the only reasons. Legal structures proved inadequate for the new commercial circumstances; there were problems with banking systems; markets lacked adequate regulation, the region was innocent of modern accounting practices, its peoples strangers to the culture of risk on which capitalism is based. These circumstances impeded privatization. How could legal titles to property be determined? What was a fair valuation? How could one tell an investor from an asset-stripper or a criminal entrepreneur? And could investment be attracted without political stability? Or political stability be achieved without a high social wage of which free-market advocates disapproved?

At first drastic economic measures such as those undertaken by the Polish government advised by American economists were in fashion. But other economists (including some Americans) believed that the strategy ignored Eastern European realities, and that a successful transition should be more gradual, and take account of social costs.[73] The quick, doctrinaire approach, though it appealed to people reared on doctrine, was certainly no magic talisman. As the World Bank warned in April 1991 even with 'big bang' policies it would take decades for the region to catch up with the West, and up to ten years to recover from the dislocations of the recent revolution. Besides, 'big bang' policies implied heavy social and political costs. The ending of housing subsidies could make rents unaffordable, bankrupting a loss-making enterprise could throw the population of an entire town out of work; and cuts in welfare encouraged voters to favour political extremists. It was at this point that doubts arose as to whether democracy was compatible with free-market reforms.

The World Bank loaned substantial sums to meet the costs of privatizing collectivized agriculture in several countries. But doctrinaire privatization harmed production in countries like Lithuania, where collectivization had ultimately proved successful. De-collectivization proved unpopular in Hungary; in Albania it was associated with land seizures; and in Bulgaria, which also had a successful collectivized agriculture, Western aid and economic doctrine led to political interference.

The USA contributed $10 million to facilitate the privatization of agriculture in Bulgaria. The United Democratic Front wanted to break up the collective farms, and they had the backing of the US government. But the Communists and Agrarians, who dominated politics in the countryside, were opposed to the plan.[74] So US agencies provided funds and personnel to undermine the local leaders and secure a victory for Zhelyu Zhelev's Union of Democratic Forces in the 1992 elections. Western aid was applied to promote privatization in Russia and the Ukraine, where it bought television-time to explain what shares were, to hype privatization, and to help political parties which supported marketization policies. Yet privatization and the return of confiscated property under Communism caused disruptions and uncertainties not only in Bulgaria but in Czechoslovakia and elsewhere – just as the offer of state and municipal assets to foreign buyers without adequate safeguards attracted crooks and asset-strippers. Even the German privatization agency Treuhand made mistakes.

In Albania $1 million was given to promote civil society by creating non-governmental organizations. This provided welcome opportunities to individual Albanians who spoke English to fulfil private agendas rather than promoting any group or social interest. Again the triumph of theory divorced from reality promoted cynicism and disillusion with the Western way.[75]

The severity of disappointment rested on the false expectations raised by Cold War propaganda, émigré communities and some former dissidents. They had encouraged the beliefs that Communism had interrupted 'normal development' and that its absence would allow people to live 'normal' lives, enjoying the living standards characteristic of the West. In fact their normality proved harsher than the propagandists had promised.[76] But another source of the disillusionment derived from the advent of inexperienced newcomers to power.

President Ion Iliescu of Romania was a rare case of a new leader with experience of government. The Lithuanian leader Landsbergis was a musicologist, President Goncz of Hungary a literatteur, and his Czech counterpart, Vaclav Havel, a man of the theatre as well as a famous and courageous dissident. But as Havel himself had written,

> A trace of the heroic dreamer, something mad and unrealistic, is hidden in the very genesis of the dissident perspective.[77]

Such men soon found that they could create no magic fairyland in reality as they had in fantasy, and several proved ill-suited to the tasks of government.

Thus, in his eagerness to end political oppression, Havel granted a wide amnesty to prisoners. This loosed common criminals on society and halted production of essential manufactures made in prisons. Havel also hastened to improve the ecology by closing polluting lignite mines where miners and their families had a very low life-expectancy – but the miners soon decided that they would rather die young than live in poverty.[78]

And in their eagerness to cut all ties with their former Soviet oppressor, Eastern Europe's new leaders rushed to wind down COMECON on 28 June 1991 – thus smashing the region's trading infrastructure and adding immeasurably to their economic problems. They assumed that the West would buy their goods instead, but the West wanted little of what they had to sell and would not import produce which competed with their own.[79] The Baltic states constitute an analogue. They severed links with Russia – and found themselves starved of energy and deprived of markets. Their Scandinavian neighbours rallied to them for a time but then encountered economic difficulties of their own.

It transpired that the countries which weathered the economic storms of post-Communism best were those, like Slovenia, which had been the most prosperous before, and which were absorbed into the German sphere. East Germans benefited from incorporation into Germany though they experienced severe cultural shock.[80] West Germans found the costs of absorbing their compatriots unexpectedly high – and this limited Germany's ability to invest in other Eastern European countries. Nevertheless Czech industry saw substantial German investments, and Czech fortunes were further boosted on 1 January 1993 by the break with the economically weaker partner, Slovakia. Poland also benefited from proximity to Germany, received financial aid to underpin the economic reforms from the United States, and was forgiven most of its hard-currency debt – the highest, per head, in the region.[81] No such leniency was applied to the others.

The countries which suffered most were the successor states to the USSR and Yugoslavia, unions which turned out to have been more profitable than exploitative. Severe though Russia's economic problems were, those of the Ukraine and Belarus turned out to be worse. Albania also suffered. Infrastructural and social breakdown promoted rising chaos and the revival of the blood feud. By 1996 at least 90 feud killings had been reported.[82]

There were other casualties of economic dislocation and institutional collapse. The old regime had encouraged a reading culture which now declined, and accumulated educational capital which was now squandered. Though philosophy had languished under the old regime and scarce resources had been wasted on Marxist-Leninist studies, many good, scholarly traditions had been preserved in education, science and the performing arts, and special provision for the unusually gifted was sustained at levels many Western countries might envy.

Scientific research in Russia attracted some Western interest. Hence German support for the Euler Mathematics Institute in St Petersburg,[83] and Boeing Corporation's contracting of much of its research and development to an aerospace research institute near Moscow. The World Bank provided funds to train Romanians in fields the old regime had neglected, like law, politics and business studies; and Western governments and foundations funded scholarships for some students to study in the West. The expatriate Hungarian multi-millionaire, George Soros, even funded a new Central European University based in Budapest, Prague and Warsaw, a research support scheme in the humanities and social sciences; and, deeming the natural sciences in Russia to be 'a great treasure for humanity', and an asset of great commercial potential, provided it with $100 million in emergency aid over the period 1993–5.[84] But the West could hardly support so large a foreign academic establishment when it could barely sustain its own.

Academy and University budgets throughout Eastern Europe were savagely cut. As a result, meagre salaries were sometimes unpaid; heating sometimes failed in winter; and libraries were starved of books and journals. There was a general flight from academe as professors took up appointments in politics, government service and the media. Those who remained had to moonlight in order to make ends meet. Such conditions encouraged a huge 'brain drain' from most countries of the region. In Russia alone 300,000 scientific researchers and engineers abandoned their posts.[85]

The post-Communist age also gave rise to one disappointment which touched Westerners more deeply than Eastern Europeans: the position of women deteriorated. As employment shrank so did opportunities for women, and whereas 30 per cent of Czech MPs under Husak had been women, there were fewer than 10 per cent under Havel.[86] There were no protests, however. Indeed many women welcomed greater domesticity. The East European experience suggested that feminism, rather than an inevitable step on the march of progress, was merely a luxury indulged in by rich societies.

* * *

In his New Year address to the nation in January 1991 President Havel reported that post-Communist reconstruction would 'take longer and cost far more than we first thought'. He attributed this disappointment squarely to Communism:

> the heritage of the past few decades [which] has proven worse than we could possible have anticipated.... What a year ago appeared to be a rundown house is in fact a ruin.[87]

There was some truth in this. Yet, as we have seen, the disappointments of post-Communism were also rooted in an unfavourable world economy, unreasonable expectations, and the errors of the successor governments. Another factor also became apparent: Post-Communism shared certain features with the pre-Communist period – in popular psychology and culture as well as politics and the economy. It was even suggested that the Communist system had served precisely to overcome problems of the sort which the region confronts today;[88] and the rising popularity of avowedly socialist politicians suggests that many who welcomed Communism's collapse now wish it would return. But what were Communism's attractions? And how far was it responsible for the region's current ills? To answer these questions we must examine the Soviet Bloc in its post-Stalinist prime.

REFERENCES

1. At a secret meeting of prominent dissidents in the High Tatras mountains in 1988 Adam Michnik eventually remarked that perhaps Gorbachev would do the job for them. He did (see *infra*).
2. W. Doyle, *The French Revolution*, Oxford, 1989, p. 401.
3. See the interesting article by Charles Maier, 'The Collapse of Communism: Approaches for a Future History', *History Workshop*, No. 31, Spring 1991, pp. 34–59.
4. Based on data supplied by Dr Roman Domaszewicz of the Cracow Academy of Economics.
5. Including East Germany, *The Financial Times*, London (hereafter *FT*) supplement, 12 March 1991.
6. Vahan Zanayan, 'After the Oil Boom', *Foreign Affairs*, November/December 1995, pp. 1–7. In 1981 crude oil reached $34 a barrel.
7. Table on resource consumption and GNP in 1966, Sik, Ota, 'The Economic Impact of Stalinism', *Problems of Communism*, May–June 1971, pp. 1–10.
8. See Marshall I. Goldman, 'Diffusion of Development: The Soviet Union', *American Economic Review*, May 1991, pp. 276–81.
9. Tatiana Zaslavskaia, 'Novosibirsk Report', *Survey*, vol. 28, no. 1, 1984, pp. 88–108. I also draw on her paper (and the subsequent discussion) presented at the IV World Congress of Slavists, Harrogate 1990.
10. *Pravda*, 9 November 1985.
11. Goldman, *loc. cit.*. Gorbachev subsequently admitted this to be a grave mistake.
12. W. Pluge 'Future Supply of Gas to Europe', *NATO Colloquium, Economic Development in Cooperation Partner Countries from a Sectoral Perspective*, Brussels, 1993, p. 169, Figure 2.
13. International Monetary Fund, *The Economy of the Former USSR in 1991*, Washington, DC, 1992.
14. It has been argued that the foreign debt was causal in that the required large hard currency loans could not be raised from countries threatened by Soviet arms. Ellman, Michael and Kontorovich, Vladimir, 'The End of the Soviet System: What we learn from the insiders', Paper presented at the V World Congress of ICCEES, Warsaw, 10 August 1995.
15. See his speech to the 27th Congress of the CPSU in February 1986.
16. See *FT*, 2 June 1989.
17. Gorbachev's speech of 6 May – see *Soviet News*, 12 July 1989.
18. See *Keesing's Record of World Events*, 1989, p. 36982; BBC, *Summary of World Broadcasts*, 3rd series, part 2 (Eastern Europe), EE 0505 c/3.
19. On 18 July 1989 – BBC, *op. cit.*, SU 0515 ci/11-4, 22 July 1989.
20. BBC, *op. cit.*, SU 0527. However, the guarantee of a Communist majority in the Congress of People's Deputies was not abolished until October (Keesing's, *op. cit.*, 1989, p. 36978); and the clause in the 1977 Constitution confirming the Communist Party's 'leading role' and centrality in politics was not formally revoked until March 1990 (*ibid.*, 1990, p. 37787).
21. Two accounts by Western observers are useful here: McElvoy, Anne, *The Saddled Cow: East Germany's Life and Legacy*, London, 1992, pp. 194–8; also Smith, Ken, *Berlin: Coming in from the Cold*, London, 1990, pp. 47–9 and 309. My account also draws on press reports, chiefly the London newspapers.
22. McElvoy, *op. cit.*, pp. 198–209; Smith, *op. cit.*, pp. 49–58. Honecker himself attributed his downfall to Gorbachev – see press reports of interview, 25 February 1991.

23. See Jarausch, Konrad H., *The Rush to German Unity*, Oxford, 1993.
24. Personal communication of a Czech witness. My account also draws on Western press reports.
25. See Brucan, Silviu, *The Wasted Generation*, Boulder, 1993, pp. 131–44 *passim*. But see also Denis Deletant's critical review, 'Myth-Making and the Romanian Revolution', *Slavonic and East European Review*, vol. 72, no. 3, July 1994, pp. 483–91. Circumstantial evidence suggests Russian involvement (though any public suggestion of this in so anti-Russian a country might have undermined the new regime's legitimacy). Several leaders of the future National Salvation Front visited Moscow before assuming power; and some were already in the building when Ceaucescu made his last speech. See also Portocala, Radu, *Autopsie du coup d'Etat Roumaine – au pays du mensonge triomphant*, Paris, 1990.
26. The best-known treatment of the Soviet Union's collapse in English, Matlock, Jack F., *Autopsy on an Empire*, New York, 1995, has the advantage of coming from a diplomatist close to the leading actors though it overestimates the importance of personalities. My analysis here has derived much from Ellman and Kontorovich (*loc. cit.*) whose study is based on interviews with a wide variety of functionaries working under the old regime in its final phase, both centrally and locally.
27. Matlock, *op. cit.*, quoted in Kennan, J., 'Witness to the Fall', *New York Review of Books* (hereafter *NYR*), 16 November 1995.
28. See the photograph in the *Montreal Gazette*, 12 March 1990.
29. The point is suggested by Ellman and Kontorovich, *loc. cit.*.
30. See Gramoz, Pashko, 'Inflation in Albania', *Communist Economies and Economic Transformation*, vol. 5, no. 1, 1993 pp. 115–26.
31. Personal observation on visits to Albania in 1989 and 1991.
32. Alia, Ramiz, Speech to the 11th Plenum of the Central Committee of the PLA (Albanian Communist Party), 7 July 1990 (separatum).
33. Gramoz, *loc. cit.*, table 2, p. 118.
34. *Zeri i populit*, 10 August 1991, p. 1 (ABREES, Albania 18895).
35. Jonas Widgren, 'East–West Migration: Economic Buffer or Security Threat', *External Economic Relations of the Central and Eastern European Countries*, NATO Colloquium, Brussels 1992, pp. 169–75.
36. For the relative poverty or affluence of the constituent republics in 1989, see *PlanEcon Report* (OECD), vol. VII, no. 9/10, 20 March 1991. A draft Academy Memorandum attributed the causes of the crisis to Yugoslavia's former leaders, Tito and Kardelj, in favouring the interests of Slovenes and Croats above those of the Serbs in constitutional and economic matters – see Pavkovic, Aleksandr, 'The Serb National Idea 1986–92', *Slavonic & East European Review*, vol. 72, no. 3, July 1994, pp. 440–55. By 1988 an almost visceral resentment of Serbs was observable among some Croats (personal observation).
37. Ciril Ribicic as quoted in *FT*, 4 February 1990.
38. Glenny, Misha, *The Fall of Yugoslavia*, London 1993, pp. 122–23 and 63 (also J. Kifner, 'The Canadian who is Croatia's Kingmaker', *NYT* January, 1991).
39. In the original, unexpurgated, version of his book *Wastelands of Historical Reality* Tudjman depicts Serbs as sub-human and blames anti-semitism on the Jews – Nora Beloff, *Sunday Times*, August 1995. Tudjman's spokesman is quoted by Gwynne Dyer in *Montreal Gazette*, 28 April 1990, copying *Bor'ba*. Also Glenny, *op. cit.*, p. 3 *passim*.
40. See *inter alia*, M. Crnobrnja, *The Yugoslav Drama*, Montreal, 1994.

41. On the Borovo Selo incidents, see Glenny, *op. cit.*, pp. 75–8.
42. My account here is based on press reports and on personal correspondence with friends and colleagues in Croatia.
43. See *inter alia* Glenny, *op. cit.*, pp. 163–4 and 188–93. Also p. 136. This view is contested in some accounts, e.g. C. Bennet, *Yugoslavia's Bloody Collapse* (London, 1995, pp. 173ff.) who castigates the other powers for listening only to the Serb point of view, and attributes the war to Serbian (or JNA) military superiority – but his first assertion is unsupported by evidence, and the second betrays a serious misunderstanding about what causes wars. In fact the fundamental issue was minority rights on which Tudjman would not yield. Even the Pope was to become disenchanted with the Croat leader, as he showed on a subsequent visit to Zagreb.
44. Donia, Robert J. and Fine, John V.A. Jr, *Bosnia and Hercegovina: A tradition Betrayed*, London, 1994, pp. 127ff. But see also Glenny, *op. cit.*, pp. 163–7. There are other versions of the outbreak. It should be noted that although I refer to Bosnian 'Serbs', 'Croats' and 'Muslims' these groupings were not ethnically distinct. Some Croats aligned with the Serbs, some Serbs with the Muslims.
45. Hence the popular impression that the Serbs were getting more than their fair share of territory in the various partition plans.
46. See Charles G. Boyd, 'Making Peace with the Guilty', *Foreign Affairs* vol. 74 Sep./Oct. 1995, pp. 22–38.
47. E.g. a senior UN officer blamed the Bosnian Muslims for 'playing a very cynical political game over refugees' – T. Butcher, *The Daily Telegraph*, 15 July 1995.
48. See Robert Block, 'Killers', *NYR*, 21 October 1993.
49. See Merlino, Jacques, *Les verités Yougoslaves ne sont pas toutes bonnes à dire*, Paris, 1993, esp. pp. 125–31. The former Assistant Secretary of State Richard Perle was retained to advise the Bosnian Muslim delegation at the talks.
50. Binder, David, 'Bosnia's Bombers', *The Nation*, 2 October 1995, pp. 356–7. Binder is on the staff of the *New York Times*. In similar fashion the media were induced to revive old footage on Serb atrocities in order to deflect attention from the Croats' ethnic cleansing of Slavonia in the summer of 1995. The popular Brian Lapping television film is misleading on this point as on others. The UN commander in Sarajevo, General MacKenzie, had previously accused all sides of shelling 'their own forces to blacken the enemy's name' (*The Independent*, 23 July 1995). The overrunning of Srebrenica which stirred public opinion against the Serbs was prompted by Muslim troops who attacked first. UN sources also alleged that it was Muslim, not Serb, troops who shot the Dutch UN soldier. The Muslim army used Srebrenica, as other 'safe zones', for military purposes, and the Serb General Mladic was right when he alleged they contained 'armed terrorists' – Nik Gowing, *The Sunday Telegraph*, 10 July 1995. Bosnian Serbs undoubtedly perpetrated grave atrocities but the singling out of Radovan Karadjic for indictment as a war criminal (overlooking the qualifications of his Bosnian Muslim and Croat counterparts) and the efforts to exclude him from politics regardless of democratic principles, is less a reflection of the strength of evidence against him than of a perception, particularly in Washington, that he might impede implementation of the Dayton accords (see *infra*).
51. On military aid to Croatia see Jonathan Eyal of the Royal United Services Institution, *The Times*, 5 August 1995.
52. The settlement allotted 49 per cent for the 'Serb Republic' and 51 per cent to the Bosnia-Hercegovinan Federation. However, the territory of the Croat

state of Herceg-Bosna was not included and the manner of division was unfavourable to the Serbs who lost territories they had always inhabited. During the Dayton talks the Muslim delegation had the advantage of being advised by a former Assistant Secretary of State, Richard Perle – James L. Graff, *Time*, 20 November 1995. See also report by the UN Commissioner for Refugees, quoted in EIU Intelligence Report, *Bosnia-Hercegovina, Croatia*, 4th quarter, 1995, p. 15.

53. EIU *Country Report: Czechoslovakia* 4th quarter 1995, p. 5: Economic Indicators; PlanEcon, OECD, figures of governmental and private consumption per capita.
54. For Romania, Poland, etc. see R. Bideleaux and Richard Taylor, *European Integration and Disintegration*, London, 1996, table 10.1, p. 194, which confirms the picture using European Bank for Reconstruction and Development and *FT* data. Also EIU Country Reports for Russia (4th quarter 1995, appendix 1, p. 37: Quarterly Indicator of Economic Activity); Ukraine, (p. 23) and Belarus and Moldova (p. 27, appendix 1). For inflation data, see Russia (1st quarter 1996, p. 39) and Ukraine (*ibid.*), p. 25.
55. In Russia the ratio was estimated at between 2:1 and 10:1 – see Peter Reddaway, *The Times*, 23 January 1996.
56. EIU, *Economies in Transition and the Former Soviet Union*, 1st quarter 1996, p. 4: 'Basic Data' table. Russian inflation is gauged by the overprinted price on a ticket to the State Hermitage Museum.
57. *UNICEF Regional Monitoring Report* (hereafter UNICEF), No. 3, Florence 1995, tables 2 and 3, pp. 128–9; EIU Country Reports for Poland, 1st quarter 1996, Appendix I, p. 2; and Romania, 4th quarter 1995, p. 19; Gaspard, Michel, 'Incomes and Living Standards' in Weichhardt, Reiner, ed., *Economic Developments in Cooperation Partner Countries from a Sectoral Perspective*, NATO Colloquium, Brussels 1993, Table II.
58. UNICEF, No. 1, November 1993, p. 8, Table 1.
59. Cornia, G.A., UNICEF, No. 2 (1994), pp. v–vi.
60. UNICEF, No. 3, Table 17: 'Crime Rate', p. 150.
61. See the interesting discussion by Katherine Verdery, 'Faith, Hope and *Caritas* in the Land of the Pyramids: Romania 1990 to 1994', *Comparative Studies in Society and History*, vol. 37 (1995), pp. 625–69.
62. Havel, V., Letter to Husak, April 1975, *The Power of the Powerless*, London 1985, p. 4.
63. EIU *Country Report: Romania*, 1st quarter 1996, p. 16.
64. See E. Gellner, *Conditions of Liberty: Civil Society and its Rivals*, London 1994. Also C.G.A. Bryant, 'Civil Society and Pluralism: a Conceptual Analysis', *Sisyphus*, Vol. I (VIII), 1992, pp. 103–19.
65. Adam Michnik, quoted by Roger Boyes, *The Times*, 8 June 1996.
66. On the Czech case, see Laber, Jeri, 'Witch Hunt in Prague', *NYR*, 23 April 1992, pp. 5–8; Havel thought it wrong, however – see Havel, V., 'Paradise Lost' (and translator Paul Wilson's note), *ibid.*, 9 April 1992, pp. 6–8. On Albania, see Laber, J., 'Slouching towards Democracy', *NYR*, 14 January 1993, pp. 24–7, a somewhat slanted report of interviews with Mme Hoxha and Ramiz Alia. Alia *was* responsible for reforms and the dissident Kadare (*loc. cit.*) pictures him as sympathetic and responsive. On East Germany, see Ash, T. Garton, 'Central Europe: The Present Past', *NYR*, 13 July 1995, pp. 21ff.
67. Elon, Amos, 'East Germany: Crime and Punishment', *NYR*, 14 May 1992, pp. 6–11.

68. *FT*, 3 October 1995; on Slovakia, Tom Gross, *Jewish Chronicle*, 10 December 1993; for Tudjman's 'reconciliation' plan (in which he reduced the number Jasenovac's Second World War victims from 200,000 to 40,000), *Montreal Gazette*, 23 April 1996.
69. See *FT* reports of 23 March 1992; and 13 June 1996. Also Helena Smith, *The Guardian*, 29 May 1996; Berisha interview with Richard Owen, *The Times*, 3 June 1996, and *ibid.*, 18 June 1996.
70. 150 people were reported killed. For a good political analysis of Yeltsin's first year in power, see P. Reddaway, 'Russia on the Brink', *NYR*, 28 January 1993, pp. 30–5.
71. Such a scheme would have yielded an estimated $100 billion – enough to set the countries of East-Central Europe on the road to recovery. See Rohatyn, Felix, 'World Capitalism: The Need and the Risks', *NYR*, 15 July 1994.
72. Nikolai Shmelev, *Izvestiia*, 19 October 1991, quoted by Abraham Brumberg, 'The Road to Minsk', *NYR*, 30 January 1992, pp. 21–6 (25).
73. See *FT Survey: Poland*, 28 April 1992; also Galbraith, J.K., 'The Rush to Capitalism', *NYR*, 25 October 1990. The effectiveness of the solutions associated with Jeffrey Sachs are still disputed.
74. In the spring of 1991 the US Ambassador to Sofia, Hugh Hill, visited the 'Polemic' debating club at Pleven and opposition leaders, in disregard of protocol. The Chairman of the United Democratic Front opened a new US cultural–information centre in Pleven – *Poletika*, Pleven, issue 5, April 1991. The author was in Bulgaria at the time.
75. On Bulgaria, Gerald Creed, 'Local, National and International Interests in the Bulgarian Political Transition'; on Russia and the Ukraine, Janice Wedel; on Albania, Steven Samson – papers given at V International Congress of Central and Eastern European Studies, Warsaw, August 1995. I am grateful to Dr Creed for a draft copy of his paper which had not appeared by the time this went to press.
76. The sources for the economic history of post-Communism generally are many and detailed. Aside from official data issued by governments they include World Bank, IMF and EBRD Reports. I have found the quarterly ERU Country Reports for the region particularly helpful.
77. Havel, *Power of the Powerless*, *op. cit.*, p. 192.
78. See *FT*, 27 and 28 October 1991.
79. See my articles '1989 and After', *SEER*, vol. 71, no. 4, October 1993, pp. 701–711, 'Eastern Europe after Communism', *European Business Review*, vol. 95, no. 5 (1995), pp. vii–x, and 'Communism's Legacy to the Balkans', *Revue de sud-est européene*, Bucharest 1996 (forthcoming). Also Wilson, Paul, 'The End of the Velvet Revolution', *NYR*, 13 August 1992, pp. 57–64, esp. p. 63. The changing patterns of interregional trade and the commerce of individual countries can be traced in the successive volumes of the UN's *Economic Bulletin for Europe*.
80. For a useful summary of the transition see 'Restructuring of East Germany', *FT* survey, 4 May 1994. The difficulties had been predicted by Stefan Heym who, early in 1990, compared the absorption of the German Democratic Republic by the German Federal Republic to a snake swallowing a hedgehog – see Adrian Bridge, *The Independent*, 18 June 1992.
81. The strange story of the separation in which the Slovak leader Meciar made the running, and which President Havel failed to contest, is described by Paul Wilson, 'Czechoslovakia: the Pain of Divorce', *NYR*, December 1992, pp. 69–75; and Draper, Theodore, 'The End of Czechoslovakia', *NYR*,

28 January 1993, pp. 20–6. On Poland's debt, N. Scott, 'East-West trade on the Threshold of the 1990s', NATO Economy database; also Aslund, A., review of Balcerowicz, L., *Society, Capitalism, Transformation* in *FT*, 29 February 1996.

82. BBC Channel 2 report by BBC correspondent, 1 June 1996.
83. I owe the information on Russia to Yakov Rabkin of the University of Montreal. The account (and what follows) also draws on interviews with academics in Poland, Czechoslovakia, Hungary and Romania carried out (thanks to an SSHRCC grant) in 1993–4.
84. See Soros interview with John Torode, *The Independent*, 25 June 1993, and Research Support Scheme, *Network Chronicle*, No. 1, 1994 and No. 2, 1996.
85. See Aubert, E., OECD, *Science in Russia: Implosion or Rebirth*, Paris, 1991.
86. See Kligman, Gail,'Women, children and the feminization of poverty' in Millar, James R. and Wolchik, Sharon L., eds, *The Social Legacy of Communism*, Washington and Cambridge 1994, pp. 252–70.
87. V. Havel, 'The New Year in Prague', trans. Paul Wilson, *NYR*, 7 March 1991, pp. 19–20.
88. S. Brucan, *The Times*, 21 October 1994.

2

The Crooked Wood of Humanity (1953–1989)

Out of the crooked wood of humanity nothing straight can be made.
Immanuel Kant

After Stalin's death in 1953 many expectations about Eastern Europe were confounded. The region did not become an earthly paradise for the working classes, and the Soviet Union did not overtake the United States in economic performance, as Nikita Khrushchev had forecast in the heady days of the sixties. Those who predicted the imminent collapse of the 'Soviet Empire' in Eastern Europe[1] were ultimately vindicated, but they were right chiefly for the wrong reasons, and the collapse when it came took most dissidents and critics by surprise.

The convergence between the worlds of East and West, much talked of in the heady days of the 1960s, did not materialize either, but a certain symmetry was observable. The Warsaw Pact mirrored NATO and COMECON the European Common Market. Even the COMECON headquarters building in Moscow bore a resemblance to its counterpart in Brussels. Eastern Bloc governments sought the latest technology from the West, and their young people were no less anxious to acquire blue jeans, hear pop music and eat 'junk' foods. Concern for the environment also grew.[2] Unfortunately, the region proved to be as vulnerable to disturbances in the world economy as it was susceptible to changes in fashion. From the mid-seventies especially, indebtedness to Western banks rose sharply in several countries of the bloc;[3] so did inflation.

Yet despite its grievous problems, and in particular its technological and developmental backwardness, Eastern Europe had been transformed since Stalin's day. Real incomes were far below those of Western countries but they had soared far above the levels of the early 1950s.[4] More and more families now owned cars and washing machines; and television had come to be taken for granted. The diet had improved, life expectations had increased and infant mortality fallen. Above all, perhaps, the old, predominately peasant way of life had almost disappeared[5] and so, for the most part, had rural poverty. Piped, fresh water and electricity, unheard-of luxuries for many even in the recent past, were generally available, and regular bus services, as well as radio and television, had broken down rural isolation. The children of peasants who could vividly recall the hardships of their village childhoods came to take the relative excitements and sophistication of city life for granted. Privation was eliminated. There was even a degree of comfort.

The rising living standards and changing lifestyles were a product of impressive economic growth. Between 1955 and 1980 industrial production rose over six and a half times, in Czechoslovakia and Hungary, eleven times in Poland, sixteen times in Bulgaria and by almost twenty times in Romania. These raw statistics were to an extent misleading, of course. Much of Czechoslovakia's industrial plant, like East Germany's and that of the USSR itself, was becoming increasingly obsolescent; the Hungarian and Bulgarian successes were based primarily on agriculture; the considerable increases in Polish living standards fell short of the population's expectations; the huge expansion of Romanian industry reflected the pitifully low base it had started from and came to be symbolized by vast stock-piles of unsaleable steel. Nonetheless, the overall picture was not one of unmitigated failure.[6]

Outside Romania the volume of production by heavy industry ceased to be the overriding priority, as it had been in Stalin's time. More was produced for the consumer and there was increasing concern for quality. Yet this trend was impeded by fundamental difficulties (in Marxist jargon, 'contradictions') in the economy, society and in political life. The apple of economic miracle turned out to contain worms.

The command economy, masterminded by central government, operated through artificial pricing. This created imbalances in the relative values of goods and led to waste. The huge bureaucracy involved produced tangles of red tape. It was also, for human reasons, inherently inflexible. Older bureaucrats and managers, accustomed over the years to one set of rules and standards, naturally resisted the introduction of change; calls for efficiency threatened people comfortably inured to inefficient practices and traditional *Schlamperei*.

Attempts to solve the problem ran into difficulties. 'Democracy in the workplace', a policy espoused by Mikhail Gorbachev in his early months in office to correct lazy and incompetent management, wasted much time with ill-informed chatter, impeding the efficient despatch of business. 'Socialist self-management', first introduced in Yugoslavia in the 1950s, had not proved an unqualified success either. Those in command confronted very difficult, sometimes impossible, choices in trying to adapt the system to new circumstances; and, since Marxist theory either failed to provide appropriate answers (or, which was worse, too many), the professional ideologists had a hard time reconciling the demands of practical government with the Marxist-Leninist canon.

Reforms called for hard choices in the social sphere, too. Efficiency implied unemployment, which threatened the maintenance of the welfare state; incentives produced bigger wage differentials than seemed decent in self-proclaimed egalitarian societies; conflicts arose between technological experts and managers on the one hand, and the established elite of the working class on the other.[7] Ultimately economic progress and the old Communist value-system proved to be incompatible.

Another contradiction had become apparent even earlier, in the relations between the Soviet Union and the other Eastern European members of the Bloc. In June 1955 Stalin's successors dropped the old principle which had given the Soviet Party the 'leading role' in the region, and substituted another:

> Mutual respect and non-intervention in the internal affairs [of other Communist states], whether for economic, political or ideological reasons, since matters of internal organization... and different forms of socialist development are solely the concern of each individual country.[8]

In October 1956 it went farther, condemning past 'errors' which 'devalued the principles of legal equality between the socialist states in their relations with each other'. A few days later Soviet tanks rolled in to crush the Hungarian revolution. The change of ideological line from the old Stalinist principle implied a contradiction between the sovereignty of the Eastern European satellites and the perceived interests of the Soviet Union.

It also complicated the Soviet Union's role as leader of the Bloc. Kadar's Hungary was subsequently permitted to adopt more liberal policies than Moscow's, but when the Soviet Union itself adopted such policies her publicly-stated principles on the question of sovereignty restricted her power to persuade hard-line regimes such as Ulbricht's East Germany or Ceaucescu's Romania to follow suit. Yet the satellites had long ceased to be Soviet clones, exactly replicating Soviet institutions, methods and policies, if ever they had been. Poland abandoned collectivization, eschewed the bureaucratic purge, and gave the Catholic Church a freedom and a role in society unparalleled elsewhere in the Bloc. Romania was tolerated despite her Stalinist internal policies, her independent diplomacy and her territorial claim to Soviet Moldavia.[9] No longer did membership of the Bloc imply automatic subservience to Soviet wishes as it had in Stalin's day. But, by the same token, it proved more difficult to hold the Bloc together. So what, other than the threat of force, was the glue that gave it some coherence?

One factor, paradoxically, was nationalism. Despite the anti-Russian sentiment that prevailed throughout most of the region the resentments that the satellite nations harboured against each other were hardly less fierce;[10] and, like the old empires of the nineteenth century, Moscow was able to exploit these to her advantage. Cooperation between armies in the

Warsaw Pact, the brotherhood of Party membership, and regular bilateral meetings between experts of all kinds, created networks of friendship among the elites of each of the countries which helped to hold the Bloc together. Propaganda also helped, and, again paradoxically, so did a general commitment to socialist principles to which many dissidents also subscribed.[11] But a more significant binding force was economic.

The economic exploitation of some of the smaller countries of Eastern Europe that had taken place under Stalin (see Chapter 3) gave way to more equitable relationships, and ultimately to a degree of Soviet beneficence. Prices of Soviet oil to friendly countries of the Bloc were kept substantially below those of OPEC, and, though Romania had to pay for her independence by tightening her belt, Poland was heavily subsidized with cheap energy and loans without repayments.[12] So, though the fact was tactfully ignored, most Bloc countries derived economic advantage from the Soviet association. The Kremlin may have been master, but it eventually became an indulgent master.

Bilateral agreements between the smaller countries were also helpful in knitting the economies of the region together. Czechoslovakia cooperated with Poland in tractor manufacture and with the East Germans in making steam boilers and textiles. Hungary cooperated with Poland in extracting coal from slack, and with Czechoslovakia on plans for a dam across the Danube (which aroused a storm of protest from conservationists in Hungary). But the chief instrument for this integration was COMECON .

In March 1954 COMECON was given the task of coordinating the economic plans of the member states. Subsequently it acquired a permanent bureaucracy and set out to eliminate technological and economic backwardness in the region. In the years that followed COMECON proceeded to rationalize machine-building, allocating thousands of items to individual member countries; pooled railway wagons; began a region-wide network of motorways; built oil and gas pipelines; set up an electric grid and a Bank for Economic Co-operation to fund industrial projects and trade. Supranational bodies were also established in Budapest, Warsaw and East Berlin to modernize steel industries and to coordinate the production of ball-bearings and chemicals.[13]

The Bloc as a whole also profited from a planned division of labour. The USSR, Hungary and Bulgaria provided food surpluses for the food-deficit countries; Hungary concentrated on providing buses and rotovators for the other members, Bulgaria produced much of their handling equipment. The communications policy was accounted a great success. COMECON was relatively successful in energy, less so in engineering, where the emphasis was mistakenly placed on the manufacture of finished products rather than parts. The pricing mechanism also presented an obstacle to efficient cooperation, making it uneconomic, for example, for one country to fulfil orders from others in excess of those planned for.

In general the smaller countries of the Bloc enjoyed the advantage of the huge Soviet market, but it was a relatively undiscriminating market which encouraged the production of many goods which would not easily be sold elsewhere. And there were needs which could not be met within the Bloc at all: hence the increased economic links with the West. The Italian Fiat company set up car plants in Poland and the USSR; Poland made deals with Krupp and Grundig; Hungary enlisted the help of Chicago agencies in developing meat production; and several countries invited Western hotel chains to open branches on their territory. Such developments reflected continuing shortages of expertize in the service sector as well as industry.

In sum, considerable changes took place in Eastern Europe between 1953 and 1989. Advances were made, yet progress was uneven, hampered by systemic problems and interrupted by rebellions. However, the major trends and the problems which culminated in the collapse of the late 1980s must be examined in the context of events, in the sequence of occurrances, and in their relationships to one another. It is therefore to chronological analysis that we now turn.

* * *

Looking back to the months following Stalin's death in March 1953, one is struck by the speed of change in some countries of Eastern Europe and the slowness of change in others. Within days Moscow announced improvements in wages, price and tax cuts, a reduction in investment for heavy industry and a boost for agriculture. Stalin's successors clearly recognized that the population had been squeezed too tightly for too long; and that the purges and the repression had gone too far. Furthermore, even as early as 1953 the Stalinist economic system was beginning to creak.[14] The consequent tempering of policies was also associated with an easing of the Cold War (the armistice that ended the Korean War was signed that July) and by relief that a post-war recession had been avoided. Nonetheless there was considerable uncertainty throughout the region as to how far and how fast the thaw might proceed, and, indeed, as to whether it would last at all.

Hungary followed Moscow's line almost immediately. The Stalinist Rakosi was demoted, and a liberal Communist, Imre Nagy, became Premier; the burdensome rate of industrialization was slowed down, investment reallocated to provide more for agriculture, prices were cut, tax arrears cancelled, and the housing programme stepped up. On the political plane some purge victims were rehabilitated, and people allowed to speak out a little. But in other countries Moscow's example was ignored. Political trials of innocent victims proceeded in Romania and Czechoslovakia,[15] and the East German leadership actually increased the pressure on its subject population.

When, in April 1953, Walter Ulbricht applied to Moscow for aid, the Soviet government took the opportunity to reproach him. He was told that his plans for reconstruction were overambitious and that he should provide more consumer goods for the hard-pressed German worker. Even though East Germany was not yet a sovereign state, Ulbricht responded by raising the work norms of the labour force by 10 per cent and inveighing against 'saboteurs'. He also increased prices, reduced social benefits and tightened the screws on what remained of the private sector. A month later, however, he began to backtrack. On the 11th the Council of Ministers abruptly admitted that a variety of 'mistakes' had been made which were alienating the people, and promised immediate rectification.[16]

Six days later the storm broke. Three hundred thousand workers took to the streets. Public buildings were occupied, portraits of Ulbricht torn down, Party offices set on fire, prisons broken into and their inmates released. The Soviet army of occupation had to be called out to restore order.

Accusations were freely traded by the press and politicians East and West. One side blamed the troubles on fascist bandits and Western agents; the other alleged that the entire population had risen in the cause of German reunification and were suppressed in a torrent of blood. None of this was true. No 'fascist bandits' or Western agents were identified; the protests had not been universal, nor were they primarily directed towards German reunification; and casualties were comparatively few – twenty-one deaths, not all of them of protesters.

In fact (as in the Russian Revolution of 1917) it was the workers in heavy industry, the Stalinist elite, who had led the protest. The very size of the plants, which distanced management from those on the shop floor, had both increased discontent and facilitated organized action. But the fuse was lit by the absence from the list of concessions published on 11 June of any mention of work norms. The protesters were swiftly crushed, yet they made their point: the intolerable increase in work norms was rescinded.

The relaxation, and the continuing option for discontented elements to escape to West Germany, kept the East Germans quiet throughout the turmoil that was to follow elsewhere in the Bloc in 1956. For the moment, however, the thaw proceeded without disturbance. In 1954 the COMINFORM, an organization ostensibly concerned with disseminating information among Communists, but regarded in the West as a dangerous instrument for the promotion of world revolution, was abolished, signalling a further reduction in East–West tensions. And in 1955, after seven years of strained relations, Yugoslavia and the Soviet Union were reconciled.

The relaxation was least marked in the Balkan countries, but East Germany gained sovereignty and celebrated it by releasing 13,000 political prisoners. In Czechoslovakia some purge victims were quietly released (though there was no posthumous rehabilitation for the most celebrated of them, Rudolf Slansky). In Poland, however, matters now went farther. Economic policies were not much changed, but in 1954 30,000 political prisoners, including a former Minister, Wladyslaw Gomulka, were released, and the collectivization programme was allowed to peter out. Marshal Rokossovsky, the Soviet soldier whom Stalin had installed as Poland's military chief as part of his scheme of controlling the country, was excluded from the Politburo; his successor, Spychalski, restored traditional-style Polish uniforms. The thaw was permitting a degree of national self-assertion.

More than that, it became possible to publish accounts of circumstances as they really were, something unheard of in the grim decade of reconstruction. The most celebrated example was Adam Wazyk's *Poem for Adults*, which encapsulated so much of the human truth involved in the frantic rush of Stalinist industrialization with its concomitants of sudden urbanization and social restructuring.

From villages, from little towns, they go in wagons,
To build a foundry, to conjure up a town,
To dig out a new Eldorado.
A pioneer army, a gathered mob,
They crowd each other in barracks, in hostels, in huts.
They plunge and whistle in the muddy streets:
The great migration, dishevelled ambition,
On their necks a little string – the Cross of Czestochowa.

With a storehouse of oaths, with a little feather pillow,
Bestial with vodka, boasting of tarts,
A distrusting soul – wrenched from the bonds,
Half-awake and half-mad,
Silent in words, singing snatches of song –
Is suddenly thrust out from mediaeval darkness....

The great migration builds new industry,
Unknown to Poland but known to history,
Is fed on great empty words, lives
Wildly from day to day in despite of preachers –
Amid coal fumes is melted in this slow torture
Into a working class.
Much is wasted, as yet only dross.[17]

With Moscow proclaiming its policy of 'non-interference' in the internal affairs of the satellite countries, it appeared that each was being allowed to find its own way to the new Eldorado. And where Poland led Hungary followed. But what gave added impetus to the reformers was Khrushchev's denunciation of Stalin's crimes at the Twentieth Congress of the Soviet Communist Party in February 1956. The former leader's 'cult of personality' was condemned; and new watchwords, 'democratism' and 'socialist legality', were proclaimed. This engendered considerable excitement.

It was reflected in a speech made to the Polish Parliament by Premier Cyrankiewicz two months later. There was a ferment of political activity, he said; yet people were afraid that 'the thaw' might not last. He reassured them; promised justice, even compensation, for purge victims; better living standards; more investment in farming, housing and social services, less in industry. He also undertook to reform the bureaucracy and to 'return initiative to the masses'. People were afraid of taking decisions and shunned responsibility, he said. Management was overcentralized and every functionary thought himself wiser than the next. Corruption, arbitrariness and 'violation of legality' was rampant. It was intolerable.[18] Cyrankiewicz had identified some of the fundamental flaws in the system. But as events were shortly to demonstrate, they were not to be corrected easily.

His speech generated great excitement. In June workers in the great ZISPO plant in Poznan (one of those whose construction Wazyk pictured in his poem), infuriated by the apparent inconsistency between the government's promises and the unresponsiveness of both management and trade unions, sent a delegation to Warsaw. Their demands were rejected, and they returned home. But before they arrived, false rumours began to circulate: it was said that they had been arrested. As a result infuriated workers downed tools and, led by a works Party secretary, marched on the town hall. Others joined them. There were calls for better living standards, 'Bread and Freedom'; some elements turned violent, attacked Party headquarters, the courts, the police headquarters and the prison. A radio station used to jam Western broadcasts was destroyed. In the afternoon tanks appeared on the streets of Poznan – but some of the troops refused to fire. More reliable units were called in. By the end of the day all was quiet in Poznan. The price was 300 wounded and as many arrests.

Next day Cyrankiewicz broadcast to the nation. Echoing Ulbricht three years earlier, he accused 'provocateurs and imperialists' of causing the trouble. However, he admitted that the ZISPO workers had some genuine grievances and subsequently agreed that they had been overtaxed and underpaid; that their wages should not have declined when their productivity had risen. The trials of those involved in the disturbance were open, the sentences light; and in October 1956 all except those convicted of homicide and looting were released.

It has been claimed that the Poznan riots occasioned a range of reforms in Poland: the setting up of workers' councils, the relaxation of censorship, the halting of collectivization, a shift to the production of consumer goods, and a degree of political liberalization. This is not true, for the reforms were already in train. However the riots did further the political career of the widely popular Gomulka, who, having been ousted from the Party and served a prison sentence for 'nationalist deviation', now returned to power, lending the regime a popular legitimacy it had not previously enjoyed. That October, having laid the blame for the 'Poznan tragedy and the profound dissatisfaction of the entire working class' squarely on the Party and the former government, he announced a new departure on the 'Polish road to Socialism'. Time would prove that Gomulka had not after all discovered the magic recipe which would secure a prosperous future while keeping the people content. Nor was anyone else to do so.

The poorest countries, Bulgaria, Romania and Albania, made no noticeable move towards liberalization at all. For them the breaking-down of village, even tribal, isolation, and the building of the nation, was as urgent as economic improvement. In these Balkan countries, then, it was nationalism which was emphasized. And in Hungary, where Rakosi had regained the helm in 1955, Nagy was disgraced and liberalization abandoned.

Rakosi's faith in forced collectivization and centralized planning was undiminished. So was his use of 'administrative means' (a euphemism for by-passing the law). However, there was rising excitement at the evening meetings of the Union of Working Youth's debating club, the 'Petofi Circle', named after the heroic poet revolutionary of the 1848 Hungarian Rising; and the tide of opinion began to run strongly against Rakosi's hard line. Support for Nagy began to be expressed openly; some sections of the press espoused the cause. Two days after the Poznan riots Rakosi acted. The firebrands of the Petofi Circle were lambasted; so were those sections of the Press which purveyed 'anti-Party views'.[19] However, the Soviet government (advised by Yuri Andropov of their Embassy in Budapest) preferred the liberalizers to Rakosi. His successor, Gerö, promptly sanctioned the posthumous rehabilitation of Laszlo Rajk, among other victims of the purges (see Chapter 3), for whose death Rakosi had been responsible. On 6 October vast crowds turned out to watch the ceremonial reinterment. The onlookers were silent but, according to a newspaper report, they 'burned with hatred' as they recalled 'the dark practices of tyranny, lawlessness, slander and defrauding of the people'.[20] But the silence was not to last long.

Crowds reappeared, and turned violent. The police lost control, and the troops who were brought in fraternized with the demonstrators. Mobs gathered outside Party offices and beat up anyone incautious enough to emerge. Members of the secret police (AVH) were lynched. Gero asked for Soviet help, but the appearance of some Soviet troops only infuriated the crowd, and, with the situation in Poland still uncertain, Moscow shrank from exacerbating the situation.

With Soviet approval Imre Nagy, who had returned as Premier, announced a 'new course'. But in a proclamation of 24 October he explained that democratization, rising living standards and, above all now, national assertion, depended on the restoration of order. 'We must not let our sacred national program be soiled by blood.' Yet though the Soviet forces withdrew at his request, Nagy could not master the situation. In the euphoria of victory, the peasants dismantled the collective farms, and though the army command under General Maleter remained loyal, most soldiers deserted. In the happy chaos that prevailed Nagy felt he had to go farther and farther to keep up with the public's mood. He abolished the AVH, dismissed several hardliners from the government and co-opted some oppositionists; promised to allow the political parties approved by the Allied Control Commission in 1945 to be re-formed, and opened the frontier, allowing foreign reporters and possibly Western agents to flock into Budapest. Warning bells began to ring in Moscow.

The Soviet government might smile on controlled liberalization, but the situation in Hungary seemed to be out of control, and Hungary was crucial to the Bloc's defences. So, on 1 November, Soviet tanks moved back towards Budapest. The Hungarians responded by declaring neutrality and leaving the Warsaw Pact[21] – to no avail. After several days of desultory fighting the revolution was crushed. As many as 25,000 died; thousands more took advantage of the confusion to flee to the West. Nagy and his colleagues were subsequently captured and eliminated.

On the day Soviet troops returned to Hungary, Janos Kadar, who had replaced Gero as the Party chief, announced a new programme. His first point, hypocritically as it seemed at the time, was to secure 'our national independence and ... sovereignty'. The Soviets had only been invited back, he explained, 'to help our nation smash the sinister forces of reaction'. But there would be reforms: a better deal for the workers, including 'worker democracy'; reforms in agriculture, including help for private farmers; support even for independent retailers and artisans.[22] At that moment 'Jani' Kadar was the most reviled man in Hungary. He was subsequently to become a national hero.

On 11 November Tito, the leader of neighbouring Yugoslavia, gave his verdict. He condemned the first Soviet intervention, but supported the second.

> Which was ... the lesser evil? – chaos, civil war, counter-revolution and a new world war, or the intervention of Soviet troops ...?[23]

There was some truth in this. The crowds had become extreme in their nationalist fervour. Order had broken down. The chaos of late October required the use of force, and this Nagy had lacked, for the Hungarian army had melted away.

It was expected that the events in Hungary would spoil Poland's chances of reform. They did not. When Khrushchev met Gomulka a few days later he agreed to cancel Poland's debts to the USSR accrued from unfavourable trade agreements made in Stalin's time (see Chapter 3); provide her with nearly one and a half million tons of Soviet grain on credit, and long-term credits of 700 million rubles with which to purchase Soviet goods. He also agreed to limit the number of Soviet troops in Poland (their presence was termed 'temporary') and to oblige them and their families 'to respect and adhere to ... Polish law'. This gave some substance to the reiterated principle of 'complete equality, respect for national integrity, national independence and sovereignty, and non-interference in internal affairs' between the two countries.[24]

* * *

It soon became clear that, despite Hungary, there would be no return to Stalinism in the Soviet Union itself, but there were still considerable policy variations among the countries of the Bloc. In Poland collectivization was shelved. In East Germany it proceeded, though at a slower pace. In Czechoslovakia 90 per cent of the arable land was already in the state sector and in Bulgaria collectivization was soon virtually complete; but in Romania the transformation of agriculture was slowest of all.

In Hungary, collectivization was reintroduced in 1959 but on a different basis from before. This time there were no compulsory delivery quotas at low fixed prices, the better farmers were appointed managers, and account was taken of different conditions in different areas. In Tokay, for example, collectives were formed for ploughing, spraying and marketing but the vineyards themselves were left in individual peasant hands. There were some failures even so, but many a new collective whose management was both expert and blessed with human skills became a roaring success; and this was to form the basis of Hungary's subsequent 'economic miracle'.[25]

While re-building the country's agriculture, the Kadar regime invested more in new technology, removed some economic decisions from the hands of the central planners, and introduced some profit sharing schemes. The introduction of modest, on the whole well-considered, practical reforms, was to continue. The approach presented a sharp contrast to the wholesale, doctrinaire rushes at economic reconstruction which had characterized the immediate post-war years. However, Kadar made few concessions in the political sphere; and Gomulka also thought it wise to rein in the younger Polish intellectuals.

The international atmosphere, meanwhile, continued to improve. Austria, hitherto under Four Power occupation, was granted independence in 1955, though Moscow insisted that she allow no foreign military bases on her territory and join no alliances; and in 1958 Soviet troops left Romania. On the other hand, the sixties began with some apparently contradictory trends in both the international and the domestic scenes. Albania defied Moscow by siding with China in the Sino-Soviet dispute; Kadar began to woo the Hungarian public; the Berlin Wall was erected; the statue to Joseph Stalin in Prague was pulled down; and Romania embarked on a Stalinist programme of forced economic growth.

The stridency of tiny Albania was, perhaps, the least surprising turn. Her foreign relations were consistently guided by hostility both to the West and to her huge neighbour Yugoslavia. Since Moscow and Belgrade were on friendly terms again, it followed that Tirana would be cool to Moscow. Furthermore, Albanians, whose language had only recently been standardized, were still disposed to think in terms of the village and the tribe rather than their country as a whole. Isolation seems to have helped Albanians find themselves as a nation. And since some economic assistance was essential, they preferred it to come from distant China rather than the USSR.

On the other hand 1962 saw a more significant turn for Hungary. Both Rakosi and Gero were expelled from the Party, and Kadar announced a new policy of tolerance with the implicit proviso that no one rock the boat too much. In March 1963 he declared an amnesty, and released even unrepentant associates of Nagy like the post-war agriculture minister Ferenc Donath. But from the moment he declared that 'who is not against us is with us' a state of truce and even co-operation began to prevail between government and people. Greater incentives were offered, parts of the black economy sanctioned, moonlighting was encouraged. The Hungarians got down to work. Output, especially in industry, increased significantly; so did living standards.[26]

By contrast to Hungary, where chains were being loosened, in East Germany they were tightened. On 13 August 1961 Ulbricht sealed the frontier with West Germany and the notorious Berlin Wall was erected. His government had good reasons for taking these oppressive steps. Since 1949 East Germany had lost 2.5 million people to the West, about 15 per cent of her population. For a time the regime had found the losses tolerable, since they rid the country of the most disaffected elements. But the migrants included too high a proportion of the young and the skilled, and the tide of migration had been increasing again. During the first half of 1961 the rate of departure had doubled.[27] The time had come to staunch the flow. Yet in 1963, following the Hungarian example, the Ulbricht regime introduced more flexible economic policies which by 1968 were to gain East Germans the highest living standards in the Bloc.

The removal of Stalin's statue from Prague in 1961 suggested the belated onset of a thaw in Czechoslovakia. Yet the waters froze over again in little more than a year. The Bulgarian purge of 1962, on the other hand, secured the appointment of Todor Zhivkov as Party Secretary against a man of harder line, while Romania adhered even more grimly to the Stalinist model. The Soviet Seven Year Plan, launched in 1959, had placed yet more emphasis on agriculture and light industry. By contrast, the Romanian Five Year Plan, unveiled in 1960, aimed to achieve a higher rate of industrial growth, especially for heavy industry, than any other country in the Bloc.

This was not welcome news to the rest of Eastern Europe, where the idea was taking hold that it was senseless to compete with each other in the sale of industrial goods. The other countries had abandoned the idea of separate, autarchic, economies such as Romania was clinging to. They now wanted a division of labour within the Bloc. COMECON, which had been set up in 1954 to coordinate the various national plans, but whose powers had hitherto been limited, now acquired considerable prominence as the instrument through which the economics of the region were to be integrated and developed. In June 1962 it announced its plan.

Instead of every member country trying to manufacture everything it needed regardless of its size and resources, each was to specialize in what it could produce most efficiently. Only the USSR, with its vast resources and infrastructure, should continue to engage on all economic fronts. This arrangement did not suit Romania; and when it was proposed that she concentrate on agriculture, or at least cut back her ambitious plans for industrial development (the new plant she planned at Galati was designed to out-produce the combined steel output of Czechoslovakia, East Germany and Poland by 1970), she flatly rejected the proposal. For a country with a population of little more than 20 million, most of them peasants, and with a very low national product, the idea of more modest development plans might be thought to have made better economic sense – but Romania feared that an inferior economic position might force her once again into a subservient political position.

Besides, the creation of a modernized socialist state demanded the urbanization of her population, and the creation of a dominant working class. When her allies suggested a regional division of labour which would include half the country in an agricultural zone along with Bulgaria and part of the USSR, and the other half in an 'intermediate' zone along with Hungary, her leaders saw a threat to split the state in two and put it at the mercy of the neighbours she had long feared. So Romania stuck to her plans, turned to West Germany for assistance and stretched out her hands to Western banks.

Khrushchev fell in October 1964. Nonetheless, no general reversion to Stalinism seemed to be in prospect. Indeed, outside Romania, rather more daring variations of approach to economic reform were noticeable, particularly in Hungary. Her 'New Economic Mechanism' (introduced in 1965–8) decentralized planning even farther. Individual production units were given more autonomy; much red tape was stripped away; profit incentives were increased and more flexibility introduced into the pricing system. Corruption was also attacked; an attempt was made to cut out dead wood (the inclusion, for example, of 'Dead Souls' on the books of an enterprise, a common practice throughout the Bloc); and collective farms were merged into larger units to promote economies and efficiencies – a practice which both Bulgaria and Czechoslovakia were subsequently to adopt. Production in Hungary soared, albeit sometimes producing wasteful gluts.[28] Exports also rose – though no less than two-thirds of the exports to the West by 1967 consisted of cattle and cattle products, as had been the case four and more centuries earlier (see Chapter 8).

These Hungarian tendencies were also to be seen in Yugoslavia where in 1965 Rankovic, the centralist police chief, was dismissed, and economic reforms were introduced which made for greater decentralization, more attention to the consumer, and freer pricing. Soon the Czechs, whose incomes had increased by only 20 per cent in the decade up to 1965, also embarked on economic reform. Yet the Czech reformers found great difficulty in raising the necessary investment with which to revive the country's obsolescent industries. Over the region as a whole optimism was maintained by a series of good harvests (1966–8). On the other hand frictions also surfaced. In 1967 Hungary, Czechoslovakia and Poland complained that the prices the Soviet Union was charging them for some products exceeded those prevailing on world markets. Moscow retorted that the goods she bought from them were below world market standards. Nevertheless, COMECON continued to promote inter-dependence within the Bloc, though Romania continued to stand aloof.

Reflecting the Romanian elite's long-standing admiration for France Nicolae Ceaucescu aped de Gaulle, asserting his country's independence in the diplomatic and military, as well as the economic, spheres. He infuriated Ulbricht by normalizing relations with West Germany, and Brezhnev by siding with Israel in the 1967 war, by calling for command of the Warsaw Pact forces (a Soviet reserve) to rotate among member countries, and for a share in the control of nuclear weapons.

At the same time, student unrest, first marked in Italy in 1966, began to spread throughout Europe, including some countries in the Bloc, while in Greece a junta of colonels staged a *coup d'état* against everything students stood for and in support of traditional values. It was ironic that Greece, despite massive injections of American aid and sizeable income from Greeks working abroad, had failed to match even neighbouring Bulgaria's increase in living standards since the war. What happened in Greece raised the question of how many Soviet Bloc countries, with their still largely traditional cultures, might have resorted to military government in the postwar era had they not been taken into the Soviet orbit. More immediately, however, it raised the question of how their governments would react to the imported Western phenomenon of student protest.

In Poland, one of the two countries most affected, there was a reaction analogous to that of the Colonels. Early in 1968 the production of a play by the nineteenth-century romantic, Mickiewicz (see Chapter 6), was banned because it included some anti-Russian remarks.[29] This provoked fierce student calls for greater freedom and 'national autonomy'. The students' zeal found an echo among many intellectuals, not least among economists who had been pressing for reform. There was no echo, however, among the working classes. Nonetheless the Interior Minister, Mieczyslaw Moczar, reacted strongly.

Like the Colonels in Greece, Moczar was cast in the old, heroic mould, and he was motivated by two traditional values in particular: nationalism and antisemitism. By extension he also disliked intellectuals and economists who were threatening the position of so many loyal, bureaucratic place-men. Moczar saw a chance of defusing tension by exploiting long-standing popular prejudices. Accordingly he arranged for students to be beaten up and for many of them to be arrested. He set up a commission to 'supervise' the handful of Jews remaining in Poland after the Holocaust, and to coordinate antisemitic propaganda. But the experiment was short-lived. In December 1968 the commission was abolished and Moczar disappeared from the stage.

In Czechoslovakia, the other country most affected by student protest, students and intellectual dissidents were not isolated. As in Hungary in 1956 there was internal ferment within the Party itself. In fact the Czech student disturbances of 1967 coincided with a bid by a combination of Party liberals and Slovak leaders to challenge the position of Gottwald's successor, Novotny. These were the essential ingredients in what was to become the 'Prague Spring', and they were rooted in widespread disillusionment, to which speeches at the Fourth Congress of Czech Writers, held in 1967, gave voice.

One speech in particular, by Vaculik, expressed the ideals of those who sought radical change. The country seemed to be unable to produce goods 'without being drowned in the by-products', he said. The economy had failed to meet the demands for housing and schools, still less created prosperity, and no attempt had been made 'to avoid the noisy and smog-infested development of our style of life'. Czechoslovakia was merely aping 'the dehumanized civilization of the American type'. Furthermore the non-democratic system was preventing 'the full assertion of man in society'; and the country had 'lost its good repute' on the international stage, too. 'I cannot see that we have given mankind any original ideas.'

This indictment reflected nostalgia for an idealized, pre-war Czechoslovakia.[30] It also represented a strong tide of sentiment within the Party. By the early weeks of 1968 this had developed to a point at which Dubcek, the young Slovak leader, replaced Novotny. At once, the activities of the security police and the censors ground almost to a standstill; and in the weeks that followed, amid mounting public excitement, a series of policy changes were introduced designed to promote 'socialism with a human face'.

The changes represented a victory for the managers and technocrats over the old Party ideologues; and of those who favoured flexibility over those who believed that only rigid centralization could prevent a descent into anarchy. But the economic and organizational changes published in Dubcek's 'April Programme' implied political transformation too. The concept of shop-floor democracy was matched by a move to openness in other spheres. A commission was set up to review the purges of the 1950s and to reveal the truth about them; and the media spoke out more and more freely, even to the extent of expressing pro-Western views.

Ulbricht, who was already concerned at the prospect of Czech economic cooperation with West Germany, became alarmed. Moscow, though still generally supportive of Dubcek, felt uncomfortable. For his part, Dubcek (no doubt mindful of Nagy's fate) seemed to welcome the Warsaw Pact manoeuvres scheduled to take place on Czech soil as a means of demonstrating loyalty to the alliance. But when the Pact forces withdrew, Dubcek's meetings with the Soviet Politburo at a frontier village, and with other Bloc leaders at Bratislava, showed how seriously his allies regarded Czech developments. They were afraid that, whatever his good intentions, he would not be able to contain the situation; that he had already opened Pandora's box and allowed the Furies to escape. Dubcek rebutted the charge, re-emphasized his loyalty to the alliance and tried to persuade Moscow that there would be no counter-revolution. The East Germans, however, proved more persuasive.

On 17 August 1968 the Soviet Politburo, by a narrow majority, decided to intervene. On the night of 20–21 August Soviet civilian aircraft landed at Prague and disgorged units of special troops, who proceeded to secure the airport and the Prague bridges. Simultaneously, Warsaw Pact forces (though not Romania's) crossed the Czech frontier. The invasion met no physical resistance – but it united the population round their leaders. Dubcek was arrested, but no one would take his place and he had to be reinstated. He was no longer a free agent, however. Eventually, in April 1969, he was replaced by one of his colleagues, another Slovak, reformer and sometime purge victim, Gustav Husak. By that time, 80,000 people, including many liberal intellectuals, had left Czechoslovakia for the West.

In the aftermath of the 'Prague Spring' of 1968 the East Germans continued to benefit from flexible economic policies and Hungarians congratulated themselves on the growing success of their own quiet revolution, while in 1969 Yugoslavia sped ahead with her plans for worker democracy. The strong nationalist tensions in Yugoslavia, reinforced as they were by substantial differences in economic development between the various constituent republics, created difficulties which most other countries of the region, the Soviet Union excepted, did not share. A resurgence of Croatian nationalism led to a purge of the Croatian Party leaders, and over-liberal Serbs were dismissed too. Yugoslavia was able, like Greece and Turkey, to export as many as a million surplus workers as *Gastarbeiter* to West Germany. This was not to prove an adequate safety valve, however.

Poland's uncollectivized agriculture continued to be both inefficient and underproductive. Years of uncertainty over agricultural policy had encouraged Poland's farmers to invest their meagre surpluses in improving their houses rather than their land or updating their equipment; and they still tended to regard their farms as a patrimony to be handed on to their descendants rather than a resource to be exploited. Poland had enjoyed several years of industrial peace, but it had been bought at the cost of high subsidy rates for comestibles. The standard of living had more than doubled since 1955. The workforce had come to take income increases for granted and were becoming impatient for more. In December 1970 there was a new wave of disturbances. Gomulka, who had endowed the regime with a degree of popular legitimacy for a time, lost credence and departed. His successor, Eduard Gierek, prescribed a 40 per cent increase in the real wages of the workers, and industrial peace returned; time would show, however, that the price paid for it was far too high.

Ulbricht soon followed Gomulka into retirement, and meanwhile Husak thought it time to emulate Kadar. On 10 September 1970, he declared that 'people who do not want to be our enemies' should not be driven into 'hostile positions.... We do not believe in "hereditary sin"'. Criticism of the Prague Spring should not be exaggerated, he said, and the purges and persecutions must cease. Husak was wooing 'the technical intelligentsia' without which the economy, as he admitted, could not be controlled or developed.[31] But though some advances were made in agriculture, the ageing industrial infrastructure and the deep demoralization of the Czechs made the outlook seem bleak.

By 1974 it seemed so in other countries too. Hungary had to draw back from the New Economic Mechanism; Yugoslavia, always more vulnerable than most to economic shock-waves emanating from the wider world, was suffering an inflation rate of 30 per cent (about the same rate as Greece) and a new flaring-up of nationalist resentments. These led Tito to replace the 1963 Constitution with one which devolved even more powers to the constituent republics. Central government retained only defence, foreign policy, certain economic decisions and the protection of minorities. It was a compromise very like that which the Habsburgs had made with the fractious Hungarians a century before (see Chapter 5). In neighbouring Greece, however, heightened discontent invited the Colonels to exploit nationalism; and this drove them into war. Their Cyprus adventure drew in the Turkish army to protect the Turkish minority on the island. In the ensuing debacle the Greek *junta* collapsed. It was, perhaps, a warning of how easily small nationalistic states could resort to arms if a Great Power was not prepared to restrain them. But the USSR was still the policeman of the rest of Eastern Europe.

* * *

The deteriorating economic climate – sluggish growth, increasing indebtedness, rising interest rates and inflation, and the unfavourable turn in terms of trade that followed the oil price rises of 1973 – brought in its wake the troubles that were to culminate in the dramatic events of 1989. However, it was not the workers but members of the intelligentsia who first expressed discontent.

In January 1977 a group of Czech intellectuals calling themselves 'Charter 77' issued a declaration complaining that their government was infringing the International Covenants of Rights which had recently been incorporated into Czech law. The occasion was the prosecution of a group of rock musicians whose performances the authorities found unsavoury, but the 'Chartists' drew attention to administrative as well as judicial infringements of the international accords on human rights made at Helsinki and Madrid. Czechoslovakia, like the USSR itself, was a signatory, yet citizens who expressed views contrary to the prevailing line were still being driven out of their professions and their children denied places at university. Independent trade unions were prevented from surfacing; the churches were still rigorously controlled (recent Vatican agreements with Poland and Yugoslavia had not extended to Czechoslovakia). The Chartists pointed out that such informal measures constituted breaches of the law, though they were careful not to put forward an alternative political or social platform of their own. However, they hoped to conduct 'a constructive dialogue with the political and state authorities' on matters involving violated 'human and civil rights'.[32]

Like the parallel Soviet movement set up by Academician Sakharov and others, 'Charter 77' was regarded as a political challenge to the establishment, and suppressed. The issue of human rights did not as yet engage most workers. They were more concerned with economic issues. But when they were stirred, as in Romania and Poland, they did not shrink from action. A coal strike in Romania had to be bought off with concessions, and the government sought to extract every vestige of political advantage from its overt anti-Soviet stance (in November 1978 it publicly refused to increase military expenditure at the request of the Warsaw Pact). In Poland the imposition of vital economic measures to dampen consumption was repeatedly baulked by popular opposition.[33] In June 1976, for example, an announcement of rises of up to 70 per cent in food prices was greeted not only by the usual run on the shops but by riots. So the government backed down – and applied for a further quarter of a billion dollars in credits with which to buy food from the United States.

'They pretend to pay us a living wage, and we pretend to work' ran the cynical joke that typified attitudes both in Poland and elsewhere; but the consequence for Poland was serious. Whatever the degree of the government's mismanagement, however stupidly resources were wasted (and both the mismanagement and the waste were considerable), the Polish people, workers included, were consuming far more wealth than they were producing. The government's policy of placating them was leading not only to an unmanageable foreign debt but to a dangerously overheated economy. Something had to give.

The crisis came in 1980. That year the huge new metallurgical works of Nowa Huta, outside Cracow, was due to reach a production of 9 million tons (three times as much as the entire country had produced fifteen years earlier), all on imported ore. A fresh wave of strikes led to the resignation of Eduard Gierek, a man of impeccable working-class credentials who had had the distinction of being expelled from France for his role in leading a miners' strike there before the war. This time, however, there were two important new ingredients in the political situation. Since September 1976 when some thirty Polish intellectuals had banded together to form a 'Workers' Defence Committee' *(KOR)* to provide practical help and advice to Polish workers who had fallen foul of the authorities, links had been forged between intellectual and working-class activists. This held out the prospect of converting strikes and demonstrations into an organized, country-wide movement of protest. The second development was the election of a Pole, Cardinal Wojtyla, as Pope, which created a mood of national exhilaration. The mixture was politically explosive.

The spark was provided by the dismissal of a woman crane operator at a Gdansk shipyard. The workers downed tools and locked themselves in. Their demands increased and the strike spread. Advised by *KOR* and with the moral support of the Catholic Church, an inter-factory strike committee was formed. The face of its chairman, Lech Walesa, with his moustache cut in the style of a Polish nobleman of the seventeenth century, was soon to be as familiar in the West as in Poland; and his watchword 'Solidarity', borrowed from the political vocabulary of the regime he confronted, soon swept the nation.

Industry ground almost to a standstill; and at last the government, at its wits' end, acceded to the strikers' demand that they negotiate and negotiate publicly. Amid great popular excitement a government delegation left Warsaw for Gdansk. On its arrival, it was handed twenty-one demands, ranging from economic concessions to greater freedom for the Church. Terms were reached on 31 August 1980 and encapsulated in a statement known as the 'Gdansk Protocol'.

In it the government acceded to the strikers' first demand for independent trade unions with their own research staff and publications, and with the right to discuss social and economic questions, including longterm plans, in public. In return, the strikers promised to recognize the leading role of the Party and not to form a political party themselves. The state also conceded the right to strike, and freedom of speech and publication, including access to the media for the Church, but preserved the rights to maintain secrecy on matters affecting the stability of the state and the health of the economy, and to use censorship to protect the susceptibilities of atheists as well as believers. The government also conceded a limited amnesty for political prisoners and promised to reinstate dismissed workers and students who had been excluded from universities for non-academic reasons. But the concessions went far beyond this.

In response to calls for 'genuine action to extricate the country from crisis', the government promised to speed up economic reforms, including 'radically increased independence of enterprises', and to encourage public discussion and union participation in the process. It also made some rather vague promises to the peasant farmers. More startling was the undertaking to raise basic wages, especially of the lowest paid and of those with large families, and to introduce inflation-linking. This ran counter to any action that could in fact extricate the economy from crisis, but it was not the only measure to do so.

The government also conceded a demand for more cheap meat, despite the huge costs of increased subsidies, restricting exports and increasing imports. The strikers' demand for lower retirement ages (fifty-five for men and fifty for women) was resisted, but others for improvements in the social wage and for work-free Saturdays were conceded in principle. On these terms the strike was called off[34] amid nation-wide scenes of popular jubilation. It seemed as if a great victory had been won not only for the workers, but for the peasants, the Catholic religion, for freedom itself. Yet the Gdansk Protocol also represented a defeat – not only of the regime, but of any realistic hope of reviving the economy.

In the months that followed the government, on the whole, honoured its promises, though 'Solidarity' was not to justify its name much longer (there were unwanted disturbances at Bydgoszcz); and though the Catholic hierarchy played an increasingly effective role as mediator between 'Solidarity' and the government, 'Solidarity' found it ever more difficult to keep the new coalition of workers, students and intellectuals together. What aided cohesion and moderation was the fear that Moscow would deploy the Red Army. It was not, in fact, to do so, but meanwhile national income slumped and the economic crisis deepened. Nor, for all the concessions, did the government gain legitimacy in the eyes of the people. In fact government and governed had reached a state of impasse similar to the impasse between the crown and the nobility that had obtained centuries earlier (see Chapter 7) and had heralded Poland's decline as a great power.

Then, suddenly, in 1981, the impasse was broken – not by Soviet troops but by the Polish army. General Jaruzelski imposed martial law and took over the government and Party. The move was not universally resented at the time. Though partly trained in the Soviet Union, Jaruzelski was a scion of the Polish noble class who commanded wide respect as a strict but honest man. Moreover many Poles retained a traditional respect for the army as bearer of the nation's honour; and there were many of the older generation who recalled another general, Marshal Pilsudski, who had saved the country from political chaos in 1926 (see Chapter 4).

Jaruzelski proceeded to replace several ministers and purge the Party and bureaucracy. He also confined Walesa and some of his associates for a time, and drove recalcitrant miners back to work, though he was careful to maintain close relations with the Catholic Church. Despite excesses by his underlings, notably the murder of an outspoken priest, Jaruzelski succeeded in restoring order. Unlike Britain's Margaret Thatcher, however, he ultimately failed to induce the Polish people to accept the hard economic facts of life. When, in 1987, he called for a referendum to endorse a desperately needed programme of belt-tightening, the Polish nation voted it down. There was no alternative but to co-opt the opposition into government. In April 1989 agreement was finally reached on forming a multi-party government.

As the eighties began to draw to a close it became clear that Poland was not the only Eastern European country in a slough of economic distress. The Hungarian regime, which had seemed for a time to have found the trick of making Communism a success and popular among the people, was also deep in debt[35] and confronting political crisis. Kadar was thrust aside in the spring of 1988, and, as the economic crisis deepened and the foreign debts continued to soar, more *apparatchiks* branched out into the private sector as a form of insurance.[36]

Romania's policy of economic autarchy had proved disastrous in a different way, though the country's problems were exacerbated by bad luck. The creation of a petro-chemicals industry dependent on imported oil, for example, had not been well-conceived, though the oil-price revolution was unforeseeable. So was a sucession of unusually severe winters which began in 1983. The task of hauling one of the most backward, peasantish, confused and anxiety-ridden societies in Europe into the modern era was a daunting task inviting drastic means; but the resort of the Ceausescu regime to obsessive national pride and grandiose theoretical designs proved costly to the people. They suffered great privation, having to do without basic foods (even bread and potatoes on occasion), which were exported to help pay the massive interest on her foreign debt; and to survive on an hour or two's electricity supply a day in winter in order to conserve expensive fuel. Bucharest acquired an underground railway system, thanks to the country's unsaleable stocks of steel, but Romania paid a grievous price for disdaining COMECON advice in the 1960s.

Yugoslavia also suffered, despite being first in the field of economic reform. The huge steelworks of Smeredovo in Serbia remained largely unoperational, a gigantic monument to ambitious folly; and in 1988 inflation reached a giddying 1,500 per cent. Attempts to dampen public demand and to make loss-making industries pay were met by worker protests and, as in Poland, government acquiescence. Though the government's economic strategies were almost the opposite to Romania's they did not prove much more successful. Devolution of economic decision-taking, as scandals emerging in the later 1980s showed, gave even more scope to corruption than centralism and did not always result in greater profitability. In these circumstances, the complex problems arising from national frictions grew worse. Both Croatia and Serbia threatened to secede, and a population explosion among the ethnic Albanians of the Kosovo region terrified the Serbs into taking violent repressive action. At the same time Soviet workers became increasingly restive and several constituent republics seemed set on abandoning the Union regardless of what the break might cost them.

Only a short time before there seemed to be some successes to set against the failures. Hungary, East Germany and Bulgaria had all contended with serious problems, yet achieved considerable increases in incomes and a degree of political calm that often attends economic betterment. For a time it seemed as if this might last. But as the People's Democracies[37] approached the fiftieth anniversaries of their foundations, it became clear that not only Stalinism but Marxism-Leninism no longer bore credence as a political prescription. Disillusionment had replaced idealism; people were coming to think more and more in terms of private gain to the exclusion of the public good; and the existing system seemed to preclude a regeneration of the economy or society. So far from stifling the voices of dissent those in command began to echo them.

* * *

Communism had outlived its uses. It had given a region notorious for its volatility greater political stability, but aroused deep resentments through its disdain of individualism. It had reduced poverty but failed to achieve acceptable standards of living; it gave chances of advancement for many who previously lacked them, but stifled much energy that might otherwise have been productive. It solved a deep-seated agrarian problem only to transform the 'sullen, alienated peasantry into a sullen, alienated proletariat'.[38] It cured some social ills, like unemployment, but encouraged others, including rampant bureaucracy. It raised living standards but whetted appetites for more than could be achieved; it raised cultural levels yet created a spiritual void.

In some ways it had come to resemble an enlightened despotism, but in treating the population as children it sometimes led them to respond like children. Popular disturbances in the region have reflected a desire for higher living standards as much as a general craving for 'Western freedom'. The intellectuals played vital parts in the protests but those who succeeded to power found themselves confronting some of the awful dilemmas their predecessors had faced. Freedom grew but so did lawlessness and sleaze. As disappointment with the new order grew some of the old sullenness returned; and nationalist assertion sometimes took on an ugly tone.

Though the great shift of 1989 was largely the work of Gorbachev, prompted by the Soviet Union's own difficulties, as we have seen it was anticipated in Poland and Hungary. The popular understanding that it reflected the bankruptcy of the Communist system was substantially correct, though there were some attendant paradoxes which are not easily explained. It might be noted, for example, that regimes in countries like Yugoslavia and Hungary which had been in the van of liberalization and reform fell into crisis and disarray, just as did those, like Romania, which had been bastions of reaction. Furthermore, but for the measures Moscow took to shift them, there was no obvious reason to expect the imminent fall of the hard-line Honecker or Husak regimes.

It was also widely believed that the great change represented a triumph for 'the people' and in particular the dissident intellectuals. Yet in retrospect this view seems exaggerated. Most of those who made the revolution worked within the system rather than outside it. Without them it is difficult to imagine the crowd and the dissidents succeeding. Indirectly, however, the people *had* played a crucial role.

In order to maintain social control and fend off industrial discontent governments had striven to improve living standards. As time went by this involved providing them with a greater variety and quality of goods and services, or simply with more money. But it became more and more evident that the economies could not meet the increasingly diverse demands placed upon it. The consequences were fateful. More foreign goods were bought on credit, building up huge debts which could not be repaid; inflation was encouraged as increasing amounts of money chased the limited quantity of desirable goods; and the black economy burgeoned in the great empty spaces which the command economy could not fill. From this perspective, then, it was an economic rock on which the regime foundered.

Yet the failure was not simply due to Communism, serious though its contribution was. The countries of Eastern Europe were characterized as 'shortage economies' throughout the period; yet the shortages may have been as much the cause as the consequence of state control. The Communist state arrogated to itself the task of allocating scarce resources and failed to do it adequately. Yet the period saw huge increases in production. The trouble was that demand grew even faster.

On the political plane Communist rule failed to replace nationalism with internationalism; and despite their institutional similarities the various countries of the Bloc retained their distinctiveness They enjoyed increasing latitude in deciding their own affairs, and some of them even exerted influence on Moscow. Gorbachev's policies of economic restructuring owed much to policies implemented in Hungary, while his ideas of 'democratization' and 'openness' drew on the Yugoslav experiment and on dissident thinking throughout the Bloc. These countries were not Soviet clones, and their divergencies reflected much more than nationalist reactions to Soviet dominance, and more than the uneven distribution of natural resources.

They were also the products of local traditions and national temperaments which were formed in the long- as well as in the short-term past. There are, for example, marked differences in the political cultures of the Balkans and the countries of East-Central Europe to the north.[39] Romania, which straddles these two sub-regions, maintained a show of unity to the outside world only at the cost of repressing the population in general and sapping the cultural distinctiveness of its Hungarian and German minorities in particular. Yugoslavia, with an even more complex national make-up, failed to resolve conflicts between north and south, Croat and Serb, Slav and Albanian. Yet neither country proved more difficult to govern than it was before the war.

Hungary and Poland, by contrast, had virtually no national minorities to contend with (though in the mid-1980s Hungarians showed increasing concern about the influx of gypsies from Yugoslavia). This allowed energies to be concentrated on other problems – an opportunity which Hungary exploited[40] but which Poland did not. For a long time their traditional work ethic and discipline helped the East Germans to outperform the others, while the Poles have been ill-served by their own traditions of revolutionary romanticism and heroic opposition. But none of these traditions was formed during the Soviet period.

* * *

The changes in the region between Stalin's death and the revolution of 1989 have demonstrated that no ideological system, however supple, can embrace humanity in all its variety and unpredictability, still less mould it;[41] and that much of the 'crooked wood of humanity' with which the Communist governments had to contend, and, indeed, many characteristics of the regimes themselves, are products of the past. Similarly the region's present difficulties derive to an extent from historical causes. But how much in the Eastern Europe that we see today remains a legacy of the Stalin period? Is it right to assume that he was determined to shape the countries of the region that came within his grasp towards the end of World War Two into small replicas of Stalinist Russia? And how much of what happened after 1944 was determined by the impact of the war itself? To answer these questions we must retrace our steps to 1944.

REFERENCES

1. For example, A. Amalrik, *Will the Soviet Union Survive to 1984?* (London 1970) and G. Ionescu, *The Break-up of the Soviet Empire in Eastern Europe* (Harmondsworth, 1965). For oracular shifts by a leading analyst see the successive editions of Z. Brzezinski's *The Soviet Bloc.*
2. E.g. C. Guirescu, *A History of the Romanian Forest* (Bucharest, 1980) especially pp. 236–7.
3. By 1980 debt-servicing accounted for half of Poland's hard-currency earnings and over 40 per cent of Romania's.
4. Between 1950 and 1980 real wages increased by 350 per cent. However there were substantial differences between countries. Poland and the Balkan states which started from particularly low bases showed the most impressive increases in terms of *per capita* gross national product, and more developed, less war-damaged countries like Czechoslovakia showed a lesser percentile,

though a greater actual, increase. See the estimates in the *World Bank Atlas* for details.

5. Although the process began in the nineteenth century (see Chapter 5) and saw its greatest spurt under Stalin (Chapter 3) it has been a continuous phenomenon. In Bulgaria the 45 per cent engaged in agriculture in 1965 was reduced to 26 per cent by 1975. In Romania the proportions were 57 per cent and 37 per cent respectively and it has since been reduced to about 25 per cent.
6. For estimated production statistics see *World Bank Atlas.* Bulgaria may not have done very much better than her neighbour Greece in the thirty years since Stalin's death, but Hungary narrowed her age-old developmental gap with the countries of Western Europe (I. Berend and G. Ranki calculate that by the late 1960s the gap was 7 per cent less). Soviet growth rates in the 1970s were reportedly higher on average than the six other leading world economies, including the USA and Japan, though the statistics took no account of technology and quality gaps (See W. Laqueur, *Europe Since Hitler* (Harmondsworth, 1982) p. 238). Of the leading seven the USSR was last in 1972 but second in 1973–4 and first in 1975. The success, however, should be gauged in relation to other countries of the European periphery, e.g. Spain, Portugal and Greece, and with Eastern Europe's historical record of economic backwardness.
7. Some of the implications are discussed in J. Szczepanski, *Polish Society* (New York, 1970) pp. 38ff.
8. F. Fejto, *A History of the People's Democracies* (Harmondsworth, 1977) p. 58.
9. See J. Gold, 'The Thorny "Non-Existent Problem"', *East European Quarterly* 13(1) pp. 47–72. Moscow would reply by hinting that it might after all return Transylvania to Hungary.
10. Most are hostile to their immediate neighbours. For historical reasons (see Chapters 4 and 5). Czechs are suspicious of Poles and Hungarians, and Romanians dislike Bulgarians and Hungarians as well as Russians. However, Hungarians and Bulgarians, having no common frontier, have tended to get on.
11. Many called for more democracy, legal rights and personal freedom without being enamoured of the Western way of life. See, for example, V. Havel *et al., The Power of the Powerless* (London, 1985); A. Michnik, *Letters from Prison and Other Essays* (Berkeley, 1985) and G. Konrad, *Antipolitics* (London, 1984). However, the range of dissident opinion tended to be wide.
12. Though most Poles would not admit it, Polish living standards were long maintained at the expense of the Soviet consumer. Before 1989 the USSR did not demand full interest payments, still less repayment, of its substantial share of Poland's huge foreign debt, and the interest it charged her was much below world market rates. Poland also enjoyed supplies of Soviet energy at low prices, and was allowed to postpone payments. I am grateful to Professor P. Hanson for information on these matters.
13 See M. Kaser, *COMECON* (London, 1967).
14. W. Brus, 'The "Thaw" and the "New Course"' in M. Kaser, ed. *The Economic History of Eastern Europe,* vol. III (Oxford, 1986) p. 41.
15. It was only after Moscow applied strong pressure that the Czech General Swoboda was released from gaol – see J. Pelikan, *The Czechoslovak Political Trials 1950–1954* (Stanford, 1971) esp. pp. 114 ff.
16. The government promised to improve living standards in general, and in particular to rescind a recent increase in the price of sugar, to restore transport concessions for various categories of the population and cease

using 'coercive measures' in collecting tax arrears. It also undertook to stop the 'administrative' punishment of withholding ration cards from those in disfavour and to review 'hardship' cases among the prison population. Other important policy changes included a slowing down of collectivization (a decree of February 1953 dispossessing more farmers was cancelled), the easing of restrictions on the non-agricultural private sector, and the encouragement of émigrés to return from the West by the promise of full civic rights, restoration of property and the provision of jobs commensurate with their qualifications. (Almost 200,000, mostly young, people had fled to West Germany in 1952 and the tide was swelling.) See the Communique of the East German Council of Ministers, 11 June 1953 in B. Ruhm von Oppen (ed.), *Documents on Germany Under Occupation 1945–1955* (Oxford, 1955) pp. 588–90.

17. *Nowa Kultura,* 19 August 1955, translated by L. Blit, *The Twentieth Century,* No. 158, pp. 504ff.
18. Cyrankiewicz's speech to the Sejm, 23 April 1956, *Trybuna Ludu,* 30 April 1956.
19. Resolution of the Central Committee of the Hungarian Workers' Party, 30 June 1956, translated in P. Zinner (ed.), *National Communism and Popular Revolt* (New York, 1956) pp. 328–31.
20. *Szabad Nep* report in Zinner, *op. cit.*, p. 385.
21. Zinner 110 – 12; *The Hungarian Quarterly,* vol. xxxiv, no. 129, 1993, pp. 107ff. Also the fresh evidence recently published by Gy. Litvan, J. Bak *et al.*
22. Programme of the 'Revolutionary Worker-Peasant Government', 4 November 1956 – Zinner *op. cit.*, pp. 476–8.
23. Tito's speech of 11 November 1956 in Zinner, *op. cit.*, pp. 527–9.
24. Communique of 18 November 1956, Zinner, *op. cit.*, pp. 306–13.
25. See I. Berend and G. Ranki, *The Twentieth Century Hungarian Economy* (London, 1985), and personal communication from I. Berend.
26. See E. Pamlenyi (ed.), *A History of Modern Hungary* (London, 1975) pp. 560–2; P. Kende, *Changes in the Economic Structure, National Income and Living Standards in Post-War Hungary* and Berend and Ranki, *Hungarian Economy, op. cit.*
27. See J. Krejer, *Social Structure of Divided Germany,* 1976, p. 118.
28. On the role of the market in N.E.M. see, *inter alia,* M. Kaser (ed.), *The Economic History of Eastern Europe 1919–1975,* vol. III (Oxford, 1986). On the agricultural reforms and pricing policy see L. Fischer and P. Uren, *The New Hungarian Agriculture* (Montreal, 1973).
29. Sensitive national pride was in evidence elsewhere too. In 1985 a production in a Budapest theatre of Shaw's *Arms and the Man* had to be cancelled after two performances following a protest by the Bulgarians.
30. See V. Kusin, *The Intellectual Origins of the Prague Spring* (Cambridge, 1971) p. 133. Thanks partly to adroit publicity, pre-war Czechoslovakia had presented itself, not altogether accurately, as a progressive, democratic liberal state in the moral van of the nations of the world – see Chapter 4.
31. Husak's speech at Ostrava, 10 September 1970 quoted in Kusin, *op. cit.*, p. 146, note 1.
32. For a translation of the Charter see Havel *et al., op. cit.*, pp. 217–21.
33. It was suggested that the problem was cyclical (see N. Asherson, *The Polish August* (London, 1981)); it turned out to be downwardly spiral.
34. For a translation of the Gdansk Protocol, see Asherson, *op. cit.*, pp. 284–94.
35. By the end of 1989 Poland owed $41 billion, and Hungary $17 billion (the largest in the Bloc per head of population).

36. E. Hankiss, *East European Alternatives* (Oxford, 1990) p. 255.
37. Ceaucescu had proclaimed Romania to be a 'Socialist Democracy', however.
38. J. Rothschild, *Return to Diversity* (Oxford, 1989).
39. By 'East-Central Europe' in this context I mean Poland, Bohemia and Hungary. Oskar Halecki used it to describe a much larger area, including the Balkans. Some émigré writers (e.g. M. Kundera) dislike the term because it suggests affinity to 'the East', i.e. Russia and prefer the term 'Central Europe' (which, following Tomas Masaryk's usage included Scandinavia as well as the Balkans) though *Mitteleuropa* is widely understood to include Germany.
40. Analysts attributed the cause of Hungary's economic and bureaucratic problems in part to the educational system which placed heavy emphasis on vocational training. The result was a large number of engineers, accountants, etc., with a vested interest in preserving obsolescent techniques and in obstructing innovation in a period of fast-changing technology. A new education bill gave emphasis to arts subjects because they promote mental flexibility. The problem was also manifest in countries other than Hungary.
41. A small indication is the ruined bridge over the Danube at Esztergom. It once linked Hungary with Czechoslovakia, but was destroyed in World War II and was never rebuilt. Locals used to refer to it dryly as a symbol of 'fraternal feeling between our two peoples'.

3

The Quest for the New Eldorado (1944–53)

The great migration builds new industry....
Is fed on great empty words ...

Adam Wazyk, Polish poet.

In 1945 Red Army units linked up with American forces on the River Elbe in Germany. After a thousand years the Slavs had almost reached the limits of their old migrations once again (see Chapter 11). By the spring of 1948 Communist governments had been imposed on all the territories occupied by Soviet forces at the end of the war, and all political opposition in them had been eliminated. Thereafter the Soviet Union proceeded to mould her satellites in her own image, restructuring their societies, imposing forced industrialization programmes upon them, collectivizing private farmers, and forcing obedience on both their Communist regimes and the population at large by means of Party discipline, secret police operations, illegal 'administrative' action, and the purge.

It is commonly assumed that Stalin had planned to do this from the moment the tides of war had changed in his favour in 1942. According to Djilas he considered it to be a law of nature that political domination should grow out of military success:

> Whoever occupies a territory [he said in June 1945] also imposes on it his own social system. Everyone imposes his own system as far as his army has the power to do so.[1]

Is it possible, however, that, had the Cold War not developed, Stalin might have been content with a sphere of influence rather than an empire in the region? After all, only eastern Poland and East Prussia were formally incorporated into the Soviet Union. Soviet troops remained in the rest of eastern Germany and in other countries, like Hungary, which had fought against them, in order to extract reparations, and pending an agreement with the Western Allies on a peace settlement which was never to be reached. They stayed in Poland and Romania primarily to ensure that their governments would not be hostile to the Soviet Union. Yet they did not occupy neighbouring Finland which had also fought against them, and soon withdrew from Czechoslovakia and Yugoslavia.[2]

Another common assumption must also be questioned: would the countries of the region have become prosperous, democratic societies, like Belgium, France or Italy, if only they had been spared Soviet attentions? The economic plight they found themselves in by the end of the war, the social transformations which had occurred in some of them as a result of Nazi domination, and the political mood of the time, all encouraged a vast increase in the power of the state and made the immediate prospects for liberty and prosperity doubtful. Indeed, it could be argued that most of these countries would have been forced into the Soviet economic sphere willy nilly.

* * *

Nazi domination, which had geared production to serve the German war effort, had sucked many of these countries dry. The fighting had taken a heavy toll in terms of ruined cities and industrial plant, while losses of livestock were such that many a farm had no horse or ox, still less a tractor, with which to till the fields. In Poland, two-thirds of whose people depended on agriculture, half the arable land lay fallow and food yields were less than two-fifths of the pre-war level. Yugoslavia had lost half her livestock, a third of her industrial plant and over a seventh of her housing stock. Hungary too, had lost half her livestock, and most of Budapest, her chief industrial centre, like Warsaw, lay in ruins. Romania's oil fields had been wrecked. Only Czechoslovakia and Bulgaria had been spared great physical damage.

In many areas communications had broken down almost completely. Departing German troops had carted as much of value away with them as they could, and invading Soviet troops (many of whom had themselves suffered great privations) were often allowed to loot and plunder freely. Severe shortages promoted rampant inflation; hordes of displaced persons added to the confusion;[3] the Hungarian currency fell to one ten-thousandth of its former value within six months.[4] Hitler's erstwhile allies, Hungary, Romania and Finland, were presented with bills for reparations and the victor's costs of occupation. To cap it all severe droughts caused famines in 1946 and 1947.

The entire region at once became dependent on the Soviet Union as the only available source of essential supplies and the only accessible market of any importance for what little export surpluses they could produce. Even Czechoslovakia, which not only had the benefit of some reparations and help from the United Nation's Relief and Rehabilitation Agency (UNRRA), like Poland and Yugoslavia, but enjoyed proximity to

Western Europe, found herself in this position. Apart from Switzerland (which bought a third of Czechoslovakia's meagre exports in the immediate post-war months) the Czechs depended on the USSR both as a market and for supplies of essential raw materials including oil, coal, wool, and cotton.

Poland's economic dependence was even greater. In 1945 nine-tenths of her exports (a mere fifth of their pre-war level) went to the USSR. The price the Soviets paid for Polish coal was well below the price on the world market, but because of an almost complete breakdown of communications Poland had no access to the world market. Soviet army lorries were virtually the only means of transportation available. According to UNRRA Poland was in a similar position with regard to essential imports:

> The problem facing the Polish Government was not so much the difficulty of obtaining supplies on favourable terms as the getting of any supplies at all. Apart from the USSR there were no alternative sources for such essential commodities as iron ore, wool, cotton and petrol.[5]

Hungary's predicament was even worse. Saddled with a reparations bill of $400 millions (payable to Czechoslovakia and Yugoslavia as well as the USSR) her industrial production was barely a fifth of what it had been before the war, and in 1946 her foreign trade was worth one seventh of the pre-war value. Much though she wanted to export to the West, she could not do so – partly because of transportation difficulties, but chiefly because the West had no use for the goods she had to offer. Czechoslovakia bought a little; for the rest she had to depend on the Soviet Union. So did Romania and Bulgaria; and even Yugoslavia, which enjoyed access to world markets through the Adriatic, was in a similar predicament: the United States accounted for only a tenth of her trade immediately after the war, while the Soviets had to provide half her imports and take two-thirds of her exports.

The manner in which this trade was conducted, through barter agreements, has been regarded as essentially Soviet and therefore sinister. Yet barter agreements, popularized by Germany before the war (see Chapter 4), had become a norm of commerce in much of the region, and the general dislocation, not least of currencies, made them a practical, if crude, means of getting economic recovery under way. Nor did the Soviet Union always perpetuate its monopoly position. Her share of Bulgaria's trade, for example, declined from 95 per cent immediately after the war to 50 per cent in 1948. Nonetheless, chiefly through force of geographic circumstances, the region was sucked into the Soviet economic sphere. The elimination of Nazi Germany, the dominant economic power there up to 1944, had left a vacuum which only the Soviet Union could fill, though much of it had also been ravaged by war.

The rebuilding of the shattered cities and industries of Eastern Europe presented a challenge beyond the scope of its weak and disorganized free enterprise system to meet. The state was obliged to intervene, whatever its political complexion, by directing labour and organizing the work. It did so by resorting to expedients normally associated with Nazi Germany and the Soviet system. The Soviet Union also involved itself in these countries' economies by setting up a series of joint companies with Romania and Hungary to get transport, industry and banking working again. Little altruism was involved, however, for without such assistance it would have taken even longer to extract reparations from these countries. The operation of similar joint companies in friendly Yugoslavia, which was already Communist-led, was to bring charges of Soviet exploitation in respect of both the valuation of the capital inputs and the profits extracted.

East Germany was a special case. Pending an agreement with the Western Powers over reparations (an agreement which was never reached), she was stripped of Nazi and *Wehrmacht* property, 15 per cent of which was handed over to the Poles. German assets were also appropriated in the other countries, and in those which had been allied to Hitler's Germany the temptation to take more was not always resisted. Nonetheless there were limits to the exploitation even of the ex-enemy countries. In 1945 the Soviet Union had shipped vast quantities of food to Bulgaria, on credit, to save the country from starvation; the following year she lent drought-stricken Romania 100,000 tons of grain and allowed her to spread her reparation payments over a longer period.

Social factors, too, suggest that the region was ill-placed to gravitate towards the West or to the 'Western way of life' even it had been left to make the choice freely. The social balance in most of the countries of Eastern Europe had long differed markedly from those in most countries to the west. Poor peasant farmers formed the overwhelming majority of the population, while the top of the social pyramid was still occupied by great landlords and traditional office-holders. The middle classes and the urban working class formed much smaller proportions of society than in the West; the entrepreneurial element had, to a large extent, been dominated by Jews and expatriate Germans, and in the Balkans by Greeks. However, the war and Nazi domination had served to distort this picture by exterminating most of the Jews and by inviting a reaction against the Eastern European Germans. Most of those in Romania, who had been settled since the Middle Ages (see Chapters 9 and 10), left with the retreating Wehrmacht or were interned by the invading Russians; and in 1945 the Czechs seized the opportunity to expel its three million

Germans, who had been among the hardest-working and most enterprising elements in the country. The most radical change, however, occurred in Poland.

The country had lost not only three million Jews but as many Poles, including a very high proportion of the educated and the skilled. The middle class had been virtually destroyed; so had the landed elite. There remained the peasants and the urban workers. As a leading Polish sociologist has remarked,

> The social classes that had traditionally supplied the leading elites were unable to reconstruct themselves, and so the new elite had to come from the working class, the peasants and the lower ranks of the intelligentsia.[6]

The agreement by the Great Powers to shift Poland's frontiers westwards involved massive population movements from territories now incorporated into the Soviet Union to areas formerly belonging to Germany, from which Germans were evicted. Like the rebuilding of cities and communications this required bureaucratic control. It also demanded an orderly distribution of land to those who had been dispossessed, while the disappearance of so many estate-owners prompted a radical land reform in favour of landless peasants and those with very small holdings. Twenty million acres were taken over; over a million peasant families benefitted. The rural proletariat at last inherited the earth that they had so long craved.

Land reform was highly popular elsewhere too. In Hungary, for example, where over half the land was in the hands of only 1 per cent of the total number of land-owners, a radical expropriation law was enacted as early as March 1945 by a provisional government dominated by the Smallholders' Party. Over half of the proceeds was allotted to landless labourers, farm servants[7] and smallholders with less than eight acres; state farms, which had existed in pre-war Hungary, were established on the rest. Czechoslovakia also introduced a land reform, exploiting the properties confiscated from expelled 'Sudeten' Germans and others. So did the Balkan states, though earlier land reforms and the structure of rural society, which differed somewhat from that to the north, made change less necessary. But in East Germany estates of over 270 acres and all land belonging to Nazis and war criminals were transferred to landless labourers and refugees from the new Poland, and in 1949 holdings were further limited to twenty acres. The *Junker* class, like the great landlords in Hungary, had been broken.

There was nothing 'Soviet' about these measures. Land reform had long been the major plank of the popular peasant parties of the region (see Chapter 4); they were also introduced in the western zones of

Germany; and state farms had been set up by the conservative regimes in power before the war. Nonetheless the social implications were significant. The millions of rural poor rejoiced in their good fortune; the once haughty and often aristocratic landowners disappeared. Many of them gravitated to white collar jobs, and in Hungary, where feeling against them was particularly intense, many a country palace was razed to the ground and the once great Count Esterhazy was reduced to eking out an existence in what had once been his stables (one of his grandsons, however, was subsequently to revive the family fortunes by becoming a star footballer). Thus the egalitarian revolution which had taken place in urban society due to the disappearance of most Jews and many Germans, had a parallel of even greater consequence in the countryside. And Communism had virtually nothing to do with it.

These social transformations fed a widespread mood of optimism despite the economic hardships and Soviet occupation. This is suggested by the birthrate, which soared to 40 per cent above the pre-war figure in 1947 and to 75 per cent above it by 1950. The young in particular sensed great opportunities in the still largely chaotic and disorienting situation. In many countries there was a rush to join the Communist Party. Liberalism, after all, was associated with a free market economy which had produced the Great Depression; fascism and Nazism (highly popular in parts of the region until 1944) were discredited; and moderation had never been characteristic of the political scene in Eastern Europe.

Furthermore, the simple egalitarianism which Communists preached had a particular appeal in the mountains zones of the Balkans, and not least Greece, where villagers tended to collectivism, while the promise to create an elite of the working class had strong attraction for the urban poor. In Yugoslavia, where Tito basked in widespread popularity due to his leadership of the successful guerilla war against the Germans and where the opposition parties, sensing that their chances of success were slim, boycotted the elections, the Communists won outright. In Czechoslovakia, where free elections were held in May 1946, the Communists won 38 per cent of the vote and took over government in coalition with the Socialists.[8]

The Communist success in Czechoslovakia owed much to popular recognition that the Soviet Union had been the only power to offer them support against Nazi Germany before the war. In other countries, however, traditional anti-Red and anti-Russian sentiment, combined with Soviet occupation and requisitioning, presented too great an obstacle. In an election held in Berlin in October 1946 the Communists gained only 5 per cent of the vote; in Austria, which was also under Four-Power control, 20 per cent; while in the Hungarian elections of November 1945 the Smallholders Party gained victory with nearly 60 per cent.

Elsewhere, too, it was the peasant parties which presented the greatest political competition to Communism. In Bulgaria the Communists succeeded in manipulating the Peasant Party with which it entered into government. The United States, which had a place on the Control Commission alongside the USSR and Britain, issued a protest, though to little effect. In the Balkans elections had usually been characterized by skullduggery, and according to a leading American expert the Communists might well have been victorious in Bulgaria even in conditions of fair play, because of traditional pro-Russian sentiment.[9]

In fact, the first case of gross political manipulation in the region was in Greece, where the British were determined to secure the election of an anti-Communist government. Had the Greek elections been free the Communists would almost certainly have won them.[10] Nevertheless the political manipulation first manifested in Greece and Bulgaria was soon to become characteristic of Hungary, Romania, Poland, and ultimately Czechoslovakia. Behind this development lay Great Power interests and the development of the Cold War. In order to answer the questions already posed and to understand why Stalinist regimes rather than any alternative came to be imposed on almost all countries of the region by the Spring of 1948, we must consider events in a broader context, in sequence, going back to World War Two itself.

* * *

The Declaration of the United Nations of April 1942, to which the USSR subscribed, laid down two principles of post-war reconstruction: there was to be no territorial aggrandizement; and the liberated nations were to have the right to choose their own forms of government. However, as Churchill had told Roosevelt, the first principle was 'not to be construed so as to deny Russia the borders she occupied when Germany attacked her' (which included sizeable tracts of northern Romania, eastern Poland, Estonia, Latvia and Lithuania, acquired since the Nazi-Soviet Pact of August 1939 – see Chapter 4); and both Britain and the United States were agreed that states neighbouring the Soviet Union must adopt 'friendly' policies towards her. This second proviso implied a possible contradiction to the principle of democracy, which was in any case the object of widely differing interpretations.

Anticipating Polish objections to Soviet annexation of what had been eastern Poland, Stalin proposed that she should be compensated with German territory to the west. The United States and Britain accepted this; the Polish government in exile in London objected. In fact the case for these frontier changes was a good one, regardless of Soviet interests. The peacemakers of 1918 had not envisaged Poland extending so far to the east; and eastern Poland, which had been won subsequently as the result of Polish victory in its war with the Soviet Union, was largely populated by Ukrainians and Belorussians who were unhappy under Polish rule. In the event, the Soviet Union, which had signed a treaty with the Polish government in exile in July 1941 in which they conceded that the Nazi-Soviet Pact had 'lost its validity' with regard to frontiers, accepted the 'Curzon Line' which had been proposed by the British Foreign Secretary in 1920. The Poles objected to this, and remained intransigent. Polish-Soviet relations did not reach crisis point, however, until April 1943 and over a different issue.

The Nazis had announced the discovery in Katyn Forest of the graves of some 14,000 Polish soldiers who had been interned by the Soviets after the invasion of Poland. Against the advice of the British, who took the view that whether or not the Soviets had been responsible for their deaths any response would play into the hands of the Nazi propagandists, the Polish government in London asked the International Red Cross to mount an investigation. Moscow then broke off diplomatic relations with the Polish government – on the grounds that it had adopted a hostile position towards the Soviet Union. It eventually transpired that the Soviet Union had been responsible for the deaths, but the *contretemps* had grave consequences for Poland's future.

As early as 1941 the Soviets had been organizing a Union of Polish Patriots. This may have been no more than a means of mobilizing Poles on Soviet territory for the war effort, but it had potential for development into an embryonic government. In 1943, when Soviet forces crossed the Curzon line to capture Lublin, a 'National Council for National Liberation' was set up, headed by a Socialist, Osobka-Morawski, but it claimed no governmental powers. In June Soviet citizens of Polish birth were 'permitted' to become Polish citizens – no doubt to swell the ranks of the pro-Communist Polish forces – and, in July 1944, the Communist Boleslaw Bierut's 'Home National Council' declared itself to be the sole source of authority in Poland. However, Moscow did not not grant it recognition as a government.

In 1944 the Polish underground 'Home Army', loyal to the government in London, staged an uprising in Warsaw against the occupying Germans. The Soviet forces, having advanced as far as the Warsaw suburb of Praga, remained on the far side of the River Vistula and gave the rising no support. At first the Soviet authorities even refused landing rights to Allied aircraft seeking to drop the insurgents essential supplies. An attempt to relieve them made by the Kosciuszko Division, fighting under Soviet command, failed, and eventually the Home Army forces in Warsaw were forced to surrender to German troops. It has been claimed that the Warsaw Rising was incited by Soviet broadcasts, and that the timing of the rising was decided by the Polish commander in the field. It is also believed that the Polish government in London wanted to establish its authority in Warsaw before Soviet troops could liberate the city, and that the Soviets wished to prevent this.

Whatever the truth of the matter, there was still a possibility of rapprochement. In October 1944 the London-based Polish Premier, Stanislaw Mikolajczyk, flew to Moscow. Stalin told him he and his colleagues were out of touch, that 'the Poles are a different people today than when you left in 1939'.[11] As we have seen, there was some substance in this. Mikolajczyk was persuaded to moderate Polish insistence on the reinstatement of the pre-war frontiers. But he could not persuade his colleagues in London, and resigned. The understandable hostility of exiled Poles to Moscow did not diminish. General Anders, commander of the Polish troops fighting with the British, urged Britain and the United States to continue their eastward advance after the defeat of Nazi Germany; others warned that the Soviets intended to swallow, not only Poland, but all Europe. If this was prophetic, however, it was a self-fulfilling prophecy.

In January 1945 Moscow at last recognized the 'National Council for the Homeland', which it had formed under the Polish Communist Bierut, as the *de facto* government of Poland. The highly popular land reform it had announced the preceding September gave it some credibility, though much of the Home Army command took the same attitude to both Moscow and the 'National Council' as their compatriots in the West. In May 1945 Marshal Zhukov invited sixteen Home Army leaders to a meeting where he had them arrested. They were subsequently imprisoned on charges of sabotage. The intransigence of the Polish government in exile had by then lost much of the sympathy of the British and American governments which it had previously enjoyed. They might have played their cards better.

The Finns, with a rather worse hand, did so. An 'enemy' rather than a 'friendly' nation, they had signed an armistice with the Soviets in September 1944, ceding all the territory Moscow demanded (some of which, however, they were subsequently to recover), and agreeing to pay considerable reparations. They also undertook to let the Finnish Communist Party operate freely and to adopt friendly policies towards their giant neighbour. On these terms Finland was left at liberty. Poland would have had to make a further concession: access for Soviet troops to eastern Germany across her territory (her refusal to countenance this in 1939 had arguably precipitated the Nazi-Soviet Pact – see Chapter 4). Had the Poles in London adopted a conciliatory attitude similar to that of the Finns, it is conceivable that Poland might have preserved a similar degree of autonomy under a non-Communist government. The Czech President Benes and the Hungarian Oskar Jaszi certainly expected as much in return for a foreign policy that was not anti-Soviet. But such a stance was inconsistent with the national temperament and Polish pride. They refused to settle for anything less than what they considered fair. As a result a process had been set in motion that was to make Poland an unwilling Soviet satellite.

The ways in which the other countries were reduced to the status of satellites differed from the Polish case. In Romania, Hitler's friend General Antonescu had been ousted in August 1944, at which Romania had changed sides. This did not avert Soviet occupation, nor the removal in March 1945 of the Premier, General Radescu, who was unsympathetic to the Communists, and his replacement by a more tractable 'Union of Patriots' government headed by Petre Groza, leader of the 'Ploughmen's Front'. As yet, however, the Communists maintained a comparatively low profile. Bulgaria, though allied to Nazi Germany, had not declared war on the Soviet Union, but in September 1944 the Soviet Union declared war on Bulgaria. In this way Moscow gained the right to participate in the peace arrangements alongside Britain and the United States with whom Bulgaria was already at war. It also allowed her to establish a sphere of influence there.

A major determinant of the post-war balance of power in the Balkans was an agreement reached in October 1944 between Britain and the USSR on a division of their respective spheres. Churchill proposed that Britain take a 90 per cent 'predominance' in Greece, and the USSR take a 90 per cent 'predominance' in Romania and 75 per cent in Bulgaria. Hungary and Yugoslavia should be split on a fifty-fifty basis between East and West. Stalin agreed. He honoured the agreement by allowing Greece to fall into the Western sphere, and as late as 1947 he could be said to have honoured the agreement in respect of Romania and Bulgaria too. This was not the case in respect of either Yugoslavia or Hungary, however; and for two main reasons.

Firstly, and no doubt to his surprise, Stalin found that he could not control Tito, who ignored his repeated urging, consonant with his agreement with Churchill, to bring back King Peter from his wartime exile in England, and who moreover persisted in assisting the Greek Communists. The second reason, which had much wider relevance, was Soviet fear of America's possession of the atomic bomb, of which Stalin was aware before President Truman broke the news to him at Potsdam in June 1945. Circumstances suggest that the Soviet Union wished to create a *cordon sanitaire* in Eastern Europe of sufficient depth to prevent American aircraft carrying the bomb from penetrating the Russian heartland. The argument had no force once a nuclear balance was established, but it was to be 1949 before the Soviet Union possessed a bomb of its own. It has been said that even before that it was unthinkable for any American politician to use the bomb against Soviet Russia, and no doubt this was so. Nevertheless Stalin had reason to suspect Allied intentions.

As early as 1943 the Western Powers had given the impression of trying to exclude the Soviet Union from peace talks with Italy. Then a Soviet request for a 6 billion dollar loan for post-war reconstruction received no answer from the United States; and in May 1945 Lease-Lend shipments to Russia were abruptly stopped, despite the Soviet commitment to go to war against Japan. In August that year Moscow renewed its request for a dollar credit. In September the Americans replied that the request had been mislaid. Roosevelt was dead, Churchill had been voted out of office, and Truman was abandoning the policy of cooperation with the USSR.

Suspicion was mutual; Western mistrust of Soviet intentions were hardly less great. The exiled Poles in particular were assuring them that Stalin intended to 'conquer the world';[12] Harry Hopkins had warned Roosevelt that 'the Soviet programme is the establishment of totalitarianism... ending liberty and democracy as we know and respect it'. Except in the case of Poland, however, Soviet actions so far fell short of this prognosis. Moscow made no attempt to use the powerful French and Italian Communist Parties to take over those countries. Indeed, it instructed the Italian Party to vote for a new Concordat with the Vatican (even though the Catholic Church in Hungary had threatened anyone voting for the Communist Party with eternal perdition).

Nor did it ignore Western representations, even over Poland. It agreed to include Mikolajczyk and five other 'democrats' in a new Government of National Unity, the price of persuading Britain and the United States to withdraw recognition from the Polish government in London. Stalin also met the West's call for 'free and unfettered elections' in Hungary (and if the Bulgarian elections were dubious, so, too, were those in Greece). Before the end of the 1945 there were further Western protests about the Soviet-Hungarian economic agreement, leading to some minor adjustments, and about Soviet actions in Romania and Bulgaria (though Moscow had delivered no such protest with regard to Greece). In March 1946 Churchill described the countries in the Soviet sphere as being subject to 'a very high and increasing measure of control from Moscow' and talked of an 'Iron Curtain' falling across Europe. Relations between the Great Powers were deteriorating fast, and the development was to have its impact on Eastern Europe.

The Powers could not agree on the terms the peace treaties with Germany and Austria should take. In July 1946 Moscow rejected an American proposal for a three-Power plan to rehabilitate Hungary economically, and declined to join the World Bank or the International Monetary Fund, no doubt because these were seen as means by which the West might penetrate the Soviet sphere. Nevertheless, in terms of political rhetoric at least, the Communist leaders of the countries within the Soviet orbit took pains to differentiate their policies from the Soviet ones. That year the Bulgarian leader Dimitrov said that his country would have no dictatorship of any kind; the Hungarian Party leader Rakosi looked forward to the implementation of socialism 'born on Hungarian soil and adapted to Hungarian conditions'; and the President of Poland, Bierut, announced the building of a new order which would differ from both Soviet and Western models. Such statements were no doubt intended to make Communism more acceptable. Meanwhile, however, steps were being taken to entrench the Communists in power whatever their national guises.

Moscow insisted that Communists in coalition governments be allotted the posts of Interior Minister. They would then use their control of the police to get rid of opponents, often on charges, spurious or true, of collaboration with the 'fascists', a term usually applied to those identified as enemies of the regime. They would also infiltrate other parties and then merge them with their own, as they did, for example, with the Bulgarian Peasant Party and, in June 1946, with the East German Socialists, picking off hostile elements with what Rakosi later termed 'salami tactics'. In this way liberals and even leftists came to be termed 'fascist bandits', though there were also others more deserving of the name. They would also gain control of the media, using them to promote their own cause and to deny publicity to their opponents. Nevertheless, the process was gradual. As late as November 1946 the Romanian Communist newspaper wished King Carol 'long life, good health and a reign rich in democratic achievements'. In fact 1947 was to be the critical year politically for most of the region.

The election held in Poland in January 1947 was anything but free and unfettered. Had it been, Mikolajczyk's Peasant Party would probably have won hands down. However, not only did another peasant party split the vote, but some of his supporters were arrested on trumped-up charges, voters were often marched to the polls waving ballot cards already made out in favour of the 'correct' list (No. 3: 'The Government Bloc'), invigilators were obstructed, and ballot boxes disappeared and then suddenly reappeared. By these means a result was obtained that was satisfactory to Moscow. Mikolajczyk fled to the West but resistance of a more violent sort continued in some parts of the country, as it did in parts of what had once been Poland and was now part of the Soviet Ukraine. Between 1945 and 1948 as many as 30,000 Polish Communists and Russians are said to have been killed. In other countries the political watershed was reached only after the United States unveiled the Marshall Plan in June of that fateful year.

The Plan was to disburse large sums of American aid for the economic regeneration of Europe. Both Poland and Czechoslovakia elected to participate, but the Soviet delegation walked out of the inaugural meeting in Paris and forced Poland and Czechoslovakia to withdraw too (Stalin had accused the Communist Premier of Czechoslovakia, Klement Gottwald, of being prepared to turn his back on the Soviet Union). In fact, as the senior State Department official, George F. Kennan, pointed out later, the Marshall Plan had been designed to be rejected by the Soviet Union. Political conditions were attached to the aid. As Secretary Marshall declared, it was designed to revive the working economy 'so as to permit the emergence of political and social conditions in which free institutions can exist'. Primarily directed at countries like Italy and France, to Moscow it appeared to be an attempt to penetrate and undermine her sphere of Europe. This outcome, however, was highly satisfactory to Washington. As Kennan put it, it was not the Americans who were to be seen to be drawing 'a line of division through Europe'.

Thereafter the United States and her allies helped to intensify the division, not only by denying other forms of aid to Eastern Europe but by reducing their negligible trade with the region too. Later in 1947 the International Bank for Reconstruction and Development refused a Polish request for a $600 million credit, and the United States rejected an appeal from Jan Masaryk, the non-Communist Czech Foreign Minister, for a grain shipment to compensate for a harvest failure. The Czechs then turned to the Soviet Union, which agreed to provide what was needed at prices below prevailing world prices; Poland also received big grain shipments from the Soviet Union, together with a $500 million credit. In December a new Czech-Soviet trade agreement, including a substantial Soviet loan, was concluded. As the Czech Minister, Ripka, subsequently confirmed in exile, the terms were very favourable to his country. In this way the economies of the two countries were meshed more closely with that of the Soviet Union.

In 1947, too, the 'Cominform' was set up to replace the Communist International, which had been disbanded during the war in deference to Western feelings. In that same year the Romanian peasant leader, Maniu, was put on trial; the Bulgarian peasant leader Petkov was shot; Hungary's Smallholder government was broken up and its leader forced into exile, as was the nine-year-old King of Bulgaria, which received a new, republican, constitution.

Czechoslovakia, though written off by the West, was still a constitutional democracy whose people enjoyed genuine freedoms. But not for much longer. The manner of the change, however, was singular. In February 1948, with an election looming, the Communists fell out with most of their partners in the government. There were disagreements over a new constitution and over unrest in Slovakia, but chiefly over accusations that the Communist Interior Minister was packing the senior posts in the police force with Communists. A constitutional crisis occurred when twelve non-Communist ministers tendered their resignations.

President Benes was reluctant to accept them. After demonstrations by workers, some of them armed, he finally did so. A new coalition government was formed, though executive power passed to a 'Central Action Committee' dominated by members of the Czechoslovak-Soviet Friendship Society, trades unionists and Communists. A widespread purge was carried out against all opponents of the new regime; clamps were applied to the press; Foreign Minister Jan Masaryk fell to his death from a high window; Benes resigned. This saved the Hungarian minority whom he was planning to eliminate.[13] Czechoslovakia became a 'People's Republic'. Kennan had foreseen that the American attempt to draw Czechoslovakia into the Western sphere would provoke some such desperate reaction.

The Cold War deepened on the economic front. The Western Powers introduced a new currency into their zones of occupied Germany in such a way as to benefit the economy of West Berlin and to destabilize that of the Soviet zone. The Soviet Union responded by insisting that only the East German currency should be used in all sectors of Berlin. The West refused and the Soviets proceeded to cut West Berlin's communications with the outside world, and its water supply. The West answered this with the Berlin airlift of 1948–9. In August 1949 NATO was founded to resist 'the Kremlin's programme of intimidation designed to attain the domination of Europe'. Yet, ironically, 1948 had seen a major defection from the Soviet Bloc.

* * *

Moscow had long disliked Yugoslavia's independent stance on several issues, but in particular its attempt, first mooted in 1946, to form a Balkan Federation with Bulgaria and Albania. In March 1948 Moscow berated Belgrade over this. Belgrade answered back. A war of words ensued, culminating in a diplomatic break in June. Yugoslavia was subjected to economic sanctions (though Hungary and Czechoslovakia found difficulty in implementing these with any speed) and Tito was excommunicated by Communist headquarters in Moscow. This suited his purpose. The Yugoslav Party had long been bedevilled by nationalist feuding,[14] as had the country as a whole. The 1946 Constitution, which had divided the country into six constituent republics and two autonomous regions, had not overcome the problem. Nor had the more recent division of the party on similar lines. But the row with Moscow placed Yugoslavia in a state of siege which helped to solidify popular support for Tito. Otherwise, however, the Soviet grip on the region was by now complete, and even Yugoslavia, while gladly accepting the offer of economic cooperation from the United States, conformed to the norms of the Bloc in domestic policy, not least in the industrial sphere.

Up to 1948 such industrial policies were as much a product of circumstances and economic fashion as of fiats issued from Moscow. A predominantly non-Communist Hungarian government nationalized the mines in 1946, the big banks in 1947, and thereafter heavy industry, power companies, food processing and all concerns employing more than 100 people. But the right-wing government before the war had brought several industrial concerns into the state sector; the Americans themselves expropriated Krupp and several other large German companies (though they handed them back after a time), while nationalization was such a cardinal tenet of Britain's post-war Labour administration that not only the coal industry but steel, railways and several other industries were taken over by the state. In general Eastern Europe followed the fashion. By the end of 1947 Bulgaria had nationalized 95 per cent of her industry, of which, however, she had very little; by 1948 60 per cent of East German industry was nationalized. Yugoslavia nationalized all concerns except small handicrafts businesses. Poland took all firms employing more than fifty workers into the state sector, and in Romania, where strong sentiment existed against foreign ownership, 85 per cent of industry was nationalized by the end of 1949. In no country were these measures unpopular.

State planning was a more obvious reflection of Soviet influence, although Poland had adopted it before the war. It undoubtedly owed something to admiration of the Soviet Union's industrial drive after 1928, and given the economic chaos of the immediate post-war period it was often seen to be essential. Czechoslovakia's Two Year Plan for 1947–8 aimed to increase industrial production by 10 per cent over the pre-war level. The Bulgarian Two Year Plan sought a much larger increase and the development of her poor communications. The Hungarian Three Year Plan envisaged reaching pre-war levels in 1947 and producing over a quarter more in 1948. The East Germans launched only a modest six-month plan, the Romanians and Poles none at all.

Nevertheless, as UNRRA reported in 1947, 'most countries' in Europe were making plans for widespread industrialization which were expected in particular to produce 'a new and large demand for the products of heavy industry'. Though they usually failed to meet their targets, these early plans did assist recovery. By 1948 Czech industrial production reached the level of 1935–8. At that point Italian production still lagged 12 per cent behind the pre-war rate, the French by 16 per cent and the Dutch by 28 per cent. Furthermore, East Germany, despite having lost a major industrial zone to Poland and having been bled for reparations, had made greater progress towards recovery than had West

Germany. Given the circumstances, state action had proved highly effective in reviving moribund economies.

After 1947, however, economic planning in Eastern Europe became more ambitious and more Stalinist in its emphasis on heavy industry at the expense of other sectors. This was in part a consequence of the Cold War. The ruthless drive to produce steel and develop heavy engineering was launched with a view to a war which Moscow told its satellites to expect within three or four years.[15] Furthermore, the Soviet method was the only one then known that could produce fast and substantial industrial growth in backward countries, as all, except western Czechoslovakia, were. The methods which subsequently produced the Indian 'miracle' which proved compatible with democracy had not yet been mooted, and the American attempt to produce an economic miracle in Greece proved to be a dismal failure.

Having taken over responsibility from the British in 1947, the United States proceeded to pour more money per capita into Greece than into any western European country. The results were disappointing. Traditional Balkan patronage systems, whereby both economic and political decisions were dictated by friendship networks and corruption, absorbed the financial inputs but defeated the American plans despite the advice of the US experts sent to Greece, Nor did democracy flourish in a Balkan country in which gerrymandering had always been rampant and democracy an arcane and alien concept to all but a few.[16] Within the Soviet Bloc countries, by contrast, much greater success was achieved at the cost of widespread privation and political terror. But at the same time a barrage of optimistic propaganda was laid on the growing working class, who were promised a heaven appropriate for the elite of the new society.

Only Tito's Yugoslavia launched a full-scale five-year plan before 1948, but it was typical in its ambitiousness – industrial production was to multiply no less than five times over the pre-war level, while the hitherto dominant agricultural sector was to form no more than a third of total income. In more developed countries percentage increases of this magnitude were impossible, but the Czech Five-Year Plan of 1949 envisaged a rise of 60 per cent in industrial production and gave the great bulk of investment to heavy industry, especially engineering. Preoccupied at first with the task of colonizing and absorbing her new western territories, Poland delayed its cavalry charge at the economy until 1951, when a Six-Year Plan was unveiled which included provision for vast projects such as a new steel complex to be built near Cracow. The East German, Hungarian and Romanian plans exhibited similar gargantuan characteristics.

While workers were encouraged to think that they were building a new proletarian Eldorado, peasants were usually burdened by heavy taxes and forced deliveries of their produce. Agricultural prices fell while prices for manufactured goods rose. At the same time the factories were manned by workers, many of whom had been hauled in from the countryside to live in temporary barrack-blocks, and subjected to strict factory discipline and ever-increasing 'production norms'.

In Hungary, workers' wages, planned to rise by 50 per cent over the period, fell by 20 per cent in real terms. Most people worked harder and ate less. The working class became disillusioned with the poor rewards. Moreover the planning, relying too much on crude theory which itself reflected a skill-shortage in many countries of the region, was inflexible and led to great waste and dislocation. Promising industrial sectors, such as precision machinery and electrical goods in Hungary, were also neglected. The results, though impressive even discounting the exaggerations of the official statistics, were unbalanced, storing up troubles for the future.

Yet however grotesque Stalinism may seem in retrospect, it also represented an heroic attempt to break the bonds of structural economic backwardness. And its failure stemmed as much from human frailty and folly and from the sheer weight of the problems bequeathed by the past, as from a deficient, skewed morality. In most countries Stalinism compensated for the shortage of experienced managers and skilled technicians by building immense plants which exploited these scarce resources to the full. It brought in surplus population from the countryside and often succeeded in overcoming their disorientation. There were, however, some unpleasant political by-products to this desperate attempt to catch up with the developed world.

Political discipline was rigid. Anyone expressing an alternative policy, or even suggesting a different way of handling some aspect of a Plan's execution, ran serious risk of denunciation and punishment. A supervisory role was accorded to Party representatives at every level from ministry to the shop floor. The membership of the Party was by then sufficient for the task. In Czechoslovakia in November 1948 a third of the adult population were Communists. Elsewhere membership was less impressive numerically, though in Hungary and East Germany in the early fifties it amounted to a tenth. In less developed Poland, Romania and Yugoslavia, however, membership totalled only about a fifth of the adult population.[17] Everywhere the proportion of young, and of educated, people tended to be high, although a great many members had merely joined the bandwagon in the expectation that it would lead to personal advancement, privilege and power. This was a reason for another feature of the Stalinist years 1948–53, the purge.

The purge, however, was not only a means of excluding undesirables from the Party, it was also a method of imposing draconian discipline through fear; a means, cloaked in transparently spurious legitimacy, of dispatching political opponents and personal enemies to prison or to execution, and, at the same time, of providing a credulous public with scapegoats. The purge owed nothing to the old imperial traditions, nor to the rough, trigger-happy, justice of the Balkans. It came straight from Moscow (see Chapter 4). So did the show trials with which it was associated.

Such practices also reflected a preoccupation with security at a time of high international tension. Moscow, which by now had control of the secret police forces of all the satellites with which to back up its dominating political influence, set out to hunt down anyone who might subvert the new order, prove susceptible to the blandishments of the hostile West, or be likely to emulate Tito's 'national deviation'. Since the new state of Israel had unexpectedly joined the American camp, a hunt for Zionists also became a feature of the period.[18] However, the purge also presented itself as a convenient means by which a party leader or faction could eliminate a rival; and, as with Senator Joseph McCarthy's witch-hunt for Communist sympathizers in the United States, it often took on a momentum of its own.

In 1949 there were purges in Bulgaria and Hungary. The Bulgarian Deputy Premier Kostov was sentenced to death on charges which included the adoption of 'an insincere and unfriendly policy towards the Soviet Union' (he had protested at the terms of trade between Bulgaria and the Soviet Union which had been selling Bulgarian attar of roses at three times the price they had paid for it). Kostov was also the chief rival of Chervenkov in the struggle for the succession to the ailing Party leader Dimitrov. Jews were among the victims in several countries. In Hungary, however, the principal victim, Interior Minister Laszlo Rajk, was not a Jew – but the man responsible for his fate, Rakosi, was. Among those imprisoned was Janos Kadar who was later to rise to the leadership.

In Poland the most prominent victims were Marian Spychalski, Zenon Kliszko and another future leader, Wladyslaw Gomulka, First Secretary of the Party and a Deputy Premier, who had envisaged the achievement of socialism without a dictatorship of the proletariat.[19] However, there were no show trials or executions, and Jews did not figure prominently among those purged, even though a number of them held high positions and despite the continuing popularity of anti-semitism.[20] In Romania, however, Vasile Luca, Georgescu and Ana Pauker, who was Jewish, were executed. The curious aspect in this case was that, according to Western observers, they represented a pro-Soviet faction. In Albania Xoxe was shot; but the show-trials were most blatant and cut deepest in Czechoslovakia.

Between 1950 and 1952, amid blazes of publicity, outrageous terms of abuse were flung at many hitherto regarded as Party stalwarts. A future

Party boss, Gustav Husak, was among those imprisoned, and no fewer than fourteen Jews including Party Secretary Rudolf Slansky, were among those executed. Yet despite the emphasis on 'Zionist conspiracy', prominent Jews including Kriegl were not touched.[21] In East Germany the victims included Paul Merker, who was a Jew, and Dahlem, who was not, though both were dangerous rivals to Walter Ulbricht. In all trials the charges of treason, Titoism, Trotskyism, Zionism and spying for the CIA were levelled rather freely. The victims included Stalinists and anti-Stalinists, nationalists and anti-nationalists, political rivals, trouble-makers, and anyone who rocked the boat or was thought by those in command to have that potential.

The vocabulary associated with the purges and show-trials reflected a political culture which had borrowed much from Christianity as well as Marx and Stalin. In fact the Party was an analogue of the Church, and in this phase it was pronouncing anathema upon its heretics. Moreover, the language it used struck chords among many simple people. Semi-literate as many of there were, they understood about demons and Antichrist, and there was a familiar logic in the view that the advent of an earthly paradise must be accompanied by a climactic struggle against the forces of evil. Images of Stalin as all-powerful and all-wise, the caring Liberator, became as ubiquitous as religious icons or the portraits of emperors in former ages. However, this was a narrow church which set its face against all rivals: the new regimes were already engaged in a *Kulturkampf* against religion. Again, though, the struggles between church and state had often started before the Communists took over.

In Hungary the Catholic hierarchy had fought the secularization of the school system, first proposed by the Smallholder government, tooth and nail. But the Communist regimes took matters farther. In Yugoslavia Archbishop Stepinac of Zagreb was tried for collaboration with the enemy soon after the war. This was not an altogether unpopular move since, though Tito's partisans had included some Franciscans, the Catholic hierarchs had either held aloof from the wartime struggles (like Stepinac) or been active in support of the Nazis and the *Ustasha* (like Archbishop Saric of Sarajevo). But elsewhere persecution of the Church did not get under way until 1948. That year Cardinal Mindszenty, Prince Primate of Hungary, was arrested on charges of treason and subsequently imprisoned for life.[22] In Czechoslovakia the state not only denied the Church publicity, but harassed it by withholding planning permission for new churches and blocking appointments to vacant sees and livings.

Similar measures were introduced in Poland from 1948 although, despite a torrent of anti-religious propaganda and such government devices as supporting movements of 'patriotic priests' like 'Pax' in order to splinter the Church, the strength of Catholicism and its close association with Polish nationalism proved too strong to be challenged directly. Even in the Orthodox Balkans where the Church had always supported the secular power of whatever colour (which may help to account for the milder nature of the anti-religious drive in Romania), the number of priests and seminarists was limited, and the young, as well as Party members, strongly discouraged from attending divine service. Everywhere watchdogs were posted to note who attended church; and everywhere the churches were impoverished by the confiscation of their landed estates. Not the least important feature of the period was a widespread (though incomplete) dissolution of the monasteries.

The great land hunger which had tormented Eastern Europe since the population explosion of the later nineteenth century (see Chapter 5) had been largely overcome by land redistribution. The Communist regimes, however, did not regard this as sufficient, and from 1948 collectivization became the order of the day. Another crude Stalinist theory was elevated to the status of a religious article of faith. Nevertheless the policy was supported by a certain logic. The crash industrialization programmes demanded the release of labour from the countryside. Furthermore the tendency, especially marked in Poland, for the peasant to regard his farm as a patrimony rather than a business led to his producing less than he might for the market; this could lead to shortages and high food prices in the cities. Besides, it was obviously more economical to farm in large units, using big machines (as they did on the prairies of North America) than in a plethora of small units employing antiquated tools.

In any case, in some areas the peasants were not as unsympathetic to collective farming as the Soviet peasants had proved themselves to be in 1929. The cooperative movement had made strides in Bulgaria between the wars; the Yugoslav *zadruga* was a kind of collective insofar as members of the extended family farmed the land in common; and some aspects of animal-rearing in eastern Hungary and among the Vlach shepherds of the Balkans savoured of collectivism. Nevertheless some regimes were somewhat sluggish in putting Stalin's model into practise. The exception was Bulgaria, where half the arable land was collectivized by 1952. Elsewhere in the Balkans the process tended to be slower. The Croatian peasant's tenacious attachment to his farm and the pointlessness of collectivization in the wild uplands of Montenegro were two reasons that induced Tito's Yugoslavia to proceed rather more slowly; and peasant resistance was so fierce in Romania that only about 15 per cent of the land had been collectivized by 1952. In Hungary the pace was much faster, but the implementation so clumsy, inefficient and unpopular that the entire edifice soon disintegrated.

Elsewhere there was a certain reluctance to spoil the honeymoon atmosphere between government and most of the rural population that had prevailed since the land reforms; and this was particularly true of Poland, where the regime was widely regarded as an alien imposition.

When Gomulka was dismissed in 1948 a programme of collectivization was implemented, but small farms were excluded and, as a result, the scheme invited evasion. Peasants with larger farms simply split them up among their relatives, creating numbers of 'small farms' which were exempt. By 1953 only 10 per cent of Poland's agriculture was run by collectives; 15 per cent was run by state farms, and the rest was in the private sector. The situation did not change much thereafter. Had that not been the case the inefficiency of the country's agriculture might not have been so great, nor such a burden on the economy as a whole. By 1960, however, most of the agricultural sector in countries other than Poland had been collectivized, often successfully. This could be regarded as Stalin's last, posthumous, triumph.

In 1952, the year the Marshall Plan ended, Stalin made his last, belated, concession to the West, proposing the holding of free elections throughout Germany, and the unification and neutralization of the country. The offer was rejected. In October the Nineteenth Congress of the Communist Party of the Soviet Union was convened in Moscow. Leaders of the satellite states mounted the rostrum in turn to deliver speeches in praise of Stalin. The scene was reminiscent of a great synod convened by a Byzantine Emperor, or of a Russian Tsar three centuries earlier (see Chapters 11 and 7). They thanked him for (among other benefits) the bestowal of 'real freedom' on their countries. Although he was aware that such talk was intended for the unsophisticated *hoi poloi*, it no doubt gave the old man some satisfaction. Some weeks later, however, he sustained a brain haemhorrage. On 5 March 1953 he died.

* * *

What does the balance-sheet of the Stalinist years add up to? A collection of Eastern European states had been converted into 'peoples' democracies' in which, however, elected assemblies had virtually no political importance, and in which high-profile 'popular councils' were but appendages to the Party. The Party itself, which had absorbed the Socialists and much of the peasant parties, enjoyed a complete monopoly of political power. Purged of the dissidents, it was an instrument in the hands of a tiny elite, and it operated through a series of bureaucratic structures, most of whose functionaries, whether Party members or not, had been frightened into obedience, terrified of losing the perks and privileges that went with their jobs. The political edifice was supported by a propaganda machine which had monopolized the media and which blared out the party line.

This political system had one major weakness, however: every grievance, every mistake tended to be blamed on the regime. The presentation of scapegoats to the public, the periodic admission of 'mistakes' and fierce anti-Western propaganda helped to deflect some of this discontent for a time, but time was to prove these measures to be no more than temporary expedients. The Kremlin kept the leaderships in line formally through the Cominform and other joint bodies, and informally through the debts of gratitude many of the leaders bore the Soviet Union, the operations of the secret police, and the ill-disguised presence of Soviet troops in all but Czechoslovakia and Yugoslavia. Nevertheless they were not quite Soviet clones. Yugoslavia had defected, Poland had not collectivized, and persistent nationalism and the differing conditions in each country demanded variations in both the content and the pace of the economic, social and cultural re-structuring which Stalin's 'Road to Socialism' called for. The achievements of this programme were not negligible, however.

Between 1948 and 1953 industrial production more than doubled in many countries of the Bloc. In the Soviet Union itself it rose by almost 50 per cent, and it is curious that deviant Yugoslavia achieved the least increase, though at a little over 25 per cent it was impressive enough. The East German economy had recovered better than the West German, Bulgaria had outpaced Greece. The successes gave rise to hopes of catching up with the West and eventually overtaking it. But the bare production statistics disguised grievous economic flaws and imbalances. The Stalinist recipe had fended off recession and laid the foundations of industry on the basis of a war economy which neglected the production of consumer goods and the short-term interests of the worker, whether rural or urban. Moreover the planning was too rigid to accommodate new technology or changing management requirements. It was in this period that the imbalances and inefficiencies, so much decried since, were built into the system. The achievements of those years were to hold the future hostage.

In social terms there was a revolution which also turned out to be flawed. Society was levelled, millions gained self-respect and opportunities that had formerly been denied them; and unemployment was eliminated, though at the cost of feather-bedding. Yet despite the deliberate social engineering, a new elite was arising in place of the elite which had been eliminated; new vested interests were created in place of the old; and the proliferation of bureaucracy not only entailed inefficiency but had the effect of nationalizing endemic corruption which had formerly operated in dispersed networks. Not least, the crude social propaganda of the Stalinist years succeeded all too well. Many of the region's subsequent troubles stemmed from an innocent belief in the truth of all those slogans.

The achievements of Stalinist educational policies were also mixed. Systems of universal education were set up and literacy was brought to the masses (though in several countries this had been in train beforehand). Scientific education saw a marked expansion at all levels while the classics and the law, formerly major features of elite education, declined sharply. Technological training received great emphasis, but succeeded in producing too many workers who could not adapt to new methods and technologies. The higher flights of scholarship suffered from their subjection to both Party ideology and bureaucratic control. On the other hand, women were given equal educational opportunities. This however, bore some unexpected fruit. As women came to occupy a high proportion of posts in medicine and the legal profession, these ceased to be premium professions in terms of pay and status.

The cultural policies of the period were the most conservative. Although the censors often laid their deadening hands on promise, artistic standards were on the whole maintained, and those in the performing arts raised. Moreover, most of the world's classics were published on a generous scale, along with propaganda, and were read avidly by millions. Aristocratic houses, transformed into 'Palaces of Culture', opened many an eye to an appreciation of the visual arts, and, although new architecture was as drab and hideous as in the West, war-damaged city centres were lovingly restored. Stalinism did not reject all aspects of the past. Indeed, since its executants were themselves the products of the pre-war era they could not help but inform the new age with some values of the old one.

Other features of the past also survived. Strong nationalist sentiment smouldered on beneath the surface of life, despite the propaganda promoting fraternity between peoples, and on occasion it erupted. Age-old clientage and favour networks persisted in the more backward areas; and even the low prices and shortages which characterized the economy were strongly reminiscent of conditions before the war. In fact, the region as a whole had always been poor; and it was this poverty which had blighted the hopes of those few who had looked forward to a Western type of development with the defeat of Nazi Germany. Democracy had been a fragile flower even in pre-war Czechoslovakia, and unsustainable elsewhere. Civil institutions were poorly developed; respect for the law, as opposed to the power of authority, comparatively limited; social and racial hatreds were too deep and passionate to allow peaceful development. All these factors had facilitated the Soviet takeover.

* * *

Nonetheless the Soviet Union would not have gained dominance over the region had it not been for the war; and there may well have been no war had the situation in Eastern Europe in the 1930s not invited Nazi aggression. But why was this so? Why did the region constitute a strategic vacuum before the war? Why had it been so poor? Why, having achieved the goal of national independence in 1918, did people not feel more secure and nationalism not lose its militancy? And why had the independent states of the region, with only one dubious exception, failed to sustain the democratic systems they had adopted, or solve their deep-seated social and economic problems? Were the chances offered them in the wake of the First World War squandered? Or were those chances deceptive, illusory and lacking substance? In order to decide these questions we must extend the enquiry back to the year of promise, 1918.

REFERENCES

1. Stalin to Djilas, June 1945 – M. Djilas, *Conversations with Stalin* (trans. M. Petrovich) (Harmondsworth, 1969) p. 90. In general on the period covered in this chapter see J. Rothschild, *Return to Diversity* (Oxford, 1989).
2. The traditional interpretation in the West attributes the onset of the Cold War to Soviet aggression. On the other hand revisionists have claimed that it was Western aggression which forced the Soviet Union to construct an empire in Eastern Europe. Both views are tendentious. A. Schlesinger suggests persuasively that the Cold War arose out of mutual misperceptions, though he attributes too much to ideology. Despite the vast amount of scholarly literature on the subject too much of relevance still lies buried in the archives of both the East and the West. The account which follows attempts to explain the origins and effects of the Cold War only in terms of circumstances and developments in Eastern Europe itself.
3. They comprised survivors of concentration camps and forced labourers returning home from Germany besides people fleeing from the advancing armies and migrating as a result of frontier changes. The frontiers of Poland were moved westwards; part of Transylvania which had been transferred to Hungary by the second 'Vienna Award' (see Chapter 4) was returned to Romania, which, however, had to cede northern Moldavia to the USSR. Czechoslovakia relinquished Subcarpathian Ruthenia to the Soviet Union on 29 June 1945. Yugoslavia gained Trieste, Zadar anal Gorizia from Italy.
4. December 1945 to June 1946. By the time the currency was stabilized in August 1946 the value of the *pengo* had slumped to a sixth of that.
5. See the quarterly UNRRA Reports on Poland, 1945 (1946).
6. J. Szczepanski, *Polish Society* (New York, 1970) pp. 40–1.
7. A resident farm labourer working on an annual contract. For a graphic description of their condition early in the century, see G. Cushing's translation of G. Illyes, *People of the Puszta* (London, 1971).
8. Benes's (anti-Nazi) National Socialists polled 18 per cent; the Catholic People's Party 16 per cent and the Social Democrats 13 per cent. Under the British electoral system the Communists would probably have gained a comfortable overall parliamentary majority.
9. R. Wolff, *The Balkans in Our Time* (Cambridge, Mass., 1956) pp. 293–304. Bulgaria's traditional sympathy for Russia derived from Russia's longstand-

ing support for the Orthodox Christians under Ottoman rule and her crucial role in the establishment of Bulgaria's independence (see Chapter 5). In the only genuine elections before the war the Communists had come second (ironically their support then derived from the cities, whereas in 1990 it derived from the countryside).

10. The 'Government of National Unity' which the British installed in Athens in October 1944, in the wake of the German withdrawal, included only five representatives of the Communist-led Popular Front. Having purged the Greek Brigade serving with the British Army of 'political unreliables', the British dissolved the Communist-led resistance force, ELAS, and fired on a crowd protesting against it. By the time elections were held in Greece in 1946 the new Greek National Guard and the police, both of which had been purged of left-wing sympathizers, procured the desired result. It should be noted that Stalin had pressured the Greek Communists into supporting the predominately right-wing 'Government of National Unity', and that when ELAS eventually tried to seize power he forbade the Communists to fire on British troops.
11. See S. Mikolajczyk, *The Pattern of Soviet Domination* (London, 1948), p. 81.
12. The phrase in Mikolajczyks's, *op. cit.*, p. ix.
13. See V. Mastny, 'The Benes Thesis: A Design for the Liquidation of National Minorities', in S. Borsody (ed.), *The Hungarians* (New Haven, Conn., 1987), pp. 231–43.
14. See P. Shoup, *Communism and the Yugoslav National Question* (New York, 1968).
15. This was subsequently reported by the Hungarian Minister, Gero.
16. The treatment of post-war Greece, see W. McNeill, *The Metamorphosis of Greece Since World War II* (Oxford, 1978). On the East German rising, see (among other works) the recent summation by Anne McElvoy, *The Saddled Cow: East Germany's Life and Legacy* (London, 1992), pp. 50–8.
17. By the end of 1945 1 per cent of Poland's population were members of the Communist Party, though there had been only 30,000 members a year before; 1.25 per cent of Romanians, 1.75 per cent of Hungarians, 2 per cent of East Germans and 5 per cent of Czechs were Party members at that stage, though in Bulgaria only 0.33 per cent were. By 1954 approximately 5 per cent of all Poles, Romanians and Yugoslavs were Party members and 10 per cent of all Czechs and Slovaks.
18. It should be remembered that the Czechs had supplied essential arms to the *Haganah* and that the Soviet Union had been the first power to grant *de jure* recognition to Israel. The historical connections between the Israeli left, which formed the first government of the new state, and the left in Russia, Israel's large agricultural collective (*kibbutz*) movement, and the Eastern European origins of most of Israel's inhabitants at that time gave rise to expectations that the new state would align with Moscow. Why it failed to do so constitutes an interesting but neglected story.
19. Gomulka had been a popular Minister for the newly-acquired Western Territories. He was expelled from the Party in 1949 and arrested in 1951 but never brought to trial. For his subsequent career see Chapter 2.
20. For example, there had been a pogrom in Kielce in 1946 in which seventy newly-returned concentration camp survivors were murdered by a mob which had gathered in response to a rumour that Jews had killed a Christian child for ritual purposes. Apologists claimed that the Communists had staged the incident in order to discredit the opposition. Bishop Wyszynski,

subsequently Cardinal Primate of Poland, failed to condemn the massacre. Wyszynski once stated that he was not convinced that Beilis, a Jew acquitted by a jury of a charge of ritual murder in pre-revolutionary Russia, had been innocent.

21. Kriegl was a veteran of the Spanish Civil War. This disposes of the theory that one of the purposes of the purges was to eliminate everyone who might have been connected with Tito, the Comintern's representative in Paris in the 1930s.
22. See J. Mindszenty, *Memoirs* (London, 1974) which, despite its tendentious tone and sarcasm, is a useful source on the *Kulturkampf* between Church and State in the early years of Communist rule. Mindszenty escaped from prison in 1956 and was long sheltered in the US embassy in Budapest. After the Vatican had reached an agreement with the Hungarian government he was allowed to move to the United States.

4

Independence and its Consequences 1918–44

Upon the Breaking and Shivering of a greate State and Empire, you may be sure to have Warres. For great Empires, while they stand, do enervate and destroy the Forces of the Natives which they have subdued ... and when they faile also, all goes to Ruine and they become a Prey.

Francis Bacon

Until 1918 most of the peoples of Eastern Europe had been dominated by great empires. By the end of that year all those empires had ceased to exist. In their place there arose a series of new, or geographically redefined states, founded on the principles of national liberation and constitutional democracy. The oppressed nations of the region had at last attained their long-sought liberty. Yet the sweets of victory very soon turned sour. After little more than two decades constitutional democracy had everywhere proved a failure and almost the entire region was in thrall to predatory Nazi Germany.

Historians commonly attribute this extraordinary collapse to the Peace Settlement which, by replacing Austria-Hungary with a gaggle of small states, turned the area into a power vacuum; to the unforeseeable resurgence of a Germany bent upon conquest; and to the wide-ranging effects of the Great Depression. All these explanations carry weight, but so do others: the destruction and dislocations produced by the Great War of 1914–18; the miscalculations of those in power; and, not least, the complicated interactions of all these factors with structural economic difficulties, social imbalance, and the region's singular political culture.

The outcome was the abject failure of the new order; but to obtain a clearer understanding of this failure, and a more accurate weighting of its causes, we need to map out the process in more detail.

* * *

The new Eastern Europe emerged piecemeal out of the chaos of the Great War itself. In the autumn of 1917 Imperial Russia collapsed under the strain. Little more than a year later Austria-Hungary and Imperial Germany collapsed too, and the last Sultan of the Ottoman Empire also disappeared from the scene. In Russia, where power was soon grasped by Lenin and the Bolsheviks, democracy lasted only a few weeks – until January 1918 when the general election produced a majority for the Social Revolutionaries rather than the Communists. Yet here alone was a great state to emerge from the crucible of civil war. It was to be somewhat smaller than the old Empire, without Finland, which gained its independence, and without its Baltic and western provinces. Nevertheless, the new federated union of nominally autonomous 'Soviet Socialist Republics' was to prove the only resilient political unit east of Germany. Everywhere else the shape of the political map was the outcome of a veritable maelstrom of conflicting interests which are difficult enough to comprehend in retrospect and which were certainly not fully understood by the main protagonists at the time.

There were many players: the various nationalist groups both within Eastern Europe and in exile; émigré communities, particularly in the United States; the Great Powers themselves – Germany and Austria-Hungary, both trying desperately to extricate themselves from the War; Britain, France, and the United States, each with its different vision of Eastern Europe's future; and, finally, the smaller states of the region, particularly Serbia, Romania and Greece. If the array of inter-acting interests and policies was bewildering, the almost breathtaking pace of events, and breakdowns in communications, added to the confusion. In attempting to follow the more significant developments, let us start with the man who is widely regarded as setting the moral tone for the Peace Settlement: Woodrow Wilson, President of the United States.

In declaring war on Germany and her allies in December 1917, President Wilson made it clear that his country had 'no wish ... to impair or rearrange the Austro-Hungarian Empire'. Only a month later, however, in his celebrated Fourteen Points speech, he called for the peoples of that Empire to be given the 'freest opportunity for autonomous development', implying that it should be reorganized into a federal state along lines of nationality; and for the resurrection of Poland which had not existed as a state since the eighteenth century.[1] The enemy took note.

In November 1918, with defeat looming, the Germans rushed the Polish nationalist leader Josef Pilsudski to Warsaw (much as they had spirited Lenin to Petrograd the year before) and set up a 'Regency Council' there as the basis for 'a free and independent Poland'. For his part, the Emperor Karl declared Austria to be a federal state, invited its subject nationalities to elect 'national councils', and sued for peace on the basis of the Fourteen Points. The offer was rejected. Only a few weeks before Wilson had committed the United States to the dismemberment of

Austria-Hungary by recognizing the 'Czech National Council' of émigrés in Paris led by Tomas Masaryk as the 'provisional government' of an independent Czech state. Having identified Austria-Hungary as the weakest link in the enemy alliance, the Western Powers had set about the task of undermining it by trying to foment rebellion among its subject peoples.[2]

The Emperor acted to pre-empt rebellion, however. Having called for the formation of National Councils, he proceeded to grant them recognition when they declared themselves independent. At the end of October he recognized the Prague Council (which was more broadly representative of the Czech people than the Provisional Government in Paris); and in the days that followed, he granted other National Councils recognition as independent states. These were acts of high responsibility designed to facilitate legitimate and orderly transfers of allegiance. But the transition was not allowed to take place so smoothly. The war was still in progress and, while it came to an abrupt end on the Western Front on 11 November, its end in Eastern Europe was to be less clearcut.

An armistice with Austria-Hungary had been signed on 3 November at Padova, but it did not include the Serbs, who continued their advance for another ten days. This allowed them to occupy Austrian Bosnia and the Hungarian Vojvodina. The same day, Austria proper, core of an Empire which had dominated so much of Eastern Europe for almost four centuries, declared itself a Republic. The Emperor gave it his blessing. Five days later he recognized the new Hungarian Republic. Then, having performed his last duty, he proceeded into exile.

Nonetheless, confusion reigned throughout most of his former possessions. The 'national sovereign state of Slovenes, Croats and Serbs' proclaimed by the Croatian parliament in October had to give way to a 'Kingdom of Serbs, Croats and Slovenes', the core of the new Yugoslavia, proclaimed with the sanction of the Allies on 1 December. The Slovak National Council was negotiating its new frontiers with Hungary, of which it had hitherto formed a part, unaware that the Allies had decided (largely under pressure of the Slovak community in the United States) to include the Slovak areas in the new Czech state.[3] The French commander in the Balkans ordered Hungary to withdraw its troops from Slovakia, and the Czechs swept in. That December Czech forces also overran the German-inhabited *Sudetenland*. Meanwhile on 13 November Soviet Russia had invited all the peoples of the region to join a Union of Soviet Republics, and, as the German armies withdrew, units of the new Red Army moved in behind them. Released prisoners-of-war were also moving westwards, many of them excited by the revolution in Russia and anxious to export it to their homelands.

On 19 January 1919 the Peace Conference began its work in Paris, but months were to pass before it handed down its decisions, and meanwhile the disorder continued. In Hungary armed bands of demoralized soldiers were plundering their way across the country, peasants were burning down manor houses and taking over the great estates, as they had done in Russia in the wake of the Tsar's departure. When, in March, the new Prime Minister, Count Michael Karolyi, resigned on learning of the extent of the territorial losses the Powers demanded of the new Republic, he was succeeded by a young Bolshevik who had been a prisoner-of-war in Russia, Béla Kun. The appearance of another Communist government promoted fears that the Bolsheviks might take over all eastern and central Europe. 'Red' elements were already challenging the Ukrainian nationalists who had formed a state under German protection, and as a civil war developed in the Ukraine as well as in Russia, an international war developed between Russia and emergent Poland.

War engulfed the Baltic region too. In April Polish troops seized Vilnius, capital of the new state of Lithuania, which had also been set up under German occupation – this on the pretext of saving it from the Russians. The month before Czech soldiers had fired on a crowd protesting against Czech rule in the Sudetenland, killing fifty-four of them. Soon the Romanian Army was advancing on Budapest, the Greeks were at war with Turkey, while in September an Italian poet, d'Annunzio, and a crowd of black-shirted followers occupied the city of Fiume to prevent it falling to Yugoslavia, and proceeded to rule it by terror. On the Western Front the firing ceased on 11 November 1918; in Eastern Europe, however, the Great War did not end in peace.

Meanwhile the statesmen gathered in Paris were building a new order designed to prevent war. Embracing the fashionable but erroneous view that the Great War had been caused by frustrated nationalism, President Wilson had formulated his famous principle of national self-determination and it had become the slogan of the hour, accepted by former emperors and invoked by Lenin himself. Its translation into practice was to prove difficult, however. Wilson intended that 'justice' should be meted out to 'all peoples and nationalities'. Yet 'justice' for one was usually to be regarded as 'injustice' by another; and the 'historically established lines of allegiance and nationality', along which the peacemakers were to redraw the political map, did not exist.[4] Besides, these principles had already been undermined by previous treaty obligations entered into by Britain and France.

In 1915, by the Treaty of London, they had promised Italy parts of the Croatian coast and of Albania as inducements to enter the war on their side. The following year they had promised Romania extensive areas of Hungary on the same condition.[5] Previous commitments to Serbia and the Czechs also led the Peace Conference to deny hearings from the Slovak and Croatian delegations, although it considered submissions from other nationalities. Furthermore it was recognized that, notwithstanding national claims to territory, the successor states (though not Hungary) must, as far as possible, have defensible frontiers and be economically viable. Finally, there were extensive areas of Eastern Europe where, despite some half-hearted attempts at military intervention, the Powers were unable to enforce their authority. In all the circumstances, the outcome of the Peace Conference represented a commendable attempt to square the circle, but it was not one that received universal acclaim in Eastern Europe, nor one that held very good prospects for avoiding war in the future.[6]

The ethnic map of Eastern Europe presented such a patchwork quilt of nationalities in many areas as to preclude the formation of relatively 'pure' nation states without wholesale and forcible population movements,[7] and virtually none of the successor states were ethnically homogenous. Indeed several of them were multi-national, like the empires they replaced. The 6 million Czechs were a minority in their own country, ruling 3.5 million Germans, three quarters of a million Hungarians and half a million Ruthenes in an uneasy association with 3 million Slovaks.

In Yugoslavia, too, the largest single nationality, the Serbs, was outnumbered by the Croats, Macedonians, Slovenes and Bosnians, and there were substantial non-Slav minorities of Albanians, Hungarians and Italians. Both Yugoslavia and Czechoslovakia confronted similar problems to those of the old Austria-Hungary. Minorities constituted nearly a third of the populations of the new Romania and Poland. It was recognized that these minorities would be subject to discrimination, if not oppression, however, and so clauses were included in the treaties signed with each state, binding it to regard certain civic rights as fundamental laws and to guarantee rights to religious minorities.[8]

Aggrieved minorities were to have the right to appeal to the newly-constituted League of Nations, whose approval was required for any change in these fundamental laws. However, the conditions accorded ill with both the jealousy which most of the Eastern European states regarded their national sovereignty and the fear with which they regarded their minorities. The Poles were among those who raised a cry of protest, but as the Conference President explained,

> The territories now being transferred both to Poland and to other States inevitably include a large population speaking languages and belonging to races different from that of the people with whom they will be incorporated. Unfortunately, the races have been estranged by long years of bitter hostility.... These populations will be more easily reconciled to their new position if they know that from the very beginning they have assured protection and adequate guarantees against any danger of unjust treatment or oppression ....

> In view of the historical development of the Jewish question and the great animosity aroused by it, special protection is necessary for the Jews.... It is believed that these stipulations will not create any obstacle to the political unity of Poland....[9]

Nevertheless, only the Czechs were to accept such conditions at all willingly and even they failed to observe their undertakings. The Ruthenes, inhabiting the tail of the country, were never to obtain their own Diet any more than the Slovaks were to have their own assembly or law courts,[10] and the administration of Ruthenia remained overwhelmingly Czech, although Ruthenes did secure most of the available jobs as road-menders.[11] Elsewhere discrimination was even more blatant. The Romanians, from the start, refused to pay Jewish and Hungarian teachers in their newly-acquired territories, while, in theirs, the Yugoslavs forced Hungarian-speaking teachers and officials out of their posts and made life difficult for their clergy. Euphoria at the attainment of national liberation and, not least, the golden opportunity it afforded to distribute official posts among members of one's own nationality, was muted by the difficulty of post-war recovery and the daunting task of nation-building.

The consequences of the war were grievous.[12] The loss of manpower in this overpopulated region was the least of them. A large proportion of the survivors were exhausted, ill-clothed and had forgotten the skills they had possessed before the war. They were also ill-fed. Losses of livestock were to take twenty years to make up. Partly as a result of the dearth of draught animals, cereal production everywhere except Bulgaria had diminished by between a quarter and a half by comparison with 1913. Even if this had not been the case, the earning potential for agricultural exports, which had been very considerable before the war, especially from Romania, Hungary and Ukraine, had fallen sharply, for, thanks to the war, the United States and Canada had become the world's granary instead of Eastern Europe. And increased production in the West had caused world prices to slump. Czech industry, among the least affected, was producing 30 per cent less than before the war; in most of the other countries production was halved. The war had also dissipated savings, so funds available for investment were scarce. Inflation grew apace, ruining many members of the middle classes; so did interest rates. Business confidence was very low.

Matters were made worse by the Peace Settlement, which allowed other criteria to override the concern to draw frontiers that made economic sense. As a result towns lost their agricultural hinterlands; villagers found their access to mountain pastures, on which they traditionally grazed their cattle, suddenly blocked by frontier posts; the headquarters and branch offices of many a firm found that, overnight, they were in different countries where different laws and taxation systems applied. Railways lines were cut off from their former termini and cities from their railway stations. Romania's newly-acquired port of Bazias had no communications to link it with the rest of the country. Hungary's second city, Szeged, once a thriving regional emporium, became a sleepy frontier town. Grass was soon growing on the once busy docks of Trieste, now part of Italy, which had no need of another port.

The new frontiers cut across communication systems in a way that made nation-building the more difficult and expensive. Resurrected Poland found herself with parts of three different railway networks, each with different gauges and signalling systems; and, since they had been built with military purposes rather than international trade in mind, they did not usually meet up with one another. In Czechoslovakia all the main lines ran north-south, radiating from the old centres of Vienna and Budapest, whereas the new country's axis lay east-west. Her predicament led to a bitter struggle with Poland for possession of Tesin (Polish Cieszyn), whose stretch of line was the only link between the head and the tail of Czechoslovakia, although Tesin's population was predominately Polish and its mines a hotly disputed prize for both countries.

Such predicaments encouraged the continuation of a 'war psychosis'. There was not only a desperate concern to protect one's territory against one's neighbours (and, if possible, to acquire more from them), but a willingness to wage economic warfare and, when opportunity offered, to loot. When, with the encouragement of the Powers who wanted to see Bela Kun's Communist regime brought down, Romanian troops occupied Budapest in August 1919, they carried away as much of the telephone equipment and railway rolling stock as they could, even if they could put it to no use. Hungary retaliated later by cutting Romania's telephone access to the West. When Romania was in dispute with Yugoslavia, she closed the locks controlling the flow of water from the Danube and so brought river traffic on the Yugoslav side to a halt. The Czechs refused to supply Hungary or Austria with coal, or to allow Polish coal to be shipped to them across her territory. The frontiers between Poland and Lithuania and between Yugoslavia and Bulgaria were repeatedly closed, and it was to take fifteen years to repair a two-mile gap in the telephone line between Belgrade and Sofia. The beggar-my-neighbour attitude was also reflected in fierce tariff wars.[13]

Such actions and reactions might be understandable psychologically, given the need to assert new national distinctions, but for the most part they were economically fruitless. And nothing was done to recreate a viable regional economy in place of the old imperial economy which had been broken up. The Austro-Hungarian common market was now divided between seven states, each of which had to be welded into an independent economic unit if its newly acquired territory was not to be sucked away, its economic life drawn into the old orbit, and its political independence not to prove ephemeral. Such, at least, was the view of most of their leaders.

The paranoia which inspired such policies was trenchantly expressed by a Prague newspaper in 1920:

> Vienna lives at the expense of others. The parasites of [imperial] Austria still live there. They see Vienna's only hope of salvation in the prospect of her again becoming a commercial centre. But their Vienna is doomed to ruin, and Czechoslovakia cannot be blamed for refusing to contribute to her preservation.[14]

Similar logic led the Czechs to contract a French company, at great expense, to build a new port on the Danube in the hope of capturing the trade of Vienna and Budapest. However, partly as a result of exaggerated protectionism, trade along the Danube in the 1920s sank to a sixth of what it had been before the war – barely a tenth of the commerce carried by Europe's other great waterway, the Rhine.

An aggressive mentality, previously associated with the Balkan peoples, was now pervasive throughout the region, and sometimes it found expression in the sort of chauvinism that had characterized the great Empires before the War. Pilsudski insisted that Poland must be a great power or none at all; Greece (until her crushing defeat by the Turks) was obsessed with the 'Great Idea' or re-creating the Byzantine Empire. All states paraded the glories of their national pasts, however dubious these glories may have been. The noble ethos of a former age was also popular, though it accorded ill with national realities and with the peasants' ideal of cosy isolationism. But the urge to achieve 'greatness', bred of a sense of inferiority and inspired by past examples of Great Power chauvinism, took a variety of forms.

Truncated Hungary, which, like Austria, nursed fierce resentment of the Treaty which had so reduced her, set out to become a great power at least in the world of sport. So did Czechoslovakia, although the greatness she was careful to present to the outside world was of the liberal and humanitarian sort that accorded well with prevalent values in the West. There were also attempts to compete with the world in terms of learning. Impoverished Hungary made big investments in higher education, and even backward Romania was producing nearly twice as many graduates as Britain by 1932. But if nationalism had benign expressions, it was often a highly divisive force which made nation-building more difficult.

This was manifest in politics where national minorities tended to opt for candidates of their own kind. In the elections held in Czechoslovakia in 1920 voters in Slovakia could choose candidates not only from the state-wide Social Democratic and Peoples Parties, but from Slovak Nationals, Slovak Christian Socialists, Hungarian Social Democrats, Hungarian Peasant, Hungarian National and Jewish Parties. Later, following further fragmentation, they could vote for German National and German Agrarian Parties too.[15] There was the same tendency in Poland, though the resentment of minorities produced so fierce a reaction there as to imperil the democratic system itself. When Poland's first President, Narutowicz, was elected, stone-throwing mobs appeared on the streets and newspapers claimed that, since he owed his success in part to the votes of minority representatives, he could not be regarded as the legitimate President of Poland. Two days after his inauguration he was assassinated by a follower of his rival, Roman Dmowski.

Fear of minorities led Poland to adopt similar policies to those of Imperial Russia. The substantial Ukrainian and Belorussian communities, patronizingly regarded as the 'little brothers' of the Poles, were urged to assimilate and, when they proved reluctant to do so, were subjected to force. As the Belorussian leader Cvikevic remarked bitterly, 'As soon as Poland had risen from the dead she began to flog Belorussia'. It was not long before the cavalry was sent in to pacify Ukrainian districts too. Such policies subsequently inclined many a frustrated Ukrainian nationalist to join the Nazis.

Nonetheless, while national minorities sometimes presented a threat to public order, they hardly threatened to undermine the state itself. Still less did Poland's Jews. Though they formed 10 per cent of the population and were becoming increasingly Zionist (both following and reacting to the nationalism of their neighbours), they were scattered geographically and politically divided between no fewer than five parties: the Jewish Populists, the Socialist Bund, Poale Zion and two (Galician Zionist Parties – one for the eastern part of that province, the other for the west. It was this general tendency to political fragmentation, rather than the multiplicity and size of national minorities, that formed the biggest obstacle to both nation-building and the survival of democracy.

Poland boasted no fewer than five Peasant Parties, reflecting regional differences rather than very divergent political aims,[16] and a hundred different parties in all. More than thirty of them gained representation in parliament in the 1920s. A similar picture presented itself in most other countries. In tiny Estonia, with its population of little more than a million, twenty-six parties fielded candidates in the 1923 election, and fourteen gained seats. In neighbouring Latvia, over 100 parties were to compete in the 1931 elections. Twenty-seven of them gained seats, though only two won more than ten. Czechoslovakia had seventeen parties in its Chamber of Deputies in 1920, the largest possessing barely a quarter of the seats.

In Yugoslavia the largest party could not muster even a quarter of all the seats, while the Serbian Democrats from the old Serbia and those from the old Austria failed to maintain a common line. Fragmentation of political opinion was evident elsewhere, too. Only in Austria was the electorate clearly and regularly divided between two chief political interests, the socialism of Vienna and the Catholic conservatism of the countryside. Elsewhere people voiced political preferences not only in terms of social and economic interests but in terms of regional, national and religious allegiances.

This led to parliaments in which the membership was so fractionalized that coalitions could take months to form and governments were easily overturned. The Czech politicians took to political dealing with relative alacrity, cheerfully sharing out the spoils of office. Elsewhere this was not the case. In Latvia the average life of a government was little more than eight months; Yugoslavia had twenty-four governments in ten years, Poland fourteen in fewer than seven. Superficially the situation resembled the political scene in France, or in Italy after World War Two. But the comparison is deceptive, for the Eastern European states in question did not enjoy heavily centralized administrations with powerful provincial prefects as in France (though several were inclining strongly to this model); nor did most of them have the strong and extensive social and economic networks of friendship and family, or the civic pride, that has given Italy coherence in times of extended political crisis.

Various explanations have been offered for the kaleidoscopic and increasingly violent character of Eastern European politics, and the chronic instability of its governments during the 1920s – that there were too many interests, bred of divergent social patterns and traditions, to be contained in a system of parliamentary democracy; that electoral systems that used proportional representation aggravated this trend; and that most of the leading politicians had learned their trade in opposition or as conspirators, whether in exile or underground.[17] All these reasons carry some weight (though Tomas Masaryk, who had also been a conspirator in exile, was nevertheless a committed democrat); but two sayings of the period shed light upon the problem: 'Everyone has a recipe for the salvation of his country'; and, to quote a Polish peasant leader, 'Everyone wants to be in opposition. No one wants to accept responsibility'.

Certainly, except in those areas which had once been part of Imperial Austria, constitutional democracy had shallow roots in the region, if any at all; and, at the same time, political principles were elevated to the status of religious beliefs which must on no account be compromised by pragmatism. As we shall see, this accorded with an increasing disposition on the part of electorates to vote for potential saviours rather than for a political programme, a disposition which may have derived in part from the persistence of patriarchalism, especially in the countryside.[18] In any case it facilitated the shift towards political authoritarianism which soon took place.

* * *

In despair at the politicians' inability to produce stable government in Poland, Marshal Pilsudski, hero of the war with Russia, staged a military *coup d'état* in 1926. Thenceforth Poland presented only an insubstantial shadow of parliamentary democracy. Before the end of the same year the army took power in Lithuania too. In the other Baltic states democracy lasted into the 1930s and was suppressed for fear that the extreme Right might take over. In Austria and Czechoslovakia democracy also survived into the 1930s. Elsewhere it collapsed sooner, despite being written into constitutions. In Bulgaria the road to authoritarian government was relatively straightforward. There, in 1923, the impolitic leader of the Agrarian Government (he had referred to the urban population as 'verminous parasites') was ousted and murdered in a military coup supported by the King. In Romania, Yugoslavia, Albania and Hungary, however, the circumstances were more complicated.

In Romania, according to one contemporary observer, the political process was the reverse of that in the Western democracies where the electorate voted a party into office so that the government was sanctioned by the 'national will':

> In Romania ... this happens the other way round: the head of state chooses the government; the government arranges the parliamentary majority and then calls on the electorate to endorse it.[19]

The elections were generally rigged (the only really free election in Romania was held in 1928). Even so, matters did not always turn out as expected. In the first post-war election of December 1919, for example, the incumbent Liberal Party, which had satisfied virtually all Romania's territorial ambitions, passed a land reform, and enjoyed a good electoral organization – as well as control of the police, censorship and 'state of siege' regulations which had survived from the war – was nevertheless defeated, gaining only 103 out of 568 seats. The victors were the Peasant Party and the representatives of newly-acquired Transylvania, who formed a coalition government commanding a comfortable parliamentary majority. Nevertheless it did not last long, partly because most of the new members were not only inexperienced and overly deferential but greedy to obtain paid office, both for themselves and their clients. In the words of Nicolae Iorga, leader of the National Democratic Party and a member of that government (as well as a distinguished historian), they were

> A patriarchal multitude of priests, provincial lawyers, doctors with small practises and professors to whom Bucharest had long represented a sort of Jerusalem, and the parliament building Solomon's Temple, in which it was not dignified or proper to make too much noise.... A bizarre conglomeration of the ambitious and the discontented .... [many of whom were ready to] change their political skins.[20]

The majority was soon diminished as members were cowed or bought off by the old Bucharest hands; the opposition raised the spectre of Bolshevism, and the King, while remaining accessible to the old Liberal and Conservative politicians, refused to receive some of his own ministers. Then, in March 1920, while the Prime Minister was on a mission abroad, the police claimed to have uncovered evidence of a plot against the King, at which the monarch dismissed the Minister of the Interior, Lupu, and the leader of the Peasant Party, Mihalache. At this the government resigned and the King asked the war hero, General Averescu, to take over. In a fresh election that May Averescu's 'League of the People' and its allies won well over 200 of 369 parliamentary seats; Romanian politics were back on their customary, bumpy course.

In Yugoslavia, democracy was imperilled from the start by the intransigence of the Croatian Peasant Party led by Stjepan Radic, a lawyer who had been a prominent anti-government demonstrator as a youth. His party had refused to ratify the Constitution, which, like the Czech one, was less devolutionary than had been hoped. Indeed, it was only fear of neighbouring Italy which had prevented the Croats from opting for independence. Nevertheless Radic's stand in the Yugoslav parliament thereafter was wholly negative, and when a former associate was arrested for sedition he fled abroad.

In Vienna he tried to organize a new 'Congress of Oppressed Nationalities' on the model of that organized by the Western Powers during the war; ho also visited Moscow to attend a 'Peasant International' and was welcomed there with open arms, the isolated Soviet government having decided to support peasant movements since peasantism was so much more popular than Bolshevism in Eastern Europe. On his return home Radic was imprisoned, and his Party, which had won half a million votes and seventy seats in the 1923 elections, was proscribed. In due course, however, he was released, the Party reinstated, and he was offered office as Minister for Education.

Office did not curb his Slavic ebullience. When he enquired sarcastically if the Croats were expected to become Orthodox like the Serbs, and adopt Arabic script like the Muslims of Bosnia, he was merely highlighting the obstacles to building a countrywide, Yugoslav, sense of identity. But his references to governmental colleagues as tyrants, gangsters and swine, though highly popular among his constituents, were less welcome to others. Leaving office in 1926 he continued his diatribes from the opposition benches – until in June 1928 when, during another parliamentary storm, a Montenegrin deputy resorted to the law of the mountains, pulled out a gun and shot Radic and four of his supporters. Radic and two others died of their wounds. The shooting precipitated a political crisis, and the Montenegrin member went to gaol, although he took pride in his 'act of patriotism' to the end of his days. A few months later King Alexander abolished all political parties and set up a monarchical dictatorship.

In neighbouring Albania, where tribal law still prevailed in the extensive mountain areas, the chances for democracy were even slimmer. Its ostensible champion, Fran Noli, came to power in 1924, but within a few weeks, he had been ousted by a shrewd tribal chief, Ahmed Zogu, with help from Yugoslavia. Four years later Zogu assumed the title King Zog. In Albania only a tiny stratum understood even the terminology of democracy and constitutions. Albanians were divided between those who spoke the Geg and Tosk dialects, and between the Muslim, Orthodox and Catholic religions. They were also caught in a power squeeze between Yugoslavia and Italy. But at least Albania was spared the deep divisions along lines of nationality that plagued most other Eastern European countries, not least the Soviet Union.[21]

Apart from Austria, the only other country so blessed was Hungary, which having experienced the trauma of the Treaty of Trianon, the Bela Kun episode, the Romanian invasion and the White Terror, built a hybrid political system which combined democratic with oligarchic elements in a manipulative fashion not unlike that in Romania, though it was to prove rather more stable. Its architect was a member of a famous Transylvanian aristocratic family, Istvan Bethlen.

When he became Premier in April 1921 Bethlen faced an unenviable situation. The economy was in ruins; the state bankrupt, yet burdened with reparations payments. The Jews, who included most of the country's entrepreneurs, were in terror of the 'White Guards' (who associated all Jews with Bolshevism); unemployment was rampant, and Budapest was crowded with ethnic Hungarian refugees from other states, most of whom were eking out a miserable existence in suburban shanty towns and ruined railway carriages. The peasant majority, sunk in a slough of ignorance and poverty, were restless after their joyful rampage against their landlords in 1919;[22] in the cities, an understandable but unhealthy mood of frustrated vengeance was in the air. The nation which had so recently ruled over others had been brought low; millions of Hungarians were now languishing in hostile states; and since the Treaty of Trianon restricted Hungary's army to only 35,000 men nothing could be done about it.

Bethlen began by buying off the more dangerous of the White Guard leaders with seats in parliament, official posts or commissions in the army, which he contrived to keep somewhat larger than the Treaty stipulated. He then set about disenfranchizing the more volatile elements of the population. The voting age was raised to twenty-four for men and thirty for women (unless they had three children or were high-school graduates), and all those without at least six years' schooling were deprived of the vote. This eliminated the uneducated and the youngest stratum of the electorate, but stable government required more – the political neutralization of the peasant masses. This was achieved by restoring the open ballot to 200 rural constituencies, which, in effect, placed peasant voters under the control of the rural elite and the police. In these ways comfortable government majorities were assured. It was not democratic, but it gave Hungary political stability and allowed civil rights to be extended to a higher proportion of the population than in some neighbouring states.

While curbing the extreme right, Bethlen offered a deal to the suppressed Social Democrats (who had shared power with Bela Kun): If they cut links with Moscow and adopted a 'patriotic' stance, their imprisoned leaders would be released, their confiscated property returned, and the government would grant freedom of the press, freedom to strike and free elections by secret ballot in the cities. The offer was accepted. Bethlen also tried to make life tolerable for the Jews, chiefly through the restoration of public order, although bombs were being thrown at them as late as 1925. He also gave them representation, along with all other major denominations, in the upper house of parliament, though he kept them out of government. And Bethlen conciliated the powerful Catholic Church by concessions in the educational sphere. In these ways Hungarians were accorded perhaps as much political freedom as circumstances allowed.

Meanwhile Bethlen was trying to promote an economic recovery. He balanced the budget, reducing the cost of the temporarily expanded civil service by cutting pay and introducing compulsory early retirement. He also stabilized the value of the currency by selling off Hungary's gold reserves and borrowing abroad. The agricultural sector provided an exportable surplus sufficient to service the foreign debt; but Bethlen was more interested in encouraging industry; and in this, too, he succeeded. By 1929 industry accounted for almost a third, instead of less than a quarter, of Hungary's national income; energy capacity had almost tripled and the value of industrial wages at last reached pre-war levels. By then Hungarians were enjoying higher levels of civic as well as political liberty than the nationals of most other Eastern European states.[23]

This was no mean achievement; but it was bought at the expense of the rural proletariat.

It is here that we encounter the basic dilemma that confronted most of the Eastern European leaders of the time. If they were to grant the peasant majority full political and civil rights, they could expect an irresistible demand for land reform. But a re-distribution of land in favour of the peasantry would not only alienate the landlord class; it seemed likely to make the agricultural sector even less efficient than it already was and to block economic modernization. The alternative was to deny the peasants their full rights. But this would not only infringe the principle of democracy, but perpetuated seething peasant discontent which could easily boil over into rebellion. The terrible peasant revolt of 1907 in northern Romania, as well as more recent outbreaks in both Russia and Hungary itself, were sharply etched in the memory. And the vocabulary of some of the peasant populist leaders added to these fears.

The root of the problem was the gross overpopulation of the Eastern European countryside. Industry and crafts employed only a third of all workers even in comparatively well-developed Czechoslovakia and Austria; in Hungary they accounted for a fifth, in Poland for a seventh, and in Romania and Yugoslavia for a mere tenth of the working population. The great majority lived in the countryside and depended on an inefficient agriculture. The picture presented a stark contrast to that of Western Europe and North America.[24] Speedy industrialization and emigration suggested themselves as potential solutions to the problem. But industrialization was restricted by the limited funds available for investment and the high cost of borrowing, while the escape valve of emigration had been shut off. Successive Immigration Acts in the United States not only imposed very severe restrictions but discriminated against Eastern Europeans; and Canada and Britain had also imposed much more severe immigration restrictions than before.[25]

Two other factors aggravated the peasant problem. Universal conscription during the war had put most able-bodied peasants into uniform, increased their expectation of land as a reward for their patriotism, and taught them how to fight for it. Secondly, as Bethlen realized, the youthfulness of the population was a force for change. Apart from Austria, where the age structure had been distorted by the influx of retired officials from the successor states which refused to pay their pensions, over half of Eastern Europe's population was under thirty, and in Poland and the Balkan countries the proportion was even higher.[26] Given these circumstances virtually every government in the region felt impelled to concede the peasants' demand for land reform.

In Hungary it was no more than a symbolic gesture: about 700,000 peasant families were granted an average of two acres apiece, while three million remained landless. In Czechoslovakia reform was a way of expropriating the alien elite rather than of benefiting the peasants. As a result of the measures enacted immediately after independence, citizens of 'enemy states' were dispossessed without compensation, but fewer than three million acres were eventually transferred in small plots to the peasants. In Poland, an inadequate reform was finally passed in 1925, in the teeth of opposition from landed interests, and by 1938 about six and a half million acres had been transferred to landless peasants and others with tiny holdings.

In Yugoslavia 200,000 peasants gained an average of four acres apiece, though many more benefited from the abolition of share-cropping rents which had been common in the south of the country. In Romania, by contrast, the 1921 reform, introduced by the Averescu government, expropriated seventeen million acres and had transferred almost ten million of them to nearly a million and a half peasant families by 1929. Even then over half a million families remained landless in Romania. Austria had no serious peasant problem; nor did Bulgaria. But elsewhere the inadequacy of land reform in the period of democracy helped lay the foundations for the victory of the Communists, who promised radical reform, after 1944.

But even in countries where there were no great estates or a substantial industrial sector a peasant problem remained. By 1937 Bulgaria and Greece were each reckoned to have surplus rural populations of a million or more; Czechoslovakia had a surplus of some two millions; Romania three and Poland between five and seven. The average size of peasant holdings over the region as a whole was about half those in Germany and France. In short they were too small, and too undercapitalized, to be efficient or even viable by international standards. Swiss peasants invested more than twice as much in their farms as their counterparts in Czechoslovakia, more than three times as much as the Polish peasants, and ten times as much as the Romanians.

The consequences were predictable. In Hungary, for example, land under wheat yielded half as much as in Denmark, the Dutch farmer raised three times as many cattle and four times as many pigs as his counterpart in Poland, while the Danish farmer raised four times as many cattle and twenty times as many pigs as the Romanian. Such were the differences between capitalized efficiency and undercapitalized inefficiency. In the United States a farmer produced enough to feed six families; in Western Europe enough for four; while the Eastern European peasant produced only enough for his own family, plus a marketable surplus of about half as much again – barely enough for such taxed necessities as salt, matches and paraffin.[27]

The mode of peasant production in Eastern Europe and poor storage facilities constituted other problems. Together they made for wide fluctuations in market prices for agricultural produce. This was disadvantageous to most peasants since they usually had to sell their surpluses when supply was greatest and prices at their lowest. The price of Yugoslav maize, for example, fluctuated by 50 per cent in the course of a season (five times as much as in the USA); and an egg would cost twice as much in winter as in summer. The situation encouraged peasant hostility to the cities, which not only harboured the officials who taxed them but the middlemen and consumers who appeared to be exploiting them. In 1919 when a peasant party came to power in Bulgaria such resentments were translated into policy. Aleksandr Stamboliisky, the leader of Bulgaria's Agrarian Union, justified it in these terms:

> The village and the town are inhabited by two different peoples.... They differ from one another, not only in ... standard of living, but in the character of the ideas and interests that animate them.... In the villages live a people who work, fight, and earn their living at the caprice of nature. In the towns live a people who earn their living, not by exploiting nature, but by exploiting the labour of others.... The way of life in the village is uniform, its members hold the same ideas in common. That accounts for the superiority of the village over the city. The city people live by deceit, by idleness, by parasitism, by perversion.[28]

If rural poverty fed political discontent, the plethora of tiny peasant farms was a drag on the economy. It was this which persuaded Stalin to collectivize Soviet agriculture by force in 1929. No such radical and destructive solution was applied in the rest of Eastern Europe. Even so, the situation of both the peasant farmer and the economy as a whole deteriorated sharply. During the later 1920s agricultural prices had dropped 30 per cent below the levels of 1923–5. Following the Wall Street Crash of 1929 they fell still farther. As a result Romania's wheat and livestock exports were halved, and, though Poland's increased in volume, they fell in value by a quarter. Price falls affected industry as well as agriculture. By 1933 the prices of raw materials as well as food had slumped by 40 per cent, and the industrial output of both Poland and Czechoslovakia fell by about the same proportion between 1929 and 1932.[29]

* * *

The year 1929 is usually regarded as an economic watershed, yet the deterioration of the Eastern European economies had set in before that, and the downward slide steepened from 1931. In May of that year *Creditsanstalt*, Vienna's major bank, failed; and in September, when Britain left the Gold Standard, twenty-five other countries quickly followed suit. These reactions to economic crisis precipitated a further series of disasters, not only economic and social, but political and international. The ultimate consequence was World War Two.

When the financial system failed there was a stampede to sell weak currencies. Loans were called in, causing a spate of bankruptcies; unemployment rose and there were further price falls. A bushel of wheat worth $1.37 fell to 92 cents in December 1932 and then to 49 cents, a third of its 1928 level. Rye slumped to a fifth of its former value. The value of Hungary's exports fell by 70 per cent. In Poland investment in 1932 was a third of its 1929 level, and in Czechoslovakia about 20 per cent of the entire adult male population was unemployed by the spring of 1932. There were fluctuations between countries, but the trend was general; and matters were worse than the statistics showed, for underemployment in the overpopulated countryside disguised the full extent of the problem. Nor was it only the lower classes who were hit. An Englishman of the time encountered a great Hungarian landowner on a train. He was carrying bundles of wood with him from his estate. Without them he could not have afforded to heat his house in Budapest.[30]

The impact of the Great Depression was even worse than in the West precisely because Eastern Europe was so much less developed and so much more dependent on the export of raw materials and food. Average incomes in Eastern Europe in 1930 were half those of France and less than a quarter those of the United States. Translated into concrete terms, this meant that an Eastern European ate a third of the amount of sugar consumed by a Westerner, used a quarter the amount of soap and could afford to buy a quarter the number of boots and shoes. Even in comparatively advanced Czechoslovakia, only 7 per cent of the population owned a radio set (barely half the rate of ownership in the West); and the provision of medical services in Romania was roughly on a par, per capita of population, with India.

As they tend to do in times of recession, statesmen gathered at international conferences to advocate a lowering of tariff barriers in order to get the world economy moving again; and to urge the poorer countries to compete more effectively in export markets. Yet, as a Yugoslav representative pointed out, the consequences of free trade would be disastrous for Eastern Europe. For it to succeed, he explained,

> We should have to create in Poland, Romania and Yugoslavia the same conditions as exist in Canada and the Argentine, where vast territories are inhabited by a scanty population and where machinery and other devices are employed.... We could not sacrifice our people by shooting them, but they would nevertheless be killed off by famine – which would amount to the same thing.[31]

The shooting, as it transpired, was not far off; but meanwhile irreplaceable resources were being squandered. The same Yugoslav visited a village where the men were cutting down their forest to sell the timber even though the price offered for it was miserable. He told them they were sacrificing their future. They replied that they knew this, but that the alternative was to die of starvation over the coming weeks. They simply could not wait for 'rational' economic decisions to bear fruit.

The parable had far more than local relevance. From 1933 onwards prices began slowly to recover, but by the time they did so it was too late: not only Yugoslavia, but several other countries had meanwhile been forced into the economic clutches of a resurgent, and Nazi, Germany. And this economic dependence threatened their political independence. At the same time right-wing extremism gained ground in many Eastern European countries. In these circumstances, the system designed by the peacemakers to maintain the peace of Europe, though shored up by France with a system of alliances, collapsed relatively swiftly.

Much of Eastern Europe would probably have fallen into Germany's economic sphere even if Hitler had not come to power. German foreign trade experts had foreseen the opportunity of regaining the economic hegemony they had enjoyed there before the Great War as early as 1932, before the Nazis took over.[32] Hungary was the first country targeted, for it had suffered more than most through the increased duties which Germany had imposed on imported foodstuffs in February 1932. The offer to buy large quantities of Hungary's grain and meat at above market prices was too good to be refused. The unusual method of transaction, which involved quotas and special payment arrangements, anticipated Soviet trade agreements with the smaller countries after World War Two. It also contravened Treaty obligations, but then both states were determined to have the peace settlement revised; and the Hungarian premier of the day, Julius Gombos, was an admirer of the Nazis.

The deal might have been expected to alarm Hungary's neighbours, Czechoslovakia, Yugoslavia and Romania, who, urged on by France, had formed an alliance called the 'Triple Entente' in the twenties to protect themselves against a vengeful Hungary.[33] Now Germany began to loom as a danger. But they were more concerned about Italy's increasing influence on Hungary than Germany's. Fear of Mussolini's Italy prompted Benes to revive the idea of Czech cooperation with Hungary and Austria which he had so bitterly opposed a few years earlier. Nevertheless, Italy's influence continued to grow. She agreed to supply Hungary with arms (in defiance of the Treaty of Trianon), and in March 1934 both Hungary and Austria allied themselves to her under the terms of the 'Rome Protocols'.

And it was not Czechoslovakia but Germany which became Italy's chief rival for influence over Hungary and Austria. For the moment Italian influence prevailed; and when Nazi sympathizers assassinated Austria's Chancellor, the Christian Social Engelbert Dolfuss, Italy rushed troops up to the frontier to fend off a Nazi *putsch*. Nonetheless Italy's influence in the region had already begun to wane – thanks to the success of Germany's foreign trade policy. And having reduced Hungary to economic dependence, Germany proceeded to draw Czechoslovakia's allies, Romania and Yugoslavia, as well as Bulgaria, into her net.

In March 1935 Romania signed the first of a series of agreements guaranteeing Germany supplies of various commodities, notably oil. At the same time Yugoslavia also entered into exchange arrangements at guaranteed prices that at the time seemed highly advantageous to her. Since these contravened the terms of the Triple Entente they were kept secret, but their effects could not be disguised. In 1933 Germany's share of Yugoslavia's foreign trade was only half that of Britain, France and Italy combined. By 1936 it was twice their combined share. Germany's overtures had come at a low point in the economic fortunes of the Balkan countries and her offers were grasped eagerly. But as world prices recovered, it proved much more difficult for these states to extricate themselves from Germany's embraces than it had been to enter into them. When Hungary baulked at a request to increase grain shipments, Germany threatened to buy not only her grain, but all her beef, from the Argentine. Hungary submitted.

Czechoslovakia, which had been trying to increase trade with her allies in the Little Entente, realized that she provided far too small a market to absorb as much of their raw material surpluses as Germany did, and so tried to build a larger trade alliance better able to compete with her larger neighbour. In 1936, therefore, the Czech Premier, Milan Hodza, proposed bringing Austria, Italy, Hungary and Poland together with the countries of the Triple Entente in order to form a vast zone of economic cooperation. As he rightly appreciated, small and medium-sized states could only deal with such a big country as Germany on equal terms on the basis of a Central European regional entente.[34]

But only Austria was receptive. Italy, whose interests lay elsewhere, insisted on a precondition: the lifting of the international sanctions imposed upon her by the League of Nations following her invasion of Abyssinia. Then she joined Germany in the 'Axis Pact'. Yugoslavia, Romania and Hungary all drew back from the Czech plan because of German pressure. So did Poland – partly because of her cool relations with Czechoslovakia which had refused to admit her to the Triple Entente earlier and had given sanctuary to Polish dissidents. Furthermore, in 1934 Poland had signed a non-aggression pact with Germany.

The Czechs had rejected the offer of a similar pact in 1934. Now seriously alarmed by the potential threat of Nazi Germany, they proposed that the Triple Entente's defensive military alliance against Hungary be applied to 'any aggressor'. But Romania and Yugoslavia had already made their own security arrangements; both were on friendly terms with Germany, and neither felt inclined to be sucked in to the defence of a Czechoslovakia which seemed more vulnerable than they were. Hodza's plan therefore came to nothing. The only alliance that promised the Czechs any security was the military pact she had concluded with the Soviet Union and France in May 1935. But France's failure to contest Germany's re-occupation of the Rhineland and continuing Western suspicion of the Soviet Union made this assurance seem somewhat fragile.

Meanwhile the hardships produced by the recession, and the growing international prestige of Nazi Germany, had lent strength to the radical Right, increasing the fanaticism of nationalists, and raising the level of political violence. In October 1934 Croatian extremists assassinated King Alexander of Yugoslavia, along with the French Foreign Minister Barthou, at Marseilles. The same year Chancellor Dolfuss had been shot dead and both Estonia and Latvia had become one-party states. In 1935 new and more illiberal constitutions were introduced into Austria and Poland. Nazi agitation reached alarming proportions in the Czech Sudetenland as well as Austria. Home-grown fascist or Nazi-type movements also gained strength in other countries. Fascism had comparatively little appeal for Poles, although an active Falangist movement attracted many teenagers, there were boycotts of Jewish businesses and, in 1936–7, pogroms which the government (now Pilsudski was dead) did little to restrain. The Czechs themselves returned a handful of fascists to parliament in 1935, but the creed of violence attracted most support in Hungary and Romania.

In Hungary the leading movement of this type, the Arrow Cross, grew out of the White Guardist secret societies (such as the Scientific Organization for the Defence of the Hungarian Race and the Blood Alliance of the Holy Cross) which had proliferated in the early 1920s, and drew support from the unemployed, not least the educated unemployed. (Over half the graduating lawyers, seven out of ten trained teachers, and nine out of ten qualified agronomists could find no jobs.) Based on extreme nationalism, anti-Communism and anti-semitism, its ideology was rooted in a misapplied social Darwinism leavened by elements of Marxism. The programme was elaborated by the movement's leader, Ferenc Szalasi, a general staff officer who was invited to leave the service when he took to politics.

Szalasi envisaged the resurrection of a greater Hungary and an ingathering of Hungarian exiles from all over the world in order to maintain ethnic Hungarian domination within it. His concept of 'workpeace' was more muddled and evasive, but proved to be attractive as rhetoric. Szalasi claimed that it would

> hold in inseparable national unity the peasant who supports the nation, the worker who builds the nation, the intelligentsia which leads the nation, the soldier who defends the nation, and those tokens of immortality: women and youth .... [It would create] economic peace which divides the profits of labour and production proportionately between the factors of production so as to abolish money capitalism and the hopeless misery of the working class; social peace which ignores the privileged classes .... and political peace which does not mislead the political nation with selfish party interests, but in which a single political idea directs the community....[35]

He also identified a 'Jewish question', a particularly popular issue for the unemployed professional classes who resented competition from Jews. He did little, however, to attract the peasant, even though a peasant fascist movement, the 'Scythe Cross', had been formed in 1931 by Zoltan Borszormeny.

The Scythe Cross reflected the ideas of peasant populism, regarded cities as essentially sinful and was as much anti-landlord as anti-Communist. Its programme, however, was even less concrete than that of the Arrow Cross movement. In 1934 a Hungarian writer met a crowd of Scythe Cross supporters carrying a banner with the slogan 'We fight for the Idea'. He asked them what the 'Idea' was. They either could not, or would not, tell him. It was yet another indication of the inhospitable soil even Hungary provided for the seeds of democracy.

In Romania, where the spirit of peasantish collectivism was strong, the fascist-type 'Legion of the Archangel Michael', forerunner of the Iron Guard, wooed the peasants from the start. It was founded by Corneliu Codreanu, a student at the University of Iasi who, with the support of Professor Cuza, had led a violent campaign against Jews in the University. Under his leadership the League's activists would ride round the villages of northern Romania, wearing turkey feathers in their hats and speaking to the peasants in a language they understood – a language of heroic imagery and religious chiliasm. They even presented their programme in the form of the Creed. Anti-semitic and anti-Communist, they believed in the socialization of industry as well as the sharing-out of all the remaining estates among the peasants, and they were fiercely anti-democratic.

In their view democracy was 'destroying the unity of the Romanian nation'. Political programmes were not only confusing and lying but divisive. Programmes should be replaced by the creation of a new, heroic type of man, a giant who would save the Romanian Nation. And the

Nation, they declared, included 'the souls and tombs of the dead' as well as the living. The ultimate goal was Romanian participation in a final climacteric,

> The resurrection of the nations in the name of Jesus Christ the Saviour. ... A time will come when all the world's nations will arise from the dead, with all their dead, with all their kings and emperors.... That *final moment*, the resurrection from the dead, is the highest and most sublime goal for which a nation can strive... .[36]

Despite severe police harassment the movement had won five seats in parliament as early as 1932, and in the elections of 1937, amid violent scenes, they captured sixty-six. A crisis was precipitated, Codreanu was arrested, and on the night of 29–30 November (the Night of the Vampires) he was either garotted in his prison cell or, according to the official communiqué, 'shot while trying to escape'. In retaliation his followers gunned down the Prime Minister. The King called on a right-wing minority leader, the antisemitic poet Goga, to form a government; then in February 1938, replaced him with the equally antisemitic Patriarch Cristea, Primate of the Romanian Orthodox Church. He then introduced a new constitution which arrogated all power to the crown and proceeded to govern with the help of the army.

Whether or not the Iron Guard would have eventually won any free election outright is a matter for speculation; so is the question of whether the Hungarian Arrow Cross might have come to power through the democratic process. By May 1939 they had a quarter of a million members. In the elections held that month they won a quarter of the votes and fifty parliamentary seats. This proved to be their high water mark, but perhaps only because of the fierce measures the government took against them.

Political repression had become commonplace in Eastern Europe. From 1936 the army, under General Zevgos, ruled Greece; and even parts of Czechoslovakia were ultimately subjected to military government. The mood of national exhilaration and the euphoria of newfound freedom which had characterized the early 1920s had turned sour, and violence was becoming the normal currency of political exchange. The kings and generals who overturned the democratic structures acted, for the most part, to prevent greater bloodletting. In any case democracy had become widely unpopular and the claims of the dictators to be the 'saviours' of their peoples echoed the desires of many simple people. It is clear that constitutional provision for free elections and parliamentary institutions were not enough to ensure the survival of democracy. Other essential ingredients were lacking – sufficient wealth sufficiently widely distributed, and the traditions of a civic polity.

Nazi Germany's economic hegemony was soon translated into political hegemony. In March 1938 the *Anschluss* with Austria took place, and Hitler returned in triumph to Vienna where, in his youth, he had imbibed his antisemitism and learned his tub-thumping brand of oratory. Schussnig, the Austrian Chancellor, had tried to forestall the union with Germany by calling a referendum, in which a combination of the Catholic peasant and Socialist votes might well have gone against *Anschluss*. But Hitler would not allow the referendum to take place. He threatened to invade. Schussnig backed down, and the Germans were invited in.

Pressure was immediately applied to Czechoslovakia to grant autonomy to the Sudetenland, and then to cede it outright to Germany. In September 1938 Britain and France insisted that she comply. On the following day, despite a Soviet threat to abrogate her non-aggression treaty with Poland if she did so, Poland delivered an ultimatum to the Czechs demanding the cessation of that part of Tesin which the Powers had granted her in the Peace Settlement. On 1 November the Czechs complied. On the following day they also accepted the 'Vienna Award', announced by Germany and Italy, according to which the Czechs were also to return a sizeable tract of territory to Hungary. The stage was set for the final dismemberment of Czechoslovakia.

This came in March 1939, when the Slovak leaders, led by Monsignor Tiso, opted for an independent Slovakia under German protection. The price was a free hand for the German army in their country and the alignment of its foreign and military policies with Germany's[37] – in short, the status of a puppet. Faced with the defection of the Slovaks and an ultimatum from Hitler, President Hacha signed away the last vestiges of Czech sovereignty, and the rump of the country became the German 'Protectorate of Bohemia and Moravia'.

This prompted Britain and France to give formal guarantees to Poland; and when in the following month, Italy invaded Albania, they extended similar guarantees to Romania and Greece. The situation might have been frozen, and war averted, had a meeting between British and French military missions with their Soviet counterpart, held in Moscow in August 1939, been successfully concluded. Aimed at coordinating military plans to protect Poland and Romania in the event of a German attack, they broke down over the issue of Soviet access to Polish territory to help repel any German invasion. This the Polish government refused to commit themselves to. Its embarrassed allies applied pressure to no effect, and could only tell the Soviets that they were 'sure' the Poles would invite them in if they were attacked.[38]

But if Colonel Beck, who had led Poland since 1935, had an inflated idea of the capacity of his cavalry armies to repulse invading German armour, the Soviet General Staff, with its knowledge gained in cooperation with the *Wehrmacht* since the 1920s, laboured under no such illusion. Though ready to defend Poland by an effective show of force, and even to fight a short war in her defence, Moscow was not prepared to make a non-reciprocal commitment which might involve her in a long war in the West, while Germany's ally, Japan, threatened to invade her from Manchuria. So when, with excellent timing, Hitler pressed an olive branch into Stalin's hand, offering him eastern Poland and the Baltic states in return for Soviet complaisance in the dismemberment of Poland, the offer was eagerly accepted. According to this reading of events Colonel Beck bore some responsibility for the conclusion of the Nazi-Soviet Pact, which was signed before the end of August. But perhaps Polish opinion had allowed him no other course of action.

Facing increasing social unrest, Beck's government had resorted to both Soviet and German devices in attempting to assuage it. In 1936 it had adopted a Four Year Plan in an attempt to revive the economy, and was on the point of enacting a law against the Jews when, on 1 September 1939, the Germans invaded. Two days later Britain and France declared war on Germany; but the Western Front was to remain quiet for several months. Meanwhile, Stalin had waited until a German victory in Poland was assured before moving in to claim his share. Then, anxious to protect his northern flank, on 30 November he attacked Finland. The other Baltic states were persuaded to accept the establishment of Soviet military bases on their territory; and in June 1940, with German and Italian consent, the Soviet Union protected its southern flank at Romania's expense by occupying Bessarabia and the Bukovina. The Germans, who had already occupied Norway, quickly overran France – at which the Soviets took the Baltic states over entirely. Only in July 1940, abandoning plans to invade Britain, did Hitler turn his attentions to the east again.

Having failed to agree on any joint measures of defence, the Balkan states presented no obstacle to Hitler's ambitions. Romania was easily persuaded to abrogate the British guarantee, and in August 1940 Hitler found a way of making her even more dependent on him, while at the same time mollifying the Hungarians. By the Second Vienna Award he presented Hungary with a third of Transylvania. A million agonized Romanians flooded across the border from the lost territory. Yet Romania was consoled by the prospect of retrieving the territories she had recently lost to the Soviet Union and, indeed, of gaining even more at her expense. In October 1940 units of the German army entered Romania to help train her army for the coming attack, as well as to protect the Ploesti oil wells from British saboteurs. And, much to the relief of General Antonescu, they were also to help him suppress an armed uprising by the Iron Guard in January 1941.

Of all the Balkan states only Greece had resisted. When, in the autumn of 1940, Italian forces invaded, they were defeated at Metsovo and forced to retreat into Albania. With Britain sending troops to her assistance, Greece threatened the southern flank of Hitler's informal empire. It had to be eliminated before the attack on the Soviet Union could proceed. Accordingly in March 1941 both King Boris of Bulgaria and Prince Paul, Regent of Yugoslavia, were persuaded to accede to the Axis Pact. This would allow German forces to cross their territory to dispose of the Greeks – but before they could move Prince Paul was ousted by a *coup d'état* staged by a group of air force colonels (probably encouraged by the British and perhaps even Soviet agents).

Germany demanded the demobilization of the Yugoslav army, which was in any case unprepared for war. The demand was rejected. On 6 April the Soviet Union issued a guarantee to Yugoslavia. Two hours later German aircraft bombed Belgrade and the country was invaded across its frontiers with Bulgaria, Romania and Hungary. Hungarian troops participated. Appalled at the infraction of a treaty of 'eternal friendship' he had only recently signed with Yugoslavia, the Hungarian Premier, Tekeli, committed suicide. Within a matter of weeks the Yugoslav army had been scattered, German and Italian forces had linked up, and Greece had been overrun. On 22 June 1941 German, Romanian and Finnish forces invaded the Soviet Union. Hungary soon followed suit. It had taken a little more than three years for Hitler to dismantle the entire edifice of the peace settlement in Eastern Europe and replace it with a new order.

* * *

In pursuit of the Nazi aim to create more *Lebensraum* for the German people, the Baltic states and Slovenia were incorporated into the Third Reich; and the 'General Government' of Poland as well as the Czech 'Protectorate' were scheduled for German settlement. German communities settled in Eastern Europe since mediaeval times were to be gathered in,[39] and territories depopulated to make room for them. Jews and gypsies were to be exterminated, and the 'inferior' Slavic peoples mobilized to work as menials in German industry. Certain changes, beyond those already mentioned, were made to the political map. Yugoslavia was carved up to provide rewards for Hitler's allies, Italy, Hungary, Romania and Bulgaria, although puppet states on the lines of Slovakia were set up in Croatia and Serbia.

In Croatia, the followers of Ante Pavelic, an extreme nationalist who expressed his love of Hitler in the most unctuous and sentimental terms, were allowed to prosecute their own racial war against the Serbian minority, mutilating as well as massacring them (often by herding them into their Orthodox Churches and burning them alive). On the whole the elimination of the Jews seems to have been a popular policy within the occupied territories. The Polish resistance saved a few Jews, but for the most part their extinction was regarded with equanimity in Poland. The Slovak nationalists enjoyed rounding up and humiliating Jews; there was no lack of volunteers among the Balts, Ukrainians, Belorussians, Bosnians, Albanians and others, either to serve in extermination units or concentration camps, while, following the traditions of the Iron Guard, Romanian troops were responsible for widespread pogroms in 'Transnistria', their zone of occupation in the Soviet Union.

Nazi racial policies were pressed on all Hitler's allies, though both the Italians and the Bulgarians refused to exterminate their Jews, and even Hungary was slow to respond. A succession of increasingly oppressive anti-Jewish laws were passed in response to strong German pressure between 1938 and 1942, but Regent Horthy, who had engineered the fall of the antisemitic Premier Bela Imredy, resisted the implementation of a 'Final Solution', which did not get under way until 1944 when Hitler dismissed Horthy and installed the Arrow Cross leader, Szalasi, as his puppet. It was ironic that in the only country where Jews could be said to have had a dominating role in the economy the government was reluctant to see them exterminated. As a result about a third of Hungary's Jews survived the war. In Romania proper, where the government had also fallen short of thoroughness in the matter, about half survived; in Bulgaria an even higher proportion. In Yugoslavia the strong resistance movement offered chances of escape; but elsewhere nine Jews out of every ten were murdered.

The elimination of a vital part of the entrepreneurial and professionally qualified classes was one of several consequences of Nazi domination that tended to favour the Communist cause afterwards. Poland in particular lost an overwhelming proportion of her educated population, both Jewish and non-Jewish, on the battlefield, in the death camps, and through forced and voluntary migrations. Furthermore, the gearing of most of Eastern Europe's economy to the German war effort, the dislocation of society, and the sheer destruction caused by the war created a situation in which the only hope of recovery, at least in the short term, lay in state domination of the economy.

There were psychological as well as social and economic effects. German occupation, often regarded as a national humiliation, tended to rally support to the Communists, especially in Yugoslavia and Czechoslovakia; and although most Romanians, Hungarians and Poles were no fonder of the Russians than they had been before the war, the defeat of Nazi Germany had the effect of discrediting the radical Right in those countries as in others. And the Czech leader, Edouard Benes, was persuaded to place his trust in the Soviet Union rather than in the Western Powers.

All this can be attributed to Nazi Germany gaining hegemony over Eastern Europe. But could the disastrous outcome have been avoided? Was Nazi penetration and subordination of the region inevitable?

* * *

If Poland and Czechoslovakia had shown a common front against him, it is doubtful if Hitler could have realized his imperial ambitions in Eastern Europe. Nor would Germany's economic penetration of Eastern Europe, which facilitated the subsequent political and military successes, have been so successful if the region had been more resilient economically. It is for this reason that analysts have focussed on the peace settlement as the primary cause of disaster which followed. Had the Austro-Hungarian Empire been converted into a federal state rather than being broken up, they argue, the region would have been much more viable economically,[40] and possessed enough military strength, perhaps, to deter a resurgent Germany. Had the rest of Poland and Romania been included in such a federal state, the Soviet Union might ultimately have been contained too.

It is very doubtful, however, if such a solution would have worked. Though economic cooperation might have helped the region withstand the buffeting of the Great Depression somewhat better, it could hardly have produced sufficient investment capital, a large enough internal market and a sufficient industrial base to absorb its surpluses of food and raw materials and, indeed, its surplus rural population. Furthermore, such a federation would have been riven, and probably undermined, by rival nationalisms. If the peoples of Czechoslovakia were unable to reconcile their differences between the wars, and if those of Yugoslavia could not regard themselves as a nation after more than seventy years of statehood, what chance of coherence would a much larger confederation have had in the shorter term?

The roots of failure, then, lie deeper. They are embedded in the period before 1918, when the peoples of Eastern Europe developed their passionate and divisive sense of nationality; when the burden of rural overpopulation was created; and when the entire region, including Russia, failed to meet the challenge of the new, industrial, age.

REFERENCES

1. For Wilson's 14 Points see *The Public Papers of Woodrow Wilson*, pp. 158–62. The reference is to point 10. The idea of converting Austria-Hungary into a federation had been mooted before the war. On the collapse of the Polish Republic in the eighteenth century, see Chapter 6.
2. The two most active proponents of national liberation in Eastern Europe were the journalist H. Wickham Steed (see his memoirs, *Through Thirty Years*, 2 vols (New York, 1924)) and the historian R. Seton Watson. See the interesting account of the latter's activities by his sons Hugh and Christopher (*The Making of New Europe* (London, 1981)) in which they seek to exonerate him.
3. The Czecho-Slovak agreement had been concluded with the American Slovaks at Pittsburgh on 30 June 1918. A similar accord with American Ruthenes led to Sub-Carpathian Ruthenia being brought into the new state. As will be seen, the Czechs failed to keep their promises to either nationality after independence. See also n. 10 below.
4. See Wilson's eleventh point, which refers to the Balkans, and the conclusion of the document.
5. Romania had been knocked out of the war by the Central Powers in 1916 but rejoined it at the eleventh hour, on 10 November 1918. This allowed her to invoke the Agreement. By a similar agreement Greece had been promised south-western Anatolia with Smyrna at the expense of Turkey.
6. The Treaty of Versailles defined the western frontiers of Poland and Czechoslovakia; that of St Germain (10 September 1919) defined Austria's frontiers with Czechoslovakia and the new Yugoslav state; that of Trianon (4 June 1920) fixed Hungary's frontiers with her neighbours, Czechoslovakia, Yugoslavia and Romania, while the Treaty of Neuilly (27 November 1919) redefined Bulgarians frontiers with Romania, Yugoslavia and Greece. The Treaty of Sevres (10 August 1920), however, failed to stick because of Greece's misadventure against the Turks in attempting to secure Anatolia (see n. 5 above) and was overtaken by the Treaty of Lausanne (24 July 1923).
7. The great map of nationalities accompanying C. Macartney's *Hungary and her Successors* (London, 1937), illustrates the fact in one sector of the region. Large-scale population movements were arranged only between Bulgaria, Greece and Turkey.
8. E.g. the rights to life, liberty, property, citizenship and religion (insofar as was consistent with public order and morals). See, for example, clauses 1–8 of the Treaty with the Serbo-Croat-Slovene State (Yugoslavia), 10 September 1919 (UK Treaty Series 1919, No. 17, Cmd. 461) and Section VI of the Treaty of Trianon (with Hungary), *British and Foreign State Papers*, 1920, Vol. XCIII. For the right of linguistic minorities to maintain private schools in their own language, see Articles XVII and XVIII of the Final Protocol between Austria and Czechoslovakia, 7 June 1921 (Article 8 of the Czech Treaty and Article 67 of the Austrian). On religious rights for Yugoslavia's Muslims, see clause 10 of its Treaty (*supra*). See also Articles 10 and 11 of the Treaty with Poland regarding the Jews.
9. Clemenceau to Paderewski, Paris, 24 June 1919.
10. For the obligations to the Ruthenes, see articles 1–12 of the Czech Treaty, 10 September 1919, UK Treaty Series 1919, No. 20, Cmd. 479. The promise to the Slovaks under the Pittsburgh Agreement (Note 3 above) was informal. In 1921 officialdom in Ruthenia was mostly Czech and Czech dominance increased thereafter (See Note 11 below).

11. See Macartney, *op. cit.*, tables on p. 225.
12. The best account of these costs, on which the following brief account is largely based, is still D. Mitrany, *The Effect of the War in South-Eastern Europe* (New Haven, 1936).
13. Tariff levels over most of the region rose by about half between 1913 and 1927, and Bulgaria's tripled. Only those of Austria and Poland saw a reduction. The only comparable rise in a Western European country occurred in Spain – see F. Hertz, *The Economic Problem of the Danubian States* (London, 1947) p. 72.
14. *Delnicke Listy*, Prague 1920, quoted in Herz *op. cit.*, p. 66.
15. Macartney, *op. cit.*, p. 118.
16. The Polish Peasant Union (PZL), the Polish Peasant Party (Piast), the Polish Peasant Party (Left), the Radical Peasant Party, and the Catholic Peasant Party.
17. R. Okey, *Eastern Europe 1740–1980: Feudalism to Communism* (London, 1982) p. 171; J. Zarnewski, *Dictatorship in East-Central Europe 1918–1939* (Wroclaw, 1983) pp. 9–26; A. Polonsky in R. Leslie (ed.), *Poland Since 1863* (Cambridge, 1980) pp. 139ff..
18. Zarnewski, *op. cit.*, p. 23.
19. A. Savu, *Sistemul partidelor politico din Romania 1919–1940* (Bucharest, 1976) p. 26 quoted in B. Valota, *Questione Agraria e vita politica in Romania (1907–1922)* (Milan, 1979) pp. 172–3.
20. N. Iorga, *O viata de om* (Bucharest, 1933), pp. 543–4, quoted by Valota, *op. cit.*, p. 198.
21. The Soviet Union, while not solving the problem, found an accommodation by granting minority nationals cultural, and a measure of political, independence, while maintaining a centralist union in practice. On the formation of Soviet nationality policy (of which Stalin was the chief architect), see R. Pipes, *The Formation of the Soviet Union*, Cambridge (Mass.) 1954.
22. For a picture of the lowest stratum, the farm servants (in some respects worse off than the serfs of former ages) see G. Illyes's fictionalized autobiography, *People of the Puszta*, (trans. G. Cushing) (London, 1971). However, particularly in south-western Hungary there were some comparatively prosperous peasants.
23. The foregoing account is based principally on A. Janos, *The Politics of Backwardness in Hungary* (Princeton, 1982).
24. These generalizations are based on A. Carr Saunders, *World Population* (Oxford, 1936) esp. col. 2 of 'Density of Population and Agricultural Employment in Europe', p. 141; *Economic Development in South-Eastern Europe*, London 1945, tables on 'Employment according to Main Branches' (p. 129), 'Density of Agrarian Population' (p. 26) and 'Yields per Hectare' (p. 29); and Hertz, *op. cit.*, esp. the table on yields 1925–9, p. 110. Carr Saunders (*op. cit.*, p. 143) calculates Poland's excess rural population at 3 millions.
25. See tables on overseas migration in *Economic Development*, *op. cit.*, p. 128; Carr Saunders, *op. cit.*, p. 147, and table on immigration under American quota legislation, p. 193.
26. Table on 'Age Distribution of Population' in *Economic Development*, *op. cit.*, p. 126.
27. Based on tables in Hertz, *The Economic Problem*, *op. cit.*; *Economic Development*, *op. cit.*; N. Forter and D. Rostovsky, *The Romanian Handbook* (London, 1931) pp. 89ff.; B. Valota, *op. cit.*. Also Hertz, pp. 114–16, D. Warriner, *Economics of*

Peasant Farming (London, 1939) and her *Revolution in Eastern Europe* (London, 1950) p. 176.

28. P. Petkov (ed.) *Aleksandr Stamboliiski: lichnost' i idei* (Sofia, 1930). See also G. Jackson, 'Peasant Political Movements in Eastern Europe' in H. Landsberger (ed.), *Rural Protest* (London, 1974) pp. 259–315. Under Stamboliiski the poor were billeted on the rich and urban dwellers forced to toil in the fields for several days each year. Traces of the latter practice were in evidence until recently, students and scientists being called out to help in the East European countryside at harvest-time.
29. The figures are drawn chiefly from G. Ranki, *Economy and Foreign Policy* (New York, 1983).
30. Generally on the resort to barter in the countryside in 1932 see Macartney, *op. cit.*, p. 472.
31. Yugoslav Foreign Minister's speech to the Commission for European Union, 1931.
32. The story of how Germany realized these plans is well told by Ranki, *op. cit.*.
33. The Little Entente had been strengthened in December 1932 by the formation of a permanent secretariat. In general on the foundation and history of the Little Entente see R. Machray, *The Little Entente* (London, 1929) and his *The Struggle for the Danube and the Little Entente 1929–1938* (London, 1938).
34. Ranki, *Economy and Foreign Policy, op. cit.*, pp. 167–9. Also Machray, *Struggle, op. cit.*.
35. F. Szalasi, *Ut es Cel* [The I and the Us] (Budapest, 1936) parts of which have been translated in E. Weber, *Varieties of Fascism* (New York, 1964) pp. 157–60, from which this rendering has been adapted.
36. C. Codreanu, *Pentru Legionari* (Bucharest, 1937) pp. 385–98, trans. S. Fischer-Galati, *Man, State and Society in Eastern European History* (New York, 1970) pp. 327–30. See also Weber, *op. cit.*, pp. 284–7.
37. The text of the Slovak-German Treaty of 18–23 March 1939 in *Prager Tageblatt*, 24 March 1939.
38. See the text in 'The Military Negotiations between the Soviet Union, Britain and France in 1939', *International Affairs*, Moscow, February 1959, pp. 119–23. Western archives corroborate the accuracy of this version.
39. By the end of the war there were only about 350,000 left in Romania (T. Schieder (ed.), *Documents on the Expulsion of the Germans from Eastern-Central Europe*, Vol. II (Bonn, 1961) p. 73) and some 200,000 in Hungary (*ibid.* vol. III, pp. 121f.), besides substantial communities in the Baltic countries and Slovenia. The 'Volga Germans', settled in Russia since the eighteenth century, were removed out of reach of the German forces.
40. See, among others, A. Basch, *The Danube Basin and the German Economic Sphere* (London, 1944). For another perspective of the problems described in this chapter see Z.A.B. Zeman, *Pursued by a Bear* (Oxford, 1989).

5

The Winding Road to Sarajevo (1848–1914)

Life has run off the old tracks and not yet found the new.
Platonov, Russian historian, 1913.

Between 1848 and 1914 the pace of change in Eastern Europe had quickened. Within the span of a single human life society was transformed: by the emancipation of the peasants and a population explosion; by railway booms which spurred industrial development and sped the growth of cities; by the spread of education, and of propaganda, which led masses to embrace the creed of nationalism. The political scene changed too. Romania, Bulgaria and Albania took their places alongside Serbia and Greece in the ranks of the new nation states; Hungary gained political autonomy within a reorganized Habsburg Empire, and most peoples of the region took their first, faltering steps in the ways of democracy.

The changes did not occur at an even pace, however, and their impact was geographically irregular. There were headlong lurches forward and no less alarming halts. Wars, and the threat of war, caused interruptions; so did outbursts of domestic violence. Yet, as the years passed, previously accepted norms of life altered almost beyond recognition and old values became skewed. In particular the habit of deference declined. It was a period of increasing disorientation (which found expression in the arts), increasing popular expectations, and increasing despair among statesmen. The culmination, as we know, was the assassination in the obscure town of Sarajevo of an Austrian archduke, which precipitated the Great War. Yet though the outcome was calamitous, the era saw many developments along what people like to call the road of 'progress'; and in retrospect many were to look back on it nostalgically as a golden age.

The region's fate in the period was determined, then, by ideas and by policies, but also by forces beyond man's capacity to control. It was moulded by clashes between states as well as by conflicts within them. In exploring the fascinating interplay of all these factors over time, the issues of peasant emancipation and demographic change, national independence and industrial development will claim particular attention. But our approach must take account of geography and chronology as well as themes. We shall therefore consider the Habsburg Empire before proceeding to the other major units into which the region was politically divided (the Russian Empire and the Balkans); and begin with the dramatic events of 1848.

* * *

In the Empire of the Habsburgs the period began, as it ended, in confusion. At the beginning of March 1848, as news of a revolution in Paris seeped in about a week after the event, crowds took to the streets of Vienna, and before long the entire Empire, from Bohemia to northern Italy, was in turmoil. In the months that followed there were uprisings in Prague, Lemberg and several other cities besides Vienna; Hungary and Venice declared themselves independent; the imperial army was driven out of Lombardy by local insurgents supported by invading forces from Piedmont, and Vienna itself had to be abandoned to the revolutionaries. Within the imperial administration there were six changes of government; two ministers were lynched; another went mad; and the Emperor abdicated. Yet by the autumn of 1849 the old order had been resurrected and the cause of revolution seemed utterly lost. What had the revolutionaries stood for? Why did they lose? And what influence did the events have both on the Empire itself and on the rest of Eastern Europe?

The Revolutions of 1848 are commonly represented as nationalist, and so to a great extent they were. Yet the call for 'freedom' as if it were a single entity embraced a variety of aims.[1] Middle-class liberals wanted the abolition of censorship, freedom of speech and assembly, and a judicial system that dispensed justice openly; radicals demanded the replacement of monarchical government by a democracy based on wide suffrage; peasants, and all progressives, wanted the abolition of serfdom; workers protested against unemployment and for more pay. After the first, heady, stages, even more interests forced themselves to the surface. Tenants struck against high rents; artisans took to the streets because new, cheap, factory-produced goods were already threatening their livelihoods; students saw an opportunity for activism, and in Prague there were anti-Jewish riots. Among the educated strata, some, like the great Hungarian landowner Szechenyi, wanted change on the lines of the British model, with economic development as the motor of social and political change. However, the slogans of the French Revolution and of the Romantic movement tended to predominate, and in particular calls for national self-expression.

The demands for national freedom, however, also took different forms. Some were founded on constitutional precedents, such as the ancient powers of the Hungarian Diet or of the Bohemian Estates, which had been sapped or overborne by imperial power. Others were based on what appeared to their proponents to be the self-evident claims of a common language and the national community which it created.[2] And there were further divisions both within the various nationalist camps and between them. Frantisek Palacky, promoter of the Czech national revival, thought in terms of a union of all the Slav peoples of the Empire, predicated on the view that, for all the myriad differences of dialect, they all spoke the same beautiful language.

This, however, was unacceptable, among others, to the Polish nationalists, who, roused by émigrés returning from France, wished to resurrect the ancient Polish Republic which had been wiped off the map only half a century before. Furthermore, the claims of one nationalist group encouraged others to assert themselves. Romanians, Serbs, Croats and Slovaks did not take kindly to the prospect of inclusion in a state dominated by Hungarians. The Ruthenes (Ukrainians) resented the Polish claims to domination in Galicia. German Bohemians feared the Czechs and some Austrians were attracted by the idea of a greater Germany.

The fast-declining sense of equality and fraternity among the revolutionaries themselves, a growing popular reaction to their extremism, and the discipline of the imperial army all helped the government to reassert its authority. The promise made on 25 April 1848 to provide a democratic constitution for Austria, and the subsequent undertaking, in response to public demand, to widen the franchise, assuaged the feelings of many democrats; the emancipation of the peasants of Bohemia and Moravia in March, and those of Galicia and the Bukovina later the same year, bought off much social discontent; and the authorities experienced little difficulty in encouraging the Croats, Serbs and Slovaks to attack the Hungarian rebels who had cavalierly rejected their modest claims to linguistic autonomy.

For the rest it was a matter of suppression. On 17 June the insurrectionaries in Prague were crushed; Vienna was recaptured at the end of October, and a rising in Lemberg put down two days later. General Windischgraetz was the imperial hero of the hour. Only the Italians and Hungarians held out. The crushing defeat inflicted by General Radetzky on the invading Piedmontese at Novara in March 1849 spelt doom to the revolution in the Italian provinces, though the resurrected 'republic' of Venice survived until August. The Hungarian rebellion lasted only a few days longer.

Unlike most of the other nationalists who merely sought more autonomy, or at most a reconstitution of the Empire as a federation of nationalities, the Hungarians had eventually followed the radical Louis Kossuth in opting for complete independence. In doing so, however, they cited the ancient constitutional ground that the Habsburgs, as Kings of Hungary, had violated their contract with their subjects.[3] They had the support of a contingent of Poles, who, perceiving a connection between the Hungarian cause and their own, drove the imperial forces out of Transylvania. Yet neither the Poles, nor the nationalistic ardour aroused by the poet Sandor Petofi, who fought in the ranks of the revolutionary army, could save them.

On 1 May, 1849, Vienna requested Russian aid in suppressing the rebellion and they responded. On 11 August Kossuth's own generals prevailed on him to resign. Two days later the remnant of the Hungarian army capitulated. It is doubtful, however, if it would have survived very much longer even without Russian intervention. The declaration of independence had frightened off many powerful aristocrats, and Kossuth's remarks about 'Serbian thieves' and 'Croat insurgents', together with his contempt for the Romanians, had alienated these nationalities. The concessions he eventually made came too late. And the Hungarian peasants whom he expected to rally patriotically to the national flag in gratitude for their emancipation simply ran away and hid at the approach of his recruiting officers. The lower orders of society, it appeared, were still 'asleep'.

In the aftermath a number of the insurgents were executed and they provided martyrs for the national cause. However, Kossuth himself escaped to the West, where he was feted by liberal society. Along with other political refugees, and not a few émigré rogues and opportunists, he helped to strengthen what were to become traditional Western prejudices against the imperial regime. Meanwhile, a new Emperor, the eighteen-year-old Francis Joseph, rejected the idea of federalizing the Empire, reimposed censorship, and insisted that Hungary pay taxes on the same basis as the rest of the realm. He also dissolved the popularly-elected *Reichstag* (parliament) which was on the point of issuing a constitution based upon the 'inalienable rights' of man.[4] Not only was the Revolution dead, it seemed, but absolutism had been reimposed.

Yet the Revolution had not, it transpired, been without its victories – only the Emperor claimed them as his own. The new government, led by Prince Felix Schwarzenberg, was genuinely reformist. The new Constitution introduced in March 1849 brought a measure of democracy and autonomy into local government, and though German remained the language of administration, local languages were permitted in elementary schools. Much more important, however, were the legal reforms and the emancipation of the serfs. The judicial reforms introduced by Alexander Bach in June 1849 modernized the legal structure by abolishing manorial courts (in which landlords could sit in judgement over their own tenants), provided trial by jury, and separated the judiciary from the executive. The administration of the law might still be authoritarian but the Empire's subjects now enjoyed civil rights.

The problem of serfdom was also addressed. Outside Hungary, 2.5 million peasants belonging to 55,000 lords were granted legal status and relieved of all dues to their former masters – dues that totalled 70 million days a year working on their lords' demesnes, 4 million gulden in cash and 40 million bushels of grain. Furthermore, they were freed with land of their own, for which they had to pay only half its value in compensation over a period of twenty years.[5] And, at the same time, the government was vigorous in stimulating economic development. All internal tariffs and tolls were reduced or abolished, and a major programme of railway-building embarked on. The show-piece was the Semmering Railway.

The first line ever to cross mountains, it was the most ambitious public project of its time. Built partly by unemployed rioters drafted in for the purpose, it left Vienna near the splendid Belvedere Palace, built for the victorious Prince Eugen over a century earlier, and ran southwards, climbing over the Alps on huge viaducts and through long tunnels, past the Semmering Pass to Graz. From Graz it wound its way to Laibach (Ljubljana) in Slovenia, and finally to Trieste on the Adriatic. Completed in 1854, the Semmering Railway was not only a breathtaking engineering achievement but of immense economic importance, providing a communications artery between Vienna (and Bohemia) and the markets of the world, encouraging an expansion of domestic trade between north and south, and giving a hefty stimulus to the mining, iron and engineering industries. Since so vast an undertaking was beyond the resources of private capital to fund, like all other European railway systems of the era (except Britain's), it was funded by the state. Along with the emancipation of the serfs it was a signal advance on the road to 'modernization'.

On the political front, however, there were further retreats from 'modernity'. At the end of 1851, less than three years after its introduction, the Constitution was revoked and representative institutions scrapped. Furthermore the Empire was being outstripped in economic development by her rival, Prussia. Then an international crisis intervened. In 1854 France and Britain attacked Russia. Russia expected the Emperor to return the favour the Tsar had done him by coming to his aid in Hungary in 1849. However, Vienna feared that intervention might invite a French attack on imperial territory in northern Italy, and that a victorious Russia might expand into the Balkans at her expense. So she remained neutral, but mobilized and occupied the Romanian principalities, Moldavia and Wallachia, which were subject to the Turks (also Russia's enemy) and constituted Russia's gateway into the Balkans. The price of this compromise turned out to be heavy.

Russia, which lost the war, was alienated; the costs of mobilization and of the occupation of the Romanian principalities (which gained independence under the Treaty of Paris which ended the war) not only forced the government to sell state assets (including the Semmering Railway) to foreign investors, but precipitated a stock market collapse in

1857. This provoked an outcry for constitutional control over the budget. And war with France came anyway in 1859, forcing the Emperor to relinquish the rich province of Lombardy and to concede a number of constitutional reforms.

The Imperial Council (*Reichsrath*) was enlarged by the inclusion of a representative element and given the right to veto certain taxation measures; and concessions were made to the Jews (the Rothschilds had floated a much-needed bank, the *Creditanstalt*, in 1855). Furthermore, the government of Hungary was restored to the more independent form it had taken before 1849, so that the imperial Ministry of Justice lost its powers to apply a common legal and judicial system throughout the Empire, a retrogressive step from a social and economic as well as a civic point of view. Nor was the concession of a parliament much appreciated by many of the beneficiaries. The Croats boycotted it in protest against the concessions made to the Hungarians, the Venetians refused to vote, and the Czech and Polish delegates walked out.

The period after 1848 was dubbed 'the era of oppression' but its achievements were impressive. Between 1848 and 1860 the railway network had expanded almost four-fold,[6] and average income per head had risen faster than in any other part of Eastern Europe. The Empire, it is true, lagged behind the European average by over 7 per cent in this respect, and by considerably more in comparison with Britain, France and Prussia.[7] Nevertheless with her improved communications, new banking system and a population free of the shackles of serfdom it seemed as if the Empire might yet meet the challenge of the industrial age, if only international problems did not interfere again. But they did.

Thanks largely to its economic predominance, Bismarck's Prussia had become the *de facto* leader of most of the German states. For a Habsburg, whose family had until 1806 provided the Emperors of the Holy Roman Empire, this was a dynastic affront as well as a strategic threat. In 1866, therefore, with promises of support from some German states, Francis Joseph decided to confront Prussia before it was too late. But this demanded Hungarian loyalty and French neutrality, both of which had to be bought. In order to placate France the Emperor was prepared to cede the Veneto, whose people had persisted in their dream of a united Italy despite all the benefits Vienna lavished on them.[8] After only a few weeks of war the armies met at Sadowa. It was a close-run contest. If the Prussian Crown Prince had brought his troops up any later than he did the Habsburgs would have triumphed and Bismark would have been discredited. As it was, however, the Habsburg army was defeated and the Emperor forced to sue for peace. The terms, which included an indemnity and acceptance of Prussia's leadership in Germany, were not onerous. But the Veneto had been ceded for nothing, and the debt to the Hungarians remained to be paid.

The price was virtually complete autonomy. As finally implemented in 1867, the *Ausgleich* (compromise) with the Hungarians divided the Empire into two parts united only by the monarch, a common army and foreign policy, and an agreed budget to fund them. A joint commission was formed to define tariffs between the two countries. Though it satisfied most Hungarians, the Ausgleich created problems for Austria-Hungary (as it must now be called) in respect of the other nationalities. The Czechs, who had been pressing for a confederation of five states rather than two, and the Poles of Austrian Galicia (the rest were ruled by Russia and Prussia) also hoped their loyalty would be rewarded. They were disappointed; and those nationalities now under Hungarian rule without hope of intercession from Vienna were resentful.

According to Hungary's 'Law on the Equality of the Nationalities' Rights' enacted in 1868, non-Hungarians were entitled to use their own languages in schools, the courts and in local government up to county level. Furthermore, Croatia was accorded a degree of political as well as linguistic autonomy. However, before long Magyarization policies were intensified to the point of eliminating all non-Hungarian place-names, while, in sharp contrast to Austria, the franchise was in effect restricted to Hungarian-speakers (and not even most of them). Hungary's chauvinistic policies were a far cry from Gottfried Herder's gentle vision of a community of distinct nationalities living happily side by side (see Chapter 6), or Palacky's Pan-Slavists, whose 1848 manifesto had insisted that

> Nature knows neither noble nor ignoble nations. It has not asked any one of them to dominate any other.... All [nations] possess the same right to develop to their utmost.[9]

Rather, it conformed to Kossuth's vision of a besieged Hungarian nation which would disappear if it did not take the offensive to defend itself; and its defence heightened the national consciousness of the nationalities whom Hungary oppressed.

As yet, nationalism was not a serious problem in the Russian Empire. A Polish rising had been crushed with comparative ease in 1863, though the russification of the courts and schools, implemented in the wake of the revolt, increased resentment. The Ukrainian elite had been successfully absorbed and the masses had still not acquired a national consciousness. Furthermore, Russians and Ukrainians together could claim to have a comfortable majority over all the other subject nationalities combined. Of much more concern was the sluggish growth of the economy. The Russian Empire at that time was in a far more backward state than Austria-Hungary – a slumbering giant, a land of backward, illiterate serfs and a largely idle and decrepit nobility; a country whose vast stores of wealth remained largely unexploited, and of primitive communications; a state ruled by officialdom under a Tsar whose chief pride was the army.

It was the defeat of the army in the Crimean War which precipitated the Russian Empire onto the path of modernization. The reform-minded Alexander II, who became Tsar in 1855, recognized that the first step must be to liberate the peasant masses from serfdom, a step often contemplated before, but never taken because of its inherent dangers. Removing the serfs from their owners' control might lead to anarchy in the countryside, and produce a fierce reaction from the former owners themselves. Furthermore, to free the serfs without land, as had been done in the Baltic provinces of Courland and Livonia in the wake of the Napoleonic Wars, would create a mass of impoverished, landless, and often workless, agricultural labourers. Yet if the serfs were to be given land on their emancipation, could they afford to pay the owners compensation?

The nettle was grasped in 1861. The serfs were to be emancipated with land; the lords would be compensated by the state which would recoup a proportion of the cost from the beneficiaries over a number of years, following the precedent set in the Habsburg Empire. However, the liberated peasants were to farm the land in the traditional, communal way (the village meeting allocating strips of land to each family according to need) and they were not to leave the village without a passport issued by the village elders and stamped by an official. Communal control was therefore substituted for manorial control. Furthermore, in the Polish provinces labour rent was not abolished until 1864. The decision was made in the wake of the 1863 rebellion, the government concluding that no purpose would be served by trying to conciliate the Polish landlords any longer. And their liberated peasants, who were mostly Ukrainians and Belorussians, would be a useful counterweight against them.[10]

The same year the serfs in the autonomous Romanian state were freed, though on much worse terms than in Austria or Russia.[11] In the remainder of the Balkans serfdom did not exist, though oppressive sharecropping arrangements on the big estates (*çiftliks*) owned by members of the Muslim elite, and the rapaciousness of the tax collectors, who leased tax farms from the government and tried to make as big a profit as possible out of them, led to periodic violent outbursts which were just as viciously suppressed. For the rest of the region, however, the die, in terms of rural reform, had been cast.

In the Russian Empire, as elsewhere, emancipation encouraged the growth of rural industry, notably textile manufacture in the central region, and made more labour available for nascent industry in the towns. It also encouraged the more enterprising of the large landowners to farm their properties more efficiently, particularly in the fertile region of Ukraine and 'New Russia' which enjoyed access to world markets through the Black Sea ports. In equally fertile Hungary, however, where peasants gained two-thirds of the arable while losing their access to common-lands, most of the big landowners despised both enterprise and agronomy. Like most of their Romanian counterparts they simply rented their estates out on short-term leases to contractors,[12] who exploited an annually contracted labour force, and often the land itself, for all they could. The labour force stemmed from the ranks of former serfs who were too poor or thriftless to survive as independent peasant farmers. Many of the smaller landlords who lacked the capital, as well as the initiative and inclination, to make their remaining land profitable, spent their compensation money, sold out and went off in search of some official job. Nonetheless, by 1870 it seemed that serfdom had been eliminated without any very serious political repercussions. It remained to be seen, however, if the rising tide of nationalism could be contained; whether industrialization could proceed and at a sufficient pace; and, even if it could, whether it would not create new and dangerous social tensions.

* * *

Darwin's new notion of the 'survival of the fittest' seemed to provide a most appropriate analogue to the nationality rivalries in Eastern Europe and to the predicament of the Hungarians in particular. Having successfully pressed their claims to Hungary's historical frontiers, while accepting the notion of the linguistic nation, they now found that the higher birthrates of the minorities threatened to overwhelm them in their own country. This led not only to the increasing drive to 'Magyarize' the subject nationalities (had not Kossuth himself and even the heroic Petofi been born half Slovak and yet chosen to be Hungarians?[13]) but to the abandonment of ancient prejudices against Germans and Jews.

As recently as 1848 three-quarters of the population of Budapest itself had been German-speaking, but from the latter years of the nineteenth century Germans and even Jews became acceptable in Hungarian society provided they spoke and wrote Magyar and identified with the nation. As it turned out even these devices were insufficient to turn the Hungarians into a majority. Rumanians, Serbs and Slovaks came increasingly to the view that the Hungarians had stolen a march over them. Moreover the fact that most Serbs and Romanians were Orthodox created further ground for discrimination against them. The situation of the Czechs, Slovenes, Poles and Ruthenes in the Austrian part of the Empire was better. They enjoyed a more broadly-based suffrage and superior educational opportunities. Nevertheless, Austrian rule was bitterly resented in nationalist circles.

The rise of nationalism everywhere was closely associated with both religion and the rise of elementary education (in which the churches often assumed leading roles). Polish nationalism, which became a creed for the masses in the later nineteenth century, was almost inextricably meshed with Polish Catholicism. Its imagery leant heavily on the imagery of Christianity. 'Poland, the Christ of Nations', the vision of the great national poet Mickiewicz, drew an analogy which gained general acceptance between the crucified Christ and a crucified Poland, and predicated a national resurrection which would save not only the Polish nation but all mankind. So far from combatting such notions as sacrilegious, the Church, particularly the parish clergy, embraced nationalism as a bastion against the encroachments, not only of secularism, but of German Protestantism and Russification (a policy which had led to the erection of a huge Orthodox Cathedral in the middle of Warsaw).

The Poles, however, constituted a special case, a nation which could not only recall an independent statehood in the relatively recent past but was homogenous in religion. The Ukrainians possessed neither of these advantages, nor even, as yet, much of a national literature, and the rise of mass nationalism there was to take much longer, though the Austrian government encouraged it in Galicia (western Ukraine) as an insurance policy against the local Poles, and to undermine Russia's hold over the Ukrainian population across the frontier. In the Balkans there were areas where the nationalities were so intermingled and intermarried that it was very difficult for an individual to decide how to identify himself nationally. However, the priests and schoolteachers, ever in the forefront of nationalist movements, helped them. As an experienced English observer was to remark at the turn of the century,

> In a school in Turkish territory you do not merely learn the usual subjects; you are taught to which nationality you really belong.

And in Macedonia the rival Bulgar, Serb, Greek and Vlah schools all reeked of propaganda.[14] What gave impetus to the 'Darwinian' nationalist rivalries in the sluggish Balkans was a consciousness that the Ottoman Empire was fast losing its grip on the region. This stimulated competitive bids for various tracts of its territory.

Yet national independence had sometimes been achieved before the rise of mass national consciousness. Such was the case of Romania. The principalities of Wallachia and Moldavia had been allowed to unite in 1861, two years after a prominent landowner, the liberal Alexandru Cuza, had been chosen as Prince by the elites in both. This unanimity indicated a degree of national consciousness, however socially restricted, and, as in Poland, the lead in this had been taken by émigrés returning from Paris fired by a variety of revolutionary ideas, of which national self-realization was the most prominent. Men of similar ilk, though of more scholarly bent, were also active in building the Romanian language on which the identity of a Romanian nation, after all, depended, for the vernacular was a plethora of local dialects, permeated with Slavonic words and forms; the language of administration had long been Greek or Old Slavonic, and the Cyrillic alphabet had been used even to record the vernacular.

The work of 'purifying' and standardizing the language had begun in Transylvania in the previous century, but it was continued under strong French influence. The builders of modern Romanian introduced a great many Gallicisms as well as neologisms. They also contributed to a deepening tension within the social elite between those, like themselves, who had been educated in France, adopted progressive ideas, and embraced an alien culture (which they regarded as a quintessential part of their nation's Romance heritage), and their traditionalist *boiar* fathers. And, as in Russia where much of the nobility preferred to speak French, their adoption of foreign ways sharpened peasant resentment.[15] But nationalist sentiment was slow to filter down the social scale unless there was a special stimulus. The mass of Romanians became nationally self-conscious sooner in Transylvania, where Hungarian dominance served as a spur and where educational facilities were superior, than in the new Romania itself.

The neighbouring Bulgarians, though also united by the Orthodox religion, had been no less linguistically divided than the Romanians. Many of the local dialects were so far removed from the literary language as to make the latter almost unintelligible to the vast majority. As late as the 1890s all seven Bulgarian grammars then available differed significantly from each other. As for the Albanians, they had no commonly accepted script in which to write their language (which was probably the oldest in Europe). The expressions of nationalism in such countries seemed far removed from those of, say, the Czechs with their pleasant provincialism centring on the theatre and the drawing room, where they would read the works of Karel Macha, sing Czech songs, or enjoy that poignant expression of national sentiment, Smetana's Second String Quartet.

So far from such gentility, life in Bulgaria verged on the brutal, and nationalism there rested as much on the old bandit tradition of the Balkans as on the activities of the few revolutionary intellectuals constrained to operate abroad. Yet when, in 1876, some of them seized an Austrian steamer on the Danube and sailed home to raise rebellion, they had been despatched as easily as had the Romanian revolutionaries who had returned home from Paris in 1848. The Bulgarian peasant masses had not been reached.

The situation soon changed. A peasant uprising in Hercegovina in 1875 spread to Bosnia and eventually inspired a rebellion in Bulgaria. The Turks responded in their wonted fashion with atrocities which stirred Gladstone to righteous condemnation (though Bulgarian atrocities against the Turks were no less cruel), and prompted intervention by Russia, which had assumed the mantle of protector of Orthodox Christians for several centuries past. Many Bulgarians participated in the ensuing Russian–Turkish war of 1877–8 with enthusiasm, and their reward was the creation of a Bulgarian state stretching from the Danube to the Aegean. But the other Powers did not welcome the creation of so large a country that was beholden to Russia, and under the terms of the Treaty of Berlin (1878) the new Bulgaria was much reduced.

As had been the case in Serbia and Greece (see Chapter 6), in Romania and Bulgaria national independence preceded the advent of mass national consciousness. The great Balkan revolts of the 1870s had been inspired as much by peasant discontent and the random oppression of Turkish rule as by nationalism. The Bosnian rising had been directed against the rapaciousness of the tax farmers and the greed of the landowning *begs*, who allowed their peasants to eke out only a miserable existence. In Romania, however, the peasant problem was divorced from the national question, though it was no less acute.

Despite the emancipation act of 1864, the intransigence of the *boiar* class prevented the peasants gaining economic as well as legal freedom, since they received too little land at too high a cost. In Hungary (whose government encouraged the peasants to believe that they owed their freedom to Kossuth rather than the Habsburgs), 75 per cent of the peasantry owned only very small plots, while some 3,000 landowners controlled half of the arable land. Even in Russia, where great care had been taken to ensure that the peasants should be adequately provided for, there were problems.

The continuation of the time-honoured Russian method of cultivating the land in scattered strips that were liable to be reallocated within the commune, was inefficient and discouraged investment in land improvement. Furthermore, as almost everywhere else, the small peasant's mode of production encouraged consumption rather than the marketing of a surplus. Levels of agricultural exports essential to the economy were only maintained thanks to the great estates. But another more serious agrarian problem was beginning to emerge – a tendency for rural areas to become congested as the population increased and individual peasant holdings became smaller.

The Western custom of primogeniture, whereby the eldest son inherited his father's farm upon his death, was practically unknown in Eastern Europe. Rather it was the custom to divide the land among all the sons, which in the case of a large family with a small farm led to its 'parcellization' into units that were too small to maintain their owner. In Russia, where the peasants owned land collectively, rising population was beginning to have a similar effect, in that the commune's allocation of arable to each member family tended to become smaller, or of poorer quality, as marginal land came to be taken under the plough. Furthermore, as more common-land came to be ploughed up peasants found that they were able to maintain fewer animals.

In Russia, as in some other countries of the region, the pressure was relieved to an extent by state-financed Land Banks which facilitated the transfer of land from impecunious lords willing to sell to peasants who would otherwise lack the capital to buy. However, towards the end of the century land prices rose steadily. This cushioned the fall of many smaller lords (whose genteel impoverishment is pictured in some of Chekhov's plays) but contributed to the rise of peasant discontent. And discontent continued to rise despite the commutation and eventual annulment of the redemption payments the former serfs were expected to pay for their land. The 'agrarian problem', as it came to be known, was becoming particularly acute in Romania and in European Russia, where there was little industry to absorb the growing population surplus from the countryside. In Russia the restriction on the peasantry's freedom of movement added to the problem. Eventually, this nettle was grasped when, in 1890, Sergei Witte was appointed Premier, though his guiding concern was not the agrarian problem but the Empire's lack of industrial development which, as he recognised, implied military weakness too. His solution was a crash industrialization programme.[16]

As in the Habsburg monarchy, the key to his strategy was railway-building – not only to encourage related industries and to stimulate the economy by developing internal markets, but to open up Siberia, with its vast mineral resources. Between 1890 and 1900 the length of the railway network in the Empire was almost doubled (from 30,600 to 53,200 kilometres) an achievement that included the completion of the celebrated Trans-Siberian track. Moreover, the production of pig-iron tripled, steel output increased ten-fold, and the production of coal and oil also shot ahead.[17] Not least, peasant migration to Siberia, previously discouraged, was now subsidised, so that by 1900 nearly 5 million people had moved there and more of its virgin land was taken under the plough. By comparison with Germany Russia was as yet only a puny industrial power, but no country in Europe rivalled its rate of industrial growth in the 1890s, and the success of Witte's programme seemed to hold out the prospect of Russia's catching up with the West, at least in terms of quantity of production, within a comparatively short time.

There were costs, however, not least to the peasant majority. Industrialization required large-scale foreign borrowing and hence a heavy burden of debt-servicing. Most of the money required was found by recourse to indirect taxation on the necessities of life like matches, tea, paraffin and tobacco, which hit the peasants harder than other sectors of society. The fiscal pressure placed upon them left them no margin to withstand periodic harvest failure; and the famine of 1901 was followed by scenes of great distress in the countryside. And meanwhile discontent was growing among the urban poor.

The new peasant recruits to industry (many of them indentured by factory owners from the communes, which received a percentage of their pay) found the overcrowded city slums an unwelcome contrast to the open aspect and freedom of life in the village, whatever its hardships; and they reacted equally badly to the work patterns demanded of them. Accustomed to a very uneven pace of work dictated by the season and the hours of light and darkness, they suddenly found themselves expected to work at an even pace throughout the year and to live a life that was dictated by the clock. Their often anarchic behaviour, bred of peasant life and culture shock, invited draconian discipline; but the rule of stick-wielding foremen and the fines imposed by many managements for unpunctuality and other misdemeanours promoted alienation, which fed a growing strike movement. The mass strike was also encouraged by the generally large scale of industrial organization (which was economical in scarce managerial resources) and by the tendency for workers to be recruited from the same rural areas, which promoted a sense of solidarity among them. Towards the end of the century the government banned both trades unions and strikes, though it also introduced factory legislation which was by no means the least humane in Europe at the time. Nevertheless, the incidence of strikes and worker demonstrations tended to increase rather than diminish.

The Russian Empire was not the last in the region to emerge from pre-industrial torpor. The Ottoman Empire was also following the fashion of promoting railway building, though its reputation for crumbling inefficiency made it difficult to attract foreign investment for the purpose. A projected line between the city of Ruse on the Danube and Varna on the Black Sea was delayed for years, but it finally got under way in the 1870s. An Englishman who helped in its construction suggests its significance:

> Up to the time the Varna and Rustchuk [Ruse] railway was made there was no such thing as a road in all Bulgaria, and ... the only way of transporting material in or out of the country, was to drag it over muddy tracks in bullock carts.[18]

For the successor states of the Ottoman Empire the promotion of railway-building was a more difficult prospect still. There, most people envisaged the fruits of national independence to be the satisfaction of the peasant's land hunger and the acquisition of an official post (preferably one that carried the right to wear a prestige-giving uniform and a sufficient salary with which to cut a little dash), rather than the creation of an industrial superstructure and efficient modernization of the country. Among the beneficiaries of Romanian independence were the petty officials known as the *Cinces* ('fivers') from the number of napoleons that made up their salaries.

> They are accused [reported a contemporary visitor] of sacrificing everything to appearance, and are said often to dispense with their meagre dinners, in order to have a little cash to pay for their seat at the play.... Sadly do they sometimes complain of the penury to which they are reduced: but how their salaries are to be raised I know not, as Romania is, *par excellence*, the land of officialism, and, small country that it is, possesses more civil servants than either France or Prussia.[19]

The proliferation of officialdom, together with the new, inflated, national armies were an almost insupportable financial burden for the independent Balkan states. Serbia went bankrupt in 1895; Bulgaria followed suit in 1901. By 1911 their foreign debts were each in excess of $100 million. While the cheapness of these countries' labour and rising world demand for their agricultural produce favoured industrialization, their shortage of capital and skills, mental attitudes and the cult of *la bella figura* constituted heavy drag-weights to development. Great joy was taken in the trappings of modern statehood – in the distinctive postage stamps, the new, imposing government buildings, the statues of national heroes, or in the fact that one's Foreign Minister was received with honour in Paris or London (his top hat, tail-coat and spats might well be exhibited in the national museum) – for such things proved that one belonged to a nation as good as any other.

But while there was a tendency to imitate more advanced (and especially Western) countries in terms of buildings, institutions, literature and the arts, and outward show of all kinds, there was little inclination to emulate the qualities on which the superiority of such countries was based. In particular, the wealthy and the educated (other than the Greeks and Jews) had a dread of commercial enterprise. This was a common trait throughout Eastern Europe and derived in large measure from an antiquated aristocratic ethos which classed business as a dishonourable pursuit (see Chapter 8). Yet where, as in Budapest, there were sufficient enterprising Jews and Germans and some investment capital, the results in terms of the speedy generation of wealth could be startling.

The boom in Budapest had its origins in Hungary's achievement of independence within the Empire. As in Belgrade, Bucharest and Sofia, a publicly-funded building programme was instituted in order to justify the city's new importance as a capital. The Cathedral was revamped to recall the glories of the mediaeval Hungarian Kingdom, and, on the Pest bank, one of the most handsome and romantic, as well as one of the largest, of all parliament buildings was erected. The building boom, together with the development of transportation along the Danube and railway-building, promoted rapid and varied industrial progress, and by 1890 well over 100,000 people were directly employed in industry (compared to 18,000 in 1848).

Much of the development was based on processing agricultural produce. There were fifteen steam-mills powering flour-processing plants, ten large distilleries and refineries, factories producing milling equipment and agricultural machinery (including a state machine factory which turned out steam-powered threshers) and tanneries which processed cattle-hides. But the development was diversified: there were also ship-building, locomotive, bridge-making and other heavy engineering plants, as well as firms exploiting the new technology; manufacturing telephone and telegraph equipment, chemicals and pharmaceuticals, and an electrical industry which lit the streets not only of Budapest itself, but of Venice, Karlsbad and Sofia and the Tsar's palace of Tsarskoe Selo. Paper, asbestos, ropes and sacking, playing cards and armaments were also made, and the brick-yards turned out over 100 million bricks a year.[20]

Similar pictures of burgeoning industry, if not always so well balanced, were to be seen in Moscow and St Petersburg as well as in Vienna, Prague and Bratislava. Yet industry was still a thin layer of icing on a vast and largely backward agrarian sector; and in Russia and the Balkans well over 80 per cent of the population were still engaged in agriculture, most of them employing the most primitive techniques. Most farmers could not afford an iron plough; but peasant conservatism, as well as their increasing poverty, held them back. As Edith Durham, who knew rural life in the Balkans well, remarked, the legacy of the past and the peasant's isolation had

> deadened his intellect, blurred his feelings, blackened his morals, but he has saved himself from extinction by developing a peculiar mulish, persistent, boring obstinacy.[21]

Often the state engaged agronomists to advise peasants how to improve their farms; often they provided credit facilities and tried to improve the education of their children. The results were usually disappointing. Towards the end of the century two agricultural secondary schools were opened in Serbia, but whether they were the sons of poor peasants funded by scholarships or the offspring of prosperous farmers, on the completion of their studies the students gravitated not to farming but to the civil service.[22] As improved communications broke down peasants' isolation, tempted them to earn more in order to buy the cheaper factory-produced goods which were becoming available, and gave them the opportunity to escape to the city, it might be thought that, in time, the problem of rural poverty might disappear, but it only became more widespread and intense. The reason was the accelerating rate of population growth.

Between 1860 and 1900 the population of Eastern Europe almost doubled. Between 1900 and 1914 it increased by at least another 20 per cent to a figure well in excess of 250 million.[23] This was a far higher growth rate than in any Western country, and it has never been adequately explained. In so far as the statistics exclude migration abroad, the situation was worse than it might seem. Mass emigration had gathered pace since 1880. By 1914 nearly 4 million had left Austria-Hungary; the rate of migration from the Russian Empire approached 100,000 a year.[24] But the migration rates from the poorest areas were the lowest (higher for Austria-Hungary than Russia, higher from Russian Poland than the rest of the Russian Empire, and lowest from Romania). However encouraging a development the population explosion might seem to chauvinistic nationalists, it brought rising despair in the countryside (where almost 60 per cent of Austria's subjects lived, 70 per cent of Hungary's and over 80 per cent over the remainder of the region). The despair at having to feed more mouths from the same small trough turned to anger in massive peasant disturbances in Russia in 1906 and a bloody Romanian uprising of 1907.[25] But the problems of the countryside were also transferred to the cities.

The population growth in most of the major cities exceeded that for the region as a whole because of urban migration. Between 1880 and 1910 the population of Prague rose by almost 40 per cent to nearly a quarter of a million; that of Budapest doubled to reach almost 900,000; those of St Petersburg and Moscow more than doubled (to 2 and 1.5 million respectively), and that of Warsaw more than tripled (to 856,000). But the most alarming increase occurred in Vienna which changed, within the span of a single generation, from a pleasant, orderly, German-speaking city of fewer than 750,000 souls to a polyglot maelstrom of over two million.[26] The city, whose ancient walls had recently been dismantled to make way for the elegant *Ringstrasse* with its modern palaces and pleasant parks where bands played Strauss waltzes, was suddenly overwhelmed by a new kind of invasion.

It was an irony of this age of nationalism that by 1910 no less than 8 per cent of all Czechs should reside in Vienna (5 per cent of all Slovaks had settled in Budapest by that time). And not only Czechs, but Serbs, Romanians, Slovenes and Ukrainians had flooded in to the new tenements and slums. The city had come to resemble a Tower of Babel, and the indigenous Viennese felt overwhelmed; their culture, their very identity seemed threatened. The popular mood, formerly easy-going, became ugly. Chief among the objects of their resentment was the most obvious group of newcomers, the Orthodox Jews from Galicia with their earlocks, beards, broad hats and coats of shiny gaberdine.

This was the context in which the demagogic Karl Lueger and Georg von Schoenerer rose to prominence on platforms of antisemitism and German nationalism – and found an admirer in the young Adolf Hitler, another immigrant from rural Linz. Three times Lueger was elected Mayor of Vienna and three times the undemocratic, but right-minded, Emperor refused to confirm him in office, though eventually he felt bound to do so. Lueger's antisemitism was culturally based. The old-established, integrated Viennese Jews were acceptable to him. Even so, the consciousness that the very foundations of society and all the norms hitherto taken for granted had become loose or skewed created severe psychological problems, not least among Vienna's Jewish establishment, and the mood of unease was reflected in the arts as well as in the politics of *fin de siècle* Vienna.[27]

In literature there were von Hofmannstahl's escapist lyric plays to set beside Schnitzler's morbid and erotic psychological dramas; in painting Klimt's rejection of realism and Kokoschka's distortions of it. In music, it is true, there were Mahler's well-crafted, albeit overblown, essays in the romantic tradition, but also the depravity depicted in Richard Strauss's *Salome*, and Schoenberg's rejection of orthodox tonality. Many of the works produced by this artistic renaissance[28] can be regarded as parables of their time and place. And if the scandalous painting 'Murderer, Hope of Women' reflected little more than a sensationalist exploitation of the disorientation experienced by the middle classes in particular, Schoenberg's *Moses and Aaron* presented a trenchant analysis of the situation. In the opera, Moses is the bearer of truth but cannot sing, and Aaron, who can communicate to the masses, distorts the truth by appealing to their primitive sensuality. It suggests the failure of reason and the rise of the masses who embrace their Golden Calf.

In the same atmosphere, Theodore Herzl developed the Zionist movement (which he modelled on the prevailing nationalism of the region), and one of the most imaginative scholars of the age, Sigmund Freud, contrived an hermetic system which sought to explain the disturbed psyches he undoubtedly found among his predominantly female middle-class patients chiefly in terms of sex. But the predicament so many middle-class Viennese found themselves in seems to have derived less from the repression of sexual urges than from the collapse of previously accepted values and the concomitant rise of anti-rationalism, anti-liberalism, and antisemitism. Freud's exploration of the individual psyche no doubt contributed a further challenge to established values, but however interesting his conclusions they reflected the general sense of malaise rather than providing a cure for it.

Elsewhere in Eastern Europe there was a similar sense of malaise, albeit less intense than in the hothouse of Vienna. In Russia there was a vigorous movement of religious revivalism, not least among intellectuals, and the poet Vladimir Solov'ev resorted to mysticism – another manifestation of the reaction against rationalism; at the same time socialism, formed in the rationalist mould, exerted noticably less attraction for the intelligentsia as a whole. But although there was a rush to find planks that seemed to offer salvation from the sea of turmoil, for the most part it was the politicians who tended to see the problems most clearly, and Austria and Russia each produced one with sufficient acuity and resource to set courses that might ultimately have led to calmer waters – Koerber and Stolypin.

* * *

Ernst von Koerber became Premier of Austria in 1900 at a time of parliamentary turmoil. One of his predecessors, Count Badeni, had given the Czech language equal status with German in Bohemia. This had mollified the Czechs but so infuriated the Germans (who saw their employment prospects threatened) as to force a *volte face*, to the outrage of the Czechs. The *Reichstag* had, in consequence, become a battleground over which Czechs and German members hurled inkwells as well as abuse at each other. The conduct of parliamentary business became impossible and ministers had to resort to government by decree. Then, in 1902, Koerber unveiled a plan for economic revival and reconciliation, and the hubbub immediately subsided. What Koerber proposed was an ambitious programme of canal-building.

Its implications were at once appreciated: it would provide much-needed employment (as the Semmering railway had done in its day), cheapen transportation costs, and provide a general boost to the economy. The creation of a large enough economic cake seemed likely to reduce the dissatisfactions on which the war between the nationalities was feeding, and even lessen the growing pressure of the masses (represented by populist demagogues like Lueger) to wrest political power from the aristocracy and middle classes. Unfortunately, the plan foundered. Koerber's own administration was divided about its financial wisdom, and the necessary capital was not provided.[29]

There was, however, some political movement after Koerber's departure from office. In particular, universal male suffrage was introduced into Austria in 1907. The Hungarian government refused to follow suit. Their fear of the national minorities and the rural poor was simply too great. Yet at the same time the ambition of the 'Kossuthites', the Hungarian extremists who had come to power at the last election, for even greater autonomy faded. Their complaints that Austria was exploiting Hungary had become increasingly shrill, though their Austrian counterparts claimed that the reverse was the case.[30] Hungary's faster rate of economic growth since 1867 suggests that the Kossuth Party was being tendentious, and it is generally recognized that the association was highly beneficial to them both. Nevertheless, this had not prevented the Hungarians from pressing, in 1906, for the creation of their own national army. The Emperor was opposed to the break-up of the imperial army, and he found a simple way to thwart the plan. He threatened to introduce universal suffrage into Hungary. The Hungarians immediately dropped their claim to military independence, for if everyone had the vote in a country where the minorities collectively constituted the majority, the basis of Hungarian dominance would be destroyed.

Nationalism, like democracy, was therefore a two-edged sword, threatening to destroy the Empire, but also helping to preserve it. Nevertheless, as Koerber understood, the stabilization of politics in that age of lurching change required economic engineering rather than constitutional tinkering – and this was no less true of the Russian Empire which was being rocked by similar forces, though nationalism was a less serious threat there and poverty a much greater one.

As the Revolution of 1905 demonstrated, both Polish and Finnish nationalism had become particularly strong. Political nationalism among the other minorities of the Russian Empire, however, was as yet only in its infancy. Furthermore, whereas in Austria-Hungary German-speakers, who constituted the largest linguistic group, formed less than a quarter of the total population, Russians and russified or nationally inert Ukrainians were the majority. By far the greater threat to the Empire's survival was the rising social discontent of the peasants and the urban poor. There was also a small, but increasingly vocal, movement for constitutional reform. Made up largely of liberally-inclined intellectuals, it was to some extent concerned about the poor but placed far greater emphasis on radical constitutional change – the abolition of the autocracy and the introduction of a constitutional and democratic form of government.

At the height of the disturbances in 1905, Tsar Nicholas II was forced to concede most of their demands, but he retained residual autocratic powers under the constitution (including the power to abrogate it). In the ensuing elections to the new parliament (*Duma*), the radical liberal party known as the Constitutional Democrats (*Kadets*) gained more seats than any other group, and to superficial observers it seemed that the Russian Empire was at last embarking on a 'modern' political course. Appearances, however, were very soon proved to be deceptive, like the apparent strength of the Russian fleet when it sailed towards its destruction at the hands of the Japanese at Tsushima. The political inexperience and theoretical dogmatism of most of the elected representatives were among the chief reasons for the failure of parliamentary democracy in Russia.

The new Premier, appointed by the Tsar, was a former provincial governor, Stolypin, and he faced an unenviable task. There was widespread demoralization following defeat in the war against Japan, chaos in many rural areas in the wake of the revolutionary upheaval of 1905–6, a more serious financial situation than ever, and now a potentially hostile parliament to face. But, like Koerber in Austria, Stolypin had a clear strategic vision. His programme had three main planks – to restore order to the country; to woo the *Kadet* Party in the *Duma* with the offer of a share in power; and to transform at least a major proportion of the peasantry into a class of prosperous farmers, creating a bulwark of stability in a society which had fallen out of kilter. With the help of military units returning from the war, order was restored relatively quickly. But his policy of cooperation with the *Duma* failed.

Euphoric after their electoral victory, and assuming that, as the majority party, they had a natural right to rule (as in any Western democratic country), they were not interested in the share in government which Stolypin offered them. Their determination was as strong as their experience of government and political nous were weak. Many of them had participated in the local authority boards, which had been set up in the 1860s and 1870s and given some responsibility for education, welfare health and other public services. These parochial concerns, however, marked the limit of their administrative experience. Their political background was also limited, chiefly confined to defending the prerogatives of local government against encroachments by ministerial officials and to reading advanced political texts. They badly needed an apprenticeship in government, and this is precisely what Stolypin offered them. They spurned it; insisted on everything – and got nothing. The electoral law was changed, then changed again, in order to procure the election of a docile parliament drawn chiefly from the ranks of the provicial gentry. The severely reduced, frustrated, liberal membership maintained its familiar stance of intransigent opposition. The constitutional experiment had failed, but the liberal *Kadets* bore much of the responsibility for the failure. It remained to be seen if Stolypin's strategy of transforming rural Russia would succeed.

The principal reform measures in this field were enacted in 1908. Peasants were allowed to consolidate their scattered strips of communal land into farms of which they, rather than the commune, would be the owners. If most members of a commune agreed to it, the village common-land could also be enclosed. Furthermore, all peasants were released from the authority of the commune and given the right to an internal passport which allowed them complete freedom of movement.

Migration to Siberia was also encouraged, and the state made the advice of trained agronomists widely available in order to encourage improvements in farming methods. This rural revolution was on the whole well-planned and implemented with a sense of equity, with the help of Land Commissions which were set up in every locality. Stolypin hoped that, given twenty years of international peace and internal quiet, these and associated measures would transform and stabilize the Russian Empire, overcome its backwardness and avert the threat of revolution. Whether it would have has been done has been a matter of hot dispute among historians,[31] for Russia was not granted the twenty years of peace that Stolypin thought necessary to success. Even so, there were hopeful indications.

By 1914 almost 3 million peasant families had become individual proprietors and well over 1.25 millions had consolidated their holdings. Furthermore, by 1915 a further 25 million acres had passed from gentry to peasant ownership, thanks largely to the operations of the state-financed Peasant Bank. As elsewhere in Eastern Europe, land under the plough increased (though in conditions of rural overpopulation it was to be expected that more marginal land and commons would be turned into arable). More significantly, crop yields per acre rose. So did agricultural prices and the rates for rural labour. The rise in peasant discontent which had erupted violently in 1905–6 seemed to have been reversed at last. On the other hand, from 1908 the level of protest by the urban proletariat began to rise again.[32] As in Austria, the main arena of social tension seemed to have moved from the countryside to the cities.

As the elections to the *Duma* showed, the Bolsheviks had already captured a majority of working-class votes in the larger cities, and, to judge by the workers' slogans in their increasingly frequent strikes, their aims were political as much as economic. On the other hand, the strikes were generally of very brief duration and, as yet, by no means general. A more serious threat to stability seemed to derive from the small group of urban terrorists who believed that the assassination of prominent politicians and administrators would somehow inaugurate a golden age of liberty. In 1911 Stolypin himself fell victim to one of these assassins while attending a performance of the Kiev opera. Such actions served little purpose other than to heighten tension and give more clout to the secret police. And the secret police were by no means out of touch with the swirling currents of public opinion, nor devoid of ideas on how to thwart the revolutionaries.

As early as 1900 a thoughtful officer in the Moscow section had the ingenious idea of capturing the illegal trade union movement from the revolutionaries and of forging an alliance between the working class and the state. Familiar with Marxist theory, he proposed that the government exploit it by playing class off against class, much as both the Russian and

Austro-Hungarian Empires sometimes played one nationality off against another. His plan was to insulate the largely middle-class revolutionary intellectuals (whom he termed the 'ideologists') from the workers, while introducing laws in favour of the working class.[33] At the same time the secret police itself set up patriotic trade unions. But the idea proved to be too clever by half.

Police-backed unionism and factory legislation hampered Russia's industrialists, on whom Russia's development largely depended; the state-inspired unions were quickly infiltrated by revolutionaries, while, thanks to poor coordination, the great demonstration by loyalist workers in St Petersburg led by Father Gapon at the beginning of 1905 (which seems to have had its genesis in secret police headquarters) had ended in a bloodbath which precipitated the revolution of that year. Thereafter, while the police hounded revolutionaries of all colours, the government made fitful attempts to encourage public expression of support for the regime by supporting 'patriotic' movements such as the ultraconservative 'Union of the Russian People', and giving intermittent and half-hearted support to diversions such as the pogroms mounted against the Jewish population by the 'Black Hundreds' (which aroused an unwelcome storm of protest abroad).

On occasion a despairing minister would sigh, as Pleve, another victim of assassins, had in 1902, for a small-scale, brief and successful war that would arouse the patriotism of the masses and stave off what they saw to be impending revolution. At the same time there was fear, despite a considerable naval build-up since 1905, that the Empire was falling behind in the arms race. Increasing militarism, and mounting expectation of a general European war was affecting Russia no less than other states. Yet, while many in high office tended to despair, other, wiser, voices made themselves heard.

In February 1914 the Minister of the Interior, P.N. Durnovo, warned the Tsar against involvement in the European war which so many felt to be inevitable and probably imminent. It would be disastrous for Russia, he wrote, regardless of whether she lost or won:

> A general European war is mortally dangerous for both Russia and Germany, no matter who wins. It is our firm conviction ... that a social revolution must inevitably break out in the defeated country which ... will spread to the country of the victory....
>
> The troubles will be of a social, and not a political, nature.... A political revolution is not possible in Russia, and any revolutionary movement must inevitably degenerate into a Socialist movement. The opponents of the Government have no popular support. The people see no difference between a government official and an intellectual. The Russian

> masses ... are not looking for political rights, which they neither want nor comprehend. The peasant dreams of obtaining a gratuitous share of somebody else's land; the workmen of getting hold of the entire capital and profits of the manufacturer. Beyond this they have no aspirations.[34]

Durnovo was to be vindicated in almost every particular; and it is clear that war would be almost equally dangerous for Austria-Hungary, though by encouraging a nationalist ferment rather than social revolution. Nevertheless, both states had been flirting with war, not least by competing with one another over the fast-disintegrating corpse of the Ottoman Empire in the Balkans, and they continued to do so.

Both Powers had conflicting aims and a mutual fear of each other in the Balkans. Russia aimed to strengthen her influence in the Slavonic-speaking areas, especially Bulgaria and Serbia, and to take Istanbul (an aim endorsed by the Western Powers as the price of Russia's alliance with them in a war with Germany). Austria-Hungary was already involved with Germany in an economic drive into the Balkans, exploiting the new rail link with Istanbul and building another to Thessaloniki. She was also determined to isolate Serbia and deny her access to the sea. Matters had come to a head in 1908 when the 'Young Turks' who had come to power in the Ottoman Empire introduced a constitution. This called for Austria to surrender her trusteeship of Bosnia-Hercegovina, which blocked Serbia's access to the Adriatic, so she immediately took preemptive action and annexed these territories. This angered Russia as well as Serbia, but the Serbs could not contest the move without Russian support, and Russia was in no position to intervene since she was still recovering from the maulings of the Japanese and the Revolution of 1905. But Vienna's triumph was to store up trouble for her in the future.

The Emperor Franz Joseph tried to justify his government's desperate opportunism in annexing Bosnia-Hercegovina by pointing to the benefits Austrian trusteeship had already brought – order and security instead of violence and oppression as under the Turks, the development of commerce and of education.[35] The building of railways and roads had opened these mountainous territories to the benefits of industrial civilization; educational facilities had indeed been much improved, and an influx of Jews had served both to develop commerce and improve medical services. The modern buildings and amenities which stand beside the minarets of Sarajevo still bear witness to some of the achievement's of Austria's brief rule. Whether the largely Muslim (though Slavonic-speaking) population regarded rule by a Christian rather than a Muslim emperor as an unmixed blessing is open to question, but certainly the Austrian promise of constitutional government for the territories had more substance than the Turkish one.

In any case, it is uncertain whether many people in the Balkans fully understood the implications of constitutional rule. The largely Muslim Albanians under Turkish rule had very little idea. Edith Durham, who was in Albania shortly after the constitution was unveiled, reports a conversation which reflected their disappointment with it:

> 'It promised to give us roads, and railways, and schools, and to keep order and justice. We have had it two whole months, and it has done none of these things....'
>
> I said no Government, however good, could do all these things [so quickly].... They shouted me down.
>
> 'It could if it chose. A Government can do just as it likes, or it is not a Government.'
>
> I urged the cost – railways for example.
>
> 'Railways, dear lady, cost nothing. They are always made by foreign companies.'
>
> 'Schools cost thousand of piastres – the house, the master, books.'
>
> 'Schools in all civilized lands cost nothing. They are all free. The Government pays for them.'
>
> 'In England', I said, 'we have to pay a great deal for schools.'
>
> They retorted that the English Government must be bad, and they did not want a poor one like that. I said, firmly, that every other land had to pay for all these things, and Albania must too, or go without. But one of the party knew as a fact that, in Austria and Italy, the Government built most beautiful things and paid for them itself.... .
>
> 'When all is set in order', they said, 'when we have' (here followed a list of all required to fit out a first-class Power and a small Utopia), 'then, if we are quite satisfied, it would be right for us to pay a little tax. But it would be silly to pay for a thing before we know how we liked it. If Konstitutzioon is not rich enough to do these things, it can go to the devil – the sooner the better.'[36]

Popular levels of understanding were not noticeably higher in other parts of the Balkans or, as Durnovo suggested, in Russia either. Elsewhere, notably in urbanized Austria, they were, but it was the backward Balkans which were to drag Austria-Hungary into war – and so ruin the chances of the entire region.

Whether headed by a native dynasty, like Serbia, or by imported German ones, like Bulgaria, Romania and Greece, most Balkan states now had constitutions. But they were window-dressing that pleased Westerners and meant little to the people, whose chief collective concern was to recapture what they imagined to be their ancient glories by extending their frontiers at their neighbours' expense. Their strivings caused repeated diplomatic alarms.

In 1912 Serbia, Bulgaria, Greece and the tiny principality of Montenegro combined in an attack on Turkish territory in the Balkans. They were largely successful. The Powers eventually imposed an armistice, but the Serbs had encroached on Albanian territory, the Albanians swore vengeance, and the other small states, though still trying to digest their recent gains, were avid for even more territory. In November 1912 a National Association proclaimed Albanian independence and this was recognized by the Powers in 1913. Then in February of that year another war broke out between Bulgaria and the Turks, and the Powers had hardly brought this to a halt than Serbia, Greece, Romania and Montenegro became embroiled in conflict with Bulgaria. This war too was stopped, but then Serbia seemed poised to attack Albania. Austria-Hungary warned her off and, reluctantly, the Serbs backed down.

By this time Austrian nerves were severely strained. As early as 1906 Conrad von Hotzendorff, the Chief of the Imperial General Staff, had advocated the partition of Serbia between Austria and Bulgaria. He was quite prepared to risk war in order to eliminate the menace of troublesome little Serbia, whose vibrant nationalism might infect the Serbs within the Empire. Until 1912 the war party had been restrained by a Foreign Minister, Alois von Aehrenthal, who believed that the Empire could protect its interests by diplomacy; but after he died in February of that year the militants gained ground. The rising tensions between Austria and Serbia was intensified by an economic war, known as 'the pig war', because of the high tariffs and veterinary restrictions the Empire imposed on the importation of Serbian pigs. This led to a rise in the price of sausage, which was almost a staple in Vienna, but had a much more serious effect in Serbia, since pigs constituted a major export and the Empire was the only major market accessible to them. Had Serbia been able to gain access to the Adriatic across Bosnia-Hercegovina or Albania she would not have suffered so badly, but Austria had contrived to cut both these exits off. Nationalist extremists in Serbia planned revenge.

In 1911 Colonel Dragutin Dmitrijevic had formed a secret organization called 'Union or Death' (otherwise known as 'The Black Hand'). In 1913 he became chief of Serbian military intelligence. In June 1914 he equipped a small group of young nationalists from Bosnia with arms and safe passage across the frontier in order to assassinate the Archduke Franz Ferdinand, who was due to make an official visit to Sarajevo. The date chosen for the visit was the anniversary of the battle of Kosovo, Serbia's national day, commemorating the destruction of the mediaeval Serbian empire five centuries before. The Austrian government was tactless, even provocative, in its choice of date, but from the moment the conspirators crossed the frontier all parties showed incompetence. Having got wind of the plot, the Serbian government tried to warn Vienna. The message did not get through. The assassins bungled their first chance and only got a second thanks to Austrian officialdom's carelessness in proceeding with the motorcade without increasing security measures. So the Archduke and his wife were murdered.

The immediate consequence was an Austrian ultimatum to the Serbian government. The Serbs promptly accepted all its demands except for one implying direct Austrian intervention in Serbian affairs which no sovereign state could have accepted.[37] Vienna rejected this response. Even so, the Great War might have been avoided, had not Russia, which had no formal treaty obligation to come to Serbia's aid and no common frontier with her, not mobilized. Nor would Vienna have taken so provocative a line without encouragement from Germany, which thought a general war to be inevitable and preferred to fight it sooner rather than later. There were voices, including that of the Hungarian Premier, Istvan Tisza, which advocated caution – but they were not heeded. For most of the decision-makers the war which was to destroy the empires of Eastern Europe seemed to be the only means of saving them.[38]

The imperial government in Vienna despaired of solving its nationality problem without eliminating Serbia; and it has since become the conventional wisdom that the Empire's survival was incompatible with rising nationalism. Yet the force promoting its coherence should not be underestimated. Loyalty to the dynasty (*Kaisertreue*) was strong, not only in the army but among the aristocracy, wide sections of the peasantry, and the Jews. There was widespread opposition, but it was disunited; and no group, however vociferous its demands for national rights, contemplated breaking up the Empire. A policy of patience and perseverance might well have succeeded. In choosing war Austria-Hungary 'committed suicide out of fear of dying'.[39]

A similar judgement might apply to Russia. A rising tide of unrest among the proletariat, reflected in the strike movement, has often been adduced to show that revolution was inevitable. But the strikers were fundamentally anarchic, and rising prosperity might well have served ultimately to reduce that threat too.[40] The economic and social progress of both Empires in the immediate pre-war period was considerable. Between 1904 and 1914 Austria's national income rose by almost 70 per cent in real terms, and Hungary's by 75 per cent. In the Russian Empire the value of production increased by 50 per cent between 1909 and 1913 alone.[41] Increasing wealth offered both Empires a chance of finding a more stable future. The Great War itself destroyed that chance.

The outcome of the war is well known, but the political changes which took place in Russia, the first Great Power to succumb, deserve further attention. The liberally-inclined Provisional Government, which assumed authority following the collapse of Tsarism early in 1917, bore out Durnovo's assessment that the political opponents of the old regime commanded no support in the country. They imagined that their legitimacy depended on their commitment to the 'democratic' cause, and therefore maintained the alliance with Britain and France, continuing a war which had become unpopular. They refused to commit themselves to land reform, which would have gained them some legitimacy, because they lacked a formal mandate to do so, yet they felt they must follow public opinion in declaring a general amnesty, proclaiming not only freedom of speech but freedom to strike, abolishing the police and refusing to use the army to maintain order.[42]

In so doing they threw away the very bases of power on which government depends. Soldiers deserted *en masse* to ensure they received their shares of the great estates, whose break-up they assumed to be the inevitable fruit of the Revolution. Workers took over their factories (at which production often ground to a standstill). Local councils (Soviets) sprang up (as they had done in 1905) and the garrison troops came to regard them, rather than the Provisional Government, as a source of authority. Yet the Soviets were only theatres that provided a stage for popular oratory and were easily manipulated by the only group which had any grasp of political reality. Within a few months, as the Provisional Government lost all grip on the situation and the country descended into chaos, the Bolsheviks were able to stage their *coup d'état*.

As Lenin knew, the Russian masses were merely confused by the vocabulary of democracy and liberalism which had been the stock-in-trade of the Provisional Government.[43] Instead, he offered a highly popular programme expressed in intelligible terms: peace, land, and bread. The available evidence, including the incomplete results of a general election which Lenin decided should be held but then ignored, suggests that the Bolsheviks' popularity in the country was rising fast, even though it was the Social Revolutionaries (in effect the peasants' party) who gained most electoral support. The evidence also suggests that participation in government spelt electoral doom for any party. But Lenin was not prepared to give way to an expression of the popular will, and so the government of Russia remained in the hands of a small, tightly-ruled group of embittered revolutionaries who had temporarily gained control over a mercurial proletariat which was itself alienated from the rest of society.[44]

* * *

The Great War had been a catalyst of change throughout Eastern Europe. Its effects might not have been so catastrophic, however, had the region been less backward industrially and its inhabitants less politically immature. Historians have pointed to more particular weaknesses embedded in the past – the sluggish development of both democracy and education in Russia from the mid-nineteenth century, and the failure to convert Austria-Hungary into a federation of nationalities.[45] But the historical weaknesses were both more wide-ranging and deep-seated. They lay in the region's economic lethargy, its social backwardness, its cultural confusion.

As we have seen, statesmen were aware of these disadvantages, and grappled with them. In the end, however, they were thwarted – by the effects, both direct and indirect, of a population explosion and the no less explosive rise of aggressive modern nationalism. Neither phenomenon had been foreseen in the later eighteenth century, although they had their genesis in that period. From another perspective, of course, it was the morass created by the progressive dissolution of the Ottoman Empire in the Balkans which eventually sucked the whole of Eastern Europe down. But the causes of Ottoman decline, like those which led to the disappearance of the once-great state of Poland, have also to be sought in the decades prior to 1848.

If we turn back to the later eighteenth century we shall find indications of a more hopeful outcome. At that time the Ottoman Empire was more stable and the rulers of all the other empires of Eastern Europe embraced the most advanced ideas of the Enlightenment. They believed in the infinite improvability of man and society, and they pursued policies designed to hasten such improvements. Yet the promise was not fulfilled. How real that promise was, and why it failed, are matters which now call for our attention.

REFERENCES

1. The point, which holds at least for the earlier stages of the development of nationalism, has been argued by E. Niederhauser, *The Rise of Nationality in Eastern Europe* (Budapest, 1981) p. 235.
2. For the powers of the old Estates, see Chapter 7; for the emergence of modern nationalism in the region and its nature, see Chapter 6.
3. Hungarian Declaration of Independence, 14 April 1849, F. Newman (ed.) *Selected Speeches of Kossuth* (London, 1853). Curiously enough Friedrich Engels, who found the Viennese radicals 'economically illiterate' and lacking in class consciousness, regarded the essentially conservative Kossuth as 'Danton and Carnot rolled into one'.
4. See K. Schneider, *Der Reichstag won Kremsier* (Prague, 1927). Since the fighting in Italy and Hungary precluded elections in many parts of these territories, they sent only a handful of representatives who were overwhelmed by Slavs and Germans. Of the 383 members, ninety-four were peasants and many of the rest were sympathetic to their cause.
5. Such measures recalled the 'Enlightened Despotism' of Joseph II in the 1780s. (See Chapter 6). In Hungary the government could not recognize Kossuth's emancipation decree, emanating as it did from an illegitimate, rebellious

regime (nor did it wish at first to displease the smaller serf-owners who, in all other matters, had been Kossuth's chief supporters). But in 1853 it began to enforce its original emancipation law. In Croatia the formal abolition of serfdom came later still, though the system had collapsed in the confusion of 1848 and could not be resurrected.

6. From 1,249 kilometres at the end of 1848 to 4,543 – C. Cipolla (ed.), *The Fontana Economic History of Europe*, vol. 4, part 2 (London, 1973) p. 792.
7. It has been calculated that the average per capita income was 40 per cent higher in 1860 than in 1800, ten times the rate of increase in the rest of Eastern Europe. See I. Berend and G. Ranki, *Underdevelopment in Europe in the Nineteenth Century* (Studia Historica No. 158) (Budapest, 1980) especially pp. 6–7.
8. John Ruskin found the passion of his Venetian friends, who could offer no rational explanation for their hatred of Austrian rule, incomprehensible.
9. I. Udal'tsov, *Ocherki iz istorii natsional'no politicheskoi bor'ba v Chekhii v 1848 godu* (Moscow, 1951) pp. 138ff. (text reproduced on pp. 140–1).
10. For a thorough analysis of peasant emancipation in the Russian Empire see J. Blum, *Lord and Peasant in Russia from the Ninth to the Nineteenth Century* (Princeton, 1961); and G. Robinson, *Russia under the Old Regime* (London, 1932).
11. D. Mitrany, *The Land and Peasant in Romania* (New York, 1968) pp. 51–62. The comparatively small class of slaves had been emancipated in the 1850s.
12. Before long as much as a fifth of all the arable in Hungary was leased.
13. See G. Illyes (trans. G. Cushing), *Petofi* (Budapest, 1973).
14. E. Durham, *The Burden of the Balkans* (London, n.d., c. 1906) p. 117.
15. These tensions are well conveyed in some of the stories of Ion Creanga, e.g. 'Goodman Ion Roata and Prince Cuza', *Memories of my Boyhood* (translated by A. Cartianu and R. Johnston) (Bucharest, 1978) pp. 118–24.
16. See A. Gerschenkron's subtle treatment of the industrialization of the Russian Empire, 'Agrarian Policies and Industrialization: Russia 1861–1917' in H. Habakkuk and M. Postan, eds, *The Cambridge Economic History of Europe* [hereafter *CEHE*] Vol. VI (Cambridge, 1965) pp. 706–800 and other contributions in Vols. VI and VII. Also Gerschenkron's *Europe in the Russian Mirror* (Cambridge, 1970).
17. See B. Mitchell in Cipolla, *op. cit.*, pp. 793–4, 773 and 775.
18. H.C. Barclay, *Bulgaria before the War* (London, 1877) p. 1.
19. J.W. Ozanne, *Three Years in Romania* (London, 1878) pp. 39–41.
20. B. Lukacs, 'Industrie und Handel in Budapest' in *Die Osterreichisch-ungarische Monarchie in Wort und Bild*, Vol. III (Vienna, 1893).
21. Durham, *op. cit.*, p. 125.
22. M. Jovanovic, *Die serbische Landwirtschaft* (Munich, 1906).
23. See A. Carr Saunders, *World Population* (Oxford, 1936) p. 20; fig. 2; C. McEvedy and R. Jones, *Atlas of World Population* (Harmondsworth, 1978); Cipolla, *op. cit.*, Vol. 2, p. 747. The Russian Empire accounts for about half the total. The alarming rise of the population as a whole was anticipated by a rise in the Jewish population from 1.6 million in 1825 to 5.1 million by 1897 despite rising emigration (data kindly furnished by Prof. G. Hundert).
24. *Ibid. Machismo* played a part in some areas. Edith Durham (*High Albania* (London, 1909) p. 252) reports a gypsy boasting that he had fathered thirty-two children, at which someone countered with the story of a Serb 'who is father of twenty-four sons, all by one mother', all grown and bearing arms. To cap this, someone told of a Muslim with forty-two children.

25. See P. Eidelberg, *The Great Romanian Peasant Revolt of 1907* (Leiden, 1974).
26. On the growth of cities, see Cipolla, *op. cit.*, Vol. IV, pt. 2, p. 750.
27. The problems have been interestingly discussed by C. Schorske whose *Fin de Siècle Vienna* (New York, 1981) has provided a basis for the discussion which follows.
28. In a BBC lecture George Steiner has termed it the finest flowering of the arts since the golden age of Athens, but this exaggeration overlooks Renaissance Florence, among much else.
29. On Koerber's policies and their fate see A. Gerschenkron, *An Economic Spurt that Failed* (London, 1977).
30. See P. Hanak, 'Hungary's Contribution to the Monarchy', in G. Ranki, ed., *Hungarian History – World History* (Budapest, 1984) pp. 165–78, and S. Eddie 'On Hungary's Contribution to the Monarchy' in *ibid.*, pp. 191–207.
31. Gerschenkron, *CEHE loc. cit.*, believes it would have succeeded; Soviet historians have tended towards the opposite conclusion.
32. See L. Haimson, 'The Problem of Social Stability in Urban Russia', *Slavic Review*, 23 (4) (1964), pp. 19–42 and 24 (1) (1965), pp. 1–22.
33. See S.V. Zubatov's Report of 9 September 1900, 'Dva dokumenta iz istorii Zubatovshchina', *Krasnyi arkhiv*, Vl (1926) p. 211.
34. P.N. Durnovo to Nicholas II, February 1914, F.A. Golder (ed.), *Documents of Russian History 1914–1917* (New York, 1927) pp. 3–23.
35. Proclamation by Franz Joseph. October, 1908. For the diplomatic preparation and consequences, L. Bittner *et al.*, eds., *Diplomatische Aktenstücke des Osterreichisch-ungarisch Ministerium der Aussen*, I, (Vienna, 1930); for Austrian evidence in support of her claim of beneficial trusteeship see *Bericht über die Verwaltung Bosnien und Hercegovina 1909* (Vienna, 1910).
36. Durham, *High Albania, op. cit.*, pp. 327–8.
37. See Austro-Hungarian Minister for Foreign Affairs Berchtold to the Austrian Minister in Belgrade, 22 July 1914, and the Serbian reply – M. Gornevin de Montgelos and W. Schucking, *Outbreak of the World War: Documents collected by Karl Kautsky* (New York, 1924) pp. 250–4. It is an indication of their political understanding that many Serbian peasants believed that the assassin, Gavrilo Princip, was the illegitimate son of the Crown Princess Stepanie, widow of the Archduke Rudolph who had committed suicide but whom they imagined had been murdered by Franz Ferdinand.
38. For a recent Hungarian contribution on the origins of the Great War, see J. Galantai, *Austria-Hungary and the War* (Studia Historica No. 162) (Budapest, 1980).
39. The phrase is Robert Kann's (*A History of the Habsburg Empire* (Berkeley, 1974), p. 519). The idea that it was nationalism that doomed Austria-Hungary is a hypothesis of A.J.P. Taylor's *The Habsburg Monarchy 1809–1918* (London, 1948).
40. Soviet historians used to interpret the increasing incidence of strikes as proof of impending revolution, but as their futile efforts to call off the general strike of August 1914 indicate, the Bolsheviks had no effective control over the workers.
41. For Austria-Hungary, see F. Herz, *The Economic Problem of the Danubian States* (London, 1947) p. 38, and I. Berend and G. Ranki, *Underdevelopment*, op. cit. For Russia, see Gerschenkron in *CEHE, loc. cit.*. Russia's growth rate of 60 per cent in the period matched that of Europe as a whole, though she ended up lagging 43 per cent behind the average in output. The economies of Romania and Greece grew by 50 per cent and 40 per cent respectively, yet

fell even farther behind in terms of output (40 per cent and 33 per cent respectively). Italy's economic progress resembled theirs.

42. Declaration by the Russian Provisional Government, 3rd–16th March 1917, *Khrestomatiia po istorii SSSR 1861–1917* (Moscow, 1970).
43. This is shown by Marc Ferro in his study of public opinion in the Revolution, see his *The Russian Revolution of 1917* (London, 1972) pp. 112ff. The general level of political sophistication is suggested by the Ural miner who claimed that a republic was really a democracy when it gave the people land and freedom.
44. The case is made by Haimson, *loc. cit.*.
45. See H. Seton-Watson in R. Pipes, ed., *Revolutionary Russia* (London, 1968) pp. 15–20; and the writings of O. Jaszi, especially *Der Zusammenbruch des Dualismus und die Zukunft der Donaustaaten* (Vienna, 1918), on the failure to create a democratic federation of Nationalities.

6

The Age of Reason and Romanticism (1770–1848)

Oh Spring! Memorable to those who witnessed it,
Oh spring of struggle and of plenty.
Oh Spring! To those who witnessed it
Flourishing with grain and grass and shining people,
Crowded with happenings, brimming with hope....

Mickiewicz, *Pan Tadeusz*, Book xi

Thou art Prometheus's only son! ...
It's not your heart the vulture pecks at,
but your brains.

Slowacki, *Pilgrimage*

The later eighteenth century was a period of great promise throughout most of Eastern Europe. This was the age of the Enlightenment, when philosophers believed that man himself, rather than chance or supernatural forces, was master of his destiny, and, at the same time, that human society was an organism capable of infinite improvement. It was an age when emperors and princes, acting on these prescriptions, set out to create a better society. It was the age of reason, when high value was attached to balance, order and refinement; a time when civilization reached a peak never attained since: when the arts flowered magnificently; when, for a member of the *beau monde*, life was truly sweet and beautiful, and when for the members of the lower orders hope of freedom and a better life first dawned.

Before the century was out, however, an antidote to Reason had developed: Romanticism. The Romantics gave primacy to the emotions rather than the mind; thought untamed Nature beautiful, and liked happy disorder, spontaneity, simple people and primitive culture. For them, order was oppressive, tamed Nature unnatural, elite culture contrived. All this caused excitement and provided further stimulus to the arts. But ideas can mutate, and, indeed, in the course of time these did so.

The idea took hold that every language of the common folk, not merely the elite languages of the time (Latin, French and German), embodied an original and valuable spirit; then that language defined nations. And this was to merge with revolutionary sentiments and concepts imported from the West: the ideology of the American Revolution, which drew heavily on the Enlightenment, and that of the French Revolution with its stress on equality and its assaults on privilege and deference. Moreover, Napoleon's campaigns served to discredit institutions and undermine order throughout much of Eastern Europe. After the Restoration of 1815 following Napoleon's defeat, governments tried to control these forces, but their success was only temporary. Enlightenment and Romanticism: thesis and antithesis. Out of the complex interactions of these powerful forces, as well as of the Industrial Revolution, the modern age, the age of democracy, nationalism and belief in endless 'progress' was created. And in the process the sweet notions of the later eighteenth century turned sour.

* * *

The civilization of the Habsburg Empire in the later eighteenth century centred on Vienna in the winter. This was a Vienna of cosmopolitan aristocracy; of noble palaces, often rented for the season but staffed by small armies of servants; of easy manners; of generous entertainments and usually well-judged patronage; the Vienna of Mozart, Gluck and Haydn. At other times of the year the scene moved to the provinces – to the great houses with their parks and libraries; to the hunting lodges; and to those comfortable residences in the smaller towns where official duties had to be performed. This gracious, pleasant style of life was shared, too, by the upper crusts of the Russian Empire and Poland-Lithuania; and it was founded very largely on the institution of serfdom.

> The ... noble [wrote a contemporary observer] ... who is so gallant that in five minutes he has bestowed fifty kisses on a lady's ungloved arm, behaves toward his servants with the utmost harshness and brutality, and if he is taking only a few steps in the morning out of his house into the village or the fields, does not hesitate to take with him a cudgel with which to visit with instant punishment anything that displeases him.[1]

There were also those, like the famous Russian general, V.I. Suvorov, who, in the interests of breeding better stock, decided which of his serfs should marry whom.[2] Even those Enlightened nobles who believed in treating their serfs well were, as a Commission of Enquiry into the condition of peasants in Bohemia concluded, often thwarted by greedy estate managers. And it was not simply the sheer weight of the demands placed on the peasant serfs, particularly in terms of labour service (*robot*), that mattered, but, as a British traveller and agricultural expert, Joseph Marshall, noted in the 1770s,[3] their irregularity – so that some serfs never knew from one season to the next what dues in cash and kind and labour might be expected of him and his family. As a result in Bohemia many

> peasants live in a condition of real slavery; they become savage and brutalized, and cultivate the land in their charge badly. They are rachitic, thin and ragged.... Even their personal effects are not safe from the greed of the great lords....[4]

The condition of serfs was not everywhere as pitiable as in Bohemia. *Droit de seigneur* was not an Eastern European institution (though it may have been practised), and most serfs even in Russia may have enjoyed a healthier diet than used to be be assumed.[5] Nonetheless, peasant discontent fed peasant flight and peasant rebellions, some of which were very costly, not only to the lords involved, but to the state.

Peasants seeking better conditions migrated from Bohemia into Prussia (where serfdom also existed); from Russia into Poland-Lithuania and then in the reverse direction; and from Poland into Prussia too. There were scattered peasant uprisings in Hungary during the 1760s, and serious agrarian disturbances in both Bohemia and Moravia in 1770–1. Considerable numbers of serfs became involved in the Cossack-led Pugachev rebellion in Russia in 1773–5, in a big uprising in Bohemia in 1775 and in the Transylvanian peasant rampage led by Horia in 1784. The state suppressed all of them and meted out draconian and public punishment to their leaders. Nonetheless, the enlightened monarchs of all the states concerned were intent on protecting the peasants and promoting their welfare. Indeed, participants in the later, more serious, rebellions were not completely inventive when they claimed to be carrying out the monarch's intentions.

All four monarchs of the period shared Enlightened principles and disliked serfdom as an institution. Frederick II of Prussia hated it, though he did little about it. Stanislaus Augustus, King of Poland since 1764, also wanted to improve the conditions of the peasantry, but was thwarted by a constitution which hobbled royal power and gave the nobility almost total freedom. Catherine II of Russia did more, though she proceeded cautiously, in the knowledge that she depended on the service nobility, most of whom, in their turn, relied on their serfs for an income. Nevertheless, in 1765 Catherine had given a prize for the best essay discussing the relative advantages of private and public landowning, to be awarded by her new foundation, the Free Economic Society. The winner (of 132 entrants) was a French scholar whose views could hardly have met with the Empress's disapproval.

> The peasants [he wrote] are the foundation of the whole state.... The poorest peasant is more useful than the idle and ignorant miser-courtier. The peasants bring profit to the State mainly from the fact that owing to them population is increased, therefore peasants should possess property inalienably, in order that they should not fear that their children might suffer hunger. Before giving him land, it is necessary to make the peasant personally free. The whole universe demands of the Sovereigns that they should emancipate the peasants....

However, the author also commended a careful approach. The bear, as he put it, had to be tamed before its chains could be removed.[6] The Empress well understood the need for caution; and though the issue was aired and some limitations placed on its extension, action on serfdom was left for the future.

In the Habsburg Monarchy, however, matters were taken farther. The Empress Maria Theresa held peasants to be 'the most numerous class of subjects and the foundation and greatest strength of the state'.[7] She imposed limitations on the ways serfs could be treated, but found that the law was evaded or ignored. Eventually she came to the view that serfdom must be abolished entirely, at least in her Austrian and Czech provinces. Her son and co-regnant, Joseph II, was more equivocal, worried about the impact of emancipation without compensation on the landlords, but nevertheless he was largely responsible for the weighty legislation introduced in Bohemia in the wake of the rebellion there in 1775 which defined, and severely limited, the serfs' obligations.[8]

In the 1780s, after his mother's death, the Emperor went farther, protecting the peasant's rights in manorial courts, and trying to prevent the fragmentation of peasant holdings. Finally, in 1789 he enacted a law introducing a single land tax throughout his dominions, including Hungary. The peasant's liability was to be limited to 30 per cent of the gross yield of his farm: this was to cover all his obligations, whether to the manor, the province or the state. The measure raised such a furore, especially among the nobility of Hungary, that it had to be rescinded.[9] But it was both radical and rational, wholly in the spirit of the Enlightenment.

Wherever it spread in Eastern Europe the Enlightenment took on different forms and emphases; and Enlightened despots like Joseph II sought to do much more than ameliorate the condition of the serfs. The reform of government, in the interests of efficiency and maximizing the state's income, was a priority for all of them; the use of government for purposes of social engineering by means of legal and educational reforms an aim of most. And some also encouraged greater freedom of expression and set out to emancipate religious minorities from long-standing discriminatory disabilities. Yet all the monarchs of the region enjoyed power that was absolute, at least in theory, as did Catherine and Frederick, or set out to acquire it, like Joseph and Stanislaus.

> I believe it to be fundamental [wrote Joseph] to direct the great machine, a single head, even though mediocre, is worth more than ten able men who have to agree among themselves in all their operations.[10]

Yet he thought it right to explain orders as well as give them; to listen to those who held contrary views and try to convince them; and he was concerned to defend his territories and promote their prosperity not simply for dynastic reasons but for his subjects' good. As he wrote in 1783,

> I have not confined myself to simply issuing orders; I have expounded and explained them. With enlightenment I have sought to weaken and with arguments overcome the abuses which had arisen out of ... deeply rooted customs. I have sought to imbue every official of the state with the love I myself feel for the wellbeing of the whole and with enthusiasm for its service .... All one's actions must be motivated by concern for the advantage and the best interests of the greatest number.[11]

At the same time he was interested in efficiency and economy. He required bureaucrats to furnish proof of their qualifications, and ordered his senior officials to submit regular reports on their subordinates (a commonplace in virtually every organization nowadays but by no means so then). He also tried to ensure that neither the bureaucracy nor the army was any larger or costlier than it need be,[12] even though the former was the instrument of his will and the latter had to be capable of withstanding both the rising power of militaristic Prussia to the north and the continuing danger from the Ottoman Empire to the south, as well as ensuring internal order.

He also tried to increase income, following both the fashionable principles of physiocracy, which stressed the importance of agriculture (hence the concern about the peasants) and the well-established ones of cameralism. Like other monarchs in the region of the period he tried to found new industries and trading enterprises, improve communications, break the power of the guilds, and generally to release the productive forces of the people. But it was also the fashion to effect improvements by authoritarian means – so that the attempted 'reconstruction' of the economy and society was accompanied by emergent bureaucracy and by police measures. It is ironic, but nevertheless the case, that the modern 'police state' owes its origins, at least in part, to the desire to improve people's behaviour and hence the civic quality of life – for, of course, the word 'police' itself derives from the civic entity known in ancient Greece as the *polis*.[13]

Police measures included the control of food prices and of vagabonds; the promotion of new crops and of coal (to save the forests); the establishment of poor-houses and orphanages, whose inmates were taught useful crafts; street-cleaning, garbage-disposal, quarantine control, traffic regulation, fire-fighting, and building regulations. Most of this conformed to an older notion of good order that would be pleasing to God,[14] though in carrying out some welfare functions the police were beginning to replace the church; and the whole was infused with a new spirit of rationality and universality. The rules, the number of which tended to increase, were repeatedly publicized and explained, and applied to everyone without exception.

The law is an obvious instrument of reform and the enlightened monarchs set out to fashion it in a rational and progressive spirit. They conjured much with Beccaria, Blackstone and Montesquieu; tried to codify existing laws and improve the administration of justice. In the end, Stanislaus of Poland, Catherine and Joseph all failed in their attempts to produce codifications. However, a Prince of Wallachia produced one in 1780; a Prussian Law Code was issued in 1794; and both Catherine and Joseph reformed the criminal law in conformity with enlightened principles.

Education was perceived not only as a way of creating cadres of potential bureaucrats but as a means of improving society by creating honest, obedient and useful citizens in much greater numbers. More schools were founded (sometimes at the church's expense) and schooling was to an extent systematized. In Russia education for the nobility was already compulsory, but the only recourse for peasants was the traditional one of the parish school (if there was one). In Poland, King Stanislaus, within a year of his accession, established the first secular school in order to educate young gentlemen in enlightened principles, and in 1773 he set up a Commission for National Education. Funded by the expropriated property of the Jesuits, whose Order had just been dissolved by the Pope, it was intended to create a system of public schools, though suitably qualified teachers as well as text books were so scarce that the great hopes of its instigators were disappointed.

Building upon a basis laid by his mother, Maria Theresa, Joseph II was much more successful. He abolished privileged noble schools but promoted elementary education on a massive scale, founding schools which would admit children regardless of class, and some especially for Serbs and Romanians. As a result a higher percentage of children received a schooling in the Habsburg domains than anywhere else in Europe. However, the Emperor was careful to control the curriculum. Anticipating his Soviet successors, he favoured science at the expense of the classics, and in the universities, too, he stressed the 'practical arts' such as engineering, economics, medicine and mining. Furthermore, conscious that his subjects spoke several different languages, he encouraged German and insisted on its use at secondary level, so that the army and the bureaucracy would be plentifully supplied with young men versed in a single administrative language. The beneficiaries tended to be grateful for the opportunities for advancement that this offered. However, the imposition of German as the administrative language of Hungary produced a fierce reaction, which was to lead to the abandonment of Latin and the emergence of a modern nationalism based on Magyar.

As in Gorbachev's Russia, ambitious reform programmes designed to promote autonomy and initiative were thought to require not only propaganda but more freedom of expression, more openness. Catherine II tried to stimulate discussion of major issues in various ways, including publication; so did Stanislaus, and in 1781 Joseph II went so far as to order censorship to be relaxed. Obscene, libellous and anti-Catholic works were to be suppressed, but criticism, even of the Emperor himself, was to be permitted, as were periodicals that contained objectionable passages provided that they were 'as a whole useful'.[15] And in pursuance of openness these monarchs did not always stand on ceremony. Joseph was notorious for his approachability, allowing anyone, of whatever rank, to accost him with his, or her, ideas and problems; and Frederick II opened his own mail rather than let his staff sift it for him. Enlightened principles also implied at least a degree of religious toleration on the ground that such minorities were also of potentially greater value to the state.

So Joseph emancipated Protestants and Orthodox Christians, and relieved the Jews of many of their disabilities. Though Catholicism remained the established church, all Christians except for adherents of the more extreme sects were now allowed to build their own churches and schools, and accorded the same rights as Catholics without having to take oaths against their consciences. Jews no longer had to pay special taxes or wear yellow bands or ribbons, and could engage in agriculture and practice any trade or profession. But this tolerance was not universally welcomed by the beneficiaries, since, in the interests of rationality they were expected to abandon Hebrew and, in effect, Yiddish, in all but strictly religious activities; and because the state threatened to interefere in the running of Jewish schools.[16]

In Protestant Prussia the church itself was receptive to the Enlightenment, and the emancipation of the Jews was at least mooted. In Orthodox Russia membership of (though not apostasy to) most other Christian churches was tolerated, and a sanctuary was created at Polotsk for Jesuits fleeing from neighbouring countries. But toleration was not extended to Jews; and in Poland, despite King Stanislaus, both

Protestants and Orthodox Christians were oppressed. This popular intolerance was to play its part in the disappearance of Poland-Lithuania, one the Europe's largest states, by the end of the century.

The partitions of Poland are popularly regarded as regressive, as violating the rights of the Polish people and the spirit of the Enlightenment. It is anachronistic, however, to apply the twentieth-century principle of national self-determination to the eighteenth, and to a population which was not yet nationally self-aware. In any case Poland-Lithuania constituted a political power vacuum which invited foreign interference. The authority of the elected kings had been so much whittled away over the centuries that they had long since enjoyed the trappings of power without the substance. They were merely 'painted monarchs'. By contrast, the power of the great landowners, the magnates, had become virtually unlimited. And many of these magnates had long looked to one or another of the neighbouring powers, rather than to their own king, for protection, thus emphasizing the centrifugal process and encouraging these powers to interfere in Poland's affairs. As a result Poland had been more or less firmly in Russia's sphere of influence for half a century.

Stanislaus Augustus, its King since 1764, had been one of Catherine's lovers, and had the support of Russian bayonets as well as the less certain backing of the powerful Czartoryski faction among the Polish nobility. Stanislaus, however, was not content to remain a 'painted monarch'. He wanted his throne to be made hereditary rather than elective, to increase his standing army, which numbered only 1,000 men, and to enact a series of constitutional reforms to strengthen central authority. His sponsor Catherine was only prepared to countenance some limited reforms, for she was anxious not to offend those Polish magnates who tended towards Russia or the Polish gentry generally who were so jealous of their 'Golden Liberty'. Nor dared she alienate her ally Frederick of Prussia (who coveted some Polish territory which separated his own dominions); and Frederick did not want a stronger Poland. It was in this context that the question of religious toleration arose.[17]

Prussia evinced concern about Protestants in Poland, Russia about the Orthodox. In 1767 parties, or Confederations, were formed in defence of both confessions. The Catholic supremists also organized, and, when the toleration of religious minorities seemed to be in the offing, created an outcry. Some of their leaders were arrested by the Russian troops on whom King Stanislaus depended. Eventually his government carried out limited constitutional reforms – but in 1769, when it seemed that Russian troops would leave the country, matters swiftly descended into chaos. An armed insurrection was organized, aimed at reasserting Catholic supremacy and reinstating the old constitution. As the movement spread, Orthodox Ukrainian peasants rose in revolt against their Polish masters – and then the Turks took the opportunity to declare war on Russia.

Russian troops, together with the tiny Polish army (which was entirely non-noble in composition), managed to restore order in the south-east, but oppositionist gentry rose against the government elsewhere, and then the Turks' ally, France, sent in money and military advisers to help them. It was the summer of 1772 before they were completely suppressed. In the three years of anarchy that intervened, innumerable private wars had been fought, chiefly between landlords over the possession of serfs; thousands of peasants had fled into neighbouring Silesia, Prussia and Russia; and Frederick had taken the opportunity of moving troops into those regions of Poland he coveted the most, including the basin of the River Vistula.

He kept them by the terms of the ensuing deal between the Powers that came to be known as the First Partition of Poland. Russia acquired western Belorussia and Habsburg Austria the southern areas, subsequently known as Galicia. Russia gained the most territorially, Austria the most population, and Prussia the most strategically; but it was also a reverse for Russia. She would have preferred to have kept Poland whole and within her sphere of influence as before. Had it not been for the Turkish war, which continued until 1774, she might have succeeded.[18] However, the King of Poland was still Catherine's friend.

The partition helped promote a revival in what remained of Poland. The loss of the Vistula basin encouraged a reorientation of trade towards the south. There was a canal-building boom and new industries developed. The population began to increase fast. That of Warsaw grew from 30,000 in the 1760s to 120,000 in the 1790s. The King accreted rather more power, the army was increased to 17,000 men and the government was partially systematized. The mid-and late 1770s also saw the tabling of other Enlightened legislation. However, reform was bitterly opposed at every step by vested interests. One conservative Polish landowner (who spoke for others of his kind not only in Poland but in Hungary and elsewhere) was convinced, with some justification, that the King's reforms would destroy the old Polish values and the dominance of his class. If the King had his way he would

> establish a new educational system so that the young would become prejudiced against [Golden] Liberty; incite the serfs in order to suppress the noble order … and place a yoke on the necks of both; extort taxes to … weaken leading personages and affluent families thus preventing … [their] coming to Freedom's rescue; question hereditary rights and noble property in order to get everyone enmeshed in the law; use … the courts to get his opponents under his thumb and fill the army with foreigners, persons with no sympathy for [golden] liberty, and have them at his call to suppress it.[19]

In 1780 parliament (*Sejm*) rejected the draft legal code which the Chancellor, Andrew Zamoyski, had submitted to it with the backing of the King, and ruled that it must never be presented again. On the other hand Stanislaus now seemed able to keep order in Poland, and so in the same year Russian troops were finally withdrawn, though the Russian ambassador continued to be a powerful influence at court.

The calm, which lasted approximately eight years, was shattered by a combination of international and domestic shifts. In 1788 the Turks made a preemptive strike against Russia; then Prussia offered Poland an alliance (in effect directed against Russia). More Polish magnates were moving into the Prussian camp, though another political element, which was both anti-Russian and reformist, had also emerged among the nobility. In October the *Sejm* voted to take over command of the army from the King's men, increase it to 100,000 men, and even to impose a tax on land. Russia protested but, embroiled in her Turkish war, was in no position to challenge what was in essence a *coup* in Prussia's interests.

That *coup* was followed in 1791 by another, this time by the reformists, an increasing number of whom were proponents of the King. The resulting Constitution restored some representation to the cities, which had been excluded from national politics for two centuries, and gave some protection to the serfs, though it emancipated neither them nor the Jews. It also made the crown hereditary, abolished the convention by which a single member of the *Sejm* could veto legislation and dissolve the assembly, and another by which a group of dissident nobles could organize a Confederation to raise a legal rebellion against the government. Nevertheless, in April 1792 furious conservatives formed just such a Confederation at Targowica in the far south-east. Large numbers of lesser gentry rallied to them – as did Catherine of Russia, whose hands had just been freed by the conclusion of a peace with the Turks.

Catherine, who had expressed satisfaction at Corsica's rebellion against France and that of the Americans against Britain, was alarmed by the radical development of the French Revolution. She did not want it echoed in Poland. Moreover Prussia (which had guaranteed Poland's integrity in 1790) now demanded compensation, at Poland's expense, for bearing the brunt of the war against revolutionary France. The upshot was the Second Partition of 1793 by which Prussia gained the rest of western Poland and Russia the remainder of Ukraine and Belorussia. However, this step, which Catherine took out of fear of revolution in Poland, in fact served to promote it.

The sense of outrage and the confusion produced by the Second Partition gave rise to more radical Polish movements. Tadeusz Kosciuszko represented a patriotic but moderate stream of opposition to the regime of the emasculated Stanislaus. A scion of minor gentry, he was a military engineer who had risen to the rank of general serving with the Americans in their War of Independence. Early in 1794, when the government began to reduce the army and arrest opponents, Kosciuszko proclaimed insurrection at Cracow and assumed dictatorial powers. He at once proclaimed a *levée en masse*, and accorded all serfs who enlisted personal freedom. He had visited Paris the year before, trying, in vain, to raise French support for a Polish revival. Yet Kosciuszko was a patriotic radical rather than a revolutionary in the new mould.

The Polish officers who took control of Wilno, however, were much more extreme. So were the members of the Jacobin Club (chiefly poor gentry, army officers, lawyers, journalists and priests) that had been formed in Warsaw. They whipped up a degree of popular revolutionary fervour, and publicly hanged a number of magnates associated with the by now notorious Confederation of Targowica, and at least one bishop. Prussian and Russian troops approached; the crowd in Warsaw became more excited; there were lynchings. Kosciuszko restored order. The siege of Warsaw was broken, the Prussian troops chased away, and Kosciuszko marched out to confront the fast-approaching Russians. He was defeated. Within a year the Final Partition was agreed between the three Powers and Poland vanished.

Most Polish landowners hastened to offer loyalty to their new sovereigns for fear of being dispossessed. Many younger Polish gentry went into exile, some to France where they formed the famous Polish Legion which was to distinguish itself in so many of Napoleon's campaigns from Italy to Russia. However, like the Irish and Scottish 'Wild Geese' of earlier times, many of them left as much out of a need to earn a livelihood as a wish to restore the old regime by fighting for another state.

As for the victors, Austria pushed her frontiers northwards again, almost as far as Warsaw; in gaining a rational frontier to the west, Russia gained vast tracts of territory and a further large accretion of population that included few Poles or Catholics, but a great many Orthodox and Jews (the Pale of Settlement was instituted at this time to prevent them migrating eastwards into Russia proper). Ironically, most of the core of the old Poland fell to Prussia, which had once been a Polish vassal. And it is ironic, too, that both historical precedent and its now huge Polish-speaking population might well have led Prussia to become as much a Polish as a German state.[20] That it did not do so is one of the many paradoxes of that extraordinary age which saw the French Revolution and the Napoleonic Wars.

These events, once viewed by liberals in a wholly positive light, now seem much less conducive to human advancement. The Revolution in France certainly invited monarchs, however enlightened, to give a higher priority to security than to reform – and especially after Louis XVI and

Marie Antoinette (sister of Joseph II) had been guillotined in 1793. Nevertheless, it was not the Revolution that forced Joseph to retract so much of his own reform programme in 1790.[21] True, he faced rebellion by his subjects in what is now Belgium, on France's doorstep. But that revolt had started in 1787 (and it was Prussia that encouraged the Belgians to declare independence in January 1790). Joseph's failure was partly due to an unfortunate concatenation of events which had only tenuous connections with France.

He faced opposition in Hungary as well as Belgium, and a war with the Turks so costly as to cause many of his subjects to become restless, even the Hungarian peasants whom he was determined to help. However, he was to a great extent the architect of his own failure. His treaty obligation to Russia obliged him to send 30,000 men against the Turks, not the 200,000 which he in fact committed at huge cost;[22] the Belgian secession might have been prevented had he made concessions earlier than November 1789; and his steadfast refusal to convoke the Hungarian Diet, knowing it to represent the mostly reactionary landlord interest, only intensified opposition to him there. In the end, by refusing to provide the recruits and supplies that were by now essential to him, the nobles forced him to yield. In January 1790 he conceded the Diet's right to a role in decision-making. He also returned the Holy Crown of Hungary, which he had never worn (since a coronation would have implied that the Diet represented an autonomous state); and revoked most of his legislation that effected Hungary. His ambition of forging a rational, unitary state remained unfulfilled. Joseph died just over three weeks later.

Hungary had been his nemesis, yet the failure was to a large extent invited. Joseph was tactless and precipitate; too much of an ideologue, too little of a politician. As one of his chief advisers commented,

> Over-hasty decisions, despotic behaviour, obsession with innovations, contempt for ... other courts, ... ambitious projects which advertized hazardous aims or gave cause for alarm aroused antipathy and distrust everywhere.[23]

His successor, Leopold II, also subscribed to the Enlightenment. He reformed the penal code, shaped the police into more of a public service than a security agency (its secret police element, recently increased, was cut back), and set about improving the educational system. He avoided both war and offending the more powerful interest groups; but retained as many of Joseph's reforms as he possibly could. Unfortunately he reigned for only two years. It was under his son, Francis, whose haunted face stares out from his portraits in Vienna's Hofburg Palace, that the rot took hold.

It was not only the French Terror that threatened the prevailing order in Eastern Europe, frightful though it was, but the philosophy of the

Revolution – in particular its rejection of accreted tradition, and its elevation of the wishes and interests of 'the people' to the status of the supreme value. It was a crude variation of the classical democratic ideal, and one which, as the contemporary Edmund Burke noted, rudely tore away 'all the decent drapery of life'.

Poland had already had a taste of Jacobin extremism but the government of Francis was determined to nip any such development in the bud. As a precaution the Freemasons were suppressed, and in 1795 two groups of subversives were brought to trial in Vienna and Budapest. The inspirer of the more serious conspiracy was Ignac Martinovics, former friar, army chaplain, professor of natural history and secret agent of the crown. His followers (as with the Polish 'Jacobins') were chiefly minor gentry and army officers. Their aim was to overthrow the Habsburgs and introduce a new republican and liberal order: peasants were to be recognized as citizens, and all citizens were to be equal regardless of class. However, the nobility would return half the members of the Diet, none but nobles would have the right to own land, and peasant serfs would continue to do labour service (*robot*) on their masters' estates. Liberty, then, was interpreted only in a collective sense, and largely in the interests of the collectivity of lesser nobles.

Yet this 'Secret Society of Reformers' was evidently intent on gaining wider support, for it drew up a catechism of questions and answers for their recruits to learn (as the Decembrist conspirators were to do in Russia a generation later). These priests of revolution were determined to educate ordinary folk in the correct secular doctrines. This was far from the practice of enlightenment and reason, and yet it was not only the influence of revolutionary France but, paradoxically, the work of enlightened despots like Joseph that inspired the ferment.

By invoking reason to justify his reforms, Joseph intimated that the human mind, and not the deity, was the ultimate sanction. But reason can be invoked by anyone to legitimate almost any action. Furthermore, although Joseph was a practising Catholic, he differed from his predecessors, who had used the Church as an instrument of state and sometimes exploited it,[24] in excluding it from the realm of public policy. This further reduced the power of divine sanction to hold his subjects in thrall. By setting off the juggernaut of 'progress', by intervening in more and more aspects of life, Enlightened governments ultimately encouraged the view that every wrong could be righted, every grievance assuaged; that the human condition was susceptible to infinite improvement – and that if the state failed to procure it, it should be replaced by another, more 'progressive' regime.

And there were other consequences of Enlightened thinking, that encouraged a different stream of opposition. In elevating reason, the emotions were neglected; and in denying religion its mystic dimension, the view was encouraged that worship was a matter of formality. This may have reduced the churches' capacity to act as safety valves for social discontent. At any rate, rationalism was coming to be regarded, not least in some intellectual and artistic circles, as too mechanical and drab; as restricting the imagination, stifling the human spirit, and rejecting the sublime. Those who thought along these lines were called Romantics. The pendulum had begun to swing away from reason.

* * *

Romanticism found expression firstly in the arts. Beethoven, the younger Pushkin and Mickiewicz were all exponents of it, and the major part of the educated classes of Eastern Europe soon became connoisseurs of the Romantic genres – the majesty of mountains, the simple beauty of a peasant's song, the emotions, not least of melancholy, induced by some newly-discovered epic (like that of the spurious Ossian). The Romantic movement encouraged respect for primitive and popular culture; it also gave rise to cultural nationalism. J.G. Herder, one of the more ardent followers of the late eighteenth-century enthusiasm for collecting folk songs, popularized the view that nations express themselves in ballads, folk-tales, customs, and traditions, and that every particular language embodied a unique spirit, without which the world would be impoverished. On a visit to Riga, he had formed the view that Latvian folklore might be drowned in the prevailing sea of German. Herder's enthusiasm for conservation caught on to become an influential source of modern nationalism.[25] But there were others, including the work of enlightened educational reformers.

Czechs benefiting from new educational opportunities learned German, for example, and were thus able to devour the classics of German Romanticism. The University of Buda Press, founded in 1777, not only printed the first good Hungarian grammars but soon began to publish in Serbian, Slovak and Romanian. A grammar was vital to the definition of a single, literary language on which a sense of linguistic nationhood could be based (a collection of contrasting dialects could form no such basis). Furthermore, publication in a variety of emerging literary languages was to help spread a consciousness of a linguistic identity.[26]

The march of the French armies into Eastern Europe also stimulated a rise of national consciousness. Napoleon's creation of a province of 'Illyria' and a Duchy of Warsaw encouraged more people to think in terms of some sort of national independence, though he disappointed the hopes of his Polish followers. Moreover his conquests stimulated patriotic reactions which, in Prussia, began to develop into a German national feeling. The repeated defeats and humiliations suffered by

Francis (who not only lost territories, but his ancient title of Holy Roman Emperor, and had to marry one of his daughters to the Corsican upstart) damaged the aura of unassailable majesty that had been carefully created around the House of Habsburg in the seventeenth century.[27] No doubt this encouraged the idea that an alternative republican, and perhaps national, form of state might be feasible. However, the Hungarians spurned Napoleon's invitation to rebel.

It should be stressed, however, that this stage of budding nationalism also drew on older concepts of group identification. Both Poles and Hungarians were to take pride in the traditions of the 'noble nation' (though not the Czechs whose nobility had been effectively Germanized). Recognizing the sense of identity (and superiority) that genealogy can give, enthusiasts set out to provide their nationalities with atavistic pedigrees, preferably ones that stretched back to ancient times. Attempts were also made to extend traditional loyalties to village and locality to all the territory inhabited by 'the folk'; and priests played an important role in the rise of Balkan and especially Polish nationalism. Indeed, in the Polish case, exiled poets were to develop the mystical notions that Poles were God's chosen people, that Poland was the Christ among nations, the crucified Messiah who would be resurrected; the saviour of mankind.

The nation-makers included philologists, historians and archaeologists as well as poets – for the people had to be persuaded to use a standard language that was, as far as possible, free from 'foreign' influences; and taught about the nation's heroic past. In most cases both the sense of the nation and loyalty to it had to be created.[28] This proved to be a slow process. For decades to come Bohemian villagers were to speak Czech and German dialects which were sometimes unintelligible to sophisticates from Prague who spoke proper Czech and *Hochdeutsch*. The first volume of the anti-German Palacky's history was published in German, not Czech; and when Hungarian enthusiasts eventually translated the *Marseillaise* they rendered it not into Magyar, but into the official language of the Hungarian Diet, Latin.

Literacy, then, was a key factor in the rise of nationalism, and in particular the literacy of the 'middle class' of poorer nobles (the magnates still tended to be cosmopolitan), junior civil servants, officers, seminarists and poorer clergy. Jacobinism had attracted elements of the same groups. Indeed Ferenc Kazinczy, one of Martinovics's co-conspirators, was to assume a pioneering role in the creation of a Hungarian literary language once he was released from gaol.[29] The size of this nascent intelligentsia continued to increase, for the Emperor Francis, determined though he was to keep revolutionary forces at bay, continued to promote education. Following in the tradition of Enlightened Despotism, he extended the educational system and even encouraged teaching in local vernaculars in order to spread 'useful knowledge'. However, the emphasis was placed firmly on technical subjects. The dissemination of ideas was severely discouraged.

As matters turned out, the policy contained two unforeseen weaknesses. At the elementary level the poorly-paid teachers constituted the sort of intellectual proletariat that was susceptible to radical ideas. Schoolteachers were to be major carriers of the nationalist virus throughout Eastern Europe. The second weakness concerned the exclusion of philosophy in favour of theology (a policy that was to be followed by Soviet regimes, too, of course). This created a hunger for forbidden fruits in people who lacked the capacity to digest them properly. Thus, Russian army officers who attended German or French universities after the Napoleonic wars, the scions of the nobility who followed them from all parts of Eastern Europe, and the as yet small number of political exiles alike tended to latch on to the more fashionable and powerful philosophical ideas without always understanding their intellectual context or being able to assess them critically. The idealist Fichte, with his stress on the importance of the ego and of nationhood, had a considerable influence, the works of his more subtle master, Kant, much less. Rousseau had a wider appeal than Montesquieu; and this preference was paralleled in the taste for poetry.

Byron enjoyed huge popularity, greater, even, than he did in England; greater probably than any other poet. It was not only the power of his poetry and the messages it carried that made him so, but the attitudes and qualities that he exemplified in his person and his life – his contempt for propriety, not least sexual propriety, his alienation from society, his defiance of authority, his contempt alike for reason, moderation and defeat, and his apparently heroic death at Missolonghi. Byron represented advanced Romanticism translated into action, and he had many imitators in Eastern Europe, Lermontov and Petofi among them, in life as well as poetry. Indeed there was hardly another region of the world where Byron made a deeper or longer-lasting impression The effects, including a pervasive sense of discontent, and tendencies to rebelliousness, cynicism and posturing, have been noticeable in dissident and nationalist movements down to our own times.

The Romantic cult of childhood also influenced the character of emergent nationalism. For Rousseau, children inhabited an ideal state of nature, unsullied by civilization. Children were pristine, spontaneous, free and therefore happy. Vuk Karadzic, who did much to create Serbian national feeling, certainly believed childhood to be the best time of life. For him it was 'the happiest condition known to mortals'. It was in childhood, when he had spent much time on the mountainside tending sheep and goats, that Vuk had learned the Serbian ballads which he was to publish for the first time. They had been sung, he tells us, 'by innocent hearts, naturally and without artifice'.[30] In the cult of childhood we find a source of the sentimentality and the wilfulness, the joy, the tantrums and the follies that have characterized nationalist movements in the twentieth century.

Emergent nationalism was also marked by a sense of inferiority. A desperate concern arose that the linguistic nation with which one felt affinity should not be shown to be culturally inferior to any other. In 1817, following the examples of James Macpherson ('Ossian') and Thomas Chatterton, Hanka manufactured some Czech mediaeval epic poetry. He intended them as proof that the Czechs were at least as advanced as Germans in the Middle Ages – and they were widely believed to be genuine. Indeed, Hanka's inventions gave such a great fillip to Czech pride that many decades were to pass before Tomas Masaryk finally persuaded nationalists that they were spurious. Nor could members of the newer nations bear to think of the ancestors of any rival clan inhabiting 'their' land before them. So Greeks were to be persuaded that they were descended directly from the ancient Greeks with no taint of Slavic blood; Romanians that they derived from the interbreeding of two distinguished stocks, Dacians and Romans; while both Romanians and Hungarians claimed historical heroes like John Hunyadi as their own.[31]

The development of communications gave further impetus to this race for national prestige. Under Napoleon the roads in Europe were much improved and, with the Restoration, came the cutting of more canals, the construction of the first railways, and the erection of more factories. In the course of these works graves were disturbed and a variety of objects unearthed, which antiquarians fell upon with great eagerness, placing them in museums and explaining them to new, local historical societies. Not infrequently these curiosities were used to 'prove' a nation's claim to prior occupation or high culture, and then to present a contrast between a glorious past and a decadent present.[32] Such beliefs both conferred a sense of self-respect upon members of a nation, and explained the pervasive sense of inferiority.

It was presumably some such sense that led Petofi to reject his mother-tongue, Slovak, in favour of Magyar, the language of the local elite. In Eastern Europe's many linguistically mixed areas nationality was still largely a matter of choice. In time competition for national recruits intensified and so did the venom with which national 'renegades' were treated. But which groups constituted which nations were as yet largely unresolved questions. Palacky, for example, envisaged not a Czech, but an homogenous Slavic state that could resist German and Hungarian alike. And paradoxically, the multi-national Empires, which Herder had regarded as monstrosities, were partly responsible for the pattern of nationalities that eventually emerged.

Fear that her Slavic-speaking subjects might succumb to the blandishments of neighbouring Russia led Austria to restore Polish to the curriculum and to encourage the teaching of Ruthenian (Ukrainian) in Galicia. It also promoted Romanian, Serbian and Slovak as a lever to use against Hungarian assertiveness. Indeed, it had been an imperial censor who first encouraged Vuk Karadzic to collect Serbian folk-songs to show Slavs, who might otherwise lean to Russia, how benign Austrian rule was. Fear of Russia also led Vienna to counter Panslavism — so it began actively to encourage Czech national culture; but it supported Ljudovit Gaj, too, when, in 1835, he launched a Croat national movement, because it promised to be another useful counterweight to the Hungarians.

Gaj's rhetoric showed how far the concept of nationalism had changed since Herder, sixty years before. Rather than cultural and conservationist, it was becoming social and aggressive; instead of envisaging a happy harmony between each nation, it preached hatred of other nations on the grounds that they threatened the survival of one's own:

> Hold together, be one! Born heroes, unfurl your banners, gird you with your swords, mount your steeds! Forward, brothers, God is with us, against us the Devil. See how the wild Tatar race, the Magyar, tramples on our tongue, our nation: but before he crushes us, let us cast him into the pit of Hell.... Let us wash our honour clean in the blood of the enemy; let each cleave one skull and our suffering will be at an end.... [33]

Gaj's words reflected a Romantic view of history; they also drew on the imagery of religious war, and in a tone familiarly associated with the Ottoman Balkans, where chaotic warring and bloodshed had become almost commonplace. And in the Ottoman Balkans of the period we encounter a singular situation in which a soldiery ceased to create mayhem among the civil population only when it was fighting Austria and Russia; and the paradox of nation states being formed before their populations had reached national consciousness. The two phenomena were associated.

The problem of the Balkans which, as we have seen, was to be a major preoccupation of the powers in the later nineteenth century, was already in evidence a century before. The Habsburg and Russian Empires, though sometimes cooperating against the Turks, were also becoming concerned that the other did not gain too much of an advantage in the Balkans. Russia regarded itself as the protector of Christians under Ottoman rule, most of whom were Orthodox, and its wars with the Turks (1768–74, 1787–92 and 1806–12) tended to take on the guise of religious warfare. The fervour of the Turks in this was no whit less than among their enemies, and the troops that were most fearsome were the janissaries. Unfortunately in times of peace they had become as much a threat to domestic order as they were to enemies in time of war.

Once highly-disciplined troops who were forbidden to marry, the janissaries had become a swollen hereditary caste (by 1800 as many as 400,000 people claimed the status). Unable to pay them adequately, the state had long since allowed them to supplement their pay by engaging in trades and crafts, but this had had an adverse effect on discipline while failing to yield all of them sufficient income.[34] When they became a threat to public order in the cities, many of them were posted to the countryside. But this served merely to spread disorder and increase the resentment of the Balkan Christians, most of whom, unlike the Muslim elite, resided in the countryside. As government dwindled the number of bandits increased (called *klephts* in the Greek, *hajduks* in the Bulgarian mountains), as did Christian self-defence units which the government sometimes licensed. But so did the size of private renegade armies run by local strong men (*ayans*).

The breakdown of order in the Ottoman Balkans, to which the janissaries contributed much, had become such a problem to the underresourced central government in Istanbul that in the last years of the eighteenth century it had little option but to co-opt some of these *ayans* into the formal structure of government and appoint them *pashas* (governors) of the districts they in fact controlled. Among them was an Albanian called Ali, who had been a bandit in youth and had since built up a power base at Janina. The Sultan appointed him *pasha* in 1788. Another, Pasvanoglu Osman, was an experienced bandit and soldier who, when the Russian war ended in 1792, formed a private army of discontented soldiers, renegades and outlaws and by 1795 controlled much of the lower Danube valley from his capital Vidin.

By 1799, thanks partly to Napoleon's foray into the Middle East which forced the government in Istanbul to divert many of its more reliable troops from the Balkans, Pasvanoglu Osman had been able to extend his power into both Serbia and the Romanian Principalities, at that time governed on behalf of the Sultan by Greeks from Istanbul (*Phanariotes*). The Sultan recognized Pasvanoglu as Pasha of Vidin. At the same time, however, he promoted Ali of Janina, who had meanwhile consolidated his control of Epirus, Thessaly and Albania, to be *pasha* of all Greece (Rumeli) – and used him against Pasvanoglu.

These *ayans* were usually able to impose order and protect their own. Matters were much worse in those localities where authority was in dispute, where rival *ayans* vied for power and gangs of janissaries and irregulars ran amuck. One such was Serbia. The Serbs had come to yearn for peace and order. So far from wanting independence, they seem to have been content with Ottoman rule – provided that rule was effective. All Istanbul could offer them, however, was an opportunity to help themselves. Towards the end of the century Ottoman Serbs were given permission to collect their own taxes and form their own militia. The Turks also promised to reform the share-cropping system which had become a source of grievance. In return for this package the Serbs were ready enough to promise loyalty.

Unfortunately the government could not deliver on its promises. The situation deteriorated and when, in 1802, janissaries seized control, civil war broke out in Serbia. The murder of some leading Serbs led to a mass flight to the mountains where, in the winter of 1803–4, they formed a scratch army under Karadjordje (Black George) Petrovic, defeated forces that moved against them, and in 1806 captured Belgrade. This was the beginning of the first successful independence movement in Eastern Europe: yet it had not been directed against the Sultan, who was widely regarded as legitimate, but against his agents. After years of chaotic struggle the Turks granted Serbia full autonomy in 1830. Even so, this was hardly a victory for nationalism. Karadjordje was a livestock dealer who had seen military service. He was a nationalist neither in the Herderian nor the modern sense.

Another rebel leader, Tudor Vladimirescu, presents a similar case. A former commander of militia (*pandouri*) and livestock dealer who often visited Habsburg territory, he was a man of wide experience but no formal education. And though a Wallachian patriot, he was hardly a Romanian nationalist. His appeal was not to a community of national culture but to economic interest:

> How long shall we suffer the dragons that swallow us alive, those above us, both clergy and politicians, to suck our blood? How long shall we be enslaved? ... Neither God nor the Sultan approves of such treatment of their faithful subjects. Therefore, brothers, come and deal out evil to bring evil to an end....[35]

Taxation being regarded as blood-sucking, Vladimirescu was appealing to peasants in the language of peasants. And the peasants that responded to his appeals betrayed no nationalist conviction. They behaved like any peasant rebels: they looted and burned down the houses of the serf-owning *boiars*.

A critical factor in the emergence of an independent Romania was Russia, which had not only maintained an ancient claim to protect all Balkan Christians, but from 1826 became the protector of the Danubian Principalities of Wallachia and Moldavia, and occupied them until 1834. But the founders of Romanian nationalism were the scions of the nobility who had been educated in Paris. The consequences were sometimes incongruous – bearded Romanian *boiars* in flowing robes being driven by coachmen dressed as hussars. In the opinion of a British visitor,

> the combination of Oriental and European manners and costume is irresistibly ludicrous. The boyar looks like a grave Mahometan, but speak to him, and he will address you in tolerable French, and talk of novels, faro and whist.[36]

The drafting of a new, foreign, elite culture upon a traditional, patriarchal and largely rural culture was to create tensions, described in some of Creanga's short stories, which persist to the present day.

Much had to be done to 'purify' the Romanian language and establish historical roots for the Romanian nation, but the Romanians at least had an indigenous elite, their *boiars*. Neighbouring Bulgarians lacked such an indigenous nobility. Increasing disorder and distress in their part of the Balkans led to continuing growth of the *hajduk* (bandit) population, but, ironically, it was not until the 1830s and 1840s, by which time the janissaries had been disbanded and the region's agriculture had begun to prosper from international trade, that national feelings associated with language began to emerge. Even then most Bulgarian journals were published in Istanbul. Moreover, it was difficult for Bulgarians to think in terms of liberation other than through the church, which was dominated by Greeks, so that Bulgarian national feeling emerged almost as much in reaction to the Greeks as to the Turks.[37]

The Greeks themselves present a different case, for they included important mercantile and administrative classes. These elements formed a cultural community of sorts, but they were distanced from the common people, who had also built up a tradition of self-defence, especially in the mountain areas and some of the islands. The Greek elite was also widely dispersed geographically. Their trading network ramified throughout the Mediterranean, the Balkans and the Black Sea littoral, while the Phanariotes staffed much of the Ottoman diplomatic service and bureaucratic machine besides ruling the Romanian principalities (often corruptly, but sometimes in the spirit of enlightened despotism). The Greek elite constituted fertile ground both for conspiracy and manipulation by foreign powers.

The Greek diaspora extended to Paris, and beyond; and French agents had been active in the Greek world since the later 1790s. Revolutionary notions were to grip members of the merchant class (though not the more substantial of them), some Orthodox clergy (though few bishops), and even an occasional potentate in the Ottoman service. But it was on Russian, not French soil, that the Greek revolution got off the ground. In 1814 expatriate Greeks formed a friendly society (*Philiki Etairia*) in Odessa. Like others founded earlier in Paris and Vienna its aims were cultural; unlike them, however, it aimed to liberate 'the motherland'.

In 1821 it mounted an attempt to do so, launching an invasion of the Danubian Principalities. But Vladimirescu's followers provided none of the support they had hoped for, and the Turks soon mopped them up. The conspirators succeeded, however, in sparking an insurgency in the Peleponnese and some of the islands. Though the Russians withdrew their ambassador from Istanbul, and Metternich opined (quite rightly as it happened) that Greece was merely a geographical expression, the Powers supported neither side. Then the Turks executed the Orthodox Patriarch of Constantinople, even though he had roundly denounced the rebellion – and the idealists of Europe rallied to the cause of Greek independence. The volunteers (including Byron), the money, and, not least the publicity which they supplied contributed greatly to the success of the cause. Albeit indirectly, they also helped to ensure that the emergent state of Greece would adopt a Western-type constitution highlv unsuitable for a society that was largely traditional and innocent of Western values. Events were to demonstrate that although the seeds of Western democratic ideas were to germinate in Eastern Europe, unlike the rampant bean-stalk of nationalism, the plants that grew out of them would be weak and spindly.

Greece's first head of state, Capodistrias, understood the problem. He was an authoritarian in the mould of the enlightened despots. He set out to build sound administrative and educational systems, to improve communications and the economy. He also favoured land reform. Anticipating Stolypin, he regarded a free and prosperous peasantry as the foundation of a stable society. Traditional interest groups, whom he held in contempt, and idealists starry-eyed with Western ways, all hated him. In 1831 he was assassinated. When the ensuing anarchy finally subsided, independent Greece found herself (thanks to an agreement between Russia, France, and Britain) with a sizeable Western loan, a Bavarian King and a small Bavarian army.[38]

The *grotesquerie* associated with the emergence of a Greek national state was matched in 1830–1 by the failure of a Polish bid for independence that had been a series of ghastly errors and misunderstandings from its very beginning.

Having pinned their hopes on the French, Poles found that in return for the formally independent Duchy of Warsaw that Napoleon granted them they had to raise, and pay for, a vast army to help fight his wars – and to send it to Spain as well as Russia. In the end, of course, they shared his defeat, and, under the terms of the Congress of Vienna in 1815, the territories of the old republic were once again partitioned between Russia, Austria and Prussia. However, Tsar Alexander I did allow a semi-independent Polish state in his zone. It became known as the Congress Kingdom, and its constitution was compiled by a prominent Polish aristocrat, Adam Czartoryski.

Its King, however, was the Tsar (represented in Warsaw by his brother Constantine), and though both the nobility and the middle classes were represented in the parliament, it was the more prosperous *szlachta* and the magnates who carried the clout. Congress Poland had its own army – but, then as now, it was a poor country. There was some economic improvement over the next fifteen years but this counted for little so far as the rising generation of young idealists, heady with the wine of Romantic nationalism, were concerned. The regime was sympathetic and the Tsar himself conciliatory – but too many Poles who hoped for the restoration of Poland as it had been before 1772, read too much into his speeches and thus stored up disappointments for themselves.[39]

Some who dreamed of revolution formed secret societies. And since the regime tolerated freemasonry the masons provided convenient cover, as did the 'National Freemasonry' association, formed in 1819. It was also fashionable, for this was an age of intrigue, not only for courtiers but for lesser noblemen, junior officers, intellectuals, poets. Many of them were beginning to feel more loyalty to a cause than to a sovereign; some of them found conspiracy to be an heroic, as well as an exciting, activity. Russians also followed the fashion. Masonic lodges in St Petersburg formed an umbrella under which revolutionaries gathered; army officers in Ukraine came together to plan a new society, and the means of achieving it. The Northern and Southern Societies, as they were called respectively, came together; representatives of the Southern Society met Kryzanowski of the Polish underground movement at Kiev in 1824. They offered to extend Poland's frontiers, but there was no agreement. Though many of their colleagues favoured a regime headed by the Grand Duke Constantine the Russians thought in terms of a republic without a monarch. The Poles, who wanted a constitutional monarchy, shrank back from the idea of regicide, and in any case the Russian conspirators were wrongfooted by the unexpected death of Alexander in December 1825.

The interregnum forced them into action they had not contemplated taking for another two to five years. Furthermore, despite a Russian tradition of army *coups*, which had brought four monarchs to the throne and killed two others over the previous century,[40] the leaders were paralyzed by doubts and confused about their plans. They turned out their troops in St Petersburg, but from that point the drama descended into farce. The soldiers themselves had no understanding of the cause they were supporting. (They shouted 'Constantine and Constitution' but imagined that 'Constitution' was the name of the Grand Duke's consort.) Those leaders who turned up did not know what to do. The rebels' troops were shot down; the conspirators were rounded up; a few of them were ultimately hanged.

In the aftermath of the Decembrist fiasco, Kryzanowski was arrested. He was arraigned before a special court which found him guilty of treason. This outraged younger Polish nationalists – subalterns, poets and military cadets; and by the end of 1828 a cadet instructor, Lieutenant Wysocki, had begun organizing a nationalist conspiracy. Two years later a rising was staged, but, like the Decembrist *coup*, it was bungled.

It only got under way by mistake; the few rebels that turned out to seize Constantine's palace failed to find him; and no senior Polish officer would join the movement, which would have collapsed had not Warsaw's poor, realizing that something was astir among the military, taken the opportunity to protest at recent rises in the price of booze. The crowd began to loot and many soldiers joined them. Meanwhile university students organized, and the most popular Polish general, for whom the mob shouted, hid himself for fear of getting involved in what he regarded as a suicidal venture. The elite was distressed at the turn of events; the government sent representatives to talk with Constantine. Eventually large Russian forces were marched towards Warsaw – but meanwhile the romantics had a hey-day.

> The Romantic Movement [so ran the leader of a new journal] by creating an intellectual revolution, called forth a political one too. With Freedom, Truth, Faith, ever more openly trampled upon by an ungenerous despotism, they found their great field of action in artistic imagination, in beauty and in literature. Lacking civil and political freedom, we [turned to] spiritual and artistic freedom. Recognizing a break with the past and with tradition to be imperative, we proclaim a future that is limitless, dreadful, sublime and enchanting.[41]

However, as most experienced Polish leaders realized, repression was to be the consequence rather than the cause of rebellion. It was really pride that was at stake. Tsar-King Nicholas had insisted, albeit tactfully, that the Poles submit to him. In response the assembly in Warsaw issued a manifesto which concluded:

> If in this last fight Poland shall lay down her freedom amid the ashes of her towns and the corpses of her defenders, the enemy will extend his dominion over yet another desert, and the true Pole will perish with joy in his heart that... he has protected the liberties of the peoples of Europe.[42]

The extremists gained the upper hand; Nicholas was declared to be deposed, and invading Russian troops were resisted. The Polish army was defeated. It regrouped and Poles rose in Lithuania and Ukraine, but the masses would not support the movement. (Polish serfs had no love for Russians but they refused to fight so long as their Polish masters insisted on keeping them in subjection.) And even libertarian Britain refused the Poles any support.

The hopeless war produced some Polish heroes, but rather more who struck heroic attitudes. The six governments that Poland had in ten months reflected not just a typical revolutionary momentum, but the fact that Poles could not cohere as a nation. Even the inevitable surrender was fumbled. Several thousand emigrated, mainly to France. But they were a tiny minority of the *szlachta* and many of them left as much in the hope of better opportunities as of political asylum. The exiles included several poets, though Mickiewicz had departed in 1829 and had not returned. Nearly a year after the debacle, however, he penned a message of hope:

> On the third day the soul will return to the body, and the nation will arise from the dead and will free all the nations of Europe from slavery. And two days have already passed: one day passed with the first taking of Warsaw [in 1795], and the second day passed with the second taking of Warsaw [in 1831], and the third day will arrive, but it will not pass away. And as with the resurrection of Christ sacrifices of blood ceased on the whole earth, so with the resurrection of the Polish nation wars will cease in Christendom.[43]

Nor was this a passing poetic fancy. In a subsequent work he likened Poles in exile to the Children of Israel in the Wilderness. When the time came

> The nations shall be redeemed by the merits of a martyred nation, and shall be re-christened in the name of God and liberty.... Truly I say unto you: ask not what the government of Poland will be. It is enough for you to know that it will be better than any you know of. Nor ask as to her frontiers, for they will be more extensive than ever before.[44]

Such Messianism signalled the advance of nationalism to the status of a secular religion In this the Poles were to be pathfinders and their creed was to prove both a blessing and a curse. It provided a source of hope, of confidence, and a consolation in times of adversity. But it also distorted their vision of the world as it is – which has forced the Polish people to live with disappointment ever since.[45]

In most of Eastern Europe, however, nationalism in the early 1840s was still a luxury indulged in by a few young people encouraged by poets, philologists and antiquarians. Except for a few unemployed graduates and officers without prospects of promotion, it did not arise from any real wish, least of all on the part of the people as a whole. After 1848, however, it was gradually to spread to the masses. But as it was transformed from an elite into a demotic phenomenon, the intellectual horizons of nationalists shrank, the soul became the property of the collective rather than the individual, and it became morally corrupting – a convenient excuse for lack of achievement, encouraging individuals and communities alike to blame their own inadequacies, misfortunes and follies on others. In this way love of one's own people came to be measured in terms of hatred of others.

Romantic nationalism stimulated artistic and poetic creativity, but, as it spread among ordinary folk, national cultures came to be reduced to slogans and symbols, to anthems and 'national costumes', and, above all, to exaggerated admiration of everything regarded as one's own, combined with xenophobia. Paradoxically, what began by drawing attention to fascinating diversity became a recipe for imposing a tedious similarity. In the process the graceful cosmopolitanism and the tolerance which characterized so much of the region were doomed in favour of narrowness and bigotry.

Demotic nationalism was also to cheapen politics. The idea of the national collective ultimately came to be thought of as sacrosanct – never to be splintered by party strife. As such it became a substitute for real political participation. So it was that democracy came to be seen as a matter not of individual, but of collective, rights, and of collective rather than individual interests. Furthermore, realization of the national dream of liberation was too often envisaged as the ultimate aim, the apocalyptic moment, the realization of utopia, the end of time itself. This was not good ground in which to root a democratic polity.

* * *

Though the ultimate development of nationalism was not foreseen, even by 1848,[46] we have been able to trace its origins. But we have yet to explore the sources of the old loyalties, which the Enlightenment and Romanticism undermined. What magic allowed the Habsburgs to hold so many disparate peoples in awe for so long? And why did the Hungarians, with their curious constitution, become such an obstacle to Habsburg policies of integration, whereas the Czechs and others did not?

How was it that the Ottomans, whose problems we have noticed, almost succeeded in capturing Vienna as recently as 1683? And, by the same token, how could the Poland of Jan Sobieski, whose army came to Vienna's defence that year, have become a Russian puppet less than four decades later? How, for that matter, could Russia, still an obscure and barbarous country to most westerners in the sixteenth century, have begun an almost inexorable rise to great power status in the second half of the seventeenth century?

How can the Polish craze of 'Sarmatism', at once a consequence of historical circumstances and an important factor in the formation of Polish mentality, be explained; or 'Tulipomania' in the Ottoman Empire? And why was Eastern Europe as a whole so unbalanced socially and poor economically by comparison with Western Europe even then?

To gain an understanding of these things we must pursue our investigation even farther back in time, to the age of the baroque.

REFERENCES

1. J.A. Demian, translated by C.A. Macartney, *The Habsburg and Hohenzollern Dynasties* (New York, 1970) p. 195.
2. P. Longworth, *The Art of Victory* (London, 1965) p. 230.
3. Joseph Marshall, *Travels through Holland, Flanders ... and Poland in the Years 1768, 1769, and 1770*, vol. III (London, 1772) p. 243.
4. 'Report of the Enquiry into the state of the peasants in Bohemia, June 1769', Macartney, *op. cit.*, pp. 173–4.
5. H. Marczali, *Hungary in the Eighteenth Century* (New York, 1971) p. 174; I. de Madariaga, *Russia in the Age of Catherine II* (London, 1982) p. 552.
6. Quoted by J. Mavor, *An Economic History of Russia* 2nd revised ed., vol. I (New York, 1965) pp. 313–5.
7. 'Instruction to the Austro-Bohemian Chancery, 1769', quoted by D. Beales, *Joseph II*, vol. I (Cambridge, 1988) p. 347.
8. *Ibid.*, pp. 352–5.
9. Macartney, *op. cit.*, pp. 174–84. How the noble class came to exercise such a disproportionate amount of power, especially in Hungary and Poland, will be discussed in Chapter 9.
10. Quoted in Beales, *op. cit.*, 1, p. 99.
11. 'Admonition of 1783', T.C.W. Blanning, *Joseph II and Enlightened Despotism* (London, 1970), p. 131.
12. Beales, *op. cit.*, I, p. 97.
13. For an original treatment of the origins and practice of the police state see M. Raeff, *The Well-Ordered Police State* (New Haven, 1981). Curiously, however, Raeff ignores the Habsburgs, though he deals with Germany, from which they acquired most of the ideas along with many of the officials to disseminate and implement them, and with eighteenth, though not seventeenth-century Russia.
14. A concept shared by Tsar Alexis and the Habsburgs of the seventeenth century, see Chapter 7.
15. Blanning, *op. cit.*, pp. 141–2.
16. C.A. Macartney, *The Habsburg Empire 1790–1918* (London, 1971) p. 121; Blanning, *op. cit.*, pp. 142–4.
17. The evolution of this unfortunate constitution will be described in Chapters 8 and 9. Non-Catholic nobles had been barred from the *Sejm* and holding public office since 1733.
18. The most convenient short account of Poland from the accession of Stanislaus Augustus to the third partition is R.F. Leslie, *The Polish Question*, Historical Association Pamphlet (London, 1971). See also H. Kaplan, *The First Partition of Poland* (New York, 1962); D. Stone, *Polish Politics and National Reform* (Boulder, Colorado, 1976); R.H. Lord, *The Seated Partition of Poland* (London, 1915), and E. Rostworowski in A. Gieysztor *et al.* (eds), *History of Poland*, 2nd ed. (Warsaw, 1979) pp. 267–334.

19. Seweryn Rzewuski. The translation is adapted from R.F. Leslie's *Polish Politics and the Revolutions of November 1830* (London, 1956) p. 24.
20. The suggestion is made by Leslie, *Polish Politics, op. cit*. See also R. von Thadden, *Prussia: The History of a Lost State* (Cambridge, 1987) p. 13.
21. A useful summary of the context is provided by Macartney, *The Habsburg Empire, op. cit.*, pp. 131–30.
22. The common notion that Joseph was a militarist has been challenged by Beales, *op. cit.*. A verdict on his direction of the war must await the second volume of Beales's study.
23. Kaunitz to Leopold II, Blanning, *op. cit.*, p. 151.
24. See Chapter 8.
25. Despite the huge corpus of literature on modern nationalism its origins have been insufficiently studied. See R.J.W. Evans, *Times Literary Supplement*, 23 June 1989, p. 699.
26. One of the shortest and best of the many treatments of emergent nationalism is E. Niederhauser, *The Rise of Nationality in Eastern Europe* (Budapest, 1982).
27. See Chapter 7.
28. Efforts have been made to find traces of modern nationalism before the late nineteenth century, but with scant success. See my 'Historians and Nationalism', *Slavonic and East European Review*, 68 (1) pp. 100–5.
29. L. Czigany, *The Oxford History of Hungarian Literature* (Oxford, 1984) pp. 105–6.
30. On Vuk Karadjic see D. Wilson, *The Life and Times of Vuk Stefanovic Karadjic 1787–1864* (Oxford, 1970).
31. On Tomas Masaryk and the Hanka forgeries, see M. Otahal, 'The Manuscript Controversy and the Czech National Revival', *Cross-Currents*, 5, 1986, pp. 247–78; on the Greek myth and the fabrications of Papparigopoulos, see R. Clogg, 'The Greeks and their Past' in D. Deletant and H. Hanak, (eds), *Historians as Nation-Builders* (London, 1988) pp. 15–31; for Hunyadi, see Chapter 9.
32. K. Sklenar, *Archaelogy in Central Europe* (Leicester, 1983) especially pp. 67–8 and 78.
33. Cited by Macartney, *The Habsburg Empire, op. cit.*, p. 254.
34. For an account of how this came about see Chapter 8.
35. A. Otetea (ed.) *The History of the Romanian People* (New York, 1970) p. 317.
36. W. MacMichael, *Journey from Moscow to Constantinople* (London, 1819) pp. 82–3.
37. See R.J. Crampton, *A Short History of Modern Bulgaria* (Cambridge, 1987) especially pp. 10–13.
38. For a convenient and perceptive account of the emergence of the Greek state, see R. Clogg, *A Short History of Modern Greece*, 2nd ed. (London, 1986) pp. 43–69.
39. For a shrewd analysis of the situation and of the events that followed, see Leslie, *Polish Politics, op. cit.*.
40. The beneficiaries were Catherine I, Elizabeth, Catherine II and Alexander himself (though he had not sought it); the victims were Peter III and Paul.
41. *Nowa Polska* [The New Poland], 5 January 1831. The rendering here is freely adapted from Leslie's translation, *Polish Politics, op. cit.*, note 1, p. 149.
42. *Ibid.*, p. 148.
43. From his *Book of the Polish Nation*, quoted in the translation by M.M. Gardner, *Poland: A Study in National Idealism* (London, 1915) pp. 35–6.
44. *Ibid.*, p. 87.

45. For a somewhat different but sympathetic treatment of the phenomenon (which was not confined to Poland), see W. Weintraub 'National Consciousness in Polish Romantic Literature', *Cross-Currents*, 6, 1987, pp. 149–58.
46. Isaiah Berlin has remarked that nationalism was the only major development of the century that had not been foreseen, see his 'Nationalism: Past Neglect and Present Power' in his *Against the Current* (New York, 1980) pp. 333–55.

7

The Imposition of Order (1648–1770)

Proud, restless, noisy, impossible to satisfy. Untrammelled license is what they want.

Montecuccoli on the nobility of Hungary

Without order there can be no security.

Alexis, Tsar of Russia

The year 1648 was an obvious turning-point in European history. That year, by the Treaty of Westphalia, the Thirty Years' War, which had devastated much of Central Europe, was brought to a merciful conclusion. But the war, and the epidemics associated with it, had reduced both the population and the economy of central Europe alarmingly. Destruction had been especially great in Germany but the disruption which the war occasioned had wider-reaching effects: trade routes had changed and markets lost; agriculture had been neglected, cities ruined, and bands of marauders, the flotsam of the war, were to plague a number of districts, not least Bohemia, for some time thereafter. For towns, countryside and governments alike, the tasks of reconstruction were daunting.

At the same time a series of upheavals took place in other parts of Europe. The Dutch and English revolutions were reaching their climaxes; and the year 1648 saw disturbances in France and Spain, revolts in Naples and in Moscow, and the great Ukrainian uprising, led by Bogdan Khmelnytsky, against the state of Poland. The middle of the seventeenth century, then, was a climacteric throughout Europe; a crisis point on which the economy, society, politics, and even the arts and attitudes, turned.[1]

Yet the effects were curiously uneven. In terms of economic advantage the fortunes of England and Holland rose, those of Spain declined, while Eastern Europe settled into a state of economic backwardness which has persisted ever since.[2] In social terms, too, the north-west corner of Europe benefited while Eastern Europe suffered: in France and England society became more pluralistic, mobile and diverse, but in Hungary and Poland-Lithuania especially, society, already unbalanced in favour of the nobility, became more rigid, while throughout Eastern Europe the mercantile class (with which north-western Europe's success was associated) remained small, and noblemen who had once shown interest in commerce came to disdain it.

In political terms, however, the configuration was different. Russia, like France, adopted an absolutist form of government; the Habsburgs also attempted to gain more authority for the crown, though with less success, while Poland took the principle of nobiliar democracy (the antithesis of absolutism) to its extreme, and England developed its pragmatically mixed constitution. The balance of power also changed. England, Prussia and Russia emerged as great European powers by the middle of the eighteenth century, while Poland and Sweden ceased to count as such.

However, despite the cultural variegation of Europe at that time, there was a tendency for East and West to share artistic styles and fashions. The baroque flowered as impressively in Prague and Vienna as it did in Borromini's Rome; the lovely new city of St Petersburg owed much to Dutch and Danish inspiration. Outside the Balkans high society throughout the Continent followed the same fashions, whether in clothes, music or the decoration of their country houses; and pursued many of the same amusements. Not even Istanbul was impervious to outside cultural influences, as the 'Tulipomania' craze of the early eighteenth century showed. The Polish adoption of Turkish styles of clothing and accoutrements was exceptional. In general, fashion tended to be generated in the West and imported into eastern Europe.

In terms of learning there was a degree of convergence, too. Poles still frequented Italian universities; the Bohemian luminary Comenius was as well known by English scholars interested in education as he was in Sarospatak in Hungary where, in the middle of the seventeenth century, he had a school; and even the Baltans proved susceptible to Western European influences to an extent: learned agents of the Vatican seeking to bring Orthodox Christians over to Rome founded schools and set up printing presses in the obscure Romanian lands, and by the early eighteenth century even isolationist Russia was sending young people to study in the West. However, while Eastern European monarchs, and especially the Habsburgs, were generous in their support of learning, it was again in north-west Europe, notably London, where the Royal Society was founded in 1662, that scientific discovery found its cutting edge.

This tendency to lag behind the West, which became noticeable in the period, has commonly been attributed by Eastern Europeans themselves to the costs of war and especially to the burden of defending the West against the hordes of Asia. This argument bears more credence in earlier periods,[3] though Eastern Europe did suffer more from wars than the rest of the continent after 1648. The Ukrainian revolt soon drew in Russia, which was to be locked in combat with Poland from 1654 to 1667. Both Russia and Poland had wars with Sweden; the Habsburgs were almost constantly preoccupied by threats from Bavaria, France and the Turks, against whom the Poles and Russians also fought; while the struggle between the Turks and Venetians for possession of Crete lasted for decades.

Then, in 1683, the advancing Turks were hurled back from the gates of Vienna. This signalled a decisive change in military fortunes. The Turks were soon to be pushed out of all Hungary and the northern Balkans. Furthermore, during the century following the Peace of Westphalia, governments began to gain control over those peripheral border areas which had been characterized by disorder for ages past. The elimination of these old war zones of the Balkans and the 'steppe frontier' meant the removal of at least one impediment to the region's progress.

On the other hand internal conflicts abounded, absorbing much of the region's energies and wasting much of its treasure. Poland's period of 'Ruin' following the Ukrainian uprising of 1648 was associated not only with foreign invasions but with the Lubomirski rebellion of 1665–6 and creeping anarchy. In Russia unrest was almost continuous: there were provincial revolts in 1650; inflation riots in 1662; a huge rebellion raised by the Cossack Stepan Razin in 1670–1; the Khovanskii mutiny of 1682, the Bulavin rebellion of 1708, and, throughout the period, pervasive religious discontent. In the Ottoman lands the government found it increasingly difficult to maintain control over society, as rising *haiduk* activity in the Balkans suggests,[4] while the Habsburgs were plagued by the persistent rebelliousness of their Hungarian subjects who rose in 1670, 1683 and yet again in 1703.

Both the maintenance of internal order and the organization of defence placed increasing demands on the state's resources. Developments in military technology and tactics led to the modernization of armies, but the costs of modernization were huge, testing the ability of governments to raise taxes, and demanding the development of bureaucracy. Furthermore the emerging wisdom of the age predicated growing wealth on the monarch's power to protect and promote commerce and industry. So pressure mounted for the state to expand its activities, improve its efficiency and vastly increase its income. In considering the period 1648–1770, then, the questions of how the various states of Eastern Europe reacted to these challenges and why the outcomes were so different should be addressed first.

* * *

Russia was the only state in Eastern Europe to move in a consistently absolutist direction. Untrammelled authority, the essence of absolutism, had long since been the objective of its rulers, and under Ivan IV in the previous century much had been done to enforce the central authority of the state, albeit through the shedding of much blood. However, at the beginning of the seventeeth century the country dissolved into anarchy, and when this abated, the new Tsar (Michael, the first of the Romanovs) was elected by an Assembly of the Land (*zemskii sobor*). This created a precedent reminiscent of the mediaeval practice of electing kings which had persisted in other parts of Eastern Europe, notably in Poland.[5] Nevertheless from the 1650s, under Tsar Alexis the scales were weighted decisively in favour of absolutism.

Like so many men of his time Alexis was almost obsessed with order – and on several planes. Not only was he concerned to enforce civil order, but to introduce orderly routines into government and even into his sport.[6] He also took more than a passing interest in music and astronomy, which were understood to be related – and subscribed to the ancient notion that the celestial order provided a model for an earthly order, an analogue for good government that would be pleasing to God. Alexis was noted for his attachment to the Orthodox Church, but his piety was to a great extent political.

Church services and ceremonial allowed him to project himself publicly as God's humble regent on earth; and the Church, with its country-wide ramifications, was invaluable not only in helping to legitimize his rule but in enforcing his will: the Tsar's *ukazy* were read out in churches (or, if the priest was illiterate, pinned to the door), and monasteries often served not only as welfare centres but as prisons for secular as well as ecclesiastical offenders, besides accommodating troops that might be needed in the district. And Alexis was well aware that a political order would be all the firmer for being underpinned by a moral order. As soon as he acceded to the throne he endorsed a movement of religious zealotry (a Russian echo of the counter-Reformation). So religion was encouraged as a means of promoting loyalty to the crown and respect for its wishes; a means of breaking down the old loyalties to clan, locality, tradition and, not least to pagan practices which were often associated with rebellion.

Alexis was also at pains to find other forms of legitimation. He claimed descent (quite spuriously) both from the Emperors of ancient Rome, and from Ivan the Terrible; he promoted Ivan's reputation, not least for cruelty, and claimed to emulate him. But aside from image-building, Alexis worked in a practical way to translate the idea of absolute rule into reality. He established a small private chancery staffed by able non-noble bureaucrats to implement his will. He used it to gain personal control of the administrative apparatus, when necessary bypassing the minister in charge; and members of its staff usually went, on promotion, to occupy the most important and sensitive posts in the bureaucracy.

The Tsar destroyed every institutional obstacle to his absolute rule. The Assembly of the Land, which many scholars have regarded as a potential parliament, was called for the last time in 1653. Alexis also reduced the role of the *Duma* or state council, in effect a cabinet consisting of the leading ministers, generals and provincial governors; promoted an increasing number of commoners to it; rarely called full meetings and forbade members to meet in his absence. He also attacked the system by which appointments and promotions were made on the basis of heredity and precedent (*mestnichestvo*). The rules were suspended for ceremonial occasions as well as for military campaigns with increasing frequency, and those who objected were subjected to humiliating punishments. Although the books of precedence were not ceremoniously burned until 1682, the system had already ceased to serve as a bulwark of aristocratic privilege. The Tsar promoted and demoted at will on the basis of ability and experience.

But the Church itself had the potential to challenge his authority, and under the Patriarch Nikon it threatened to do so.[7] According to the Orthodox Christian ideal, church and state worked together in symphony. In practice, however, differences arose between them from time to time. Most Byzantine precedents, from which the Russian derived their understandings, favoured the emperor over the patriarch.[8] Nevertheless, when Alexis and Nikon fell out in 1658 it proved very difficult to depose the Patriarch canonically. This was eventually achieved in 1666 with less than scrupulous regard to the rules, and with the advice of an ecclesiastical expert who, it transpired, was an agent of the Vatican. Nonetheless after that the Russian Church was very careful to meet the Tsar's every wish.

Alexis's unexpected death in 1676 and that of his successor, the twenty-one year old Fedor, six years later, threw doubt on the permanence of the achievement. However, in the event no Russian social stratum, political grouping or institution proved capable of mounting any serious challenge to the new order. Alexis's youngest son, Peter the Great, found no great difficulty in asserting his autocratic powers; and he followed very largely in his father's footsteps.

In Russia it was the huge size of the country, the very difficult communications, and the low educational level (which created a chronic shortage of administrators, especially for the provinces) that impeded the monarch's exercise of power – not institutions, vested class interests or constitutional law. In neighbouring Poland, by contrast, the powers of the crown were severely restricted by law, and by a significant section of the nobility, which was adamantly opposed to any change. Nevertheless under the able Jan II Casimir (1648–68), a former Jesuit, the attempt was made to gain more power for the crown.

The occasion was a series of military disasters: defeat by the Ukrainian rebels in 1648; the loss of a large part of Lithuania, including Vilna, to the Russians in the campaigns of 1654–5, and the Swedish army's sweep through almost all of the rest of Poland in 1655. In 1656–7 much ground was recovered, largely because of a surge of patriotism associated with what came to be regarded as the miraculous defence of the monastery-citadel of Czestochowa, but also to the Russian offensive of 1656 against the Swedes. Nevertheless the King recognized that a larger, better-trained and better-equipped army was needed, and that this demanded a much bigger income than he could obtain from the sources over which he had control – the royal free cities (as opposed to those wholly owned by the great landlords) which he could tax, the crown estates which he could lease, and the offices within his gift which he could use to buy political compliance. Yet any general taxation required the approval of the *Sejm* (parliament) which was dominated by noblemen and gentry who believed any imposition of taxation upon them, their property, or on the population subject to them, to be an unconstitutional infringement of their liberty. And approval was all the less likely without reforming the parliamentary rules, because since 1652 the veto of a single member had been sufficient to defeat a bill and prorogue the session.[9]

The shock of the defeats, however, rallied some powerful support to the King, and in 1660 a reform programme was compiled, mooting a two-thirds majority as sufficient to pass legislation, a reduction in the powers of the local assemblies (*sejmiki*), and the taxation of the nobility. At the same time some reformers sought to overcome the uncertainties implicit in a system of elective kingship by trying to have an heir apparent elected (French and even Russian candidacies were considered). This, however, raised fears of creeping absolutism even among moderates, while the defenders of localism and republicans were outraged by the very prospect of reforms which threatened their 'Golden Liberty'. Thus, when the reform bills were tabled in 1661–2 they were comprehensively defeated. Nonetheless the King persisted, and had the leader of the opposition, Jerzy Lubomirski, successfully prosecuted for treason. But Lubomirski responded by raising rebellion (1665–6), and, though he was eventually forced to submit, the victory was Pyrrhic. In 1668 King Jan II, concluding that the cause of constitutional reform, still less absolutism, was hopeless, abdicated and left for France.[10]

The emergence of absolutist Prussia presents a dramatic contrast to Poland. Its founder, the Elector Frederick William (1640–88) ruled a ramshackle collection of German territories (he was Margrave of Brandenburg, Duke in Prussia and Pomerania, etc.). Indeed, as ruler of Prussia he was a vassal of the Polish king. And he, too, was largely dependent for taxation income on the Estates which were naturally reluctant to vote him money. Nonetheless, Frederick William succeeded where Jan II had failed. Not only did he understand a permanent standing army to be the key both to effective defence and the centralization of his territories; he was both determined and unscrupulous in pursuit of his objectives.

In 1653 he persuaded the Brandenburg Estates to grant funds for the maintenance of a standing army for a period of six years, regardless of whether there was war or not. This was a significant precedent, though one bought with considerable concessions of rights to the nobility. In Prussia, too, over which he won outright title from Poland by the Treaty of Wehlau in 1657, he was granted taxes in return for privileges. However, the 'Great Elector' did not scruple to use his troops to extract what he needed, regardless of his undertakings. The Estates continued to exist, as did many of the ancient institutions associated with autonomy, but they came to resemble mere tokens, their members unable, or simply afraid, to exercise their former rights. By 1701, when the Hohenzollerns became Kings in Prussia, the monarch was all but supreme, ruling through a centralizing bureaucracy which was an outgrowth of his military commissariat. On their estates, however, the Junkers, the Prussian equivalent to the Russian service gentry, themselves enjoyed almost absolute power over their serfs.[11]

Attempts to assert the power of the crown over the estates had failed in Poland but had succeeded in Prussia. In Russia, where social institutions were weaker and the Byzantine tradition respected, the victory was even more complete. But in the Habsburg territories of Eastern Europe the circumstances were more complicated and the outcome much less clear-cut than in the other cases.

Like the Hohenzollerns of Prussia, the Habsburgs had a variety of rights and powers in many different lands. They were Archdukes of Austria, hereditary Kings of Bohemia, traditional candidates to the elective throne of Hungary (though the Turks occupied much of it and Transylvania was an autonomous principality); and, besides holding a plethora of other titles, were Emperors of the Holy Roman Empire (again as hereditary candidates), a position which gave them little direct power, but a great deal of prestige and not a little patronage. The Habsburgs, then, governed in various ways at once – sometimes exerting direct authority backed up by force; more often abiding by precedents, negotiating, persuading, exerting influence through their powers to grant titles and make appointments.

Theirs was a ramshackle empire, which had expended much of its wealth and sustained much damage during the Thirty Years' War; and it was still threatened by powerful enemies, notably Ottoman Turkey and France. Furthermore, although the Habsburgs had been the chief protagonist of the Catholic cause in the war, and although the peace sanctioned their imposing it on all their subjects, it was not practicable to do so in Hungary, where there were many Protestants; and the suppression of Protestantism elsewhere, as in Bohemia, tended to promote sullen resentment which might be exploited in the cause of rebellion. How, then, were these obstacles to Habsburg authority to be overcome? What glue could be found to bind these disparate peoples and territories into a cohesive body politic?

According to a leading authority[12] the recipe called for the mutual support of the dynasty, the Counter-Reformation Church and a cosmopolitanized aristocracy, who formed a community of interest; and the use of religious mysteries, the mystique of kingship and the magic of the arts to hold people in thrall. But the military was also important.

The Habsburgs emerged from the war with a permanent standing army and thereafter strove to enlarge it, though as late as 1683 the establishment was only 36,000.[13] Since this was a professional, disciplined, force which did not normally live off the land, it did not arouse the resentment of the population in the localities where it was stationed, as had formerly been the case. Indeed, in time, the army came to promote loyalty to the dynasty not only among those who served in it (the new permanent armies presented welcome new career opportunities to gentlemen and commoners alike), but among a wider public. The sight of neat ranks of men in attractive uniforms marching by to the invigorating sound of flutes and drums tended to arouse popular enthusiasm, and when the army won victories the dynasty gained prestige.

Nonetheless, as in Russia, the practice of religion and the institution of the Church were recognized as being of prime importance in legitimating the dynasty and promoting deference among its subjects. Both Ferdinand III and his successor Leopold I (1657–1705) were personally devout and, like Alexis of Russia, made public show of it.[14] Leopold often made pilgrimages, visited monasteries three or four times a week and dispensed a great deal of charity to the needy. He also believed oaths, including those he himself swore, to be binding. Yet, like Alexis, insofar as he showed himself to be as pious as any prelate, he felt entitled to interfere in church affairs. Not only did he control the more important ecclesiastical appointments, order special prayers to be said and proclaim religious holidays by decree, he imposed taxes on the clergy and milked the church of funds, plate and valuables as the need arose. One can therefore understand the wry comment of the papal nuncio who wished the Emperor were not quite so pious.

For the Habsburgs of this period the Catholic religion was at once an ideology with which to justify the dynasty and underpin the state; an instrument of God-pleasing order; and, not least, a test of loyalty. Ferdinand III's councillors had to swear that they believed in the Immaculate Conception (as did university graduates). In his reign, and that of his successor, Catholics were ordered to take communion at Easter and obtain a certificate proving they had done so. 'Reformation Commissions', often escorted by military, would tour suspect parts of his domains to enforce conformity; and assaults were launched against Protestants. Article I of the Proposals to the Bohemian Diet of 1651 insisted that all clergy be of the Catholic faith. Both in Bohemia and elsewhere, Protestant churches and chapels were closed down, their preachers expelled, their marriage and funeral rites forbidden.

This drive towards exclusivity for the state's religion was part of a general trend. In 1653 the Catholic Church, not to mention the Arians, Anabaptists and others, was banned in Brandenburg. (In Prussia Catholics were specifically protected by the Treaty of Wehlau.) In Russia the dissenting 'Old Believers' were excommunicated in 1667. Their leader, Avvakum, was burned at the stake in 1682. Even in decentralized Poland, which had a reputation 'for religious toleration, life was tending to become difficult for Protestants and Orthodox alike; in 1658 the Arians were banned; ten years later it became a capital offence for a Catholic to abandon the faith; later some Lutherans were to be executed for sacrilege, and by 1733 non-Catholics were barred from the *Sejm* and from holding office.

Yet though the Habsburgs succeeded in introducing Catholic conformity into most of their territories, they were to fail in Hungary. This was to thwart immediate plans to centralize their holdings in East-Central Europe, and (as we have noted earlier) to constitute a very grave long-term impediment to the integration of the Habsburg Empire. Not that the attempt was not made, or that there was no foundation to build on. Leopold himself was determined to make Hungary as Catholic as its designation 'Apostolic' suggested; powerful members of the Hungarian elite were now Catholics; and about 1,000 members of the Jesuit Order, the vanguard of the Counter-Reformation, were soon active in Hungary. Furthermore, from 1662 he refused to call an Hungarian Diet, in effect denying the lesser nobles and gentry, many of them Protestants, any say in the conduct of affairs. But what was to defeat Leopold was not so much the strength of Protestant feeling as fear that the Habsburgs might impose absolute rule in Hungary (as they had in Bohemia in 1627) and, at the same time, doubts as to his ability and will to defend Hungary effectively.

Hungarians were particularly aggrieved that the famous Habsburg general, Raimondo Montecuccoli, did not exploit his defensive victory over the Turkish invaders at Szentgotthard (at the extreme western edge of Hungary) in 1664 and that, afraid of France, Leopold immediately concluded the unfavourable Peace of Vasvar which left the enemy in possession of most of their gains. Resentments coalesced into an anti-Habsburg conspiracy, formed by some of the most powerful magnates, including Catholics, egged on by the French ambassador and by Protestant gentry. But the plotters were half-hearted, unrealistic, and indiscreet; and when, in 1670, some of them seemed about to pledge allegiance to the Turks (rather than merely discussing the possibilities of electing a Hungarian or even a Frenchman as king) the ring-leaders were arrested, sentenced to death and their estates confiscated. Others who had already died, were tried posthumously so that their estates could also be expropriated to the benefit of the Habsburg exchequer. Others again fled into Turkish territory and Transylvania from where, with a small army of displaced soldiers and peasants who came to be called 'crusaders' (*kurucz*), they launched marauding expeditions into Habsburg territory.

The conspiracy provided Vienna with the justification for severity. The Hungarian constitution was suspended and direct rule imposed. The Hungarians were forced to pay half the costs of occupation; special courts were set up and a purge of dissenters carried out. In 1674 over 300 Protestant preachers were tried for treason. All were found guilty and sentenced to death unless they became Catholics. Then a combination of internal reactions and international pressures intervened. The harsh regime in Hungary was alienating both the magnates who had remained loyal to Leopold and the Protestant powers whose help he needed against France. In 1676 the special courts were abolished and the surviving prisoners released; in 1681 direct rule was abandoned altogether and a meeting of the Hungarian Diet was called at last.

The Habsburgs' problems in Hungary stemmed not only from the rebels but from the Turks who were giving them asylum and encouragement.[15] To many Hungarians of the time the Turks seemed more powerful, and therefore more effective, protectors than the Habsburgs. For the Ottoman government had also been following the trend of reform, and the reforms were paying dividends in an accretion of military strength.

The problems of the Ottoman state differed from the others we have considered, since the Sultan's authority was already absolute, albeit usually delegated to viziers (ministers), and the Empire was already a centralized state with a complex bureaucratic organization. However, the Sultan's palace at Topkapi had become a centre of intrigue between rival factions of officials, many of whom were appointed on grounds of favour rather than ability, and too often dismissed (and executed) because of some *canard* put about by their enemies and competitors. In these circumstances ministers tended to be as occupied with trying to guard their positions, and lining their pockets while they could, as with addressing problems of state. But 1656 saw the initiation of a period of reform associated with the Koprulu Viziers.[16] Mehmet Koprulu, who hailed from Albania, had acquired considerable experience by the time he became Grand Vizier at the age of seventy-one. He also enjoyed a reputation for integrity, and showed great energy and ruthlessness during his five years of office. He dismissed many incompetent and corrupt officials, executed the disobedient (and indeed anyone who endangered his position) and ensured that men he trusted occupied all posts of importance. He pruned expenditures, reduced the number of office-holders, interfered with the religious establishment and suppressed the Muslim fundamentalists. Both the solvency of the state and the efficiency of government began to improve.

On Mehmet's death in 1661 his son Fazil Ahmet succeeded him, and more stress came to be placed on military affairs. The Cretan War was at last brought to a succesful conclusion; Janos Kemeny, the hostile Prince of Transylvania, was defeated and replaced by Michael Apafy who recognized Ottoman suzereinty; the Habsburgs were forced to conclude a peace on terms satisfactorily to the Porte; and a war with Poland ended in 1676 with the acquisition of Podolia and western Ukraine. That year Fazil Ahmet died and was succeeded by his foster brother Kara Mustafa. But the tide of Ottoman military success continued to rise. In 1682 the Turks supported the candidature of the *kuruc* leader and political entrepreneur Imre Thokolly to be King of Hungary, and his forces overran Upper Hungary (Slovakia). The following year, while Thokolly's Hungarians guarded its flank and the Crimean Tatars swept westwards to join them, Kara Mustafa led a vast Turkish army to Vienna and laid siege to the city.

The rout of the Ottoman army and the relief of Vienna, with the help of the Polish army and contingents from some German states, have been described often and well by historians so there is no need to repeat the story here.[17] At the time the event inspired the publication of dozens of fly-sheets announcing the victory and describing how it was won – and the news sparked great excitement in the more literate regions of Christian Europe. Ever since, the siege of Vienna has been regarded as a great watershed, as the decisive historical event which finally halted the Turkish advance into Europe that had begun in the fourteenth century. Subsequent events suggest that it turned the tide. By 1699 the Turks had been chased out of Hungary and Podolia, and they were to lose ground steadily to the Christian powers thereafter. Yet set in a broader historical context the battle for Vienna in 1683, dramatic and important as it was, seems rather less of a turning-point than popular opinion of the time, and since, believed.

The display of Turkish military strength in 1683 belied the ability of the Ottoman Empire to sustain it. The Koprulu reforms, beneficial though they had been, had not addressed the deep structural flaws in the Ottoman system that had appeared in the sixteenth century; and the accretion of strength which the reforms had brought was squandered by Kara Mustafa's excessive ambition and overconfidence. Even if the Turks had taken Vienna it is difficult to imagine their being able to sustain and exploit the success. The mere acquisition and despoilation of more territory was no solution to the daunting problems of structural decline. The Koprolu reforms had improved governmental management but had failed to address systemic problems. Hence, from a long-term perspective they only served to delay the process of reintegration a little. The Ottoman state was in decline before 1683, and the decline continued thereafter.

Nor, on the other hand, did Poland's contribution to the relief of Vienna signal any significant change in her circumstances or prospects. Jan III Sobieski's part in the victory, valuable though it was, has been somewhat exaggerated. He brought to the field fewer than a third of the 40,000 men that he had promised; and though they constituted the right of the line, it was Charles of Lorraine who planned the battle, and the troops in the centre and on the left that bore the brunt of it (not to mention the gallant defenders of Vienna itself under von Starhemberg). Thereafter the Polish troops played a rather less distinguished role, plundering the Turkish camp and sustaining a defeat at Parkany during the pursuit. The legend that Vienna was saved largely through Polish efforts owes much to a publicity campaign mounted by Sobieski himself to enhance his own reputation and give a sorely-needed fillip to Polish morale. Hence the ceremonial entry he made into Vienna before the Emperor himself could arrive; and the publication of the letter to his consort giving his own tendentious account of the battle.[18]

By the Treaty of Carlowitz in 1699, to be sure, Poland was finally to retrieve the territories she had lost to the Turks in the 1670s, but she owed this more to her association with a broad alliance of Christian powers[19] than to her obsolescent and underfunded army, and she was never to regain the territories lost to Russia. Like the Ottoman Empire, the Polish state of the late seventeenth century suffered from deep structural problems: an unreformed constitution which made her vulnerable to foreign interference; demographic decline; and economic weaknesses accentuated by the wars in the middle of the century, from which the recovery was both slow and incomplete.[20]

For the Habsburgs, however, the relief of Vienna initiated a run of successes. In 1686 their troops captured Buda and before long virtually all Hungary, and Transylvania, was in their hands. Furthermore the Hungarian Diet summoned in 1687 was docile, voting Leopold 2 million gulden and agreeing to the crown of Hungary becoming an hereditary Habsburg possession. But the Hungarians would not remain so tractable; the territory which the crown had gained from the Turks remained to be integrated; and continuing efforts were required to consolidate the dynasty and make its government more effective.

The Habsburg administrative machine was a bewildering hotchpotch of chanceries and councils, most of them dealing with individual territories, and some with awkward overlaps in their responsibilities. There were rival departments for Austria and the (German) Empire, for example; and the Supreme War Council (*Hofkriegsrath*) supervised diplomatic relations with the Turks as well as administering the army and the

'Military Frontier' districts in the south. The Emperor's decision was final, his authority potentially supreme. He might have emulated Alexis or Frederick William of Prussia but, except fitfully in Hungary, he did not. Leopold was a traditionalist who, perhaps wisely, preferred to court rather than confront regional interests. So localism remained strong, the defict permanent, and the running of affairs largely decentralized, often lax and sometimes corrupt. While one central institution, the War Council, continued to swallow resources another, the Court Chamber (*Hofkammer*), worked to find them. This office administered the royal free cities, supervised indirect taxation and collected revenues from Bohemia. It now set about exploiting parts of newly-occupied Hungary.

The search for new sources of income was by no means a novelty for the Habsburg court or any other, of course. It had long employed alchemists who might find a way of manufacturing gold. But some of the cameralist (or mercantilist) ideas for raising more money by promoting trade and general prosperity which it now adopted promised better success. The Habsburg court was inspired by Colbert's schemes to promote the foreign trade of France, and by the successes of the English and Dutch merchant venturers. So were other Eastern European governments. Thus Alexis of Russia built a flotilla at Astrakhan to protect his commerce with Persia and find a new trade route to the East Indies across the Caspian (which German scholars assured him must be possible).

Frederick William of Prussia also built a little fleet and founded a trading company to run a colony in West Africa, but his, too, was a failure. And the 'Oriental Trading Company' founded by the Habsburg court in 1666 to promote trade with the Ottoman Empire along the Danube, proved no more successful.[21] These disappointments were mostly due to a shortage of merchant enterprise capital and to disorders: predatory *haiduk* and then war interrupted commerce along the Danube; the rebel Razin burned the flotilla at Astrakhan. But geography also played a part: the states of Eastern Europe were simply too far away from the Atlantic to share in world trade or build profitable colonial empires.

Internal colonization, however, offered better prospects of success. Siberia provided Russia with tremendous potential for development; the Prussian government resettled depopulated regions and encouraged the immigration of skilled foreigners, notably Huguenots. Some Polish magnates, like Laski, followed similar policies on their estates, giving asylum to religious refugees from Bohemia and Moravia and encouraging Jews to build new towns. There was an agricultural parallel in the Ottoman Balkans where, in the seventeenth century especially, enterprising notables would found sheep-farms, cattle ranches or share-cropping estates on wasteland.[22] In similar fashion, from the 1680s the Habsburg government set about making war-torn Hungary more productive.

The method was to encourage settlement, especially of Germans, by offering land and immunity from taxation for a time to help them to establish themselves. This provoked another storm of protest from the Hungarians, but (though exasperated at their apparent intractability and wilfulness) Vienna had not been motivated simply by arrogance and prejudice. Germans, even then, had a reputation for hard work and discipline. The response was excellent and gathered momentum in the early eighteenth century. They moved in from Silesia, Moravia, Wurtemberg, and Bavaria. Orthodox Serbs came too, and even Spaniards. Sometimes, as in the Banat, servicemen were encouraged to settle and (as with the French in North America) girls would be recruited and sent out to them as brides. And Germans came to populate towns as well as countryside. As a result, by 1740 Buda was completely German-speaking and many other towns largely so. Indeed, one can still find distinctive 'Swabian' villages in the Hungarian countryside, even though the descendents of those who built them have long since been absorbed linguistically or else driven away.[23]

By such means Hungary was made much more productive, but it was still the Achilles' heel in the Habsburg body politic, as the rebellion of Ferenc II Rakocsi (1703–11) showed. The fact that the bulk of Rakocsi's support derived from Calvinists led to a new drive to Catholicize the country once the rebellion had been suppressed. The Hungarian Estates remained loyal on that occasion, and the handful of great landowners like the Eszterhazy were Catholic and dependable. Nevertheless, by the Treaty on Szatmar (1711) which ended the rebellion, the Habsburgs conceded that the Estates had rights to grant or deny taxes in Hungary. The Hungarians never seemed to be quite as beguiled by the glamour of the Habsburg court as their Austrian or Bohemian counterparts; and, like the Catholic Church, the court had become a major ingredient in the glue that helped the empire in eastern Europe to hold together.

This glamour did not derive solely from the formalities of what was essentially Spanish court protocol, nor from the prestige of possessing the crown of Charlemagne and the most ancient of all chivalric orders, the Golden Fleece. There was another, more complex, element associated with the baroque movement in the arts. Elaborate equestrian ballets (in which notables like General Montecuccoli participated), and magnificent stagings of operas and plays, like those performed in celebration of Leopold's marriage in 1666–7, for example, helped to indoctrinate courtiers and other spectators, asserting, by means of allegory, the virtues of the monarch and the glory of the dynasty. But the chief glories of the Habsburg Baroque were to come later, and they were to reinforce loyalty to the regime among much wider circles than the court itself.

The relief of Vienna in 1683 and the series of military successes which followed inspired a surge of confidence which found exuberant expression in the arts, especially architecture. The development came to be associated above all with Johann Fischer von Erlach (1656–1723), Imperial Inspector of Buildings for the Court and Festivities from 1705, and Johann von Hildebrandt (1663–1745), trained town planner and military engineer who became Court Architect and later succeeded Fischer in post.[24] As the title suggests, they were concerned not merely with buildings but with the design of temporary structures like triumphal arches for ceremonial entrances into Vienna, and designs for firework displays which comprised not just, as nowadays, a series of pretty (but momentary and meaningless) cascades in the sky, but entire scenes which lasted for several minutes. Here, then, was a series of media capable of educating the observer, not least politically. It was one of several means, secular and religious, to promote awe of the dynasty, deference to masters and obedience to the church.

In the characteristic way of the baroque, this was done with a degree of flamboyance – but elliptically, through the suggestive use of symbols and by exploiting allegory, in the knowledge that anyone with a basic education would be familiar with the gods and heroes of classical antiquity, and that even the illiterate might be expected to recognize a number of saints as well as major biblical characters. The paintings and sculpture with which buildings were adorned exploited this repertoire in order to draw attention and to convey messages to viewers (to the effect that, for example, the Emperor was benign and valiant; that he combined in his person both the Christian and the classical virtues; or that Austria, Bohemia and Hungary represented a terrestial Trinity). Furthermore, the design of buildings themselves was contrived to affect the emotions, not only by weightiness or the harmonious rhythm of a facade, but through the contrivance of spaces to create illusions, and the exploitation of light and shadow for dramatic effect.

Music, too, was important. This, after all, was the age of Bach (and of his well-tempered clavier, itself an expression of order); and along with the other arts, music made churchgoing a pleasurable experience, lent mystique to the dynasty, and helped to glamorize its cosmopolitan court. Art also advertised the manner in which the dynasty rewarded its ablest and most devoted servitors – for the Belvedere, designed by Hildebrandt and arguably one of the most beautiful architectural ensembles in the world, was built for Prince Eugen, victor of Zenta and Blenheim, Peterwardein and Belgrade. And the arts helped to make Vienna popular as a centre of fashion as well as of administration. Most families of account built palaces there in which to reside during the season. Most Hungarians, however, still stood aloof and culturally suspicious, their horizons bounded by their estates, their district or their county. Nevertheless, the arts constituted a generally effective means, along with patronage and compulsion, by which the Habsburgs held their still somewhat ramshackle Empire in East-Central Europe together.

In Prussia the Elector Frederick III (who was at last crowned as a king with appropriate pomp in 1701) employed an architect and sculptor who had been trained in Danzig, Andreas Schlueter, to ensure that his palace should have a magnificence appropriate to his station. In Russia, however, where some baroque features were evident in the wooden palace of Tsar Alexis at Kolomenskoe, it was only under Peter (d.1725) that prevailing European fashions were whole-heartedly and publicly embraced. Indeed in 1714 Schlueter was persuaded to move to St Petersburg, though he died soon after his arrival. In any case, despite creating the greatest architectural monument of the age, the new city of St Petersburg, Peter himself had no liking for formal living in grand palaces and, as the most absolute of all the monarchs in Eastern Europe, had no need of conspicuous magnificence, other than to maintain his imperial prestige abroad.

Poland, too, shared in the baroque, though rather than helping to bolster any absolutist tendency on the part of the crown, it emphasized the process of decentralization – partly because it was adopted by magnates wanting to enhance their own prestige; partly through the development of Sarmatism, the myth, at once escapist and justificatory, that the Polish nobility were genetically distinct from the population of the country as a whole by virtue of their descent from the Sarmatians of Roman times. As we shall see, this provided a justification for serfdom, but at the same time it asserted, in overblown baroque style, the exceptional quality of the Polish nobility and the superiority of Poland to any other state. Its constitution, so it was claimed, was perfect – modelled on that of the Roman Republic and with no trace of tyranny. Furthermore, it was Poland that had defended Christendom and rescued Europe from the Turks. As the poet Wespasian Kochowski, who had accompanied Jan Sobieski to Vienna, wrote:

A neighbour saved the throne of the West
From being overthrown;
The sword of the Sarmatian rescuers
Avenged the vineyards of Hungary.

Since Poland, as it was believed, had achieved perfection, it followed that it had no need of improvement. Since the *szlachta* had achieved success through following their ancient, chivalrous way of life, innovation could only be harmful. Since they were strong and self-sufficient, there was no call for Poles to borrow from the West. Foreigners, indeed, came to be regarded as inferior, even contemptible. Xenophobia grew along with intolerance (attitudes which were not formerly much in evidence), and educational standards declined. In such ways Sarmatism, a form of escapism born of national disaster, served only to reinforce Poland's failure to address the challenge of the age, her backwardness, and her separation from the West.[25]

At the same time the already-existing tendency to adopt oriental and particularly Turkish fashions intensified – not only in weaponry design, clothing and hair-styles, but in furnishings and interior decoration. The baroque taste for the exotic was also reflected in some Polish translations of oriental tales. Yet while Poland, rejecting absolutist France, adopted fashions from the Turks, the Turks themselves were beginning to imitate French fashions and import western artists to decorate their palace walls. Polish Sarmatism had its antithesis in Ottoman 'Tulipomania'.

Tulipomania, a phenomenon associated with Damad Ibrahim Pasha, Grand Vizier from 1718 to 1730, denotes far more than a horticultural fad for growing rare forms of a flower. Originating in an attempt by the Vizier to keep the Sultan amused (and so, no doubt, to allow himself a freer hand), it involved the building of a 'Palace of Happiness', surrounded by gardens, at the very tip of the Golden Horn, which became the scene of frivolous, elegant and lavish entertainments. Nevertheless Tulipomania was important – because it signalled a cultural revival and the breaking down of the Ottoman Empire's cultural isolation.

The court poet Ahmed Nedun sang joyfully of love, but at the same time translations were made of Arabic and Persian histories, public libraries were opened and the first Turkish printing press (established by an Hungarian Protestant convert to Islam) began to publish books on geography and science. Tortoises ambled round the tulip-beds at night with candles on their backs, but for the first time the Sultan sent resident ambassadors to European courts and the West was scoured for ideas and technology from which the Empire might benefit.[26] The essay in hedonism, inspired by drawings of the French king's palace at Fontainbleau, its gardens and its furniture, and the new, Western, vogue for *chinoiserie*, was associated with a revival of learning and developed into a 'Westernizing' trend that might, had it been sustained (and sufficiently well funded), have helped to revive the state.

It seems doubtful if this development was inspired by Russia's 'Westernization' under Peter the Great. In 1711 Ottoman forces had comprehensively defeated Peter's army on the River Pruth and might easily have taken the Tsar himself captive. Yet this event is not counted among the decisive battles in history, whereas Peter's victory over the Swedes and their ally Mazeppa, the Ukrainian counterpart of Thokolly, at Poltava in 1709 is, and rightly so. In the long run, the reverse at the Pruth turned out merely to have delayed the Russian advance towards the Balkans a little. On the other hand, although it was to take several more years and a great naval victory at Hango to establish the fact in a formal treaty, Poltava signalled Russia's arrival as a great power and the dominant force in Northern and Eastern Europe.

There were considerable consequences for the balance of power in the Balkans too. Just as the rise of Prussia was to threaten Habsburg predominance in Germany (and from 1740, when Frederick the Great marched into Silesia, even their hereditary lands), so the rise of Russia was to threaten Habsburg interests in the Balkans, notwithstanding their frequent cooperation against the Turks. Russia enjoyed the considerable advantage of sharing the same Orthodox faith as the great majority of the Balkan population, who tended to look on her as their protector. For its part, the Habsburg government encouraged the Uniat Church, which though Orthodox in ritual recognized the supremacy of Rome, giving its members equal rights with Catholics in 1699; it granted privileges, too, to immigrant Serbs whom it needed; and eventually, in 1759, it went so far as to compromise its own Catholic principles by emancipating its Orthodox subjects.[27] Nevertheless Russia was to gain the predominate influence on the Balkans.

Though Poltava had taken most foreign observers by surprise it should not have done so. The assumption, nourished by the reports of generations of Western travellers,[28] that because Russia was isolated, backward and barbaric it could be of little account, was mistaken. But was Russia's emergence a consequence of her 'Westernization', a reflection of burgeoning economic strength, or due to the absolutism of her governmental system?

It could be argued that the success stemmed from a combination of all three. Certainly, the Swedish army had been a model of effectiveness that had swept all before it early in the Thirty Years' War; in order to overcome them the Russians had to adopt Western military organization and techniques. In fact the Kremlin had long since recognized the need to do so. Individual Western explosives experts had been engaged as early as the mid-sixteenth century; under Boris Godunov entire units of Western mercenaries had been employed; and by the 1660s not only did a substantial portion of the field army consist of 'regiments of new formation', but a Western drill-book for infantry had been published in Russian. The Dutch, who had been among the chief creators of the military revolution, were prominent among Tsar Alexis's military advisers, they supervised the armaments manufacturing centre at Tula, and acted as midwife at the birth of the ill-fated Caspian flotilla as later to the Russian navy proper. Peter's success, then, rested in part on policies of military Westernization which were already well-established.

But the success was also predicated on a resilient Russian economy which had recovered surprisingly well from the costly wars and civil disturbances of the later seventeenth century and from Peter's own early defeats. This mysterious resilience needs explaining, but a convincing explanation is hard to find. The country (which by the turn of the century included all Siberia) was underpopulated, overwhelmingly agrarian, and with its vast mineral resources as yet largely untapped. Like the Habsburgs and Prussian rulers of the eighteenth century, the Russian state even before Peter had encouraged trade and industry. However, the state also accounted for the lion's share of foreign trade, and founded and ran industries, by no means all of which were strategic, or profitable. Whether the state encouraged or inhibited economic development is debatable. In any case before Peter's reign it is difficult to distinguish between the private and state sectors, since the chief merchants of the realm constituted a special order whose members acted as financial administrators for the state, and entrepreneurs, like the Stroganovs, who had opened up Siberia, operated under special licence from the Tsar.

It has been suggested that the Russian economy owed its resilience to its isolation from the 'world economy'; that it was therefore insulated from the price inflation, deriving from the influx of Spanish silver from the Americas, which had had such devastating effects on the rest of Europe.[29] Yet the economy was not so isolated, the value of Russian money was related to the *Joachimsthaler*, the widely respected German currency, and a crisis of financial confidence had indeed occurred in the 1660s, though the cause was internal, the currency reform launched in 1654. A more convincing explanation may lie in the fact that the country possessed in Moscow one of the largest cities in Europe with a population numbering about 200,000 souls. So large a concentration is likely to have been an economic generator of considerable magnitude. If so, this was a fruit, in part, of long-standing governmental policy in, for example, requiring merchants of conquered cities to move there. Yet the building of St Petersburg offers an even better example of the association of Westernization, absolutism and economic development.[30]

The victory at Poltava was important largely because it ensured that Russia would keep the marshy site on which the construction of a new city, St Petersburg, had already begun. St Petersburg was to be Peter's crowning achievement. It at last realized his predecessors' ambition to acquire a Baltic port (and hence much easier access to the West and to world markets than were available overland or via the perilous northern route from Archangel). But Peter not only made it an important commercial centre but his capital and the show-piece of Westernization in Russia, both in the design of its buildings and the institutions that it housed: the Admiralty, the new Colleges which replaced the former ministries (*prikazy*), the museum (*Kunstkammer*) and, ultimately, the Imperial Academy of Sciences, which, unlike its forerunner, the Academy founded in Moscow in the 1680s, was exclusively Western in orientation and predominately German in its staffing.[31]

St Petersburg was built, of course, by forced labour and on the bones of many dead; and the bulk of its population did not move there voluntarily but in response to government fiat. Without compulsion, however, the project would have foundered. It could hardly have been built by a Habsburg Emperor in negotiation with Estates, however docile. Absolutism, then, was the *sine qua non* of St Petersburg and all it stood for.

At this point, however, we confront a paradox. Absolutism represented political modernism. It had been the prevailing trend in the West (in Tudor England as well as the France of Louis XIV); and Russia had become the most absolute state in Eastern Europe. Furthermore (for all the attempts of successive Tsars to enlarge the spirit of enterprise among their subjects and give it direction) the state, like its Western couterparts, had become the largest entrepreneur in the land. Yet though elsewhere absolutism was to give way to some form of political plurality, in Russia it was to remain entrenched. And the Russian economy was ultimately to be outpaced by that of almost every other state, not only in Western but in Eastern Europe. Why?

According to an eminent Hungarian historian,[32] this was partly because in the West some institutional elements that had a potential for changing the absolutist political structure were preserved, whereas in Russia this was not the case. There, absolutism provided the framework within which all change had to be contained; and this was associated with a distinctive mentality for, in asserting its predominance over the Church, the Russian state claimed, in effect, to possess a monopoly of truth and moral authority. Dissenters who would not submit were therefore forced into a stance which was as absolute and as uncompromising as the state which they confronted. Hence the Old Believers who, in the later seventeenth century, burned themselves to death in their churches rather than accept Westernization or the liturgical revisions that had been ordained; hence the bogus 'tsars' who appeared with increasing frequency after 1600 to claim the throne of Russia.[33] Yet this absolutist political culture (noticeable throughout Eastern Europe in the Communist period and even today in the tendency to associate moral and political considerations) was not confined to Orthodox countries that had inherited the Byzantine political tradition; they found some resonance in the Habsburg regime in Bohemia, in the Polish *liberum veto* and the intransigence of so many of the Hungarian, as well as Polish, gentry.

Westerners have customarily attributed Russia's economic failures to its absolutist system. The explanation will not quite do, however. As we have seen, Russia, like the absolute regimes of the West, implemented cameralist policies yet did not reap comparable benefits from them. The Habsburgs and Prussia had similarly sad experiences. They lacked some essential ingredient for success. In the West it was sufficient for governments to organize and protect companies of merchant venturers and entrepreneurs; in Eastern Europe as a whole men of wealth who were willing to risk it on such enterprises were lacking, so the state usually found itself providing all the enterprise and capital. The General Directorate to promote industry and commerce which the Habsburgs established in 1746 initiated and acted rather than merely supporting; and the state took a lead, too, in agricultural improvement, setting an example in the newly-conquered territories, draining marshes and introducing clover as a crop. The Polish crown introduced some reforms on its estates in Lithuania – but landlords interested in introducing new crops and agricultural techniques had become as rare as urban entrepreneurs.

Yet Eastern Europe had not always been so short of entrepreneurs. In Poland and Hungary, for example, there had once been thriving communities of merchants; and noblemen themselves had once (and not so long before) engaged enthusiastically in business. All that had changed, however. The merchant class had become much weaker; the richest of them had either lost their wealth or, like the Thurzo family (by now great magnates in Hungary), had invested in land and bought their way into the noble class. And the enterprising noblemen, having lost their taste for business, now viewed commerce as a deceitful, ignoble, pursuit fit enough for Jews, Armenians or Greeks (whom they might engage to do any such dirty work that might be necessary) but inconsistent with their own status as noblemen. At the same time their outlook on life had tended to become rigid[34] – as inflexible as society itself.

This freezing of society, a comparatively recent phenomenon, had much to do with the political and economic singularities that we have noticed. Service to the state, whether direct or indirect (through serving those who served) had become the basis of society in Russia; and, except in the vastnesses of Siberia where people could escape the arm of the state, there was no social autonomy. (Subsequent attempts to create autonomous institutions in Catherine II's reign were to wilt, just as Peter's attempts to instill a mercantile spirit into men of means had wilted.) Society and administration had become confused with one another. But even in those parts of Eastern Europe where there were groups that enjoyed rights and a measure of autonomy, society was much less variegated, mobile and swelling with wealth than that of north-western Europe. It was also less flexible and more imbalanced. Social mobility had all but ceased; the middle classes had declined both in power and as a proportion of the population; the nobility, including the service nobility of Russia, were the dominant grouping, and in Hungary and Poland extraordinarily numerous.[35] And everywhere outside the Ottoman Balkans, the peasantry, by far the most numerous social category, were mostly serfs at the mercy of their lords.

From the middle of the seventeenth century an economic boom had been gathering momentum; but Eastern Europe was not deriving much benefit from it. As we have seen, the incidence and intensity of wars, and Eastern Europe's isolation from the main arteries of world trade do not fully account for this; societal differences clearly had some bearing on it, and serfdom was closely associated with the other social peculiarities that we have noted. It also helped to form some of those distinctive traits in the mentality of noblemen; and, it had profound economic implications too. It was serfdom above all else, perhaps, which distinguished the two halves of Europe. Yet serfdom was a comparatively recent institution, finally entrenched in Russia as late as 1649 as part of a new Code of Laws which was itself an instrument of centralizing absolutism.

* * *

How and why serfdom was imposed is one vital piece of the puzzle we are trying to reconstruct. But it is not the only one. How did the noble class gain their preponderance, and why did their ethos change so fundamentally in so short a time? Furthermore the causes of Ottoman decline, the origins of the Polish constitution, and the strange impact of the Reformation on Eastern Europe have yet to be explored. Demographic trends and the incidence and intensity of wars may also help to account for the different rhythms and tempi of regional development that we have already noticed. All these questions draw attention to the sixteenth century, when the colonial period was only in its infancy, when Habsburg Spain was the chief exploiter of the New World; and when a huge growth in demand for the produce of Eastern Europe gave it a considerable economic stimulus. Here, seemingly, was a period of opportunity. Perhaps, after all, the sixteenth and early seventeenth century constituted the critical time, when the destinies of east and west began to diverge.

REFERENCES

1. The idea that the seventeenth century saw a 'general crisis' has long been current among historians (see T. Aston (ed.), *Crisis* in *Europe 1550–1660* (London, 1970)) though they differ about its nature and causes. There are differences, too, about its timing: e.g. for Paul Hazard it starts about 1680, Theodore Rabb places it in the period 1630–75, while Ronald Mousnier dates it c.1620–c.1660. Remarkably little attention, however, has been paid by Western historians to the crisis in Eastern Europe. For the origins and earlier stages, see Chapter 8.
2. According to one of the most distinguished students of the war, J.V. Polisensky (*The Thirty Years War*, London, 1974), it contributed to the rise of the West as well as the relative decline of Eastern Europe. More particularly it promoted the economic rise of the Netherlands and England; destroyed the middle classes; discouraged enterprise among the nobility in

Central Europe; and exaggerated the move towards serfdom in Eastern Europe. All this gave the West advantages over the East and hence promoted the separation of the two parts of the continent (p. 260).

3. See Chapter 8.
4. See the appropriate maps plotting the incidence of *haiduk* activity in B. Cvetkova, *Hajdutstvoto v blgarskite zemi* (Sofia, 1971).
5. The Assembly of the Land was hardly a nascent parliament, however – see L. Cherepnin, *Zemskie sobory russkogo gosudarstva v xvi–xvii vv* (Moscow, 1978).
6. See the rules for his falcon hunt in my *Alexis, Tsar of All the Russias* (London, 1984) pp. 118–20.
7. *Alexis, op. cit., passim* but especially Chapter X; also 'The Emergence of Absolutism in Russia' in John Miller (ed.), *Absolutism in Seventeenth Century Europe* (London, 1990) pp. 75–93.
8. See Chapter 11.
9. This was the *liberum veto*. The first to exercise it was one Wladyslaw Sicinski.
10. Aside from J. Tazbir in A. Gieysztor *et al.* (eds), *History of Poland*, 2nd ed. (Warsaw, 1979) esp. pp. 218–19, see the valuable essay by A. Kaminski, 'The *Szlachta* of the Polish-Lithuanian Commonwealth and Their Government' in I. Banac and P. Bushkovitch (eds), *The Nobility in Russia and Eastern Europe* (New Haven, 1983) pp. 17–46. On the implications for the Polish army in the decades that followed, see J.A. Gierowski, 'The Polish-Lithuanian Armies in the Confederations and Insurrections of the Eighteenth Century' in G. Rothenberg *et al.* (eds), *East-Central European Society and War in the Pre-Revolutionary Eighteenth Century* (New York, 1982) pp. 215–38.
11. F. Carsten, *The Origins of Prussia* (Oxford, 1968); also C.A. Macartney (ed.), *The Habsburg and Hohenzollern Dynasties* (New York, 1970) pp. 209ff. and H. Rosenberg, *Bureaucracy, Aristocracy and Autocracy* (Boston, 1966) pp. 34ff.
12. R.J.W. Evans, *The Making of the Habsburg Monarchy 1550–1700* (Oxford, 1979).
13. Largely because of the expense, not only of uniforms and equipment but of barracks and supply, so that the troops should not alienate and impoverish Habsburg subjects as the much smaller and inadequately-financed Polish army did (see Gierowski, *loc. cit.*). The Habsburgs also disposed of defence forces on the southern frontier of Slavonia who, like Cossacks, were rewarded in land and tax exemption rather than pay. See G. Rothenberg, *The Austrian Military Border in Croatia* (Urbana, 1960). Also Chapter 8.
14. On this, and for much of what follows, see J.P. Spielman, *Leopold I of Austria* (London, 1977) as well as Evans, *op. cit.*, and J. Bérenger, 'The Austrian Lands: Hapsburg Absolutism under the Emperor Leopold I', in Miller, *op. cit.*, pp. 157–74.
15. Notably Imre Thokolly, ambitious rebel and leader of *kuruc*. On Thokolly, see the works of L. Benczedi, including his essay on Hungarian sentiment of the period in *Harvard Ukrainian Studies* X (3–4), December 1986, pp. 424–37. Also Bérenger, *loc. cit.*.
16. On the Koprolu reforms see Stanford J. Shaw, *History of the Ottoman Empire and Modern Turkey* vol. I (Cambridge, 1978) pp. 207–16 (in which he chiefly follows the Turkish chronicler Naima); also A. Kurat, 'The Reign of Mehmet IV' in M.A. Cook (ed.), *A History of the Ottoman Empire to 1730* (Cambridge 1976) pp. 163ff., and P. Sugar, *Southeastern Europe under Ottoman Rule* (Seattle, 1977) pp. 198ff..
17. E.g. Thomas M. Barker, *Double Eagle and Crescent* (New York, 1967); John Stoye, *The Siege of Vienna* (London, 1964).
18. Reproduced in Macartney, *op. cit.*, pp. 67–76.

19. On inter-state relations in eastern Europe at the turn of the seventeenth and eighteenth centuries, see B. Sumner, *Peter the Great and the Ottoman Empire* (Oxford, 1949).
20. Although overtaken in detail, Jan Rutkowski's *Histoire Economique de la Pologne Avant les Partages* (Paris, 1927) still provides a generally sound overview, esp. pp. 89–92, 159–60.
21. Evans, *op. cit.* pp. 146–52, Spielman, *op. cit.*, pp. 22–6.
22. See *inter alia* Fikret Adanir, 'Tradition and Rural Change in Southeastern Europe during Ottoman Rule' in D. Chirot (ed.), *The Origins of Backwardness in Eastern Europe* (Berkeley, California, 1989) pp. 131–76.
23. See H. Marczali, *Hungary in the Eighteenth Century* (New York, 1971) pp. 207–12. These are not to be confused, however, with various German settlements in Transylvania which originated much earlier (See Chapter 10).
24. Spielman, *op. cit.*, pp. 54–5; Eberhard Hempel, *Baroque Art and Architecture in Central Europe* (Harmondsworth, 1965) especially pp. 88–98.
25. J. Tazbir, 'Culture of the Baroque in Poland' in A. Maczak, H. Samsonowicz and P. Burke (eds), *East-Central Europe in Transition* (Cambridge, 1985) pp. 167–80; also in Gieysztor, *op. cit.*, pp. 226–8; J. Michalski, 'Le sarmatisme et le probleme d'europeisation de la Pologne' in V. Zimanyi (ed.), *La Pologne et la Hongrie aux xvi–xviii siècle* (Budapest, 1981) pp. 113ff., J. Krzyzanowski *History of Polish Literature* (Warsaw, 1978) pp. 133–7. Something of the mentality of the lesser gentry of the period can be gauged from the autobiography of Jan Pasek, *Memoirs of the Polish Baroque* (ed. C. Leach) (Berkeley, California, 1976).
26. Shaw, *op. cit.*, I, pp. 234–8; A. Kurat and J. Bromley, 'The Retreat of the Turks 1683–1730' in Cook, *op. cit.*, pp. 215–16.
27. The Uniats could also be used as a counterweight to the Hungarians. The indirect result was the first stirring of Romanian nationalism when, in the 1740s, Uniat Bishop Ion Klein found a way of legitimizing his flock's claim to equality with the three historical Hungarian 'nations' (Hungarians, Saxons and Szeklers) by claiming they were descended from the ancient Dacians. See K. Hitchens, 'Religious Tradition and National Consciousness Among the Romanians of Transilvania', *Harvard Ukrainian Studies*, X (3–4), December 1986, pp. 542–58. Meanwhile, as a direct consequence of the failure of Peter's offensive against the Turks, in conjunction with Dimitru Cantemir, the ruler of Orthodox Moldavia, the Turks installed 'Phanariot' rulers both there and in Wallachia (1714), considering administrators of Greek culture more reliable.
28. This is certainly the case, with rare exceptions, of the English travellers, whether merchants or diplomatists, from the Elizabethans (e.g. Giles Fletcher, *Of the Russe Commonwealth* (London, 1591) but see also R. Hakluyt, *The Principal Navigations, Voyages, Traffiques and Discoveries of the English Nation* (Glasgow, 1903) II, pp. 248ff. and III) to Charles Howard, Earl of Carlisle (see G. Miege, *A Relation of Three Embassies….* (London, 1669).
29. See Chapter 8.
30. On the encouragement and regulation of trade see the New Trade Statute, *Alexis, op. cit.*, pp. 191–2, and note 18, p. 273; on whether the state helped or hindered the economy in the seventeenth century see S. Baron *(Muscovite Russia*, London, 1980), who changes his mind on the question. For the idea that the Russian economy was insulated from world trends of price inflation, see B. Mironov, 'Revoliutsiia tsen v Rossii xviii v' (cyclostyle), 1989. On price inflation in the sixteenth century, see Cap. 8. For the history of pre-Petrine

monetary policy (and the monetary reform of 1654–63), see A. Mel'nikova, *Russkie monety ot Ivana Groznogo do Petra Pervogo* (Moscow, 1989). Some reflections of S. Troitskii are also pertinent. See his *Russkii absoliutizm i dvorianstvo v xviii v* (Moscow, 1974). On forced migrations of merchants to Moscow (not always effective), see P. Bushkovitch, *The Merchants of Muscovy* (Cambridge, 1980).

31. The Academy founded by Tsar Fedor, though largely Greek in orientation, did embrace Latin culture, however, and its chief luminaries, the Likudi brothers, had Venetian connections. For a translation of part of the old Academy's charter, see G. Vernadsky *et al.*, eds., *Source-Book For Russian History*, vol. I (New Haven, Conn., 1972) p. 248.
32. J. Szucs, 'The Three Historical Regions of Europe', *Acta Historica Academiae Scientiarum Hungaricae*, 29 (2–4) 1983, esp. pp. 161–7. He errs, however, in accepting P. Anderson's notion that in the East absolutism was merely 'a device for the consolidation of serfdom'. The serfdom question will be addressed in Chapter 8.
33. On Pretenders, see P. Skrynnikov, *Samozvantsy v Rossii v nachale xvii veka* (Moscow, 1990) (more particularly on the imposture of G. Otrep'ev), and the works referred to in my 'The Pretender Phenomenon in Eighteenth Century Russia', *Past & Present*, 66, 1975, pp. 61–83.
34. On the nobility's changing views of business, see P.L. Pach, in *Etudes Historiques Hongroises* (Budapest, 1985) vol. II, pp. 131ff.; also Marczali, op. *cit.*, pp. 86–7.
35. The nobility (including the 'sandalled' gentry) accounted for about 10 per cent of the population of Poland-Lithuania and a good 5 per cent of Hungary's, although in some counties (including those of Szatmar and Bihar, where noble status had been granted collectively to the entire population of certain settlements) it was as high as 20 per cent.

8

Metamorphoses (1526–1648)

Henceforth these regions accustomed to the ringing of church bells will hear the cry of the muezzin….

Proclamation of Suleyman the Magnificent, 1541.

On Christmas night according to the Lutheran calendar the Devil himself came to Church, and sat on a throne near the altar. He wore black silk clothes in the German fashion … and a black silk cap on each of his nine heads.

Confession of witchcraft in sixteenth-century Riga.

On the evening of 29 August 1526 Louis II, twenty-year-old King of Hungary and Bohemia, fell into a swollen stream while fleeing from the battlefield at Mohacz and drowned. The heavy armour which weighed him down symbolized the obsolescence of his army which had been overwhelmed by the superior fire-power and discipline of the Ottoman force under Sultan Suleiman the Magnificent.[1] It being late in the campaigning season, the Turks soon turned for home. Nevertheless, their victory was to have serious consequences.

There were far-reaching effects in the sphere of religion, for example. The deaths at Mohacs of both Hungarian archbishops and five of the country's fourteen bishops weakened the administration and the authority of Hungary's Church. Even more significant, however, was the effect on faith. The Turks' military successes encouraged Christians to doubt the potency of their Catholic religion. Martin Luther had described the Turks as a scourge sent by God to punish Christendom for its sins; and the Turks themselves began to encourage Protestantism in territories under their control. There was soon much wavering in belief: a number of Catholic bishops became Protestants; some Orthodox prelates were also attracted; and a variety of differing confessions within the Protestant camp each drew adherents. This was the heyday of the Reformation in Eastern Europe. But it was not to last long. The attractions of reformed Catholicism; the force applied by its political backers; the confusion created by the Protestants themselves; and changing perceptions of the advantages to be gained by embracing one or another of the alternative doctrines, eventually combined to sweep Protestantism almost entirely away or underground – except in Hungary.

For a time it seemed that this religious struggle might bring about a truce in another, the long-standing confrontation between Catholic and Orthodox. Both Tsar Ivan the Terrible and the Pope concentrated fire against the Protestants. But the Counter-Reformation Church not only sought to recapture the souls lost to Protestantism but to bring the Orthodox of Russia, Lithuania and the Ottoman Empire into obedience to the Pope. For a time this effort, too, had some success. Then the iron curtains of mutual intolerance descended once again.

The political consequences of the battle of Mohacz were also considerable. Louis II had died childless; and the Habsburgs of Austria, long-sighted dynastic politicians and shrewd diplomatists, became the leading contenders for the thrones of both Hungary and Bohemia, and soon gained both. But in Hungary there was strong backing for a local candidate, John Zapolyai, and he, too, was crowned king. This political division weakened resistance to the Turks, who by the end of 1541 had occupied the southern and central parts of the country, including the capital Buda; and gained suzereinty over the east, which became a largely autonomous principality, Transylvania.

The death of Louis had ended one Eastern European dynasty. Two others failed to survive the sixteenth century. The last Jagiellonian King of Poland-Lithuania died in 1572; the last of Russia's ancient Riurikid dynasty in 1598. In both instances political hiatus encouraged tumults, though, as we have seen, the long term outcomes were quite dissimilar. While Russia returned to dynastic rule, Poland abandoned it. In this respect she came to resemble the smaller polities in the region, the Danubian Principalities, self-governing tributaries to the Turk, which also lacked dynastic rule: The instability of their domestic politics is suggested by the fact that, in the course of one century Wallachia had twenty-four, and Moldavia no fewer than forty, changes of ruling prince. or *hospodar*.[2]

These religious and political changes were obvious to contemporaries. But there were other shifts, no less profound in their effects, which were much less noticeable at the time, or recognized only in retrospect.

Europe's centre of economic gravity had been moving from the Mediterranean to the countries bordering on the North Atlantic; from the basin of the River Po to that of the Rhine (where it has remained); and from the emporia of Istanbul and Venice to that of Amsterdam. Furthermore, a surge in the population of Western Europe, and in particular of its cities, was stimulating a sharply increasing demand, and hence higher prices, for imported foodstuffs which Eastern Europe was able to supply. This was to have marked social as well as economic effects, especially on those regions with access to the Baltic, not least in encouraging the rise of serfdom.

At the same time the importation of silver from the Americas was promoting a sharp increase in the money supply and hence serious inflation. This was to throw the finely-tuned mechanisms of the Ottoman state out of kilter and prove a major factor in its subsequent decline. And there was one change perceived by very few, if at all, the indirect effects of which were felt by almost everyone. This was 'the little ice age', a slight but insidious drop in the average temperature beginning late in the sixteenth century. By restricting the latitude and height at which agriculture was viable this precipitated famines, population movements and the great disorders which were to overtake most of Eastern Europe at the turn of the century, turning the frontierlands especially into a crucible of violence.

And there was a plethora of other factors which intervened at various points with varying intensity to influence the course things took. Linguistic differences, for example, sometimes fed into religious and political struggles; and social classes sometimes gained or lost constitutional rights according to the religion they embraced at a particular moment. Low population density in Poland-Lithuania contributed to the enserfment of the peasant; yet high population density in the Ottoman Empire contributed to the disruption of that state. Sometimes the effects seem paradoxical. The Turkish presence, so often assumed to be a wholly negative influence, slowed down and even reversed the process of enserfment in Hungary for a time. The Baltic grain boom had helped to promote serfdom, yet the end of the boom around the turn of the century served not to remove serfdom, but to entrench it. And though Protestantism is often associated with the origins of modern science Copernicus was a priest whom Polish Protestants rejected, while the patron of Tycho Brahe and Kepler was a Habsburg. The interactions of circumstances and catalysts that shaped Eastern Europe in the period from 1526 to 1648 far exceeded in complexity the most complicated transmutation process in any alchemists's laboratory. But to gain a better understanding of the processes that took place we have to consider the salient developments in more detail, in their appropriate context, and with regard to the order of events.

* * *

In 1526 Ferdinand of Habsburg succeeded to two fragile crowns, those of Bohemia and Hungary. That of Bohemia gave lordship over extensive and quite prosperous territories that included Moravia, Silesia and Lusatia besides Bohemia itself; and a population of some two million people. On the other hand, the royal powers, strong enough on paper, had grown weak for lack of exercise; the Czech nobility was notoriously haughty and the population as a whole inclined to disorder. Furthermore, Bohemia was deeply affected by the Hussite tradition and hence vulnerable to Protestant reformism.[3] Hungary was in even worse condition: a shattered state. In 1529 John Zapolyai of Transylvania swore homage to the Sultan. The same year Suleyman's troops reached Vienna. This attack was staved off but others followed. Three years later the Turks were stopped again, at Koszeg; but in 1541 they took Buda, then Szekesferhervar, and they organized the Hungarian territories they had conquered into provinces of their empire. The war zone crept northwards; the pressure seemed unremitting. At this juncture, then, the Turks constituted a greater threat to Habsburg interests than Protestantism.

As records still extant in the archives of Vienna and Budapest show,[4] the Habsburgs invested great energy and resources in shoring up their vulnerable southern front. In 1538 they formed a Holy League with the Pope and the Republic of Venice, whose Mediterranean Empire was also threatened by the Turk. But their financial needs were huge and a very large proportion of their income had to be coaxed out of the Estates. In time this was to make Protestantism as insidious a financial as it was an ideological threat to Habsburg fortunes.

In 1530 the arrival of Lutherans was noted in Bohemia and Austria. They were soon active in Hungary too, where not only the German-speaking 'Saxons' of Transylvania but many Hungarian nobles gave them a ready welcome. Lutheranism was also spreading through Poland, introduced by preachers trained at the universities of Heidelberg and Wittenberg (Luther's city), then from centres like Konigsberg. Meanwhile Calvinist ministers, some of them trained in Geneva or Basel, were gaining adherents and setting up schools. Soon more extreme sects blossomed: Arians who could not abide the notion of the Trinity; extremist Anabaptists; the Bohemian Brethren. And all the while there was disunity within the demoralized Catholic Church itself, some insisting on customary authority and rights or simply clinging to the familiar; others pushing for reform. By the middle of the century Eastern Europe outside Russia and the Balkans resembled a religious Tower of Babel.

The ferment owed less to printing than is often imagined, for printed books were still expensive. But it owed much, in Eastern no less than Western Europe, to the tone of open-minded curiosity and tolerance that was characteristic of late Renaissance Humanism; to the dissatisfaction of intellectuals with a somnolent Catholic Church; to the covetousness of those who wanted its property and who resented the jurisdiction of its courts; to the hopes of the poor (encouraged by some of the more radical sects); and not least, of course, to a straightforward concern to live and worship in a correct manner.

Protestantism first presented an open challenge to the established order in Bohemia in 1543; but Ferdinand handled the reformers firmly.

Then, early in 1547, the burghers and commoners of Prague rebelled, and they received support, albeit mostly tacit, from the nobility. They too were crushed. The upshot was a restriction of Bohemians' constitutional rights *vis à vis* the crown and the expulsion of the Bohemian Brethren in 1548. Ferdinand was fortunate in being able to deal with the religious and constitutional challenges separately. Nonetheless he succeeded; and he had another success in 1547 when a Hungarian Assembly declared itself subject to Ferdinand and his successors 'for ever'. However, Ferdinand thought it wise to have his son, Maximilian, crowned king in his own lifetime, and it was 1563 before the Hungarians would agree to that. Maximilian was to prove more tolerant in matters of religion; but, as time would show, the Habsburgs' problems with Bohemians and Hungarians were by no means over.

Nevertheless, the humanist Maximilian was more representative of his age than Ferdinand. The mid-sixteenth century saw the high point of the Renaissance as well as the Reformation in Eastern Europe. In shattered Hungary the glories of Matthias Corvinus's Renaissance court (see Chapter 9) might only be the object of occasional wistful reminiscence, but the Habsburgs employed many Italians; some of the Kremlin's most famous buildings were designed by Aristotele Fioraventi from Bologna; and Sigismund I of Poland was married to a Sforza from Milan, who naturally attracted Italians as well as Polish men of learning to the court. Renaissance influences may have arrived late, affected few and been uneven in effect (devotees appreciated architecture better than the works of Machiavelli). Nevertheless humanism helped to create the atmosphere which allowed so much religious diversity.

The story of two Eastern European scholars of the time provides an illustration. Andija Dudic was one of a handful of young Hungarians who in the 1550s attended that great centre of the classical tradition, the University of Padua.[5] There he became the close friend of another student, Jan Kochanowski from Poland. They subsequently travelled to France together; and they were to remain lifelong friends. It is their subsequent careers and their positions on religion which are of interest in this context, however.

Kochanowski was soon recognized as Poland's greatest poet, and the first to write in Polish rather than the humanist *lingua franca,* Latin. Though he translated some psalms he showed no great enthusiasm for religion and was never ordained a priest. Nevertheless he lived very comfortably as the incumbent of more than one ecclesiastical living (a corrupt church can be a generous sponsor of the arts).[6] Dudic, on the other hand, took holy orders, became Bishop of Pecs in Hungary, and then Habsburg ambassador to Poland. There, however, he abandoned Catholicism for marriage, and became in turn a Lutheran, a Socinian and, finally, a Calvinist. The two friends exemplify on the one hand an easygoing openness; and, on the other, a restless, questioning, and wilful spirit. Dudic and Kochanowski belonged to a tiny intellectual elite, of course. Nevertheless in the middle years of the sixteenth century there were households that proclaimed their open-mindedness, doubts or internal divisions by employing both a Catholic chaplain and a Protestant preacher.[7]

In Poland Lutheranism had made most ground in the still predominately German-speaking cities. But resentment of German city culture accounts only in part for the greater appeal of Calvinism for the nobility. Like other reformist creeds Calvinism challenged the legitimacy of the Catholic Church and hence its rights to property and jurisdiction; but, unlike Lutheranism, which gave the monarch primacy in religious matters, Calvinism taught that lay leaders should control religion. By the 1560s a substantial proportion of the nobility were Calvinists, including the great Lithuanian magnate Nicholas Radziwill and some former Orthodox nobles; and the movement was particularly marked among the better-educated, richer and more influential members of the noble class.

This change was soon reflected in legislation. In 1562–3 the Catholic Church's juridical authority was reduced when the civil authorities ceased to enforce verdicts of ecclesiastical courts against laymen in cases involving property; and clergy were forced to pay the land tax. Then, in 1573, the introduction of religious toleration in effect gave individual lords authority over the churches on their estates. The change in the balance of power between church and nobility was accompanied by a change in the relative power of the king and the Estates.

Although historians disagree about which point might have been decisive in the long transition of the Polish constitution to a gentry dominated republic headed by a 'painted monarch', the death in 1572 of Sigismund Augustus, last of the Jagiellonians, was undoubtedly a critical moment. From then on the crown became wholly elective and its powers much reduced. Furthermore, during the long interregnum which ensued the gentry emerged with a political clout they had never formerly possessed. This was partly a result of a miscalculation by Catholic prelates who favoured a wider franchise in electing a new king. They believed they could influence the gentry, especially those who lived closest to Warsaw who would have the least expense in attending, against the predominately non-Catholic magnates and senators. But a growing movement inspired by Ciceronian republicanism among the gentry themselves was also important, as was the intervention of the future Chancellor of Poland, Jan Zamoyski.

The *Sejm* then proceeded not only to pass over the candidacies of a Habsburg and Tsar Ivan IV, who were considered too authoritarian, to elect Henry of Valois; but Henry was forced to accept severe restrictions on his powers. The *pacta conventa* and the Henrician Articles obliged the

King to maintain an army out of the crown's own resources; to call no general levy, and impose no tax or duty, without parliamentary consent; and to call a *Sejm* at least once every two years. Furthermore if the King were to ignore the laws of the land, infringe the established liberties of his subjects, or neglect any of the conditions placed upon him, then the nobility would be relieved of their oaths of fealty and obedience, and might legitimately rebel against him.

Soon afterwards Henry made a bolt for France in order to secure his succession to the French throne. This occasioned another interregnum in Poland which served to entrench the new constitutional precedents. It has been argued that the crown retained significant powers even after 1574, and the periodic reaffirmations of the restrictions placed upon it suggests that it had at least the potential to claw back some of its former authority; but it was not, in fact, to do so. The new king, Stefan Bathory of Transylvania, was diverted by the rebellion of Gdansk and war with Russia; and though some of his successors tried, none was to succeed. It has also been argued that the constitutional change was good because it enlarged the social base of power; and that the tragedy of Poland's subsequent decline stemmed from the mutual obstruction of king and *Sejm* rather than from the dominance of one over the other. Yet, with the cities now counting for almost nothing politically, and with the clergy having lost the clout they had once carried, the social base was still very restricted. Furthermore, power had not only moved from the Senate to the *Sejm*, it was moving steadily into the hands of gentry who had not been educated in the responsibilities of office. The deliberations of local assembles *(sejmiki)* were becoming increasingly important too, suggesting centrifugal tendencies, a peripheralization of power. And a perilous insistence on unanimous rather than majority decisions in law-making was already apparent.[8]

The mid-sixteenth century was also a watershed for the Ottoman Empire, although the roots of its decline lay in different soil from that of Poland's. Historians differ as to whether the decline set in before or after the death of Suleyman the Magnificent in 1566, and as to which causal factors were the most important. Nonetheless there is general agreement that it was still a well-run and highly successful state in the mid-sixteenth century, and that by about 1600 it was showing signs of disorder and decay. As a chronicler of the time lamented, the lower orders *(reaya)* had become disobedient, and even

> the soldiers turned against the Sultan. There was no respect for the authorities, who were attacked with blows as well as by words. All behaved as they pleased. As tyranny and injustice increased people began to flee to Istanbul. The old order and harmony declined and when these have finally collapsed catastrophe will surely follow.[9]

Both the description of symptoms and the prognosis are accurate enough, though the chronicler, like most of his contemporaries, is vague about the sources of the trouble. Given the advantage of long hindsight historians now have a much clearer sense of what the causes were, although they disagree about their relative importance.[10]

The inflation which affected the entire Mediterranean world in the mid-sixteenth century was undoubtedly one of them. It is sometimes maintained that, like its Byzantine predecessor (See Chapter 10), the Ottoman Empire pursued autarchic policies and constituted a self-contained system which was largely immune from disturbances in the world economy. But, for all the government's belief in protectionism and price control, particularly on basic foodstuffs, this was not the case. Commerce, including overseas trade, was encouraged and so inflation was imported. At the same time high Western demand and ever-increasing prices for foodstuffs and raw materials began to suck these commodities, including precious metals, out of the Empire, creating shortages, particularly in the cities; and the importation of manufactured goods, particularly cheap cloth and metal goods, from the West, threatened craftsmen with loss of livelihood. These constituted a recipe for popular discontent. But there were other ingredients too.

Short of specie and facing high expenditures, in 1584 the government reduced the silver content of its currency, the *akce*, by nearly 40 per cent, a devaluation of 50 per cent in terms of gold; and counterfeiting and debasement of the coinage served to accelerate the inflation. The impact was all the greater for the fact that the long-term value of the *akce* had been very stable, the silver content falling by less than 10 per cent in the eight decades prior to 1565. Population growth may also have contributed. Earlier in the century the Ottoman government had been concerned that the population level was too low, and the increase stemmed in part from deliberate policies, but there is evidence to suggest that, in the Balkans at least, it was associated with spontaneous migration from uplands to plains. As the population grew, so did brigandage and migration to the cities, whose population almost doubled in the course of the century,[11] increasing urban misery and discontent.

Overpopulation and the fixity of governmental mechanism combined to transform inflation into a wasting, and ultimately terminal, disease for the Ottoman state. Since salaries were fixed, officials and servicemen at all levels soon found the cost of living fast outrunning their incomes. This encouraged rebellion and corruption. In 1589 the janissary corps rebelled, stormed the palace and beheaded the minister responsible for the devaluation. Three years later the household cavalry (*sipahis* of the Porte) mutinied; and discontent over pay fired other serious disturbances in 1600 and 1603. Meanwhile more and more officials accepted bribes, resorted to fraud by, for example, registering some property as a charitable endowment exempt from tax *(vakif)*, and, especially in the more remote districts, extorted money from the unfortunates in their power.

Shortage of funds drove the government to take measures which were to do more harm. The practice of tax-farming, which had not yet reached the European provinces, was extended; the janissaries were mollified by allowing their sons to enlist in the corps and by granting them privileges as urban traders. Military commanders tended to spend less time in post and more time between postings. More governors were appointed who had career backgrounds in Istanbul, fewer who had experience in the provinces; and promotions directly up the old ladders of command became the exceptions rather than the norm.[12] Ottoman institutions generally lost their fine tuning. Morale fell; graft increased.

Some of the forces at work in the Balkans were also evident elsewhere in Eastern Europe, particularly the rising demand for foodstuffs in the West. This led to increased prices being offered for Eastern European grain, which in turn stimulated agricultural production for export, especially in areas with access to cheap water-borne transportation to Baltic ports, especially Gdansk at the mouth of the great River Vistula (for grain was far too bulky to be carried westward overland). This development of increased production for the international market had serious social consequences for the peasants, however, intensifying serfdom at a time, ironically, when the equivalent Western institution, villeinage, was fast disappearing. As we have already noticed, serfdom cast a dark shadow over most of Eastern Europe that has reached down to modern times.

Serfdom, sometimes questionably referred to as 'the second serfdom'[13] ascribed a peasant to his lord (whether secular or spiritual) or to the land, denying him the freedom to move without the lord's permission. It also subjected him very largely to the lord's jurisdiction, for although he often retained a theoretical right of appeal to the crown this was usually worthless in practice, and in any case was shortly to be removed. It therefore allowed the lord to extract whatever payment from the serf that he saw fit, whether in money or in kind or, as was becoming increasingly common, in *robot* or labour service. Often difficult to distinguish from slavery, it was nonetheless distinct institutionally, and often far removed from it in practice. In Russia there were men who bound themselves as slaves willingly, sometimes to a relative, to avoid service obligations or the repayment of a debt; and most of the highest potentates in the Ottoman Empire were formally slaves of the Sultan. In the Danubian Principalities the peasants' legal position is obscure but since they rarely had a means of defending themselves, except as elsewhere, by flight or by rebellion, they are hardly distinguishable from serfs.

Serfdom was largely the product of the economic forces already mentioned. In the later sixteenth century bread grains, chiefly rye, from the

Baltic region accounted for at least half the total value of East–West trade, and from the end of the century for about three-quarters of Poland's exports to the West. Yet yields were pitifully meagre, usually little more than three grains harvested for every grain sown. Nearly a third of this had to be saved as seed and most of the rest was consumed by the peasants who produced it. Since the lords' households and the cities of the region had to be fed out of the balance, the export of a quarter of a million tons a year from Gdansk alone (a figure achieved early in the seventeenth century) is remarkable.[14] Without some form of serfdom, however, it could hardly have been achieved, for most peasants were inclined to economic autarchy and isolationism, tended to consume all they produced, and were not disposed to grow disposable surpluses unless coerced.

Rising prices certainly encouraged landlords and even some peasants to sell more grain for cash, but the readiest means of increasing production at the time was to take more land under cultivation, and there was still plenty of wasteland that could be cleared and ploughed. On the other hand there was a scarcity of people to do the work. In England the population shortage following the Black Death in the fourteenth century had had the effect of freeing peasants; in Poland, Prussia, Russia and the Habsburg territories, on the other hand, the relative scarcity of labour served to complete their subjection and intensify their exploitation.

The paradox can be explained in part by considering the relative strengths of the money economy and of the cities. In England the scarcity had driven up the wages of free hired labour; but in sixteenth-century Poland prices were notoriously low and very little money circulated. In England, as elsewhere in the West, 'the city made free', but in Poland the landlord interest succeeded in curbing the liberties of cities. Since production could not be raised sufficiently by monetary inducements, lords adopted the simpler method of extending their demesne and working it with forced labour, particularly in areas where their peasants had small plots and were under-employed.[15]

The intensification of serfdom began in countries bordering the southern shores of the Baltic, in Prussia and Poland; but then spread farther afield, though, as we shall see, not always for similar reasons. In Russia, legislation limiting peasant movement was gradually extended in the late sixteenth century, though serfdom was not to be fully entrenched in law until 1649. There the state intervened in order to preserve the livelihoods of the service gentry whose serfs were flitting to the frontierlands or, more frequently, to great estates whose owners could afford to offer them better terms.

In Bohemia agricultural exports played a lesser role than brewing, an industry in the hands of the bigger landlords which consumed grain in considerable quantities. In Hungary food exports took the form of cattle driven to the cities of south Germany and to Venice, and wine for which Poland provided increasing demand. Neither cattle-raising nor viniculture lend themselves to forced labour, yet in Hungary, too, the size of demesnes and the use of serf labour increased – encouraged by the demand for grain from the frontier garrisons. In the 1540s proximity to areas under Turkish occupation had encouraged the restoration of peasant liberties and limited the obligations of serfs but, as conditions in Ottoman territory deteriorated and more labour came to be demanded of peasants there, the process was reversed. Meanwhile in Transylvania the Szekels, frontier guards of an earlier age, were being reduced to the status of serfs while their chiefs gained noble status,[16] and rising demand for grain to feed the growing population of Istanbul and other Balkan cities increased the pressures on the peasants of Wallachia.

Nowhere outside the Ottoman Empire did the state make any serious attempt to protect the peasants' interests, but in this they were sometimes guided by administrative convenience rather than by powerlessness. The administration of justice and the maintenance of order are disproportionately expensive in large countries with low population densities and poor communications. Governments were sometimes relieved, therefore, to devolve much of their responsibility in these spheres to local potentates and even cease to act as umpire in lord peasant disputes. Early in the century the royal courts in Poland had been forbidden to hear such cases; in the mid-seventeenth century it became a serious offence for a peasant to petition the sovereign. The consequences for the peasantry were generally unfortunate. According to a Polish humanist of the time, by 1599 lords in the Baltic provinces had arrogated

> the right to decide on the life and death of the peasant, and this without their referring to any law or justice, or appealing to reason, but acting according to their whims and moods, frequently venting their fury on them in fits of unbridled wrath and even killing them. The peasant has no opportunity to lodge his complaint with higher authorities. In order to guard his life and keep his possessions, he has no other means of defence than to rely on the chance of finding a humane and benevolent lord....[17]

It should be added, however, that the violence was not always one-sided. Landlords were murdered and country houses set ablaze. A few years later another witness in the Baltic area remarked that

> Serfdom did not exist in our territory fifty or a hundred years ago ... but latterly it has been introduced on a large scale with the help of the authorities.... [As a result] a peasant may not sue his landlord without special permission, nor send his children to the towns to learn a trade

> … nor give them dowries, have them marry or leave them an inheritance…. [Yet the peasant] must aid and support the lord against his enemies; … and accept his judgement even when he is party to the case. He is obliged to plough, harrow, sow, reap and thresh on his lord's demesne, even to the neglect of his own plot, or, in default of service, make payment in lieu whether in coin or in kind.[18]

This was a city alderman whose interests had been adversely affected by the rise of serfdom and of the gentry whose interests they served. Yet in the Baltic area the burghers had at least contested the development.

Overall, however, they failed not only to protect the peasant's interests but their own. Rather than forming a common front with the burgher interest elsewhere, the prosperous city of Gdansk fought for representation in the Senate rather than the *Sejm,* and then sought Danish protection in a vain attempt to break away from the Polish crown. Many cities, in Bohemia, Poland and elsewhere, had failed to send the representatives to parliaments that they were entitled to because of the expense involved – and so their concerns were weakly voiced and brushed aside. But the cities were hampered by their small size and by increasing competition from the private towns, which usually enjoyed immunities from taxation, that had been set up by great magnates on their own land. In time they were to outnumber the royal free cities by almost two to one. And in both Poland and, after 1547, in Bohemia the 'free cities' were controlled by crown officials, rather than by their citizens.

In the more prosperous western provinces of Poland-Lithuania, barely a fifth of the population was urbanized by the end of the century; in the more prosperous parts of northern Italy over half the population was. By the end of the century the population of Gdansk had reached 50,000 and was still growing, but there were probably no more than ten cities in the entire state with populations of 10,000 souls or more. Prague, in which the Habsburg Emperor Rudolph II had his residence, was at least as populous as Gdansk but the other cities of Bohemia were tiny. In the opinion of one specialist in urban history 'the urban backwardness of East-Central Europe as compared with the West was increasing' and the enserfment of the peasantry was a major cause of it not only because it impeded migration to the cities but because it restricted demand for what the city produced. Craftsmen, though organized in guilds, tended to be poor, and foreign capitalists were already much in evidence. Entrepreneurs from southern Germany, Holland and England were prominent in commerce, manufacturing and mining, as were enterprising nobles.

This suggests a serious shortage of capital. There were a few wealthy merchants in Gdansk and Prague, though none to compare to the Fuggers. Burghers were hampered to an increasing extent by restrictions placed on their own freedoms and by competition from the landed nobility and from their private towns, both of which enjoyed exemption from taxes. But in any case there were signs of a looming crisis of business confidence. The great Prague banker Mordechai Meisl left a considerable part of his fortune in cash; and the more successful merchants seem to have been increasingly inclined to invest their fortunes in land. Prosperous businessmen have always tended to buy country estates, of course, but in Holland or England this had no very serious adverse effect on the cities' capital resources. In East-Central Europe, however, it did.[19]

Burghers were eventually to lose their right to buy landed property in the countryside; but by then a number of local entrepreneurs and capitalists had already entered the ranks of the landed nobility. The ancestor of Imre Thokolly, the Hungarian rebel of the 1680s, Sebestyan, had made his money in the cattle trade; the prominent Hungarian magnates, the Thurzos, were descended from Polish entrepreneurs who had been prominent in the mining industry; and the aristocratic houses of Rakocszy, Illeshazy and Palffy, among others, all date from the later sixteenth century.[20] In their fight for supremacy the nobility of Poland and Hungary reduced the cities and pre-empted the merchants' role as entrepreneurs (though, as we shall see, their taste for business was not to last). But the religious movement of the Counter-Reformation also played a role in the decline of the middle classes of East-Central Europe.

* * *

The movement was spearheaded by the Jesuits whose first representative arrived in Austria in 1550, Bohemia in 1551, Poland in 1560 and Hungary in 1565, two years after the great Council called to find ways of revivifying the Catholic Church concluded its deliberations at Trento in the Italian Alps close to the frontier with Austria. They faced an uphill struggle. In Poland the atmosphere was tolerant and at Breslau (Wroclaw), for example, Catholic bishop and Lutheran burghers got on well together. In many areas parishes were vacant for lack of men and money, and both Catholics and Protestants held services in the great cathedral church at Esztergom in Hungary. Furthermore the first Jesuit missionaries to Hungary and Bohemia could not speak Hungarian or Czech.

Hungary was soon abandoned but the Jesuits in the other countries persevered, opening schools, appealing to students, and indoctrinating them, by such means as amateur dramatics; and sending promising boys to study in the new or revitalized colleges in Rome. They also set out to recapture adults for the faith. In Poland they began by embracing the causes of the burghers and the serfs, and pressing for a strong, hereditary monarchy instead of a weak, elective one. Alliance with burghers and yeomen could, if the experience of England was anything to go by, make a monarch strong; and a strong monarch could be an invaluable ally in their battle to eliminate heresy. Then, realizing the political landscape to be quite unlike those of Western Europe, they changed their tune, began to praise 'Golden Liberty', practise philanthropy among the urban poor, and encourage hostility towards the burghers. In Cracow in 1591 merchant shops were looted and Protestant churches set on fire. Similar events were to follow in other Polish cities.

The Counter-Reformation was to triumph in most Protestant areas, and for many reasons. Some Protestants were won back to the Catholic fold through the persuasive force and charitable work of the orders – principally the Jesuits, though the Dominicans, the Paulines and the Piarists, the Franciscans and the Theatines, each with its speciality, each with its particular appeal to a social category or taste, also played an important part. The Catholic Church was better-organized and more confident than before, and also more attractive – partly because it adopted some of its opponents' methods such as popular preaching in the vernacular; partly because it adopted the tone and cosmopolitanism of humanism as well as much of its learning. Furthermore, the Catholic revival profited from Protestant disunity and from the continuing Turkish threat, which (so Hungarians were told) was due to the Lutherans, destroying six centuries of grace accumulated by good Catholic Hungarians.

Victory or defeat often turned on local circumstances. In Upper Austria, for example, the association of Protestants with radicalism and peasant rebellion, and a desire to please the government which had suppressed an uprising in 1597, persuaded many of the local Protestant nobility to return to the Catholic fold. Yet in Bohemia, despite Ferdinand's support for the Jesuits and the Pope's concession of wine as well as wafer in the administration of the sacrament to laymen (an issue at the heart of religious discontent there since the Hussite movement over a century earlier) the forces of dissent, including Lutheranism, continued to make gains and Catholicism to wither. In Poland the Church's new association with the cause of the triumphant nobility was important in the rout of Calvinism. On the other hand, in Hungary the proximity of the Turks still helped the cause of Protestantism despite increasingly energetic and partly successful efforts of the Catholic Church to win back the elite.[21] In the longer run, however, the Catholic cause profited more than its competitors from the general malaise which set in during the last decade of the sixteenth century.

This malaise was associated with the onset of the 'Little Ice Age', the resumption of war between the Habsburgs and the Turks (1593–1606), and a severe economic recession. At the same time there was a great welling-up of social discontents and political upheavals. The entire frontier zone from Ukraine to the Adriatic was affected by the troubles as well as Russia and the Ottoman Balkans; and there were reverberations in Poland and for the Habsburgs. The crisis was the confluence of many streams and was expressed in many forms, but one of its most frightening manifestations were the bands of undisciplined and ruthless soldiery who plagued both sides of the frontier in Hungary.

The Turks had long used a variety of paramilitary forces (*armartolos, derbentsy, akinji, vojnuki,* etc.) as auxiliary troops, frontier raiders, mountain-pass guards and the like; as we have seen, the Habsburgs had followed suit; and the Cossacks constitute a parallel in Ukraine and southern Russia.[22] Such troops usually received some pay and also rations or plots of land, but by no means always. There was an Ottoman category known as *deli,* young men noted for their dare-devilry who would take part in campaigns and sieges for no reward whatsoever, except the opportunity to share in any plundering. Another such type of predatory soldiery was known as *haramia.* These had an equivalent on the other side of the frontier in the unpaid *heyducks* and *uskoks (venturitni)* attached to the 'official' groups of *heyducks* and *uskoks* employed by the Habsburgs to garrison frontier forts and stations, and the unregistered Cossacks of the Ukraine who were to play such a prominent role in the Khmelnytsky rising of 1648.

Evidence from a wide variety of sources suggests that the numbers of such freelance warriors increased sharply in the later sixteenth century, despite a general increase in the numbers employed not only by governments but in the private armies of noblemen, like the Wisniowieckis in Ukraine, the Bathorys in Transylvania or the Frankopans in Croatia.

This increase in the soldiery, both freelance and employed, and the tumults they promoted were linked to the endemic warfare of the frontier, which created both a demand for such troops and, by disrupting the economy of entire districts, a supply of them from among the ranks of the homeless and indigent. But the phenomenon was also related to the huge increase in the population of the Balkans and to the imposition of serfdom. The demographic explosion which doubled the population of Balkan cities also fed migration northwards and eastwards across the frontier, mostly, it seems, through the gap of Timisoara.

The subsequent economic difficulties and the onset of disorders no doubt increased the flow. In any case the numbers of heyducks called 'Racz' registered in Eastern Hungary (and there were units in which nearly two-thirds of the men bore that name) points to a sizeable migration northwards from the Balkans, for *racz* in Magyar *(rat* in Romanian) means 'Serb'. Their names also indicate that, although most were or became linguistic Hungarians, some heyducks had originated in Slovakia *(toth),* Romania *(vlach, olah)* and Ukraine *(kozak, rusnak)* as well as in Hungary and the Balkans. And there were Hungarian, Romanian and

Tatar names among the Zaporozh'e Cossacks, though most had migrated from Belorussia, Ukraine and Russia. Circumstances suggest that a proportion of these were peasants escaping serfdom, and this was also the case with the recently enserfed Szekels whose support for Michael 'the Brave' when he invaded Transylvania regained them their freedom as frontier servicemen.[23]

As late as the 1580s heyducks are reported in groups of up to a few hundred, or, occasionally, of a thousand; but by the turn of the century no fewer than 8,000 unpaid heyducks were reported to be serving Michael 'the Brave', Prince of Wallachia, alone.[24] The growth of the phenomenon is suggested by the extremity of their behaviour as well as increasing numbers. Compared with them, Elizabethan England's problem with sturdy beggars pales into insignificance. In some areas heyducks claimed to be Calvinist, yet they would kill Calvinist priests without compunction; and the Transylvanian Saxons have left matter-of-fact, but eloquent testimony in their memoirs and diaries to the heartless bestiality of the heyducks.

> In the summer of 1603 [runs one such contemporary account], the Serbs and heyducks went farther and burned the market at Udvarhely.... The cruel Serbs and heyducks spared no-one whether enemy or friend....

According to another,

> On 18th July [1603] the heyducks burned Rothbach and cut down fifty-two people, young and old, and robbed my place of four horses, two cows and the pigs besides my clothes and a few good books.

At about ten o'clock on the evening of 17 February 1612 'the heyducks came to Weidenbach and Neustadt and cut down many people but also led some few away alive....' Nine weeks later, on Good Friday, they raided the old city of Brasso, kidnapping many people and driving off cattle. And so the bloody catalogue continued – as it did in many other sectors of the frontier zone. Hoefnagel's representation of seven refugees, presumably would-be heyducks suspected of spying, being impaled by garrison heyducks at Pappa in northern Hungary provides graphic witness to the violence that was becoming commonplace almost everywhere along the frontier.[25]

Heyducks or *hadju*, haramia or *martolos*, Cossacks and uskoks – they had many names, depending on the area and the language of the witness, but they all belonged to the same genus. Uprooted, savage, desperate men and boys with no expectation of longevity and a contempt for death, they fought on all sides in every struggle.

> Peasant thieves ... without faith who by robberies ruinate all the country ... [and] care not for any paine, travaile or daunger.

Thus a French contemporary[26] described them in a book published the year that Michael 'the Brave' exploited a favourable moment in the war between the great powers to confront the Turks, become Prince of both Wallachia and Moldavia, and, albeit briefly, lord of Transylvania as well – all with the aid of a substantial heyduck following which, in the course of events, attracted yet more to their ranks. Michael was assassinated by a Habsburg agent, but then, in 1604, Stephen Bocskay of Transylvania backed by another huge heyduck army rebelled against Rudolph II. A heyduck rebellion occurred in eastern Hungary in 1607–8; and they were to be involved in more troubles subsequently.

The frequency of the disturbances and the great effort Bocskay made to settle several thousand of them in underpopulated areas he owned near Debrecen and to accord them corporate privileges as gentry, suggest that these infestations of unpaid soldiers and sturdy beggars had themselves become a factor promoting war. Princes and magnates found it necessary to employ some, sometimes many of them, to protect their property against the rest; and to occupy them on some violent enterprise when they seemed likely to become unruly. Nor was the phenomenon confined to Hungary and the Romanian lands. It extended like a thick and angry weal across the whole of Eastern Europe.

In the extreme Western sector, in Slovenia and Croatia-Slavonia, where the Habsburgs had a firm grip, life was more orderly; but farther south Uskoks had made a pirate base out of the little port of Senj on the northern Adriatic, and when, after numerous complaints of their preying on Venetian as well as Turkish shipping, the government attempted to bring them to heel, they overran the castle and butchered the Habsburg commander. Eventually a major operation had to be mounted to regain control of the place and to round up those Uskoks who did not succeed in making good their escape and deport and resettle them inland. Even so, Uskok pirates and smugglers were to plague the sea-lanes and littoral farther to the south for decades afterwards, and to give as much trouble to the governors of the Venetian islands of the Adriatic and the Ragusans as they did to the Turks.[27]

The troubles extended eastwards, too, into Ukraine and southern Russia. In 1591 and again in 1595 there had been rampages by Cossacks and peasants in the Ukraine; and, except when war intervened to suck up Cossack energies and increase Poland's demand for fighting men, the pestilence became endemic – fed by a constant inflow both of peasant runaways and by gentry with land claims and in need of peasant labour. In 1606 Poland was disturbed by a legal rebellion against the king which was to take over two years to suppress. But in Russia the crisis produced more terrible disorders.

These, too, were fed by many causes. The climatic cooling which had set in around 1590 produced famines and population movements which, in turn, increased demands from the service gentry to prevent their peasants leaving. The political background had been troubled too. Ivan IV had earned his nickname 'the Terrible' through his ruthless severity in dealing with his opponents, although his reign (1547–83) had witnessed important achievements as well as failures: the conquest of the Tatar khanates of Kazan, Astrakhan and Siberia; an attempt at law codification; the assertion of monarchical authority over the selfish interests of the traditional nobility; and the promotion of a service gentry which inherited land along with obligations to the state. Ivan also introduced a wide measure of self-government, and was the founder of the *zemskii sobor*, which liberal historians, much though they revile Ivan, have recognized to be the only precedent for a parliament before the establishment of the Duma in 1906. And, for all his cruelty, ordinary Russians were to remember him as a good Tsar.[28]

Ivan had killed his eldest son in a fit of rage, but two others survived him. Unfortunately both were to die without issue. The situation might yet have been saved by Boris Godunov, the able brother-in-law of Ivan's son, Fedor. Boris was crowned Tsar in 1598. But it was in his reign that the discontents came to a head, encouraging doubts about his legitimacy. The story retailed by Pushkin and Mussorgskii that holds Boris responsible for the death of the Tsarevich Dmitrii is founded in malicious rumour. On the other hand Tsar Dmitrii, who came to the throne in 1606 with help from the Poles and the Russian service gentry, was certainly an impostor. Neither he, nor his successor Vasily Shuiskii lasted long, however, and the general turmoil abated only in 1613 when Michael Romanov was elected Tsar.[29] Ironically, Cossacks from the Don who had played an active part in the troubles also played a part in stabilizing the situation.

The restoration of order in Russia owed much to a patriotic reaction against the Poles who had backed the False Dmitrii, but since there was no modern sense of national self-consciousness, nor any comprehension of secular ideology, this patriotism was inspired by Orthodox religious feeling and anti-Catholicism. Indeed, the troubles had a religious dimension almost everywhere. The rebellion led by Stephen Bocskay was fed in part by resentment of militant Jesuit revivalists who had returned to Hungary in the late 1580s; and the perennial disturbances in the Ukraine were informed by religious frictions between Orthodox and Catholics and, since 1596, between Orthodox and Uniats.

Uniats were Christians of the Orthodox rite who nevertheless acknowledged the authority of the Pope. Agreement on this union had been reached between most of the Orthodox bishops of Lithuania and the Ukraine (under some pressure from the Polish crown) and representatives of the Vatican at a synod held at Brest-Litovsk in October 1596. Although two bishops and the abbot of the great Monastery of the Caves in Kiev stood out against the arrangement, the Union of Brest was a triumph for the Catholic cause. It gave a great boost to the missionizing spirit, and revived ancient hopes of bringing the entire Eastern Orthodox Church into obedience to Rome – hopes which seemed to have materialized at the Council of Florence more than a century before, but which had soon been disappointed.[30]

Rome's war of persuasion with the Orthodox is a dimension of the Counter-Reformation which is too often neglected. It was waged with no less skill than the war against the Protestants; and considerable resources were invested in it, including the foundation in 1577 by Pope Gregory XIII of a new College in Rome, St Athanasius, to train Greeks, some of whom were later to serve as missionaries in the Orthodox territories. However, it met with more instinctive opposition from the masses, and therefore tended to take on the character of a secret war, in which Rome infiltrated undercover agents into the Ottoman Balkans, the Romanian Principalities and Russia in attempts to convert the powerful, both ecclesiastical and secular, including the Tsars of Russia themselves. But Ivan IV could stand his ground in disputation with a Jesuit[31] just as he did against Protestants, despite his fondness of the Protestant English; and after the Polish intervention during the Time of Troubles chances of winning Russia over became even slimmer. In fact the triumph of Brest was to mark the limit of Catholic penetration of Eastern Europe; and this limit constituted a cultural as well as a religious frontier. It was not quite an impervious Iron Curtain. Nevertheless it impeded acceptance of humanism, Latin culture and Western ideas, confirming an ideological divide that would be recalled by, and contribute to, the Cold War of the twentieth century.

Meanwhile, Catholic revivalists had been finding the going hard in Bohemia too. Rudolph II, Habsburg Emperor at the turn of the century, and great patron of the arts, sciences and arcane learning of every kind, had made Prague his capital and the looming Hradshchin castle and airy summer palace he built close to it his residences. Brought up at the Spanish court, which was noted alike for its stiff protocol and Catholic devotion, Rudolph was nevertheless a troubled soul afflicted by the many divisions, religious and political, within his realms. He disliked making choices in matters of religion, and, given the delicacy of the religious balance by 1600 his prevarications are understandable. Emperors had never been very fond of Popes, but Protestantism had long been associated with opposition to Habsburg authority. The Counter-Reformation was winning ground, especially among the elite, yet the

Protestants were still strong in Hungary, and a rising force in Bohemia itself.

The rebellion of Stephen Bocskay with his heyducks, and the disloyalty of Rudolph's own ambitious brother, Matthias, who allied himself with the opposition, eventually forced Rudolph to make peace with the Turks, grant liberty to the Protestants of Hungary in 1606, and hand over all his realms, except Bohemia, to Matthias. Then, by the Letter of Majesty of 1609, he conceded religious liberty in Bohemia as well.[32] But the compromise did not hold. The Protestants remained suspicious; neither the mentally unstable Rudolph (who died in 1612) nor Matthias (who resided in Vienna) could be relied on to implement their undertakings; and provocative behaviour by some champions of the Counter-Reformation increased the tension.

It finally broke on 23 May 1618 when, amidst pandemonium, leading notables in the Bohemian Estates, including a Lobkowicz and a Kinsky, seized the representatives of the new Emperor, Ferdinand II, Jaroslav Martinic and Vilem Slavata, and hurled them out of a window of the Hradschin Castle. They fell over 150 feet and survived. But the act precipitated outright rebellion against Habsburg rule; the election in 1619 of a new king, the impeccably Protestant Frederick, Elector Palantine; and the outbreak of the Thirty Years War.[33]

So far as Bohemia was concerned the issue was soon settled. In November 1620 a small force loyal to Ferdinand II met Frederick's troops at the so-called 'White Mountain', in fact an area of modestly high ground outside Prague, and put them to flight. In retrospect the victory can be recognized as decisive, though at the time the final outcome seemed rather less certain. Even so, a few months later twenty-seven leading rebels were executed; and this seemed to take the heart out of the movement for Hungarian independence which had crystallized around Gabor Bethlen, Prince of Transylvania. In the autumn of 1621 his support simply melted away. Meanwhile Bohemia witnessed a display of 'salami tactics' that anticipated the methods of Communist leaders in Stalin's last years.

First the Calvinist clergy were expelled, and afterwards the Lutherans; the cities were picked off (except for Pilsen and Budweis which had remained loyal and which were therefore exempt from the hefty tax on beer that was soon imposed); and then the nobility was purged, pressured into conformity or ordered to leave the country. Yet almost seven years were to pass before Ferdinand formally imposed a new constitution upon Bohemia. According to this the Habsburgs became hereditary Kings of Bohemia instead of hereditary candidates, and their constitutional powers increased. Furthermore, in order that

> All occasions for such most abominable rebellions as have recently occurred shall forever be prevented, We [Ferdinand II] enact, ordain

> and will that should one or more of Our subjects, of whatever dignity, rank, or nature, now or in the future, again venture to revive, by words or deeds, the pretexts ... misinterpretations, and sophistries invented and adduced against Our hereditary right by the rebels, ... they shall be deemed ... to have committed the felony of *lese-majeste* and open rebellion, and shall forfeit their life, honour and goods.[34]

Under Ferdinand II, and from 1637 his successor Ferdinand III, both of them convinced Catholic revivalists, all the doubts, hesitations and reversals of line that had characterized his predecessors vanished. Loyalty became synonymous with Catholic, and Protestant with treason.[35] The tide of fortune was to turn against the Habsburgs and from 1639 until the end of the war forces hostile to them made frequent incursions into Bohemia and occupied large parts of it at times. The economic and demographic losses were considerable.[36] However, the commanding position gained there in 1620 was not to be fundamentally affected; and in the long run the construction of an alliance between the Habsburg monarchy, the Catholic Church, and the great nobility was to stick – not only in Bohemia but in Austria and the other territories; even to an extent in Hungary.

The victory owed much to the work of the new generation of Catholic intellectuals and administrators such as Ernest Harrach, Cardinal Archbishop of Prague, and that mighty proponent of education and conformity, the Primate of Hungary, Peter Pazmany. But the disarray of the Protestants also contributed to their defeat. And if the glamour built up around the court inspired awe and the Church consolidated this respect with its celebrations, disciplines and cults, there was also a nastier side to the restoration of order – the campaigns of terror used against nonconformists, the allegations of devilry and witchcraft levelled against the unreliable poor.

Charges of diabolism could be used as an ideological weapon against Protestants since Lutheranism, for example, had been branded as a creation of the Devil. Hence an Estonian arraigned in Riga might be persuaded to describe a terrifying vision of a 'Lutheran' devil with nine Mongoloid faces, wearing black skull caps like Jews and clothes such as German merchants wore. Prosecutions for witchcraft had been made in Calvinist areas of Hungary as early as the 1560s; in the 1580s there had been a series of such trials in Austria; and charges of witchcraft became more frequent thereafter, peaking in the Habsburg lands after 1648 and in Poland and Russia later still. Such prosecutions were not simply a rampage against women, as feminists claim; but a useful weapon for the restoration of order.

Charges of witchcraft could be used to combat traces of paganism, itself a dangerous form of nonconformity which was still deeply entrenched among the common people, especially in mountain areas; to root out secret Protestants; to fight rebels of any sort, whether protesters against serfdom or those who infringed against social conventions. And even if there were no real witches the charges could be psychologically acute, in accordance with common understandings and even some observable facts. Terrifying plague epidemics had traditionally been explained away with references to evil forces. Besides, subversive elements might be expected to meet at night as in a coven, or flit about the country as if by means of magic; in Slovenia there actually was a cult of 'Leapers' whose devotees apparently practised pagan rites; and there were people who claimed to conjure up spirits.

Martin Laimbauer, for example, leader of a great peasant revolt in Austria which broke out in 1634 and took two years to suppress, claimed to have conjured the mediaeval Emperor Frederick Barbarossa up from the dead. As is so often the case war encouraged the lower orders of society and provided opportunities for protest that would not usually occur. In Austria alone Laimbauer's revolt had been preceded by Fadinger's in 1626 (the biggest, it was said, since the German 'Peasant War' of 1525) and Greimbl's in 1632. Such frequent and fearsome threats to order called for a social antidote and the witch crazes of Eastern Europe were part of the response. They could purge the fears of common folk while purging society of potential threats to the social, political and religious order.

The fears of intellectuals, however, ran just as deep and were less easily purged. Instability of faith was one manifestation of it and Bishop Dudic was by no means an isolated example of such a waverer. Among the more notorious examples were James Palaeologus, descendent of Orthodox Byzantine Emperors who became a Dominican and then Protestant; and Antonio de Dominis, Archbishop of Split, but 'a man for many masters', who became an Anglican and for a time enjoyed the patronage of King James I as Dean of Windsor. Cyril Lucaris was another. Like Dudic, Lucaris was a graduate of Padua; he also knew the city of Vilnius, visited the Principality of Moldavia, had Dutch friends and corresponded with de Dominis. In 1620 Lucaris became Patriarch of Constantinople and thus Primate of the Orthodox Church. At this late stage he was discovered to be a Calvinist and deposed, Calvinism being as objectionable to traditional Orthodox Christians as it was to Jesuits. Lucaris was restored as Patriarch but finally deposed again in 1635.[37]

Meanwhile another career was getting under way, this time of a firm anti-Protestant, but waverer between Orthodoxy and Catholicism, Paisios Ligarides. Graduate of St Athanasius Greek College, where he subsequently taught, and ordained a priest by Raphael Korsak, Uniat Metropolitan of Ukraine, he soon set out on a career as missionary to the Orthodox in the Balkans and secret agent of the Propaganda Fide in

Rome. All things to all men, as secret agents often have to be, he ingratiated himself with the Orthodox hierarch and became confessor and ecclesiastical adviser to Matei Basarab, Prince of Wallachia; subsequently to Vasili Lupu of Moldavia, and, ultimately, to Tsar Alexis of Russia.

Ligarides, one of several Vatican agents infiltrated into the Orthodox East in the first half of the seventeenth century, was as important as an educator as well as a player in the 'Great Game' of his era, for he opened a school in the Wallachian capital and was associated with the local printing press which had recently been set up there. Printing was as yet confined to church books which he helped to correct; but he was also one of those few who introduced elements of late humanist learning into the Balkans, as later to the Russian court. His reputation, however, is unenviable. Almost everyone came to distrust him as a renegade, an opportunist and a money-grabber. Yet even in the ambiguity of his beliefs and loyalties, he was a representative figure of his age.

Ligarides was a would-be reconciler at a time when religious positions had become entrenched and compromise impossible. His interests, including divination, were typical of learned people of the day; even his greed reflected a material insecurity that was familiar to many scholars who were his contemporaries. Furthermore he recognized that he lived at a harsh and unpleasant juncture in history. In the 'Book of Prophecies' he wrote to ingratiate himself with some powerful patron, he compared the state of the world to a dying man whose body is exhausted by struggles; who cannot stomach his [spiritual] food, but who pulls his clothing to him for fear it will be stolen.[38]

But the world had turned sour for others besides impecunious scholars. Wars and civil strife had taken heavy toll in Bohemia and the frontierlands; both the Ottoman state and Russia were licking their wounds; the grain boom had ended by the 1620s (the West was finding other sources of food), the Polish lead mines which had done well out of the wars were exhausted, and by the 1640s a deep recession had descended over the entire region. It might be thought that, since rising prices for grain had contributed to the enserfment of the peasants, falling prices might result in their liberation But this did not occur. On the contrary, as landlords sought to maintain their living standards in unfavourable market conditions, they tended to work their serfs all the harder, hoping to compensate for falling prices by selling yet more grain. Meanwhile many a city merchant had been hurt by competition from the noble class, and many a lord ceased to be entrepreneurial.

This was the case in Hungary as well as Poland. Peace with the Turks cut demand from the frontier garrisons, while the Thirty Years War depressed prices for Hungarian beef. But here there was less of a tendency to increase production for the market. Rather there was a tendency, as in Bohemia, to use excess grain to brew beer, for which one's serfs supplied a captive market; and, as during the Great Depression of the 1930s, to aim at autarchy – producing virtually everything one's family, staffs and retainers needed on one's own estates with one's own labour. This led to some diversification of labour skills in the countryside but tended to starve the towns of business. At the same time, especially in the more isolated areas, it led to the building of palaces by craftsmen of inadequate training who, much to the frustration of the hopeful owner (as Miklos Bethlen reports in his autobiography), proved incapable of building a straight wall or a level ceiling.

Changes of mentality have also been noted. In 1542 a Hungarian nobleman, George Hedervary, like many of his generation, provident but outward-looking, eager to embrace opportunities and to introduce improvements, had written enthusiastically of his

> ambition to buy a boat on which I could ship off a thousand bushels of barley and wheat ... [and] carry ... flour and other victuals [for sale] too.

By 1642 outlooks had changed so radically that one of his descendents, complacent, self-indulgent and traditional as so many of his class had become, could boast of

> the great show I made at my wedding, for which I could not be reproached. My late father also regarded his income as sufficient so long as he could keep a good table appropriate to his birth and honour. So I, too, cannot live otherwise, for I am my father's son.[39]

A change in attitudes was also marked among the Polish elite, whose taste for imported luxuries, encouraged by the grain boom, did not diminish when it ended. In Poland, too, there had been no lack of noblemen in the sixteenth century who had shown commercial initiative, an entrepreneurial spirit, and a certain adventurousness in matters of religion. Yet by the middle of the seventeenth their staunchly Catholic descendants, though inclined to ancestor-worship, were coming to despise these things, and leave them to their Jews. As in Hungary (or Spain) trade had come to be regarded as inconsistent with patrician status.[40] The attitude eventually travelled east to Russia and down the generations, contributing to the torpor of 'the class without a role'. And, particularly in Poland, where the seventeenth-century nobleman came to be regarded as the icon of the nation, it was to have an effect upon the lower classes too.

What caused this transformation of mentalities? Serfdom obviously had much to do with it; but so did other factors. The sudden change of economic climate in the first quarter of the seventeenth century forced sensible men of property to retrench; and the length of the economic trough encouraged a certain inertia and fixity of outlook. The change of religious climate encouraged conformity and a narrowness of view; and this was related, perhaps, to a decline in educational standards since the heyday of the humanist intellectual when attendance at Italian and German universities had been both easier and more popular. But all this bears on broader issues of Eastern Europe's backwardness by contrast to the West.

* * *

As we have seen, the imposition of serfdom was related to the lower population densities that prevailed east of the River Elbe. The sixteenth century had been a period of demographic growth in the region but then war and the 'times of troubles' affected every state of the region except Poland. Her period of troubles would only begin in the 1650s. It has been argued that these losses were the more serious in their implications for the region's long-term economic fortunes in coming when they did, at a moment when population was most needed. Furthermore changes in climate had adverse ecological effects not only in restricting agriculture in the higher altitudes but in, for example rendering the flood country of Upper Hungary, which had formerly yielded rich crops, unfit for agriculture.[41] By 1648 the region as a whole was already confirmed as one which exported raw materials and imported manufactured goods – only its position had deteriorated since the West had less need of Eastern Europe's foodstuffs while parts of the region had developed a demand for expensive Western imports. In this respect the region's predicament in the mid-seventeenth century anticipates its predicament at the end of the twentieth.

The economic backwardness established by the mid-seventeenth century had a parallel in a deepening social backwardness. By 1650 several states in the region possessed a swollen noble class and an underdeveloped bourgeoisie, while, except for the Ottoman Balkans and parts of the frontier zone which had their own idiosyncratic social systems, serfdom had been imposed throughout the region. At the same time avenues which had formerly allowed successful burghers to become landed magnates and peasants to become burghers, churchmen and even squires, were blocked. As a result the social structure was petrified at the same time as it was skewed. Yet serfdom could hardly have been imposed nor social mobility stopped had the nobility not wielded such great political clout or had the monarchies of East-Central Europe not been so much weaker than their Western counterparts; and these conditions had their origins in constitutional and social debilities which date back before 1526.

New questions have also arisen which draw attention to the earlier period and to cultural and religious even more than social and economic concerns. Since the population of the Balkans was overwhelmingly Christian and serfdom was unknown there, for example, can Ottoman rule justly be regarded as the prime cause of the region's backwardness, as is commonly alleged? What kinds of regime did the Turks replace and how much discontinuity did the change of government imply? What effects did the differences between the Catholic and Orthodox Churches have on mentalities and intellectual traditions of their respective flocks? And why had the Czechs, so quiescent after 1620, been so insistent in matters of doctrine and political rights previously? We have noticed that humanism had a limited effect on the region, but we need to know why earlier Renaissance influences had so restricted an impact and why Eastern Europe found it so difficult to establish and sustain universities.

These questions among others invite us to review the later fourteenth century when Lithuania and Poland became associated under a common king, and when the Turks first gained a foothold in Europe; and the fifteenth, the age of Skanderbeg and Dracula, when the Czech dissident, John Huss, was burned at the stake, when King Matthias the Raven presided over the Renaissance court of Hungary, when the last Emperor of Byzantium died defending his city against the Turks, and when the Grand Dukes of Muscovy thought of claiming their imperial heritage.

REFERENCES

1. See the eye-witness account by the Chancellor of Hungary and Bishop of Syrmia, Stephanus Brodericus [Istvan Broderics]: P. Kulcsar (ed.), *De Conflictu Hungarorum Solymano Turcarum imperatore ad Mohach historia Verissima* [Bibliotheca scriptorum medii recentisque aevorum, series nova vol. VI] (Budapest, 1985) especially pp. 52–6. For recent analyses in English by military specialists, see G. Perjes, *The Fall of the Mediaeval Kingdom of Hungary* (Boulder, 1989) and L. Alfoldi, 'The Battle of Mohacs, 1526' in J. Bak and B. Kiraly (eds.), *From Hunyadi to Rakocsi: War and Society in Late Mediaeval and Early Modern Hungary* [East European Monographs, No. CIV] (New York, 1982) pp. 189–203.
2. For the career of Petru Rares, ruler of Moldavia 1527–38 and 1541–6, at the inception of this period, and the difficulties he faced, both internally from his own boiars and internationally as head of a shuttlecock state poised between the Habsburgs, Poland and the Turks (to whom they were formally subject), see L. Simanschi (ed.), *Petru Rares* (Bucharest, 1978).
3. For the constitutional position in the lands of the Bohemian crown see K.J. Dillon, *King and Estates in the Bohemian Lands 1526–1564* [Studies presented to the International Commission for the History of Representative and Parliamentary Institutions, No. LVII] (Brussels, 1976) especially pp. 19–21.
4. For the western flank, Kriegsarchiv, Vienna, especially the Alte Feldakten records which date back to 1528 and are voluminous from 1540; also

Steiermarkische Landesarchiv, Graz: Meiller akten, and K. Kaser, *Freie Bauer und Soldat* (Graz, 1986) especially pp. 18–60 on the settlement of Slav and other fugitives (*uskoci*, vlachs) from the 1550s, the origins of the Military Frontier in Croatia-Slavonia. The records in the Budapest State Archive [Magyar Orszagos Leveltar] dealing with the eastern, Hungarian, sector are predictably spottier, though some telling detail relating to the defences of Hungarian border towns, muster and pay lists is provided, for instance in E 210: Militaria (see also n. 23 *infra*). However, the destructive effects of war have sometimes been exaggerated – see V. Zimanyi, *Economy and Society in Sixteenth and Seventeenth Century Hungary (1526–1650)* [Studia Historica Academiae Scientiarum Hungaricae, 188] (Budapest, 1987) pp. 9 and 14.

5. A. Veress (ed.), *Matricula et Acta Hungarorum in Universitatibus Italiae studentium* [Monumenta Hungariae Italica, Vol. III] (Budapest, 1941) pp. 182–96 for Padua 1536–60; also pp. 317–19 for Dudic's association with Verona.
6. See A. Kadic, 'Jan Kochanowski in Croatian Literature', in S. Fiszman (ed.) *The Polish Renaissance in its European Context* (Bloomington, 1988) pp. 421–8 and other essays in the same volume.
7. On the Reformation in general, see A.G. Dickens, *Reformation and Society in Sixteenth Century Europe* (New York, 1966), for East-Central Europe, R. Betts in *The New Cambridge Modern History* vol. II (Cambridge, 1961) pp. 186–209 and R.J.W. Evans, *The Making* of *the Habsburg Monarchy* (Oxford, 1979) especially pp. 3–40; for Bohemia, Dillon, *op. cit.*, pp. 71ff.; for Poland J. Tazbir in S. Kieniewicz (chief ed.), *History of Poland*, 2nd ed. (Warsaw 1979) pp. 158ff.
8. On constitutional developments in Poland see in particular A. Wyczanski in A. Maczak *et al.* (eds.), *East-Central Europe in Transition* (Cambridge, 1985) pp. 142ff. Also Tazbir in Kieniewicz, *op. cit.*, pp. 160–7, and H. Roos, 'Standewesen und Parlamentarische Verfassung in Polen', D. Gerhard (ed.) *Standische Vertretung in Europa von 17. und 18 Jahrhundert* (Gottingen, 1969) pp. 310–67.
9. Mustafa Selaniki, *Tarih-i Selaniki: Die Chronik des Selaniki* (Freiburg, 1970). Translation adapted from a forgotten source.
10. The account which follow draws on *inter alia* O. Barkan, 'The Price Revolution of the Sixteenth Century', *International Journal of Middle Eastern Studies*, 6, 1975, pp. 3–28; V.J. Parry, 'The Successors of Suleyman, 1566–1617' in M.A. Cook (ed.), A *History of the Ottoman Empire to 1730* (Cambridge, 1976) pp. 103–32; S.J. Shaw, *History of the Ottoman Empire and Modern Turkey*, vol. I pp. 107ff. and for the useful bibliography, pp. 317ff. Also C. Kafadar 'When Coins Turned into Drops of Dew and Bankers became Robbers of Shadows', McGill University doctoral thesis, 1986.
11. S. Pulaha *On the Demographic and Ethnical Situation of the Albanian Territory (15th–16th Centuries)*, (Tirana, 1988), pp. 31–3, suggests that the drying-up of migration from Albania to Italy contributed to the increase. On urban population growth, O. Barkan in N. Todorov (ed.), *La Ville Baklanique xv–xix ss* (Sofia, 1970) p. 181.
12. I.M. Kunt, *The Sultan's Servants 1550–1650*: *The transformation of Ottoman Provincial Government* (New York, 1983) especially Tables 4.1, 4.8, 4.9, 4.11, and 4.12.
13. The 'second serfdom' is a Marxist notion supported by little evidence. In Ceaucescu's time David Prodan once challenged his colleagues in the Academy by promising to accept the notion if they could demonstrate the existence of an earlier 'first serfdom'. Their response was to expel him. For further discussion, see Chapter 10 and p. x above.

14. See the useful discussion by M. Bogucka in V. Zimanyi (ed.), *La Pologne et la Hongrie aux xvi–xvii siècles* (Budapest, 1981) especially pp. 11–18.
15. L. Zytkowicz, 'The Peasant's Farm and the Landlord's Farm in Poland from the Sixteenth to the Middle of the Eighteenth Century', *Journal of European Economic History*, I, 1 1972, pp. 135–54; also A. Maczak, 'Polish Society and Power System,' in S. Fiszman, *op. cit.* pp. 17–33. For a general introduction to the phenomenon of serfdom, see J. Blum, 'The Rise of Serfdom in Eastern Europe', *The American Historical Review* 42 (4), 1957, pp. 807–36, who believes the chief cause of this divergence from the Western European experience was political. For Russia, J. Blum, *Lord and Peasant in Russia from the Ninth to the Nineteenth-Century* (Princeton, 1961); and J. Mavor, *An Economic History of Russia*, I (New York, 1965) which draws on the considerable expertise of V.I. Semevskii.
16 Zimanyi, *Economy and Society*, *op. cit.* pp. 30–8.
17. A. Wolanis's speech is quoted by A. Spekke, *History of Latvia* (Stockholm, 1951) p. 198.
18. Alderman Prutze of Stralsund 1614, quoted by H. Kamen, *The Iron Century* (London, 1971) pp. 219–20.
19. M. Bogucka, 'The Towns of East-Central Europe from the Fourteenth to the Seventeenth Century', A. Maczak *et al.*, (eds.), *East-Central Europe in Transition* (Cambridge, 1985) pp. 97–108 (the quoted extract is on p. 101).
20. Zimanyi, *op. cit.*, pp. 69–70. She rightly points out that the number of new-comers to the aristocracy was no greater than in England. However, the numbers of substantial merchants and yeomen were considerably less. A closer analogy lies, perhaps, with the merchants of Venice who showed a marked change in their investment policies in the same period, buying estates in the hinterland rather than putting money into commercial ventures which had become both riskier and less profitable.
21. Dillon, *op. cit.*, pp. 159ff.; Evans, *op. cit.*, pp. 39ff.; also his *Rudolf II and his World* (Oxford, 1973) pp. 157–8; A.F. Pollard, *The Jesuits in Poland* (Oxford, 1892).
22. A useful summary of such Ottoman military categories is provided by O. Zirojevic, *Tursko vojno urecenje u srbji 1459–1683* [Istorijski institut posebna izdana, kn. 18] (Beograd, 1974) esp. pp. 158ff. Despite the title the categories described apply to Ottoman-governed Balkan areas other than Serbia. See also my 'Conclusions' in G. Rothenberg *et al.* (eds.), *East-Central European Society and War* (Boulder, 1982) pp. 507–12. More specifically on the origins of the Cossacks, see Chapter I of my *The Cossacks* (London, 1969).
23. The Ottoman register of Timisoara [Temesvar] for 1566–7 (Basbakanli Arsivi, Istanbul, TD no. 17) may throw more light on this. For registers of units with a high proportion of men called Racz, see Hungarian State Archive E 210, 123t., 51cs., especially Jus Bassa's company (sixty-five out of 100), and Farkas Rats (twenty-one out of fifty). Also names such as U[z]beg (=runaway), Pribek (=refugee), Kozak, Rusnak, Torok, etc. Many south Slavs also found their way into the Romanian lands (as witness names and references to refugees) e.g. ms. 721 in Bucharest State Archive. See also L. Makkai, 'Istvan Bockai's Insurrectionary Army' in Bak and Kiraly, *op. cit.*, p. 277. For the origins of the Szekels, see Chapter 9. It is impossible to standardize the spelling and italicization of words such as *uskok*, *heyduck/haiduk*, *martolos*, etc., there is no standard form in English. See *OED*.
24. On the evidence of Cossacks' names see S. Luber, *Die Herkunft von Zaporoger Kosaken des 17 Jahrhunderts nach Personennamen* (Berlin [Freie Universität,

Osteuropa Institut: Slawische Veröffentlichungen, 56], 1983), also the report from Alba Julia, the capital of Transylvania, December 1597, in A. Veress (ed.), *Epistolae et Acta Jesuitarum Transylvaniae temporibus … Bathory (1571–1613)* [Fontes rerum Transylvanicarum] 1911.

25. I owe the reference to their killing Calvinist pastors whose faith they professed to Ferenc Szakkai (personal communication). For the data on heyduck depredations, G. Kemeny (ed.), *Deutsche Fundgruben der Geschichte Siebenburgens* , 2 vols (Klausenberg [Cluj], 1839–40) I, p. 189 and T. Tatler's record in *Quellen zur Geschichte der Stadt Brasso*, vol. IV [=Chroniken und Tagebucher, I] (Brasso, 1918), pp. 160 and 165–6 (but one wonders what use heyducks might have found for the books). The print referred to is in Braun and Hohenberg, *Theatre totius Mundi* no. 35 (Pappa, 1597). For an example of heyducks plundering villages in Wallachia in 1611, see Romanian State Archive, Bucharest, M-rea Tismara XCII, 152.
26. M. Fumee, *Historie of the Troubles in Hungary* (London, 1600), p. 323. The French edition was published in the same year. For a useful collation of documents of Michael 'the Brave', see I. Ardeleanu *et al., Mihai Viteazul in Constiinta Europeana*, pt. 4 (Bucharest, 1986).
27. For cases of Uskok activity around Trau [Trogir] at the turn of the century: Zadar: Historijski archiv, Archiv Trogira, k. 25, sv. xxvii, 11, ff. 2476r–7v. See my 'The Senj Uskoks Reconsidered', *Slavonic & East European Review*, 57 (3), 1979, pp. 348–68; B. Desnica, *Istorija kotarskih uskoka*, 2 vols (Beograd, 1950–4); also W. Bracewell in Rothenberg *et al., op. cit.*, pp. 431–47.
28. The manipulation of Ivan's image by both Stalinists and anti-Stalinists has stood in the way of any fair assessment of him. Ian Grey's *Ivan the Terrible*, (London, 1964) is in parts outdated; R. Skrynnikov's study is too brief. For a summary in English, see Fennel in *The New Cambridge Modern History* (hereafter *NCMH*) II, pp. 551–61. But a good new biography is sorely needed.
29. The recently discovered evidence of an eye-witness leaves no doubt that the report of the original investigation was correct and not a white-wash. Dmitrii's death in a play-fight with another child was accidental. The part peasant rebels played in Russia's 'Time of Troubles' is nowadays downplayed. See R. Skrynnikov, *Rossiia v nachale xvii v: 'smuta'* (Moscow, 1988) and his *Samozvantsy v Rossii v nachale xvii veka* (Novosibirsk, 1990).
30. See O. Halecki, *From Florence to Brest (1439–1596)* (Rome, 1958) parts III and IV, esp. pp. 366–91, and see Chapter 9.
31. The Jesuit, Antonio Possevino, left an account of his experiences, *Moscovia* (1587).
32. R.J.W. Evans, *Rudolph II and His World* (Oxford, 1973) especially pp. 60 and 70; and his *Making of the Habsburg Monarchy* (Oxford, 1979) pp. 51ff. A translation of the text of the Letter of Majesty is to be found in C.A. Macartney, *The Habsburg and Hohenzollern Dynasties* (New York, 1970) pp. 24–32.
33. The classic assertion of the rights of the Bohemian Estates is P. Stransky, *Republica Bohemiae* (Leyden, 1634); for an account of the defenestration, see Macartney, *op. cit.*, pp. 33–7; and for some useful background and bibliography, Evans, *Making, op. cit.*, pp. 66ff..
34. See the translation in Macartney, *op. cit.*, pp. 37–45.
35. Evans, *Making, op. cit.*, pp. 71–3 *passim.* At the same time legitimations of Habsburg power were disseminated. For an example of Habsburg display on behalf of Ferdinand III which anticipates the age of the Baroque with its puns associating the House of Austria with a star, see P. Ostermann, *Iustus Romaio-Basilikos Stephanos* (1640).

36. As Father Dvornik points out, cultural damage was done too insofar as Czech literature was associated with Protestantism [*The Slavs in European History and Civilization* (New Brunswick, 1962) pp. 456ff.].
37. S. Runciman, *The Great Church in Captivity* (Cambridge, 1968) pp. 259ff. The phrase characterizing de Dominis is Richard Neile's, see his *M. Antonio de Dominis ... His Shiftings in Religion* (1624) which contains the text of a letter to Lucaris.
38. On Ligarides see V. Grumel in *Dictionnaire de Théologie Catholiqiue*, IX (Paris, 1926) and R. Salomon in *Zeitschrift für Osteuropäische Geschichte*, V, 1931 (both hostile), besides much else in Greek and Russian. For his letters from Romania 1647–8, Rome: Archivio della Propaganda Fide, SOCG Nos. 64 and 177. For translation of passages from his 'Book of Prophecies' see H. Hionides, *Paisios Ligarides* (New York, 1972).
39. Zs.P. Pach, *Die Ungarische Agrarentwicklung im 16–17 Jahrhundert* (Budapest, 1964) pp. 91–2. This work is devoted to exploring the differences between Hungarian and West European agrarian development. See also Zimanyi, *Economy*, *op. cit.*, pp. 75ff. and L. Zytkowicz (*inter alia*) in Maczak *et al.*, *op. cit.*, pp. 59–83, whose qualifications do not substantially alter the general force of the summations made here.
40. On the strange story of the rise and decline of business mentality among the nobles of East-Central Europe, see Zs.P. Pach, *Etudes Historiques Hongroises*, 3 vols (Budapest, 1985), vol. II, pp. 131ff. At the same time the fact that St Isidore had been a farm manager was suppressed in Poland (see J. Tazbir in *Poland at the 14th International Congress of Historical Sciences in San Francisco* (Wroclaw, 1975) p. 107) and the word 'peasant' became a term of abuse in Hungary.
41. These points are argued by E. Fugedi in Maczak *et al.*, *op. cit.*, *p.* 54 and L. Makkai, *ibid.*, p. 31.

9

The Clashing of Cultures and Religions (1352–1526)

Be Patriarch and good fortune attend you. You are assured of Our goodwill and will retain all the privileges which your predecessors enjoyed.
Mehmet II to the new Patriarch of Constantinople, 1454

'The Muses fall silent amid the clash of arms' as the saying goes, and we are almost constantly at war. Never the less we devote what little leisure we have to the enjoyment of literature, which affords us much solace and delight.
King Matthias of Hungary to a humanist, 1471

In 1352 an earthquake damaged the ramparts of the harbour town of Gallipoli, facilitating its capture by the Turks. Thus the Ottoman Sultans gained their first base on the continent of Europe. The arrival of the Turks and their subsequent advances presented Christendom with a cultural and religious, as well as a political challenge. Yet Christendom itself remained divided. In the decades that followed, the longstanding differences between Catholics and Orthodox proved irreconcilable. The Orthodox camp itself tended to division between the proponents of asceticism and of more worldly views, while Catholics split between the devotees of rival Popes, and soon faced a serious religious rebellion in Bohemia. At the same time linguistic separatism first emerged as a cultural and political force, and Latin began its long decline as a Catholic *lingua franca*. This was also the age of the Black Death. Yet, for all these threats and divisions, the later fourteenth and fifteenth centuries were not devoid of opportunities for Eastern Europe.

The bubonic plague struck regularly throughout the period but its demographic effects were less serious than in the West. North-western Europe was not to make up its population losses until the early sixteenth century; but the Russian lands recovered earlier, Bohemia's losses were in any case small, and Poland's population seems actually to have increased during the period. The damage may have been less because the population of Eastern Europe was less dense and less urbanized than that of England and the Low Countries. But in any case the region as a whole began to catch up with the West during this period, and not only demographically but in terms of urbanization and economic development. By 1500 Prague and Gdansk as well as Istanbul and Moscow were among the twenty largest cities in Europe with populations of 30,000 or more; and most parts of the region had begun to produce commodities as well as agricultural goods.

Even an apparently adverse development like the Turkish occupation of Byzantium (Constantinople) in 1453 had beneficial effects: the once-great city which had fallen into a sad state of decline and dereliction was quickly repopulated and refurbished; demand for foodstuffs increased stimulating agricultural production in the Balkans; and the Genoese merchants based at Keffa in the Crimea were prompted to re-route their trade through Poland, to the benefit of its economy. Less positive, at least in its long-term effects, was the decline of the Hansa League which controlled the sea-borne trade from the Baltic and included some East European cities in its membership; and the advent of the Dutch to pre-eminence in shipping. But despite these threatening developments, the economic pace, albeit sluggish, was quickening and the region as a whole was narrowing the economic gap with the West.[1]

There were opportunities, too, to heal the religious divisions between Christians. In 1436 at Basel and Jihlava a compromise was struck which promised to establish religious peace in a Bohemia that had been racked by civil war; and at Florence in 1439 it seemed for a moment as if the great schism between the Orthodox and Catholics had finally been healed. In the sphere of cultural development the period was one of even greater promise. For decades before it fell to the Turks Byzantium had been an impoverished city, a splendid shell long since deprived of its former wealth and glory. Nevertheless it was the heir to and preserver of a great tradition. Its once immense empire had shrunk to almost nothing, yet it was still the acknowledged centre of an informal cultural empire that included Russia and the Balkans.[2] Not only did it preserve the art, learning and literature of classical antiquity; it was still culturally vibrant, productive in literature and art, and its scholars were much respected in the West, where they were to play a vital role in the development of the Renaissance.

Yet the cultural exchanges were by no means one-sided. Western influences on Eastern Europe were also strong. The glories of the Kremlin owe a great deal to the architects and craftsmen brought to Moscow from northern Italy in the fifteenth century; Russians were influenced by Maxim the Greek, who had been associated with the famous printer Aldo Manutio in Venice, had studied in Florence, knew the work of Pico della Mirandola and had heard Savaranola preach;[3] entire streets in the city of Buda were peopled by Frenchmen and Italians; Magdeburg law provided the legal basis for dozens of East-Central European cities; Venetian influence was strong in Dalmatia in the period and universities were founded in Cracow, Pecs and Bratislava to rival those of Oxford, Paris and Bologna.

The Turks, though committed to their Islamic culture, made considerable contributions to European civilization in the period particularly in the fields of decorative art, music and fine cooking. They also borrowed much from the Byzantines, whom they supplanted, in terms of administrative skills as well as science and architecture. Like the Russians, they employed many skilled Westerners, and Sultan Mehmet II's sense of cultural superiority did not prevent his having his portrait painted by one of the greatest Western artists of the day, Giacomo Bellini. This reciprocity was furthered by a widespread, though not universal, spirit of tolerance that was most evident in Poland, least so in Russia and Bohemia. In short this was a period when cultural understanding often transcended political differences, a time of widespread cross-fertilization in the realm of culture, though the crops were to be of uncertain size and flavour.

* * *

The 1350s had inaugurated a period of great political upheaval. Much as the geological plates that form the earth's crust accommodate themselves to disturbances beneath by grinding up against each other, so Eastern Europe had to make adjustments to sharp changes in the balance of power: the appearance of the Turks; the withdrawal of the Tatars from the line of the Danube; and the decline of the Teutonic Orders which controlled much of the southern shore-line of the Baltic. At the same time new powers had been emerging: Lithuania, which had gained coherence as a state earlier in the fourteenth century in angry reaction to the Teutonic Knights who were enslaving as well as converting the pagan peoples of the Baltic; and the Romanian principalities, Wallachia and Moldavia, which originated as frontier marches formed by the Kingdom of Hungary on territory which had been Tatar marauding grounds.[4] These developments created serious uncertainties. Would Lithuania, for example, align itself with its eastern neighbours, the Russians, upholders of the Orthodox cause, or with Poland and Catholicism? Would Catholic Hungary be able to retain the fealty of Danubian principalities whose populations were largely Orthodox? Even the issue of which among the various Russian principalities would emerge pre-eminent over the rest, had not yet been settled beyond question. The scene of the first great disturbance to claim our attention, however, was the Balkans.

The death in 1355 of Dushan, Tsar of Serbia and would-be Emperor of a revived Byzantine Empire, precipitated the break-up of the largest and most powerful state in the Balkans into a rabble of small, warring political entities – a situation which both facilitated and invited the Ottoman intrusion into Europe. The view that the Turkish advance destroyed a viable political order in the Balkans is therefore as much a myth[5] as the complaint that it hampered the region's development. It can be equally well argued that by re-establishing order in the peninsula the Ottomans were a force for good.

The later fourteenth century saw a steady Ottoman advance due as much to the disarray of the Christian states as their own military strength and political skills, considerable though these were. By 1370 they had taken Adrianople in Thrace[6] which because of its important strategic position they made their capital. Meanwhile a desperate Emperor of Byzantium, John V, volunteered to compromise his own church in return for Western aid. In 1355 he had promised the Pope in Avignon to bring his people into obedience within six months and offered his own son, Manuel, as a hostage to his good faith – if only the Pope would supply him with twenty ships and 1500 soldiers.[7] In 1366 he journeyed to Hungary to beg aid from its king, but the only substantial help he received was from his cousin, Amadeo of Savoy, who recaptured Gallipoli for him. In 1369 John actually kissed the Pope's feet, symbolizing the union of the two Churches – but most Orthodox clerics immediately repudiated the act. Two years later the same Emperor concluded that he had no alternative but to submit to the Sultan Murad and become his vassal.

Byzantium was virtually helpless, weakened by the Black Death, plagued by party strife, and bankrupt. The crown jewels were in pawn in Venice; and the money the Grand Duke of Muscovy had sent in 1350 to repair the ruined basilica of St Sophia had been misappropriated for more urgent purposes. Unable to obtain sufficient aid from abroad Byzantium was in no better position to assert its independence than the other principalities of the region, several of whose princes, Slav and Greek, also submitted to the Turks following the defeat of the strongest of them at the battle of the River Marica in 1371. For the time being the Ottomans were content to manipulate vassals and collect tribute from them rather than administer the conquered lands directly. The result was a certain blurring of cultural and political dividing lines. Thus Christian troops would be mustered to fight for the Sultan, just as Byzantium itself had employed Turkish troops when funds afforded.

The Ottoman advance continued. In 1383 they took Sofia, in 1385 Kastoria in Albania and Nis, in 1387 Thessaloniki. From time to time the Turks would experience a reverse at the hands of one or other of the bubble states of the Balkans or some combination of them, but then on 15 June 1389 (a date still commemorated with passion in the region more than six centuries later) a Turkish army routed a coalition of Serbs, Albanians, Bosnians and Romanians led by Lazar Hrebeljanovic at Kosovo. The advance continued. In 1391 Skopje was taken; in 1396 the Hungarians were defeated at Nicopolis and Ottoman influence reached Wallachia. Three years later the Emperor of Byzantium set out on another tour of the West, including England, in an attempt to translate sympathy into material support. Yet though salvation soon came, it did not emanate from the West but from the Orient. In 1402 at Ankara the Turks themselves were routed by the Mongols under the mighty Tamerlane. The pressure, for a time, was off.

Ironically, although many of the Sultan's Muslim troops deserted him at Ankara, his Christian troops had remained loyal. After the battle, however, there was a tendency for many lords in the western Balkans to transfer their allegiance to the Venetians, while others gravitated to Suleyman, son of the former Sultan who appeared likely to win the struggle with his brothers for the succession. Indeed, in order to cement an alliance with him the Byzantine Emperor Manuel II offered him his daughter in marriage (not the first time such a dynastic union had been contemplated: in 1345 the Sultan Orkhan had married a daughter of John VI). Though Suleyman did not, in fact, emerge victorious, Byzantium contrived to align itself with the eventual victor, Mehmet I, in time. However, this brought only a temporary respite.

Byzantium was as helpless militarily and politically as it was financially. Yet its plight gave impetus to a new surge of spiritual strength, which found expression in hesychasm, a monastic movement centred at Mount Athos, which emphasized Christian learning, mystic quietism and contemplation, employing certain techniques since associated with yoga and with zen. And Byzantium was still the centre of a vast spiritual empire, so that, at a time when all its political power was spent, it still wielded great influence far afield through the Orthodox Church. It had been playing a particularly important role as arbiter in a dispute between Muscovy and emergent Lithuania.

By the middle of the fourteenth century the state of Lithuania had grown to include the whole of the valley of the middle Dnieper and, after a victory over the Tatars in 1368, most of the territory of the former principality of Kiev too. Like the Turks and the Tatars, Olgerd, Prince of Lithuania, ruled for the most part through a system of vassalage and, as throughout the rest of mediaeval Europe, relied much upon the church as an agency of control and government. Lithuania's rulers had embraced Orthodoxy and in 1354, through the agency of the then independent Bulgarian Patriarchate, had obtained their own metropolitan see, which was of great help in asserting Lithuania's independence as a state. However, in 1361, thanks to Moscow's intervention this see had been suppressed. Since then the Lithuanian bishops had been subject to the Metropolitan of Kiev and all Russia who since 1328 had been based in Moscow and naturally tended to support its ruling prince. This provided a compelling reason for Olgerd to persuade the Patriarch in Byzantium to have the Metropolitan see removed to its original home in Kiev, which was now in his territory, or else sanction the re-establishment of a separate one for Lithuania.

The Orthodox Primate in Byzantium was therefore faced with an unenviable choice. To accede to the request would displease Muscovy, the most powerful of the Orthodox states; but to reject it might well alienate Lithuania, a welcome newcomer to the Orthodox community. At last in 1375 he responded by appointing his special envoy to the area, Cyprian, Metropolitan of Kiev and Lithuania – but with a patent to succeed the then Metropolitan of All Russia, Alexius, upon his death.[8] Clearly the Patriarch preferred to keep both countries under the same spiritual leadership, and this would be much more easily accomplished if they had the same political leader too. In all probability, then, Cyprian played a part in a deal struck in 1377, when Olgerd of Lithuania died, between his widow and Prince Dmitry of Moscow, according to which Dmitry's daughter was to marry Olgerd's son, Jagiello.

Had the deal stuck the result might well have been a vast Orthodox state of Muscovy-Lithuania. However, Lithuania soon made an extraordinary about-face. In 1386 Jagiello married not the Muscovite princess but the twelve-year old Jadwiga, heiress to the now defunct male line of Piast, and 'King' of Poland since 1384. Jagiello himself was now elected King and baptized a Catholic. Meanwhile Cyprian, who had become Metropolitan in Moscow, proved too independent for Moscow's prince, Prince Dmitry, who had him replaced, evidently by means of fraud, and the matter was only satisfactorily resolved in 1390, after Dmitry's death. But meanwhile Lithuania as a state was lost to the Orthodox camp. Many of its noble *boyar* class were long to remain loyal to Orthodoxy but pressures on them to convert soon became manifest. From 1413, for example, Lithuanian *boyars* could be 'adopted' by Polish noble families and given their coats of arms, and forty-seven soon availed themselves of the opportunity – but the privilege was limited to Catholics.[9]

Jadwiga, an enthusiastic *religieuse*, was remarkable, too, as a patroness of learning. She founded a Lithuanian College for the training of missionary priests at Prague, where a university had been established in 1348, and she revived the University of Cracow. This had been founded by Casimir the Great in 1364, with faculties of philosophy, medicine and law like Bologna; but it had collapsed a few years later for lack of students, teachers and money. Jadwiga, however, arranged for it to be modestly but suitably housed and endowed, and for a faculty of theology to be added. Thanks largely to her efforts, the project succeeded at the second attempt. In the year 1400 over 200 students graduated, and 18,000 were to register there in the course of the fifteenth century. Copernicus was to be one of its more distinguished *alumni.*[10]

By no means all the foundations of the age were so fortunate, however. The University of Vienna, established in 1365, was to survive, but that of Pecs in Hungary, founded by King Louis I and confirmed by Pope Urban V in 1367, foundered, and that of Prague[11] was soon the scene of great dissention and violence. Both Czech nationalists and Communists have seized on this story as gloriously justifying their beliefs, but in doing so have ripped it out of its mediaeval context, for the so-called 'Hussite Revolution' had primarily to do not with nationalism in a modern sense nor any secular idea of social justice, but with the reform of religion, of the church in Bohemia, and of the University of Prague.[12] It came to comprise many other struggles, however: not only between religious reformers and the religious establishment and between rebels at the University and its administration, but of local patriots against interlopers; of land-hungry noblemen and peasants against a land-rich Church; of assertive burghers against other estates; of the poor of Prague against the city's patricians; of the powerless against authority in general.

John Hus himself, the figure at the eye of the storm, had been born in 1371, graduated at the University, and was appointed a lecturer there in 1398. Two years later he was ordained a priest, and then became the Dean of Arts, meanwhile building a popular reputation with his sermons at the Bethlehem Chapel in which he denounced abuses in the Church: the practice of drawing fat incomes from several benefices at once but leaving services to be performed by curates who were paid a pittance; the sale of indulgences granting absolution for sins in return for contributions to the papal treasury; the greed, corruption and immorality of so many of the clergy. In this fashion Hus started on the road of dissent which was to lead to his martyrdom, burned at the stake in 1415.

The story is no simple morality tale, however. Hus can be regarded as a representative Eastern European figure; the dissident *avant la lettre.* In the judgement of one, not unsympathetic, historian, he was undoubtedly sincere in his desire for Church reform and always considered himself to be a good Catholic. But

> his zeal led him to overstep the mark. There was in him a mystical desire to suffer and to die for his convictions.... He seems to have been excessively proud of his own moral conduct, and the admiration and devotion of his faithful followers made him blind to the consequences to which some of his exaggerated views and teachings could lead.[13]

Much of the inspiration for this teaching undoubtedly derived from the West, from the teachings of John Wycliffe at Oxford, yet the Hussite movement was also fed by a sense of Bohemian grievance against immigrant Germans who dominated the university and seemed to obtain the best of the church livings. Such, at least, were the views of Jerome of Prague, another rebel hauled before the Council of Constance in 1416, the year after Hus was executed. In a speech defending himself Jerome implicitly recalled the fact that it had been Greek Byzantine missionaries who first introduced Czechs to Christianity even though the Church in Bohemia was organized along strictly German lines (see Chapter 11):

> I am condemned by ... the German Bohemians; the reason for their hatred is this: the Czechs are descended from the Greeks and as there was hatred between the Greeks and the Teutons. So it continued until the kingdom came into the hands of the Emperor Charles IV [who] ... saw that it was a rich country... lacking... only in educated men.... Wishing to endow the kingdom of Bohemia and the city of Prague, [he] founded ... a university.... [But] many Germans secured prebends and fellowship, so that the Czechs had nothing. And when a Czech had graduated ... he had to earn his living by teaching in some private school. The Germans were in complete control of the University of Prague and of all its benefices. Also they had three votes in the University, namely the Bavarian and the Saxon and more than half the Polish vote, for the Silesians ... were all [linguistic] Germans. Whatever the Germans wanted in the university was as good as done. The Bohemians could do nothing.[14]

The Hussites had succeeded in promoting an exodus of the German masters. Patriots interpret all this as the Czech nation leading the progressive forces of the West towards the Reformation, as proof positive that the Czechs not only belong to the West but played an essential role in the creation of Western civilization. In fact, however, the Hussites included many Bohemian Germans, the movement gained many supporters in the German lands proper, and its enemies included linguistic Czechs. Furthermore, the reputation of the university had depended in large measure on scholars from Germany, and the linguistic tensions that had been aroused discouraged foreign students and banished that happy ecumenical spirit which makes a university. The net result of the Hussite movement was to turn Prague from one of Christendom's leading intellectual centres into a stagnant backwater, cut off from the mainstream of Europe's intellectual and cultural life, until the later fifteenth century.

The Hussite victory had owed much to Bohemia's King, Wenceslas IV, who exploited the dissention for his own ends. He had been deposed from the imperial throne of Germany and wanted to regain it. Most of the cardinals had promised their support to this end, provided he supported their choice for Pope rather than those already ensconced in Rome and Avignon. However, the German masters who ran the university had opposed him. Hence the Decree of Kutna Hora of 1409 by which Wenceslas increased the franchise of the 'Bohemian nation' in the university, and, when this was resisted, its takeover by royal officials. It was this which had precipitated the exodus of German scholars from Prague.

Furthermore, the Hussites gained widespread support from society as well as from the king. Hus's death provoked a storm of protest in Bohemia and there was a general refusal to accept the interdict which the Cardinals placed upon Prague. Nearly 500 noblemen formed a league in defence of free preaching; calls came for an end to the church's temporal authority. Then when Wenceslas, afraid of becoming isolated diplomatically, began to trim, there was a massive protest in Prague. The king died and his successor, Sigismund, led a 'Crusade' to regain the kingdom, thus precipitating the Hussite Wars. He was ably opposed by John Zizka, a minor noble and competent general who established his headquarters camp at a place they named 'Tabor' after the Biblical mountain which joined heaven to earth.

The movement radicalized. The burghers of Prague seized the opportunity to assert their primacy in the Estates in 1421; peasants and the urban poor went on the rampage; a sect known as the Adamites went so far as to propound the view that women should be held in common. The situation descended into chaos.

> When I contemplate the present extensive ruin [wrote the contemporary chronicler Lawrence of Brezov] and the calamities which have befallen the once fortunate and famous Kingdom of Bohemia, now devastated ... by strife, my understanding becomes dull, and my mind, bewildered by sorrow, loses its intellectual vigour.[15]

At last, in 1434, the radical extremists were routed by the forces of the King, and at Basel two years later a compromise was forged: henceforth preaching in Bohemia was to be free and its subjects could take wine as well as the wafer at Communion; the church there was shorn of its secular powers and the clergy's right to own property was limited.[16] Gradually the dust settled, though, as we shall see, it did not disappear.

The Council of Basel seemed to have settled a serious but essentially local crisis. Much more was at stake at another Council which began at Siena two years later and concluded at Florence in 1439 – for this attempted to heal the great schism between the Orthodox and the Catholics (who had at last recovered from the schism in their own ranks). As we have seen, it was no novelty for a Byzantine Emperor to promise obedience to the Pope in the expectation of material aid, but such undertakings had always been repudiated afterwards. This time, however, the attempt at rapprochement was rather better prepared and promised better chances of success. The Emperor, John VIII, was accompanied by the Patriarch Joseph II and by some leading clerics, although others had declined to come; and considerable mutual respect was evident among scholars in both delegations.

The Emperor and his suite were feted on their arrival in Venice and the splendour of their welcome in Tuscany by the ruling Duke, Cosimo de' Medici, is still to be observed in the vivid frescoes by Pinturicchio on the walls of the Gozzoli Chapel in Florence. The negotiations themselves, however, were less satisfactory. The Patriarch behaved in a confused and ineffectual way, and then died in the middle of the proceedings. Union of the churches was eventually agreed upon, but on terms that made few concessions to the Orthodox, and it was not to gain widespread acceptance among them.[17] One signatory of the accord, Bessarion, Metropolitan of Nicaea, eventually abandoned his see, settled in Italy, received a Cardinal's hat, and gave his collection of some 600 Greek manuscripts to Venice, where they form the nucleus of the great Marciana Library. The celebrated neo-Platonist scholar George Plethon contrived to withhold his signature, but Isidore, Metropolitan of Kiev and All Russia, who did sign it, was imprisoned on his return to Muscovy on grounds of apostasy. The only benefit was the belated mounting of a 'Crusade' against the Turks who had reassumed an aggressive stance towards Byzantium.

At first it was successful. Hungary, Poland, and Venice all participated. So did many Serbs. Together they won a victory over the Turks at Nish and occupied Belgrade. These successes attracted yet more support to the Crusade, most notably from George Kastriota, one of the more important Turkish vassals. Although a Christian prince, Kastriota had been partly educated as a hostage of the Turks who called him Iskander Bey (General Alexander). He was to become better-known, however, by a corruption of that name: 'Skanderbeg'. From his stronghold at Kruje in central Albania and in the mountains to the north and east of it, Skanderbeg was to fight on against his former friends for a quarter of a century; but meanwhile in November 1444 the crusade had ended in disaster on a battlefield near Varna. Both Wladyslaw III, King of Poland and Hungary, and the Pope's envoy, Cardinal Cesarini, were among those who perished. When the Hungarians, under the able general John Hunyadi, were overwhelmed by the Turks at Kosovo in 1448 all hope for the remnant of the Byzantine Empire and its capital, Constantinople, seemed to have vanished. Yet five years were to pass before the Turks were able to mass their forces outside the city.

The Sultan, Mehmet II, demanded its surrender. When this was refused, a siege began that was to last seven weeks, for poverty-stricken and depopulated though the city was its magnificent position and still strong walls made it eminently defensible. In the end the Turks succeeded only by transporting a flotilla of small ships overland and launching them in the Golden Horn, bypassing its protective chain; by laying down a fierce artillery bombardment, and launching a costly assault from the landward side. The Pope, Genoa and Venice made contributions to the defence. The galleys Venice sent arrived too late, however, although Venetians guarding their commercial interests in Byzantium took part in the fighting. Some of them survived, escaping by sea at the eleventh hour, and one left an account of the battle and of how the last Emperor, called Constantine after the city's founder, died upon its walls.[18]

Mehmet II had had no alternative but to conquer the city. As he himself remarked,

> Situated as it is in the middle of our dominions, [it] protects the enemies of our state and incites them against us. The conquest of the city is, therefore, essential to the future and the safety of the Ottoman state.[19]

In accordance with convention Byzantium, having refused surrender terms, was given over to the victorious troops to pillage, and the Sultan himself entered the great and ancient Basilica of the Holy Wisdom and personally dismantled its high altar. It has been a mosque ever since. Nevertheless the continuities between the old and the new regimes, like those in twentieth-century Eastern Europe, were almost as remarkable as the changes which historians commonly stress.

* * *

There had been a good deal of peaceful interchange as well as fighting between Byzantium and the Ottomans in the decades preceding 1453; and not a little intermarriage. Mehmet's own ancestors included Byzantine Christians. Besides he entertained considerable respect for some aspects of the Byzantine tradition; he was invited to think of himself as 'Emperor of the Romans', like the Byzantine Emperors of old, and came to believe that he could unite all Christendom under his rule. More immediately he used certain Byzantine institutions as models for the system he set up to run his Empire. Thus the Byzantine fief seems to have been the inspiration of the *sipahi* system; Byzantine offices, taxes and even ceremonials became bases for Ottoman administrative and court practices,[20] and certain posts, particularly those involving foreign affairs, became almost a monopoly of Greeks. This is not to suggest, however, that much about the new regime was not alien and burdensome.

The Ottoman state was run by a system of slavery, even though the Sultan's slaves constituted an administrative and military elite. Furthermore, the Turks took an irregular levy of children (*devshirme*) from their subject Christian population and made Muslims of them, even though they also trained them for their service and set them on ladders of opportunity which enabled them to reach the highest offices of state.

Furthermore, Christians were made to feel their inferiority. They were forbidden to wear green or to paint their houses in bright colours, forbidden to ride horseback in the presence of Muslims, and restricted in the number and the height of their churches.

On the other hand there was freedom of worship; non-Muslims were not obliged to do military service; and they were largely subject to their own justice within their own religious *millets*, of which by far the largest was the Orthodox, administered by the Patriarchate of Constantinople whose latest incumbent was invested in office by the Sultan himself. The Great Church was largely in captivity, but it retained most of its autonomy. The monasteries of Mount Athos were not disturbed, and the Turks did not distract the monk Gabriel of Rila from his life's work, a vast compilation of the sayings of St John Chrysostomos.[21]

The Ottoman Turks also breathed new life into decrepit Byzantine cities and above all into Constantinople which they called Istanbul. Christians, Muslims, Armenians and Jews were brought from all over the Empire and settled there. Hence the population which had shrunk to about 10,000 in the immediate aftermath of its fall increased by as much as tenfold within thirty years. Most came voluntarily recognizing opportunity or responding to concessions, though some were forcibly resettled; and huge building and rebuilding projects were soon under way. Water supplies, sewage disposal, street-paving and street furniture were soon renewed or supplied for the first time; ruined structures were rebuilt, others restored and new palaces, fountains, public baths and hospitals erected. Also a great bazaar – for the Ottomans had long recognized the importance of commerce.[22]

In the Balkan countryside Ottoman domination replaced uncertainty and periodic anarchy with an orderly system that did not at first always unduly disturb existing social relationships. Local lords who submitted to the sultan were generally left in possession of their estates, provided they served the Ottomans as loyal vassals. They were encouraged to convert to Islam and embrace Ottoman culture, of course, but pressures to do so tended to be applied gradually over a period of two or three generations, by which time many had gravitated naturally to the ways of the new elite.[23] Lower down the scale peasants could gain privileges such as certain tax exemptions by serving as military auxiliaries or local police; most monasteries that had not earned the Sultan's displeasure continued in the possession of most of their estates; and the populations of some regions, notably the heretical Bogomils of Bosnia, positively welcomed the Turks.

In two other respects the Ottoman system can be regarded as superior to some others in the Europe of the time. It was unequivocal about the ultimate ownership of property belonging to the state, eliminating powerful lordships, bases of individual power which could be exercised capriciously; and it did not permit the military class to become too numerous. Christian servicemen surplus to requirements were reduced in status and lost their privileges. This was not the case in Poland and Hungary, where, as we have seen, a swollen nobility and the virtually unrestricted power of lords were to be conducive to great harm. Furthermore the Turks provided security for the great majority of the Balkan population to live in tranquility in accordance with a familiar culture. By uprooting and changing Byzantine institutions, it has been said to have decapitated Byzantine high culture.[24] On the other hand, as we have seen, Byzantine civilization had made some impression on the Turks themselves; and its cultural legacies, to both Eastern and Western Europe, were particularly rich.

The Byzantine-Russian connection was one of long standing; and in time the fall of Constantinople was to encourage the Grand Dukes of Moscow to regard themselves as successors to the Emperors. Since the Council of Florence, it is true, Moscow always insisted on a Russian rather than a Greek as Metropolitan; and the question of how far the Russian Church and the Slavonic liturgy diverged from the Byzantine ideal was to become a major issue for a considerable time to come. On the other hand, the collapse brought many prominent Greeks, some of them with valuable experience in government, military affairs, diplomacy and commerce to Muscovy, where they tended to receive preferment and wield influence; and they brought a good deal of cultural baggage with them too. Furthermore in 1472 Ivan III married Zoe Palaeologus, niece of Constantine XI, the last Emperor, thereby adding a genetic component to Russia's Byzantine heritage.[25]

Byzantium's legacy to the West had less spiritual content and smaller political, ceremonial and institutional constituents; but it had more to do with learning. Men like Bessarion and Plethon had been feted in Italy because their scholarship was much admired, because they belonged to a people who had preserved the language and the literature of ancient Greece as well as those of late Rome and the Byzantine Empire – for the rediscovery of classical Greece was a major stimulus to the Renaissance, as much in literature and philosophy as in art and architecture.

One brilliant product of this new atmosphere was Aenius Silvius Piccolomini, who hailed from a poor little village in Tuscany, yet became one of the most complete of humanists, a learned bibliophile, an elegant stylist, an adroit diplomatist and politician and, as a visit to his country house at Pienza will show, a lover of both nature and the classical arts. He rose to become Bishop of Siena, chief diplomatic adviser to the German Emperor, in which capacity he became well-acquainted with post-Hussite Bohemia (and thought of writing its history); and in 1458 he was elected Pope, taking the title Pius II.

It was his great ambition as Pope to mount a successful Crusade against the Turks, and, as one of his principal helpers in this enterprise, he looked to another Renaissance Prince, Matthias Hunyadi, called

Matthias Corvinus (the Raven), son of the great soldier, who was elected King of Hungary at the age of fifteen in the same year that Pius became Pope. The two apparently had much in common. Both were devotees of humanism and patrons of the arts and learning. Matthias had Fra Filippo Lippi and Andrea Mantegna paint his portrait (the latter from memory), formed a splendid library of manuscripts and printed books, each magnificently bound,[26] founded a university at Pozsony [Bratislava] and had passions for speed, for building and for luxury. He extended and refurbished the castle palaces at Buda, another (one of three summer palaces) at Visegrad on a height overlooking the Danube bend, and a third in Vienna which he occupied in 1486 towards the end of his reign. According to a contemporary observer:

> He had spacious reception rooms ... ceilings embellished with gilt bosses and doors with intarsia. The mantlepieces were ornamented with carved chariots and the walls decorated with other Roman emblems.... The upper dining room in the new palace [at Buda] is decorated with the twelve signs of the Zodiac which is wondrous to behold, and the floors covered with mosaic patterns ... There are bathrooms supplied with hot and cold water.... In the palace yard the visitor is greeted by three statues of armed men on horseback, the central one of which is Matthias himself.... The pedestals are decorated with emblems of victory.[27]

Two Rennaissance men, a warrior and a spiritual leader – they seem happily complementary figures; and one finds further suggestions of it in their correspondence, as when, for example, the experienced Pius offers the young king good advice, hinting (despite his dislike of the Orthodox 'heresy') that Matthias would do well to master Greek in order to gain a better understanding of his subjects, so many of whom, particularly in the archdiocese of Kalocsa, still had a vestigial sympathy for Orthodoxy. Yet Matthias proved to be a disappointment as a crusader. Time and again he was urged to action against the Turks; he even accepted contributions towards the costs of war against them. Yet for all his frequent expressions of good faith and commitment to the cause, the good intentions were not translated into action.

It was not troops that Matthias lacked: he was to build up a force of nearly 30,000 crack mercenaries, chiefly Czechs and Germans (the famous 'Black Army') in addition to the traditional call-out of the noble cavalry in time of war. Nor did he lack income, profligate spender though he was. During his reign, in fact, he contrived to increase his predecessor's income of 200,000 gold florins a year to five times that figure; and earned some notoriety for imposing a stiff household tax which was doubled in time of war.[28] Internal challenges to his authority precluded foreign adventures early in his reign, however, and later he was much more interested in empire-building to the north than fighting the Turks in the south. Only briefly in 1463 did he respond to the Pope's entreaties, undertaking a half-hearted campaign against the Turks in Bosnia. Pius died that year, a disappointed man. But there was another victim, the Romanian prince Vlad III Tepes, Vlad the Impaler, since better known as Dracula.

The nickname Dracul ('the Dragon') probably derives from his father's membership of the Hungarian chivalric Order of the Dragon, although in Romanian it takes on the meaning of a devil, and Vlad was certainly to earn the name with his draconian behaviour. A member of the ruling house of Basarab, he had, like Skanderbeg, been a hostage of the Turks, then turned against them, serving with John Hunyadi, and he was related by blood to King Matthias. Becoming *Hospodar* (lord) of Wallachia in 1448, he was promptly ousted by a rival, but in 1456 he regained power and this time took better care to keep it.

He built up a personal army of retainers, executed a number of hostile *boiars* [nobles] and took harsh measures against anyone else who opposed his will. He also tried to promote commerce, established Bucharest as the country's capital, and in 1459 responded positively to Pius II's call for a Crusade against the Turks. He withheld the Sultan's tribute, killed Ottoman emissaries sent to deal with him, and then, in the winter of 1461–2, carried out a devastating assault into Ottoman territory. In a night attack, he routed an Ottoman force that had driven him back across the Danube – an occasion marked by a great slaughter of Turks.

At this point Vlad's luck began to change. The Turks supported a bid by his half-brother Radu the Handsome to replace him and the movement gained increasing support within Wallachia, partly because of party interests, not least because it promised peace. Then, late in 1462, when the reluctant crusader King Matthias at last reached the 'Saxon' city of Brasov in Transylvania at the head of his troops, Vlad went to meet him, expecting, as did the Pope himself, that they would launch a joint operation against the Turks. Instead, Matthias arrested Vlad, took him back to Buda and kept him imprisoned there for thirteen years.[29]

Vlad's diminishing support in Wallachia no doubt prompted Matthias to have second thoughts about the crusading action he had promised the Pope, though there was another consideration: in an attempt to enrich Wallachia, Vlad had tried to regain territories that had been lost and wrest control of the profitable oriental trade from the 'Saxon' cities of Transylvania (which supported pretenders to his throne) and even attacked them. A new Turkish-backed regime in Wallachia promised to restore the old pattern of trade and, for his part, Matthias was anxious to reassure them, for Transylvania, and the prosperous Saxon cities in particular, constituted an important source of income to the Hungarian treasury. However, he now had to justify his actions to the Pope. This he did by mounting a highly effective campaign of disinformation against Vlad, incidentally drawing our attention to a facet of humanist activity that is sometimes overlooked: the manufacture of propaganda. In fact the Dracula legend was largely the creation of humanist officials at Matthias's court.[30]

The motive was both strong and simple: Pope Pius had to be convinced that, so far from being a doughty Crusader, Vlad was an oppressor, a murderer, a sadist – a disgrace to the Christian cause, from whom he should at all costs distance himself. To this end Janos Vitez, who was to become Primate as well as Chancellor of Hungary, Janus Pannonius, later Bishop of Pecs, and other literary talents at the court of Matthias were set to work. They used the complaints made by the Saxon merchants and stories put about by Vlad's enemies in Wallachia in their apparently successful attempts to convince Pius; and these stories were essentially true. Vlad had undoubtedly had many people impaled (it was a commonplace form of execution in the region); he had fired many villages (as part of a scorched earth policy in the war against the Turks) and put many Ottoman subjects to death (though Matthias's own father had once slaughtered a thousand Turkish prisoners).

However, by carefully ignoring the reasons for his actions, and by inventing new tales (for example about his allegedly favourite pastime in prison: slowly picking off the limbs of live insects) they were able to create the impression that Vlad was a traitor, a capricious despot, a sadist and a psychopath. A Latin poem by Pannonius picturing Vlad as a tyrant gained wide currency, and in 1463, as part of a wider propaganda effort, the printing, in German, of the 'Story of Prince Dracula' was arranged. It proved highly popular and was subsequently republished many times with embellishments and in several languages. Ultimately it was to provide Bram Stoker with the inspiration to invent a modern, fictional, Dracula. Opinion manipulators of our own times would have had little new to teach a Renaissance humanist.

Pius died in 1464 and his successor Paul II was not deceived. Indeed he accused Matthias of misappropriating the money he had accepted as a subsidy for the crusade. However, he was also concerned about the situation in Bohemia, which since 1458 had been ruled by George of Podebrady, the 'Hussite King'. George has since earned a respected place in the pantheon of Czech national heroes as a Renaissance monarch who showed Europe the way forward by promoting plans for a 'Perpetual Union' of Christian princes to counter the Turkish threat, and for the abolition of war in Europe. However, though expressed in rhetorical terms which were commonplace in that age, George's purposes were immediate and practical: to gain allies, notably France, against the Emperor, and to defend the Bohemian Hussites (now called Utraquists) against an increasingly hostile Papacy. Rather than demonstrating that George was a European statesman of central importance and the Czech Utraquists heralds of a united Europe, it suggests that they were politically, as well as culturally, isolated.[31]

For his part, Paul II, who had come to consider George and the Utraquists to be as great a threat to Christendom as the Turks, encouraged Matthias's attempts at empire-building at George's expense. In May 1469 Matthias (who had married George's daughter) was actually elected King of Bohemia at Olomouc, although George retained possession of the crown. When George died in 1471, the Bohemian Estates did not choose Matthias as king, nor his rival the Emperor Frederick III of Habsburg, but a Jagiellonian, Wladyslaw of Poland. Nevertheless, a deal was eventually struck that left Matthias in possession of Moravia, Silesia and Lusatia. He also occupied a great deal of Austria; and in 1476, in conjunction with Stephen the Great of Moldavia, he struck against the Turks at last, releasing Vlad from gaol and supporting his claim to the throne of Wallachia.

It ended in disaster. Within weeks of regaining his throne Vlad was ousted and hacked to death. Yet, vile though the reputation that Matthias had manufactured for him was, in the Romanian lands he was to be remembered for good, as an admittedly stern and crafty but nevertheless just and patriotic monarch. The stories were picked up by the envoy of Muscovy's Ivan III to Matthias, Fedor Kuritsyn, who reached Buda via Moldavia in the 1480s. In this case, however, it was the moral of the stories that held interest: the notions that the monarch enjoyed an untrammelled right to reward and punish, that he treated all his subjects, of whatever rank, equally, and that he combined severity with justice. So in due course these components of the Dracula legend came to be used in the ideological underpinning of the Russian autocracy.[32]

Ivan III is often regarded as the real founder of the Russian state. He forced the Principalities of Yaroslavl and Rostov to recognize his supremacy; he subjected Novgorod too, breaking the Hansa League's long-standing strangle-hold on its commerce. He annexed the Grand Duchy of Tver, finally ended the last formal vestige of Mongol-Tatar suzereinty, and incorporated the lands of several Lithuanian notables who defected to him. In 1494 Ivan proclaimed his success by adding the words 'of all Russia' to his titles. But his success was a matter of financial and administrative engineering as well as territorial annexation, and it was celebrated in building as well as the accumulation of titles.

The compilation of land registers of all the state's territories, and on a more thorough basis than before, played a significant part in the consolidation of the new Russia, facilitating the continuing effort to bring the peasantry into the tax-net of central government, regardless of what lord, lay or clerical, stood in between.[33] The absorption of the nobilities of all the newly-incorporated territories presented another major challenge.

Appointments in Moscow's service sufficient to their energies and sense of honour were found for most of the newcomer elite without offending too many of the older servitors. And although many of the newcomers, including princes who could trace no less an impeccable descent from the legendary Riurik than Ivan himself, had wielded formidable power under the old regimes, membership of the central executive, the Boyar Council, was kept very low.[34] These were major achievements. At the same time Muscovy was by no means isolated from the rest of Europe even before the English appeared there in the 1550s; nor was it immune to Renaissance influences.

Italian craftsmen, some of whom had arrived with the Greek refugees from Byzantium, were employed to remodel the Kremlin for Ivan III. Among them were Alvise Novi of Milan who designed the Cathedral of the Archangel Michael, the mausoleum of Russia's rulers, and Aristotele Fioravanti da Ridolfo, engineer (and counterfeiter) from Bologna, who built the great Cathedral of the Dormition – which is why both monuments have an Italianate feel while conforming to the canon of Greek Orthodox architecture. And in secular buildings of the period Renaissance influences are more obvious still: in, for example, Ivan's new venue for state receptions, the Hall of Facets, and the new Kremlin walls, both designed by the Solari brothers from Milan in styles strikingly similar to those of contemporary Ferrara. Nor were Renaissance influences confined to architecture or, indeed, to Moscow. Alvise Lamberta de Montagnana was a Venetian sculptor who reached Moscow in 1504 from the Crimea; and other Italian craftsmen worked at Dorogobuzh, Nizhnii Novgorod and Pskov.[35]

Nevertheless, though the Muscovite government kept well abreast of European affairs and had secular books, including some scientific tracts, translated, Renaissance humanism, like its representational art, had a negligible influence in the country, not only because of the generally low level of literacy in Russia, but because the linguistic medium of the Renaissance, Latin, was associated with Catholic heresy which implicitly challenged Muscovy's emerging sense of destiny, not simply as heir to Byzantium but as the centre of a future universal empire. It was at the turn of the sixteenth century, after all, that the messianic notion of Moscow as the 'Third Rome' was elaborated.[36] This factor was added to existing forces: the isolationism that vast spaces, low population densities and pervasive ignorance of the wider world tend to breed; and the mystic tendencies and popular hatred of the West that Russians inherited from late Byzantium. Together they helped to mould a distinctive mind-set which had much in common with those to be found in other Orthodox regions of Europe, but which found great difficulty in absorbing humanist ideas.

Yet Renaissance influences even on non-Orthodox areas of Eastern Europe were either limited compared to the Low Countries and France, or else delayed, or both. In Bohemia Hussite nonconformity, and, apparently, the decline of Latin, had the effect of delaying the impact for the better part of a century. As for Poland, though her churchmen encountered humanists at the Councils of Constance (where they tended to sympathize with Hus), Ferrara and Florence, and there were various other contacts through diplomacy and travel, the early fifteenth century was in the opinion of one specialist, 'spiritually and intellectually still a deeply mediaeval period' in Poland. Humanism had but little impact until the 1470s when the first printing press was set up at Cracow, and even then, like Renaissance art, it remained a restricted currency, principally dependent on court patronage. The University of Cracow flourished, thanks partly to an influx of students from abroad, not least from Bohemia and Hungary,[37] but the greatest sculptor working in Poland in this period was Veit Stoss. In terms of learning as well as art Poland, like Bohemia, was more indebted to the Germans than the Italians.

Hungary had been the only country of the region to be strongly influenced by the Renaissance at an early stage. Yet again the achievement was centred on the royal court; and it proved short-lived – not simply because of the Turkish advance but because it was unaffordable. The great blossoming had occurred suddenly under Matthias Corvinus, but the plant quickly wilted after he died in 1490. The professional army on which he had depended was destroyed and most of the Italian craftsmen departed. The university he had founded at Pozsony had collapsed even earlier for lack of support. Like that other master of *Realpolitik*, Ivan III of Moscow, Matthias had been a successful state-builder; but unlike Ivan he had not succeeded in making his achievement last. Much earlier in his career he had solemnly recognized Frederick III Habsburg as his heir should he die childless. In fact Frederick predeceased him and Matthias tried to establish his illegitimate son as his heir, but in vain. Of the several candidates who declared themselves upon his death it was Wladyslaw Jagiello, King of Bohemia, who won the election.

Jagiellonian Poland also seemed highly successful. Not only had it succeeded in weaning Lithuania away from the Orthodox camp, but it was in this period that it broke through to the Baltic, received the submission of the Teutonic Knights, whose last Grand Master, Albrecht of Hohenzollern, became a Polish vassal Duke in 1525, and absorbed several Hansa towns. In all, the Jagiellonians were at least as successful in the struggle for power in East-Central Europe as the royal houses of Anjou and Luxembourg had been in the fourteenth. They have therefore attracted a good deal of attention in the older-fashioned histories. However, the Angevins and Luxembourgers failed to establish their dynasties very firmly, and Wladyslaw won the crown of Bohemia because he promised to be a weak king, not a strong one. Rather than representing dynastic success, therefore, the phenomenon suggests that there may have been some institutional weakness, some flaw or imbalance in the political structure of these states even at this early date. But in order to trace the fault and define its extent we must examine the powers of the crown, and its relationships with both the cities and the nobility.

As both Matthias and Ivan showed, a monarch's political success was chiefly dependent on his ability to raise money. But in Poland, Bohemia and even Hungary the barons had been able to limit the crown's powers to tax them, while the fact that royal bureaucrats tended to be appointed from the ranks of the higher clergy placed informal limitations on the monarch's ability to tax the Church. Furthermore, as in Russia and the Ottoman lands, custom and sentiment also placed effective bounds on the monarch's ability to raise money at the expense of religious foundations. It is often pointed out that Western monarchies were cramped by similar limitations, and this is true. However, whereas in East-Central Europe the powers of the crown tended to decline, in the West, and in Russia, they were already tending to grow.

There was a curious difference in timing too. *Magna Carta*, which marked the high point of noble privilege *vis à vis* the crown of England was signed in 1215. The Polish equivalent, the Statute of Nieszawa, by which the king undertook to seek the approval of the nobility before introducing new laws or going to war, is dated 1454, and that for Lithuania in 1492. Around the turn of the century the two-chamber parliamentary system became established, the idea took hold that Poland was a republic; then, at the Diet of Radom in 1505 the *nihil novi* law was enacted which deprived the monarchy of the right to legislate without the consent of both parliamentary chambers.[38] This suggests that Poland was in advance of other states in creating a balanced constitution, but such a reading would be superficial. In fact the cities were being effectively squeezed out of parliament, and the political forces in the country generally were falling seriously out of balance. So far from heralding the emergence of a healthy body politic, the new development marked the onset of political artero-sclerosis.

Poland lacked a common law such as the Normans had introduced into England, and the prevalent customary law varied from district to district, each of which had its own law courts.[38] The central government now became incapable of countering this localism, though attempts were to be made to do so. This political debility of Poland's kings which increased sharply from the later fifteenth century had several causes: the property structure that prevailed in Lithuania, the difficulty of communication in the enlarged kingdom and the nobility's acquisition of extensive privileges. This latter problem in turn stemmed in part from the gradual accretion of local power, and clients, by the more substantial landlords and their increasing coherence, through marriage as well as interest, as a political force;[39] and in large measure from the practice of elective kingship. As early as 1374 Jagiello, founder of the new dynasty, had been forced to grant the nobility complete freedom from taxation as the price of his election. But there are other dimensions to the story.

Whereas in later fifteenth-century England a monarch like Richard III could find a powerful ally in the city of London, the Kings of Poland, Bohemia and Hungary had no city of such great wealth and influence to turn to. True, Matthias Corvinus and the city of Buda seem to have had a mutually supportive relationship,[40] but on the whole the cities of East-Central Europe were not quite the mainstays of royal power that they tended to be in the West. Artisans tended to be few, urban populations as a whole were linguistically divided, and often alienated from the population of their hinterlands. Furthermore, although towns in all three states enjoyed a considerable degree of legal autonomy under Magdeburg Law (see Chapter 10) developments in the period tended to bleed them of political power and hence reduce their independence and their economic prospects too.

Bohemia constitutes an exception. Wenceslas IV had brought burghers into his inner council but had been forced to discontinue the practice. Then in 1419 the royal free towns gained full rights of consultation in the Estates, though in the constitutional order laid down by Charles IV in 1438 no place was found for them. The Code of 1500 barred the cities from the Diet. However, the right was regained in 1508. Clearly burghers in Bohemia could not take their political rights for granted; and it is understandable, though still curious, that in order to support their claims the burghers of Prague should have borrowed the nobility's traditional argument of genetic inheritance, the right of blood.[41] In Poland most cities were effectively deprived of political representation in 1505; and their economic rights were being eroded too. In 1496 the Polish peasantry was denied freedom of movement, and the nobility gained exclusive right to make and sell beer on their estates. Furthermore, around 1500 townsmen in Hungary and Poland were forbidden to hold rural land. These laws hit the cities hard.

Until this point burghers had tended to invest at least part of their profits in land. In this they were no different from their Western counterparts, though they seem to have accumulated significantly less capital – a circumstance which may help to account for their apparent demographic weakness. Only half the merchant patricians of Cracow who died between 1490 and 1526 left a male heir, and only one in ten a living grandson. No doubt disease was partly responsible, but a desire to preserve their comparatively small fortunes may well have led them to limit their families.[42] The burghers may not have lacked an understanding of civic virtue but they could not play the essential role for which the bourgeoisie in the West had been cast. Nor was this the only aspect of social and political imbalance which prevented these countries developing in ways more similar to those of the West.

Whereas in the West the nobility made up about 1 per cent of the population, in Hungary it comprised upwards of 4, and in Poland upwards of 7 per cent; and it was continuing to grow as more elements who had no other obvious place in the social order gravitated to it rather than to the towns as was the case in the West. Some were only, in effect, substantial peasants, but so far from having the virtues and the literacy of fifteenth-century English yeomen like the Pastons, they constituted (in the words of one of their latter-day compatriots) a 'most noxious phenomenon'.[43] Furthermore, the 1490s saw the first legislative acts depriving peasants of their freedom everywhere in Eastern Europe except the Ottoman Balkans.

In Poland resistance was sporadic; but in Hungary a fierce revolt flared up in 1514. The peasants' grievances make the outbreak easily comprehensible: but the occasion was curious – the calling of a popular crusade against the Turks. Franciscans and Dominicans (orders traditionally close to the people) stomped the country gaining an enthusiastic response. However, the authorities became alarmed at the gathering of large, armed crowds and called the crusade off. At this, hostility against the Turks was quickly deflected towards the nobility, the peasants' oppressors who were now seen to be neglecting the only responsibility which entitled them to a privileged position in society: defending the country against foreign enemies.[44] Under the leadership of George Dozsa, evidently an experienced frontier soldier, 'the people of God' as they called themselves, set about the task, taking control of large tracts of countryside for nearly two months and laying siege to several towns. Their heyday was of brief duration, however, and when Dozsa was caught he was roasted on a red-hot throne while a red-hot crown was forced down upon his head. Some of his followers were obliged to eat pieces of his charred flesh before they themselves were hanged.

The same year Istvan Werboczi completed a summary of his country's laws which was quickly confirmed by the Hungarian Diet. In defining the extensive rights of the nobility, they declared all nobles to be equal, and collectively equal to the King in government. It also condemned the peasantry to 'eternal servitude'.[45] This was a provision which could not be implemented for some time (see Chapter 8), but, enacted at a time when serfdom had all but disappeared in the West, it was to remain law, and a heritage for future generations, in Hungary.

* * *

As we have seen, the occupation of Byzantium by the Ottoman Turks did not destroy a civilization, nor did its conquest of the Balkans displace any viable political and social order. By these tokens the Balkans were already 'backward' before the Turks arrived. At the same time neither Hungary nor Poland (still less Bohemia) can fairly be said to have been thrown off a 'Western' course of development in this period by the Turks or Russians. Rather it was social imbalance and institutional weakness which condemned them to a different course of development.

They certainly shared in the heritage of the Renaissance which contributed so much to 'Western civilization'. However, as we have seen, these influences were cut short in Hungary due to an inability to sustain strong government and generate sufficient wealth; they came late to Poland, and later still to Bohemia where the turmoil of the Hussite period proved culturally as well as economically debilitating. Nonetheless, in all these countries a small, educated stratum came to share a common Catholic and humanistic culture with the West, from which the Orthodox regions were largely excluded. This difference promoted divergence between elite mentality in Russia on the one hand and Poland and Hungary on the other. Whether, and to what extent, they promoted differences in popular culture, however, is less certain.

At the same time we have noted new aspects of divergence both within Eastern Europe, and between it and the West. Why did the Byzantine Empire, which bequeathed such rich cultural and religious heritages to both Eastern and Western Europe, fall into such a sorry state of decrepitude? And why did sympathy for the Orthodox Church linger as strongly as it did in Hungary, Bohemia and Poland? How had the Catholic Church in Eastern Europe come to differ so much in character from the Church in Italy? And how had so many foreigners, Germans in particular, come to settle in Eastern Europe in such large numbers and dominate so much of it for so long? What did the Slavs of Eastern Europe have in common in terms of customs and institutions as well as language, and why did Western institutions, whether legal or political, so often wilt on being transplanted into Eastern Europe's soil?

For answers to these questions we must turn to the high middle ages, between the middle of the eleventh century when the Byzantine Empire was a great world power and the *Drang nach Osten* got under way, to the middle of the fourteenth: to the age of the Crusades and of the Mongol invasion.

REFERENCES

1. According to Henryk Samsonowicz's calculation of population densities in fourteenth-century Europe, Poland, Bohemia and the Balkans averaged about ten people per square kilometre and Hungary eight. The figure for Russia and Lithuania, as for Sweden, is only two people per square kilometre. See H. Samsonowicz and A. Maczak, 'Feudalism and capitalism: a balance of changes in East-Central Europe' in A. Maczak *et al.* (eds), *East-Central Europe*

in Transition: from the Fourteenth to the Seventeenth Century (Cambridge, 1985) pp. 8–10. The uneven impact of the Black Death is considered to have helped Moscow gain preeminence over the other Russian principalities. See R. Crummey, *The Formation of Muscovy 1304–1613* (London, 1987) pp. 42–3; also p. 25 on its overtaking Novgorod in size of population.

2. D. Obolensky, *The Byzantine Commonwealth* (Oxford, 1971).
3. On Maxim Trivolis's activities in Venice and Florence see E. Denisoff, *Maxime le Grec et l'Occident* (Paris, 1943); also D. Obolensky, 'Maximos the Greek' in his *Six Byzantine Portraits* (Oxford, 1988) pp. 201–19. Aside from Italians and Greeks the Russians of the period also brought in experts from Germany, Denmark, Scotland and Hungary. See A. Khoroshkevich, *Russkoe gosudarstvo v slsteme mezhdunarodnykh otnoshenii* (Moscow, 1980) p. 224.
4. On the emergence of Moldavia which seems to have become independent under Prince Bogdan in 1363, see D. Deletant in Deletant and H. Hanak (eds.), *Historians as Nation-Builders* (London, 1988) pp. 32–45; but see the discussion in V. Spinei, *Moldavia in the 11th–14th Centuries* (Bucharest, 1986) pp. 200ff.
5. See J. Fine, *The Late Medieval Balkans* (Ann Arbor, Michigan, 1987) pp. 345–77.
6. The precise date has been disputed for reasons described by E. Zachariadou, 'The Conquest of Adrianople by the Turks' in her *Romania and the Turks c.1300–c.1500* (London, 1985) pp. xii, 211–17. ('Romania' in this context is the Balkans south of the Danube, not present-day Romania.)
7. G. Ostrogorsky in J. Hussey (ed.) *The Cambridge Medieval History*, vol. IV, part 1 (Cambridge, 1975) p. 368.
8. 'Cyprian of Kiev and Moscow' in Obolensky, *Portraits*, *op. cit.*, pp. 173–200.
9. F. Dvornik, *The Slavs in European History and Civilization* (New Brunswick, New Jersey, 1962) p. 343.
10. P. Knoll, 'The Urban Development of Medieval Poland with Particular Reference to Krakow', S. Fiszman (ed.), *The Polish Renaissance in its European Context* (Bloomington, 1988) pp. 63–136, especially 123–4; and on the academic operation of the University, A. Wroblewski, 'The Cracovian Background of Copernicus' in *ibid.*, pp. 147ff.
11. Another Hungarian foundation of the period, the University of Obuda, also foundered. On the early history of Prague University, see R. Betts, 'The University of Prague: the First Sixty Years' in R. Seton-Watson (ed.), *Prague Essays* (Oxford, 1949) pp. 53–68.
12. F. Seibt, *Hussitenstudien* [Veröffentlichungen des Collegium Carolinum, 60] (Munich, 1987) especially pp. 123–4.
13. Dvornik, *op. cit.*, p. 196.
14. Quoted by Betts in Seton-Watson, *op. cit.*, p. 64. The sentiment that still attached to the Old Church Slavonic liturgy led the Bohemian crown in the later fourteenth century to attempt the foundation of several monasteries that would use it; but the Pope would only sanction one.
15. Translation adapted from Count Lutzow, *Lectures on the Historians of Bohemia* (London 1905) p. 37.
16. See *inter alia* E. Jacob, 'The Bohemians at the Council of Basel, 1433' in Seton-Watson, *op. cit.*, pp. 81–123.
17. For a convenient account, see S. Runciman, *The Fall of Constantinople* (Cambridge, 1990) pp. 16ff.
18. See Runciman, *op. cit.*, pp. 86–144.
19. Cited by H. Inalcik in 'The Rise of the Ottoman Empire' in M.A. Cook (ed.), *A History of the Ottoman Empire to 1730* (Cambridge, 1976) p. 40.

20. Inalcik, *loc. cit.*, pp. 41–2; S.J. Shaw, *History of the Ottoman Empire and Modern Turkey*, vol. I (Cambridge, 1978) pp. 23–4.
21. A useful summary of the Ottoman system is to be found in P. Sugar, *Southeastern Europe Under Ottoman Rule 1354–1804* (Seattle, 1977). See especially the diagram on p. 32. On the status of the Orthodox Church see Runciman, *The Great Church in Captivity* (Cambridge, 1985) especially pp. 171–2. On Gabriel of Rila, see D. Petkanov and G. Neshev in D. Kosev *et al.* (eds.), *Istorii na Bulgariia,* IV (ed. D. Gandev *et al.*) (Sofia, 1983) p. 262, col. 2.
22. Shaw, *op. cit.*, I, pp. 59–60; also Inalcik in Cook, *op. cit.*, pp. 51–3; also Inalcik's 'The Foundations of the Ottoman Economico-Social [*sic.*] System' in N. Todorov (ed.), *La Ville Balkanique xve-xixss.* (Sofia, 1970) pp. 17–24.
23. Practice and timing tended to vary, however. For a useful study of landholding in Albania see S. Pulaha, *Pronesia Feudale ne Tokat Squiptare* (Tirane, 1988) (French summary, pp. 441–512).
24. The analogy is A. Bryer's in 'Rural Society in Matzouka' in A. Bryer and R. Lowry (eds.), *Continuity and Change in Late Byzantine and Early Ottoman Society* (Birmingham, 1986) pp. 53–95.
25. See R. Crosskey, 'Byzantine Greeks in Late Fifteenth and Early Sixteenth Century Russia' [separatum], pp. 33–56.
26. The Library was dispersed after his death. For a partial reconstruction of it see L. Csapodi *et al., Bibliotheca Corviniana* (Budapest, 1967).
27. A. Bonfini, *Rerum Ungaricarum Decades* (Basel, 1568) p. 654. Some pertinent extracts from this work (indifferently translated) can be found in A. Kubinyi, ed., *Saecula Hungariae 1438–1526* (Budapest, 1985).
28. For a recent, succinct, discussion see J. Bak in P. Sugar (ed.) *A History of Hungary* (Bloomington, Indiana, 1990) especially pp. 70–6.
29. On Vlad Tepes (Dracula) see N. Stoiescu, *Vlad Tepes* (Bucuresti, 1976).
30. On the formation of the Dracula legend see M. Cazacu, *L'Histoire du Prince-Dracula en Europe Centrale et Orientale* [Ecole pratique des hautes études – ive section, V' (Hautes études médiévales et modernes) 61] (Genève, 1988). On Vitez and Pannonius as humanists, see L. Czigany, *The Oxford History of Hungarian Literature* (Oxford, 1984) pp. 28–32.
31. For the details see O. Odlozilik, *The Hussite King: Bohemia in European Affairs 1440–1471* (New Brunswick, New Jersey, 1965) especially pp. 151–89. Though Francis Dvornik was a Catholic priest as well as a Czech patriot, he was right to point out (*The Slavs, op. cit.*, pp. 290–3) that the Czech humanists were mostly Catholics (and opposed to George), and that the reformed University of Prague constituted an obstacle to the penetration of humanistic learning until the later sixteenth century.
32. See *inter alia* Cazacu, *op. cit.*, pp. 55–81.
33. S. Kashtanov, *Finansy srednevekovoi rusi* (Moscow, 1988) pp. 22–40 and 244.
34. A.A. Zimin, *Formirovanie boiarskoi aristokratii v Rossii* (Moscow, 1988) pp. 283–4 and 297–8. Kliuchevskii was mistaken in holding that many of the newly-subject princes were included in the Duma.
35. Khoroshevich, *op. cit.*, pp. 243–5; Crummey, *op. cit.*, pp. 196–7.
36. As Vasily III was informed, 'You are the only Caesar of Christians in all the world.... All the Christian realms have been gathered into thy realm. After this we await the eternal kingdom.... Two Romes have fallen but the third stands and there will not be a fourth'.
37. T. Ulewicz, 'Polish Humanism and its Italian Sources', in S. Fiszman (ed.) *The Polish Renaissance in its European Context* (Bloomington, Indiana, 1988) pp. 215–35, especially 216 and 222; also his *Wsrod impresrow krakowskich dobu*

Renesansu (Cracow, 1977); also J. Bialostocki in Fiszman, *op. cit.*, p. 281 and his 'The East-Central European Renaissance' in Maczak, *op. cit.*, pp. 153–66.

38. F. Sigel, *Lectures on Slavonic Law* (London, 1902) pp. 110–21; J. Tazbir in Gieysztor *et al.*, *History of Poland* (Warsaw, 1979) pp. 149–50.
39. See A. Maczak, 'The Commonwealth of Poland-Lithuania' in *Economy and Culture in the Baltic 1650–1700* [Acta Visbyensia VIII], pp. 8 and 16.
40. M. Rady, *Medieval Buda*, pp. 75 and 112.
41. Seibt, *op. cit.*, pp. 61ff., 127 and 148.
42. See M. Bogucka in Maczak, *East-Central Europe*, *op. cit.*, p. 105 (plus the source on the demographic decline of the merchants of Cracow). Similar considerations may help to explain the extinction of earlier dynasties such as the Premyslids of Bohemia who had died out in 1306, for primogeniture was not practised among the Slavs – see Chapter 10.
43. F. Maksay, 'Le pays de la noblesse nombreuse', *Etudes Historiques Hongroises*, 1980, vol. I, pp. 167–90; I. Bibo quoted by J. Szucs, 'The Three Historical Regions of Europe', *Acta Historica Academiae Scientiarum Hungaricae*, 29 (2–4) 1983, p. 155.
44. For a wider context see J. Bak in J. Bak and B. Kiraly (eds.), *From Hunyadi to Rakoczi* (New York, 1982) pp. 12–13, and for Dozsa his article in *East-Central Europe*, I, 1974, pp. 153–67.
45. *Tripartitum opus iuris consuetudinarii*, 1514.

10

The Age of Crusades (1071–1352)

The damned Latins ... Lust for our possessions and would like to destroy our race ... A wide gulf of hatred divides us from them. Our outlooks are completely different; our roads lead in opposite directions.

Nicetas Choniates, Byzantine chronicler

In the mid-eleventh century Byzantium was Europe's greatest city and the Byzantine Emperor claimed to rule the entire civilized world. In terms of precedent and potential this claim was not wholly ridiculous. The empire stretched from the heel of Italy in the West to Armenia and Syria in the east, and from Crete in the south to the Crimea in the north. It included the Balkans south of the Danube but its sphere of influence extended far beyond, and both Russia and Venice were counted among its clients. The Byzantine Empire was the continuation of the Roman Empire, and though its Emperors had long since abandoned Latin for Greek they called themselves *Romanoi* and still thought of themselves as Romans.

They called Byzantium 'New Rome' and all roads still seemed to lead to it. Travel might be slow. It took six to eight weeks to sail from Venice to Byzantium (and two from Wolin at the mouth of the River Oder to Novgorod in north-west Russia). Nevertheless, contacts with the periphery were by no means infrequent. Recruits from England, Sweden and Russia served in the Emperor's Varangian Guard; monks from Mount Athos found their way to Poland, Russians visited Western shrines like Hildesheim, and once the Holy Land fell into Christian hands again, Eastern as well as Western Europeans made pilgrimages to Jerusalem. Europe itself was criss-crossed by commercial routes which linked all parts of the Continent, and there were marital links too, not least between ruling families. Vladimir Monomakh, Prince of Kiev early in the twelfth century, provides a convenient example. He married the daughter of the unfortunate King Harold of England; his uncle married the King of Poland's daughter, his aunts the Kings of Hungary, Norway and France. He himself was the grandson of one Byzantine Emperor, Constantine IX, and his grand-daughter was to marry another.

Exchanges between Eastern and Western Europe were hardly less frequent in proportion to the size of population than they have sometimes been in modern times, and mutual comprehension was certainly no worse. True, Rome was struggling with Byzantium for the spiritual leadership of Christendom, and the German and Greek Emperors were usually in competition for temporal supremacy, but though official relationships were generally cool there were areas of shared understanding; and despite cultural divergencies mutual influences, in the realms of literature and learning for example, tended to increase. These circumstances have led an historian to remark that

> In the medieval period it seemed that Eastern Europe would follow a course similar to that of Western Europe. The major division in European civilization was not on a West-East, but on a North-South axis, with the Mediterranean culture more advanced. ...[1]

Europe's economic, as well as cultural, centre of gravity also lay in the south. However, this potential was not to be fulfilled. Between the eleventh and the fourteenth centuries the weight of economic advantage shifted decisively from the eastern to the western Mediterranean, and then northwards across the Alps to the basin of the River Rhine, the state of Burgundy and cities like Bruges. The political and military preponderance gradually moved in similar directions. In 1204 a coalition of Venetians and French and Flemish knights conquered Byzantium, plundered its treasure, and divided its territories between them. In due course the Emperors returned to their city but as feeble heirs of a great tradition, supplicants of the West, the rulers of a diminished and embittered population.

Eastern Europe was to be struck a second blow in the thirteenth century, this time from the East rather than the West. It was delivered by the Mongol-Tatar horde and Russians were by no means the only victims. The Tatar impact is often said to have 'orientalized' the eastern Slavs and stunted their political development; and the economic and psychological effects were undoubtedly severe. However, the indirect consequences were probably even more significant; and, as we shall see, they were not entirely negative.

There was a third important foreign impact, that of the Germans and Flemings. To a large extent this was a peaceful phenomenon – the eastward migration, chiefly into Poland, Bohemia and Hungary, of industrious people possessed of skills, including that of deep-ploughing, for the local peasants with their scratch-ploughs could not break heavy soils and had to leave much fertile land uncultivated. This eastward migration, which had begun in the earlier period, now grew apace, encouraged by monarchs who needed merchants, miners and artisans of every kind, as well as farmers, to help develop their territories and generate prosperity.

At the same time, however, Germans of the Hansa League took a stranglehold of commerce through the Baltic, just as Italians did of the trade-routes running down the Adriatic and through the Aegean and Black Seas; and the thirteenth century also saw the entrenchment on the southern Baltic of well-organized but aggressive German crusading orders, intent on Christianizing, and enslaving, the pagan peoples of the hinterland. It was in reaction to this that the state of Lithuania was to emerge.

As we have seen, the long-term effects of the *Drang nach Osten* were varied and often negative. But it was associated with one development of particular promise: the introduction of 'German Law' into East-Central Europe. This encouraged the development of commerce and the growth of towns. It might also have established urban autonomy as a normal feature of the scene, and, over the course of time, nurtured a sense of civic responsibility parallel to that which became characteristic of many Western countries. The period was generally important for the growth and regularization of the law; and the monarchs of Eastern Europe were no less interested in developing their legal systems and codifying laws than their counterparts in the West. The age which saw the introduction of the Common Law into Norman England also witnessed the compilations of 'the Russian Law' (*Russkaia pravda*), King Ladislas's overhaul of the laws of Hungary, and the issue of a Law Code by Stefan Dusan, King of Serbia. Yet the law and legal culture were not to develop in altogether similar fashion to the West; nor were institutions generally. An explanation for this divergence must be sought, at least in part, in the fateful epoch on which we now embark.

* * *

Some time in the 1070s a 'magician' is said to have appeared in Kiev, the leading Russian city at that time,[2] and to have prophesied to its people. The great River Dnieper which flowed past them, he said, would start to flow backwards, in the opposite direction, so that 'the Greek land [Byzantium] will be where Russia was, and Russia where the Greek land was'.[3] If the story is true the 'magician's' metaphor was indeed prophetic; and the timing of the prophecy is intriguing too, for in 1071 the Byzantine Empire suffered two reverses which together signalled the decisive turning-point in its fortunes, even though this was not the general perception at the time. That year the city of Bari, its last stronghold in Italy, was captured by the Norman, Robert Guiscard; and in the east the Byzantine army was defeated at Manzikert. The loss of Bari reduced Byzantium's leverage with the Pope, and increased her dependence on Venetian sea-power to protect the Balkan coastline against the Normans.[4] But the Battle of Manzikert, fought in August 1071, commands interest not only because of its serious consequences but because it indicates causes of Byzantium's decline.

The battle itself was an odd affair. The Byzantine forces, led by the Emperor Romanus IV, were pitted against those of the Seljuks who had emerged as the most powerful of the Turkish tribes in Asia Minor. However, the Seljuk Sultan, anxious to reach an accommodation with the Emperor, did not seek battle, and the two armies seem to have stumbled across each other by chance, neither aware of the other's presence in the vicinity. Furthermore, the Emperor commanded the stronger force. Some Pecheneg mercenaries and a contingent of Armenians, who harboured a religious grievance, deserted. Even so Romanus would probably have won but for the treachery of Andronicus Ducas, commander of his rearguard. The battle had hardly commenced when Ducas spread a rumour that it had been lost, and promptly withdrew. The rumour was false, but caused many of the remaining troops to flee in panic. The battle was lost, the Emperor captured.[5]

Ducas's motive throws light on one source of the Empire's decline: political rivalry. His uncle had been emperor and he wanted another member of his family on the throne. But this dynastic feuding overlay a larger struggle for power between two factions of the Byzantine elite: 'the generals', represented by Romanus IV, who were associated with the great landowners; and 'the bureaucrats', including the Ducas clan, who represented the urban elite. Earlier in the century this competition had been kept under control and emperors had been able to slap down overmighty subjects, but more recently this had not proved possible.[6]

Behind all this, however, lay more fundamental problems. A deep economic crisis had set in during the eleventh century. There had been a succession of droughts and then a series of damaging incursions into the European provinces by barbarian Pechenegs and Uzes. This problem was eventually controlled, and some of the raiders employed as mercenaries or settled in depopulated areas. But in the meantime, agricultural production in many European provinces had slumped. So had land prices, while demographic decline created a shortage of manpower. Hence the rising competition between lords and government for the available labour.[7]

Meanwhile the old provincial military system, by which many farmers had held land in return for military service, collapsed. In its place a class of local warlords had arisen who were progressively less inclined to obey the government's mobilization calls. This increased both the need for mercenaries, who were not always reliable, and for funds with which to pay them. A vicious spiral set in whereby the government repeatedly devalued the coinage and became ever more extortionate in its demands for taxes. Rising numbers of rural taxpayers were forced to seek protection from local lords, which increased the pressure on those who did not.

And the urban economy was very adversely affected too. After 1071, however, the Empire's problems became worse.

Manzikert and the deposition of the Emperor Romanus heralded a decade of political chaos and civil war. The Serbs seized their opportunity to assert independence; so did the Croats under their leader Svinimir (Zvonimir); and in 1077 Jerusalem was lost as well. From 1081, when the Comneni family established a dynasty, the Empire staged a recovery. Order was restored, territories regained. Yet the cost of these repairs was sometimes heavy, and the structural faults that had appeared in the system proved beyond its capacity to repair. From the 1070s, for example, the Venetians helped Byzantium defend Dalmatia against the Normans, but the price exacted was high, including a charter of privileges which was to serve as a cornerstone of Venice's colonial empire; the grant of property in Byzantium, and of rights to trade there free of tax.[8] This presented Byzantine merchants with unwelcome competition on unequal terms, and implied a further decline of revenue for the state. The economy continued on its downward path.

So did the powers of central government. At a time when the Kings of England and of France were beginning to create centralized states and bring the feudal nobility under control, the Byzantine emperors found themselves losing control of the increasingly powerful lords. They tried to rectify the situation by extending *pronoia,* a system akin to that of the Ottoman *timar* by which the dues from certain lands were allocated to military men in return for their service; but in practice the *pronoia* tended to become hereditary and their holders to serve themselves rather than the state. Yet the Byzantine Empire was by no means the only state in eastern Europe which failed to cope with noble disobedience.

In 1076 Boleslaw II had himself crowned King of Poland in the city of Gniezno. With the support of the Papacy, he set about putting the organization of the church in Poland on a sounder footing and improving the efficiency of the royal bureaucracy. However, these developments were ill-received by lords who saw in them a threat to their independence. A rebellion was staged. One of its organizers, a bishop, was executed, but Boleslaw could not regain effective control and in 1079 he fled to Hungary where he soon met his death. His successor did not even claim the royal title; in 1138 Poland began to dissolve into a collection of duchies. The centrifugal tendencies that had been interrupted in the eleventh century prevailed once more.[9]

The problem of royal power in Poland was related to the absence of primogeniture among the Slavs. According to their customary law all sons had a right to a share in an inheritance. The custom also prevailed in the Russian lands where the effects were similar. Indeed, the existence of two competing dynasties, the Olgovichi and the Monomakhs, made matters worse. Despite the existence of a pecking order by which princes came to rule successively more important cities as they rose in seniority within the family, it became increasingly difficult to calculate seniority as the family tree became ever more extensive. Largely as a result of this the Russian lands fell into chaos by the later twelfth century, after which the city of Kiev alone changed hands at least thirty times in seventy years. The only effective unifying force for the Russians, as for the Poles, in this period was the church.[10]

Of the South Slavs, the Serbs were also divided between a number of principalities. By the year 1100 that of Duklja was in disarray and that of Raska, the strongest of them, had been forced to submit to Byzantium again. Meanwhile Croatia had crumbled into a state of 'noble anarchy' and soon came under the control of Hungary and Venice.[11] Hungary itself was rather more stable politically and more successful strategically. Under Ladislas I (1077–95) and his successors it intervened regularly in Russian as well as Bohemian, Polish and Croatian affairs. Even Hungary had problems, however. It was invaded by a nomadic people known as Cumans, for example. They were defeated, their leaders executed and the rest settled in the regions they had devastated,[12] but then, in 1096, Peter the Hermit's motley horde, the vanguard of the first Crusade, arrived in Hungary on their way to the Holy Land. They seem to have behaved no better than the Cumans. According to a contemporary account,

> The uncouth crowds ... began to treat the meek natives rapaciously, with violent, unrestrained excess.... The inhabitants ... gladly brought them all kinds of produce for sale but, unable to curb their greed and ignoring the natives' gracious hospitality and goodwill [they] fell upon them violently.[13]

Fortunately Peter's followers were seen out of his kingdom relatively quickly, and King Coloman was able to turn the crusade to diplomatic advantage. But from Hungary the crusaders moved on to Byzantium.

The Byzantine government was equal to the challenge. They speedily arranged for Peter's followers to be transported across the Bosphorus into Asia where the Seljuk Turks were waiting to massacre them. By that time the more respectable crusaders had arrived – lords and knights from France, Flanders and other states in north-west Europe, with their retainers. Their leaders were persuaded to take oaths of allegiance to the emperor, and they promised to hand over to him any cities they might recapture from the Muslims. But though they took Antioch in 1098 and Jerusalem itself in 1099 they reneged on their promises. Bohemond the Norman held on to Antioch, and Jerusalem became the capital of a new kingdom ruled by Geoffrey of Bouillon. These new 'Latin' states in the Levant were not to last long; but the Crusade had increased Byzantine acquaintance with Westerners, and the experience was not conducive to their good relations.

Since 1082 Byzantines had watched the Venetians ensconced in their city enriching themselves at their expense. Now they had had occasion to observe the behaviour of the Western rabble, and betrayal by members of its noble elite, who struck the urbane Greeks as little better. Furthermore, unlike the Orthodox priesthood which abjured violence, the Latin clergy had been observed to be shockingly belligerent and warlike.

> Your Latin barbarian will at the same time handle sacred objects, fasten a shield to his left arm and grasp a spear in his right.... He will give Communion while watching bloodshed and become himself 'a man of blood'.... [A Latin seemed to be] more man of action, then, than priest.[14]

Even so, the Byzantine government nurtured good relations with the 'Latin' Kingdom of Hungary. This policy was dictated in the main by short-term strategic considerations. Nevertheless the prospect of weaning Hungary away from Rome might not have seemed quite so hopeless at the time as it was to do in retrospect. As recently as the 1070s Hungary's King Geza I had accepted his crown from Byzantium. Its inscription, 'Geza, faithful King of Turkia [Hungary]', suggests that Byzantium still exerted a powerful influence. It was manifest in the continuing strength of the Orthodox Church in eastern and southern Hungary; in the number of Greek loan words in Hungarian, the popularity there of Byzantine names, and the frequency with which Byzantine motifs are to be found in Hungarian literature and art. Hungarian interest in the Russian principalities, especially Halich, Volhynia and Kiev, and increasing involvement with the Serbs, reinforced the eastward orientation. So did the marriage in 1104 of the orphaned daughter of Ladislas I to the Byzantine heir apparent.[15]

By the middle of the twelfth century, however, Geza II of Hungary was ranged with Iazaslav of Kiev and Stefan Uros II, Grand Zupan of Serbia, alongside Byzantium's enemies, the Normans and the Pope. Byzantium, under its Emperor Manuel I Comnenus, emerged victorious and by 1155 his forces were established in Italy once again, apparently stronger than before.[16] This great revival was bought at crippling expense, however, and proved to be short-lived, though the final crisis set in only after 1170.

In 1171 long-brewing troubles with Venice seethed over. In 1119 Byzantium had refused to renew the charter of privileges it had granted its former underling. Six years later Venetians on their way back from the Holy Land had plundered Byzantine islands. Despite a brief episode of cooperation against the Normans on Corfu, relations continued their downward slide. Venetians consolidated their reputations for greed and insolence, and in 1170 Byzantium granted commercial privileges to Venice's rivals and Genoese and Pisans. Venetians in Byzantium countered by attacking the Genoese quarter there. In retaliation, in March 1771 the Byzantine authorities arrested all Venetians on their territory and froze all their assets, including their ships. The Doge, Vitale Michiel, responded by mounting an unsuccessful assault against Byzantine possessions in Dalmatia. Then a Venetian emissary to Byzantium got involved in a fight in which he lost most of his eyesight. His name was Enrico Dandolo, and he had not forgotten his injury by the time he himself became Doge in 1192.[17]

Meanwhile in 1176 a Byzantine army under Manuel's command had been crushed by the Seljuk Turks at Myriocephalum. Manuel escaped but Byzantium lost its grip on Anatolia, which had been its breadbasket; and it became clear that the aggressive policies which had been pursued in Italy and Asia as well as in the Balkans had been unaffordable. Furthermore Byzantium had ceased to be an effective sea power. The Empire's decline now became precipitous; and with the advent of the weak Angeli dynasty in 1185 and Saladin's capture of Jerusalem two years later, the stage was almost set for the Fourth Crusade.

The story of that crusade, its culmination in the capture of Byzantium in 1204 by Dandolo's Venetians and the 'Latin' knights from France and Flanders, and the subsequent division of what remained of its Empire between them, has often been recounted[18] and the details need not be repeated here. According to a participant, Geoffroy de Villehardouin, the capture of the city was followed by

> a scene of massacre and pillage: on every hand the Greeks were cut down, their horses ... and other possessions snatched as booty. So great was the number of killed and wounded that no man could count them.... [The loot] included gold and silver, table-services and precious stones, satin and silk, mantles of ... ermine and miniver, and every choicest thing to be found on this earth.... So much booty had never been gained in any city since the creation of the world.[19]

He omitted to mention the desecration of churches, the wrecking of great works of art, the destruction of libraries, the rape of nuns. Reports of it led Pope Innocent III himself to exclaim

> How can we expect the Greek Church ... to return to ecclesiastical unity and devotion to the Holy See when all it sees of the Latins is an example of utter depravity and the works of darkness?[20]

The Fourth Crusade is, or ought to be, a source of very deep embarrassment to proponents of 'Western civilization', and not only because of the Crusaders' bestial behaviour (which compared very badly with that of the Saracens at Jerusalem). Aside from all else the sack of Byzantium represented the rape of a superior culture by representatives of one which in most respects was still inferior. Furthermore the Crusaders had no appreciation of the Empire's function nor of what exactly they had captured, other than a vast collection of luxury goods and some valuable real estate. Hence, in the words of R.W. Southern,

> They fell on it as savages might fall on a watch – giving the case to one, the jewels to another, and the disjointed mechanism to a third.... The Crusaders were accustomed to the splitting up of fiefs and they adopted the plan of division as the only possible one under the circumstances. Fifty-seven years of miserable life were to teach them what it meant to hold the gateway to the western world....[21]

* * *

While some Crusaders were ravishing Christian territories in the Balkans, others had begun to operate far to the north in lands bordering on the southern Baltic, between the mouths of the Rivers Vistula and Neva. The region concerned was inhabited by Prussians, Letts, Lithuanians and other peoples who were neither German nor Slavonic, most of whom still clung to pagan practices and beliefs. They were coming under increasing threat, however, as German traders, colonists and missionaries moved in amongst them.

The first missionaries had made little headway with either Letts or Prussians; and it was the merchants of Bremen, anxious to establish a safe trading route into the Russian lands, who first established themselves firmly in the region. About the year 1200, they built a fortified trading post at the mouth of the River Dvina which soon became the city of Riga. At about the same time Bishop Albert of Livonia had the idea of setting up a new crusading order – not to fight for the Holy Land but to subdue the pagan peoples of the region. By 1204 the idea had been realized in the Order of the Brethren of the Sword. Headed by Albert, it consisted chiefly of German knights, and they soon succeeded in subduing the Letts and, with the help of the Danes, in taking control of the area that is now Estonia, including a Russian trading settlement called Yur'ev, which was re-named Dorpat (now Tartu) and made the centre of a German bishopric

Another German crusading order, that of the Teutonic Knights, had been formed in Palestine in the 1190s. Their operations were not confined to the Levant, however, and when the Saracens reoccupied most of the

Holy Land more were constrained to find a livelihood elsewhere. In 1211, some were engaged by the King of Hungary to subdue and settle the territory of Transylvania. After fourteen years they were invited to leave Hungary, but an alternative offer soon came from a Polish duke, Conrad of Mazovia, who needed military help in conquering the Prussians and gaining an outlet on the Baltic for his duchy. Hermann von Salza, the shrewd head of the Order, accepted, but he also obtained a charter from his friend the German Emperor, Frederick II, issued in 1226, entitling his order to sovereignty under the emperor of any territory it might conquer.

Meanwhile the Knights of the Sword had been engaging the pagan Lithuanians, but they received such a bad mauling from them in 1236 that the survivors had to be merged with the Teutonic Order, which also took over its responsibilities. There were repeated uprisings by the conquered peoples, continuing warfare with the Prussians and the Lithuanians and intermittent hostilities with both Danes and Russians. Yet the Knights were largely successful – partly because of their superior technology, partly because of a continual influx of new recruits from the ranks of landless knights and of those who were guilty of some violent crime, for entry into the Order earned remission for such sins.

Terror also helped, apparently. A member of the Teutonic Order left an account of a winter campaign against the Prussians:

> The hearts of the Crusaders burned to break the Prussians' spirit. They entered the Reisen district, slaying and capturing many.... [And soon] met a great host which ... stood ready to give battle.... Then in their wrath they destroyed those sinners.... The flashing sword of Christian chivalry consumed the flesh of the unbelievers.... So ensued a great bath of blood among the Prussian people.[22]

They did not always have things their own way, however. The Prussians were to maintain a grim resistance for many years; in 1243 the Order sustained a serious defeat at the hands of the Russians under Alexander Nevskii in the famous battle on the ice of Lake Peipus; and the Lithuanians also proved formidable opponents. In the 1240s a great leader Mindaugas (or Mendovg) succeeded in uniting them, became a Christian, and gained the Pope's approval for being crowned a king (1253). His conversion bought peace with the Knights – and freed his hands to fight the Russians. But he soon reverted to paganism and the warring with the Knights continued throughout the remainder of the century and into the next.

Meanwhile the German hold over the coast was consolidated and extended. Rostock had been founded in 1218, Gdansk (Danzig) about 1230, and in 1237 the port of Elbing was established on the site of an old Prussian harbour, Truso; the city of Klaipeda (Memel) was founded in 1242, that of Konigsberg in 1255. Torun (Thorn), Marienburg and other towns centred on the forts the Knights had built also filled up with immigrants from the overcrowded West, and especially from northern Germany. Meanwhile Germans seeking opportunities had also been moving into Poland to develop cities and a mining industry – and in general they were welcome. In 1237 special rights were granted to the German merchants of Szczecin (Stettin), and Germans who settled in Wroclaw, Poznan, Cracow and other cities were accorded privileged status too. Meanwhile Germans, especially from Saxony, had also been migrating into Bohemia and Hungary.

Attitudes then were unlike those of later ages. Hungarians of the nineteenth century were to combine their xenophobia with a terrible complacency encapsulated in a Latin tag which proclaimed that nothing really worthwhile existed beyond the country's frontiers (*extra Hungariam non est vita; si est vita none est ita*). But in the eleventh and twelfth centuries the admonition of the great St Stephen, Hungary's first king, to the effect that a country with only one language and one culture must be poor and backward (*regnum unius linguae uniusque moris fragile et imbecilus est*) was still respected. Thus, for example, in 1244 King Bela IV granted the city of Buda the rights of self-government, including that of administering its own laws in its own courts. The beneficiaries were largely German and the source was German, the celebrated Magdeburg Law. Indeed, like Magdeburg, Buda was to become a 'mother city', deciding disputes in other urban settlements which had been granted the same liberties.[23] However, though industrious Germans were welcome in Hungary, the Mongols and their Tatar adherents were not.

The Mongols, who had attacked China in 1215 and taken Pekin, first turned their attentions to Europe in 1222. The following year a reconnaisance force annihilated an army of Cumans and Russians in a battle on the River Kalka in the steppes. Then the Mongols withdrew and did not reappear for fourteen years. In 1237, however, they returned in strength under their leader Baty Khan, subdued the basin of the River Volga, captured Kiev in the winter of 1240–1 and sped on into Poland and Hungary. The following winter the Danube froze over and they were able to cross it, strike out to the Adriatic, besiege Esztergom, ravage Austria, plunder Silesia and threaten the rest of Germany, Bohemia and Italy.

Bloodcurdling stories were told of their savagery, and they were certainly cruel, though the stories also reflected the widespread sense of shock and terror at the suddenness and power of their attack. There was no doubting their fighting qualities, however. As a contemporary reported,

> They ride fast bound unto their horses, which are ... exceedingly strong, and maintained with little provender. They ... fight constantly with javelins, maces, battle-axes, and swords. But specially they are excellent archers, and cunning warriers with their bowes....

Vanquished, they asked no favour, and vanquishing, they shew no compassion ....[24]

Then, as a stronger, better-coordinated, defence was organized against them, the Mongols suddenly withdrew. For decades they were expected to mount another massive assault. It did not materialize. Nevertheless, they had only retreated across the Carpathians, not from Europe. They attacked Poland in 1259, engaged the Teutonic Knights in Prussia in 1260, ravaged Hungary again in 1285 and remained a force to be reckoned with in the Balkans too.[25] Their regular stamping-grounds, however, were north of the Danube and east of the Carpathians, in the territories which were to form the core of modern Romania and in the steppe zone to the east, including the Crimea. Baty Khan himself had established his base at Sarai on the Volga, and from there the Mongols and their Tatar associates, with whom they came to be identified, battened onto the Russians.

There is no doubting that the Tatars did great damage. They are believed to have destroyed as many as four out of every five villages in eastern Hungary, and according to thirteenth-century Western travellers they turned the area of southern Ukraine to the east into a virtual desert. They also introduced the gypsies, skilled Indians whom they had captured and enslaved, into Eastern Europe. The region's backwardness has often been attributed in large measure to the Mongols; and it is generally agreed that their impact on the Russians, and on the development of Russia, was greatest of all. They certainly terrorized the Russian principalities into paying them tribute on a regular basis and providing contingents to help fight their wars. How decisive the long-term political and cultural effects of Mongol domination were, however, is a matter of dispute.

Though separate Russian principalities had sometimes joined forces in regional alliances before the arrival of the Mongols, they showed even less inclination to form a unitary state than did the Polish duchies. Their interests pulled them in opposite directions. In Novgorod they were preoccupied with the tasks of keeping the route to the Baltic open and defending themselves against the Lithuanians and the Teutonic Knights. In Suzdal and Vladimir the Volga Bulgars seemed the greater menace, in Chernigov the Hungarians and Poles. In fact it was Mongol domination itself that constituted the great spur of Russian unity; and the Mongols also provided the Russians with some essential tools for state-building.

They introduced them to the census, for example, and, as loan-words to the language suggest, to customs duties, sales tax and the post. The Mongols also taught Russians an oriental form of obeisance to the sovereign which involved knocking one's head upon the ground in front of him in token of obedience;[26] and Russians borrowed words for shackles and a particular kind of whip from Asiatic sources. However to suggest that Mongol domination 'orientalized' the Russians and set the Russian state on a course towards 'oriental despotism'[27] is a reflection of long-standing Western prejudice, encouraged by the Cold War, based on a selective and exaggerated reading of the evidence.

As we have seen, Russia's autocratic political system stemmed not from the Mongols but from Byzantium. The brutality that so often characterized social relationships derived from the state's need to extract a surplus from a recalcitrant peasantry and from the related institution of serfdom. But serfdom was an importation from the West, not from the Orient. The Mongols did not interfere with the Russians' church, had but a marginal influence on their language, and a negligible impact on their law. However, in subjecting most of the Russian principalities it imposed a form of unity upon them, and it unwittingly created circumstances that facilitated the building of a unitary state.

Moscow, under which this state was to cohere, was a comparatively obscure principality, of which virtually nothing is known for nearly fifty years after the Mongol invasion.[28] By the turn of the century, under Daniel, the youngest son of Alexander Nevskii, it had become, along with Tver, one of the two chief contestants for leadership in north-east Russia (for Mongol domination did not extend as far as Novgorod). By 1331, when Ivan I became Grand Prince, it had become the leader, at least for the moment. Since all Russian princes in the region ruled by permission of the Mongol Khan at Sarai, Moscow owed its success, at least in part, to being a more reliable agent for the Mongols than its rivals. However, its princes also seem to have been more adroit in manipulating their overlords; and their role as intermediaries made them as much the spokesmen and negotiators for the Russians as agents for the Mongols. Furthermore, they received remarkably consistent support from the church, whose Metropolitan established himself in Moscow in 1326.

Moscow's growing strength is suggested by the grant in 1346 of a considerable sum for the reconstruction of the great church of Saint Sophia, part of which had collapsed; and by Grand Prince Dmitrii's rebellion against Khan Mamai in 1380 which culminated in his rout of Mamai's army at Kulikovo near the River Don. Mamai's successor sacked Moscow and brought Dmitrii to heel again. Nevertheless the Mongols had been shown to be vulnerable and the Grand Princes of Moscow had established themselves, among all else, as patriotic heroes.

Dmitrii also had a posthumous achievement. In his will he bequeathed all his territories and his title to his eldest son. This was an important step along the difficult road away from the apanage tradition of partible inheritance, which vitiated the prospects of continuously stable central government and encouraged the flowering of noble anarchy. As we have seen, both Kievan Rus' and Poland had suffered from this customary institution of the Slavs. Yet the practice of shared inheritance was by no means the only cause of political instability. The Hungarians were not Slavs, yet in the thirteenth century Hungary also entered a period of anarchy.

The rot had set in even before the Tatar invasions with Andrew II who was overgenerous both in his gifts of crown lands, and his confirmation of noble privileges. These included immunity from taxation, which by his 'Golden Bull' of 1222 were extended to royal servitors. He also curtailed the income and power of the church which, as elsewhere, was the great support of mediaeval monarchy, providing literates to staff the palace chanceries. Andrew's successor, Bela IV, tried to retrieve the situation, but with little success. Noble opposition sprang from resentment of the royal bureaucracy as well as from defence of economic privileges; and the noble interest tended to prevail. During the century small landholders, including many soldiers serving in the royal castles, gained the privileges of noble status, and at the same time the counties, into which the kingdom was divided for administrative convenience, tended to become the instruments of local oligarchs rather than of the king and his bureaucrats.[29]

Ladislas IV went so far in his attempt to assert royal power as to ally himself with the pagan Cumans and then call in the Mongols. His reward was assassination, and when his successor, last of the Hungarian royal line, died childless in 1301, noble anarchy became complete. Bohemian and Bavarian princes were sent packing; former royal servitors joined baronial retinues, local oligarchs turned their properties into little principalities, negotiated with foreign powers, issued their own coinage. One even waged war against the Primate of the Hungarian Church. When the dust finally settled an Angevin from Naples, Caroberto, or Charles, was King. But he had to be crowned three times and to find new foundations for his authority.

Charles concentrated his energies on the military and on developing his financial base. The new army was based on the private armies of ecclesiastics and lay lords, subordinate to the crown as in the feudal West. However, he also had a force under his direct command, financed from the royal treasury. The key was the development of the financial base chiefly through a more efficient exploitation of royal property and the development of social elements, notably the burghers, who were independent of the great magnates of the land. This opened up the prospect of raising greater revenues from the towns and trade, including customs duty; but it required a sound monetary system. The 1320s saw both a monetary reform and a great fillip to the mining industry. This was the basis of wider reforms that marked a significant recovery of royal power in Hungary. There was predictably fierce opposition, but the crown found useful allies in the elements alienated by the magnates; and it was fortunate in possessing valuable deposits of precious metals.[30] On this basis Hungary became a great power in Eastern Europe in the later fourteenth century.

Meanwhile Poland had entered an even deeper trough of disunity and disorder. With local support from the German urban elite and clerical elements Wenceslas II of Bohemia conquered the southern region known as 'Little Poland' centring on Cracow; and became king from 1300 until 1305. Meanwhile in 1308–9 the Teutonic Knights captured Gdansk, which competed with their own port of Elblag, killing many of its German merchants, and subdued Little Pomerania. Then, in the later 1320s, Bohemia began to take over the duchies of Silesia. After 1333, when Casimir III (The Great) became king, Poland's fortunes revived. Casimir failed to break through to the Baltic and in 1335 recognized the loss of most of Silesia, but he imposed unity on the rest of his landlocked kingdom, and extended it south-eastwards into the Ukraine, though after 1370 there were to be renewed signs of noble anarchy.[31]

Bohemia's experience was not dissimilar, though she enjoyed certain advantages over her neighbour. The Slavonic principle of apanage entitling all of a ruler's sons to a share in government prevailed among the Czechs, too, but the Premyslid dynasty did not produce as many competitors for power as did the Polish Piasts; and though there had been times when dynastic rivalries threatened the dissolution of Bohemia, the apanage system disappeared early in the thirteenth century. Furthermore, Bohemia had rich deposits of silver.

On the other hand, as elsewhere, the higher nobility obtained guarantees of privilege; and in 1215 the church also obtained limited immunities from taxation and other obligations to the state, while the towns gained the rights of Magdeburg or Nuremburg Law. Noble anarchy did not take hold in Bohemia as it did in other countries of the region. Nor, however, did the Western feudal principle by which nobles were obliged to serve the head of state. Like their counterparts in Poland, Russia and even Hungary, the Bohemian nobility wanted hereditary tenure of both lands and offices, and showed little interest in fiefs which were non-hereditary.[32] Partly because of this, the royal absolutism which characterized France in the high Middle Ages, and the England of Henry II, had no parallel in the region.

The Byzantine Empire had known the service estate, however; its emperors had been absolute, and it still provided the model of authority to which local potentates in the Balkans aspired. After the fall of Byzantium to the crusaders a government had continued to function in exile at Nicaea. While the Latin occupiers fell into increasing disarray it accreted strength; and in 1261 succeeded in recapturing Byzantium. The emperors represented only a shadow of the power their predecessors had once possessed. Nevertheless, they had not entirely lost their governmental cunning. In 1282 they masterminded the 'Sicilian Vespers', a great revolt against the Angevin regime in Sicily. This destabilizing operation effectively thwarted enemy plans to mount a counter-offensive against them, and stands as a tribute to continuing Byzantine skill at sophisticated covert operations which are so often, and mistakenly, regarded as a twentieth-century phenomenon.[33]

Even so, in the late thirteenth and early fourteenth century the Byzantine Empire and the Balkans as a whole constituted a zone of political weakness. As the Tatar menace began to decline, Hungary began to push out tentatively in their wake. In 1324 a Hungarian vassal state known as Wallachia emerged,[34] and its importance was acknowledged by the Orthodox Church in 1359 when a metropolitan see was established for it. Meanwhile the struggle between Venice, Hungary and south Slav states for control of Dalmatia had been continuing; and there was intermittent warfare between Byzantium, Serbia and Bulgaria. The conflict between the last two states was decided in the summer of 1330 by the battle of Velbuzhd, in which the Serbs destroyed Michael Sisman's army, and subjected the last independent Bulgarian state before the nineteenth century to Serbian hegemony.[35]

As a result the new Tsar of Serbia, Stefan Dusan (1331–55), commanded a state of considerable size. He claimed sovereignty over Greeks as well as Slavs; and he saw himself as an emperor in the Byzantine mould. Imperial claims were not new to Serbia. Dusan's grandfather, Stefan Uros II, had claimed to rule the entire terrain between the Adriatic to the Danube, although his Serbia was politically unstable and it soon lost its holdings in Dalmatia. Stefan Dusan, however, extended his empire to embrace not only Serbia and Albania but Macedonia, Bulgaria, and northern Greece. So long as he lived he also managed to stamp his authority on the region. Byzantium provided a convenient model for the organization of his empire.

As Michael Sisman of Bulgaria had done, Stefan Dusan wore a crown modelled on a Byzantine diadem and a purple robe. He also styled himself 'Autocrat', adopted elements of Byzantine court ceremonial, organized his government in partial imitation of the Byzantine central administration, and, no doubt because he had acquired so many Greek subjects, adopted Byzantine laws and institutions (for example the *pronoia* or service estate). In May 1349 he issued a Law Code (*Zakonik*), to which he added over fifty clauses five years later.[36] This work, several copies of which have survived, constitutes a major source for the Balkans in his time. It also draws attention to the law as a reflection of society and as a factor in development.

* * *

So far we have searched for the origins of Eastern Europe's distinctiveness and the sources of its difference from the West chiefly in terms of its economic fortunes, its social formation, its culture and its politics; but the development of its laws and legal system, especially in this mediaeval period, demand attention too. The operation of a legal system, after all, reflects the nature of the state. Laws help to shape society, maintain a political order, and establish the rights and obligations of both individuals and institutions. Churches, monarchies, estates, cities and institutions of all kinds are defined by law – which is no doubt why the law is so often regarded as the cornerstone of civilization. However, the state of the law may be imperfect; it may even inhibit civilization; and it can differ greatly in its character and its effects from one region to another. Certainly, differences, perhaps critical differences, between Eastern Europe and the West can be detected in the relative coherence of the laws, the firmness of their application and the respect for the judicial process even as early as the Middle Ages.

Of all the states in Eastern Europe the Byzantine Empire had by far the richest legal inheritance, Roman law. However, it had seen many changes since the days of the Emperor Justinian. Christianity had had an incremental but profound effect upon it; so had the need to adapt to different circumstances over the course of centuries. As a result much judicial authority had been devolved on institutions, especially the church. Some elements of Roman law were passed on to other Orthodox states (the *Basilica*, or re-codification of Leo VI, for example, influenced Russia, as did Byzantine canon law); and both Roman law and canon law also influenced the West, especially the Papacy.

However, there was nothing in any Eastern European state to compare with the common law which the Normans imposed on England,[37] that is, a system of laws for the entire state applied in the same way in all localities. Indeed, it was the desire to establish just such sets of norms covering entire kingdoms that was a prime motive in the several efforts made to codify laws and have them enforced, for a standard set of laws uniformly applied overcomes divisive localism and promotes the good of the wider community.

Customary law, that is traditional rules or understandings often conveyed orally rather than set down in writing and specific to a particular locality in at least some respects, was the most prevalent kind of law in Eastern Europe outside the Byzantine Empire. Traditional understandings of the laws of property, the ways in which people should behave to one another, and the manner in which conflict should be resolved constituted a serious obstacle to the broader interests of the state, for they could vary considerably from area to area, cause confusion and impede the effective administration of the prince's justice. Furthermore, certain widespread customary laws were harmful. The apanage system governing princely inheritance, for example, had once been an effective way of keeping peace within a family, yet became a source of political fragmentation and strife.

The blood feud was an even worse evil, an affront to the state. This form of law had evolved as a customary means of settling disputes between tribes in the absence of any superior judicial authority. It was to persist, particularly in isolated mountain areas with tendencies to overpopulation, such as northern Albania and Montenegro, into the twentieth century.[38] On the other hand, the difficulty of communications in the larger states which stood in greatest need of standard laws and legal process made the imposition of a truly common law extremely difficult. The dominance of customary law, therefore, both motivated such attempts and impeded them.

Codifications of law were issued in Hungary early in the reign of Ladislas I (d. 1095), legislation which, it has been suggested, was tantamount to the introduction of common law into Hungary[39] but it would be going too far to equate legal development in Hungary with that in England. The routine recording of judicial decisions in writing was only introduced by Bela III in 1181; and the legal trend in Hungary, as in Bohemia and Poland and unlike England and France, was away from absolutism and the uniformity associated with it.

In both Eastern and Western Europe, however, the church exercised broad legal powers and influenced legal development. Throughout the continent it was a considerable landowner; and canon law was often applicable not only to clerics but to peasants and other laymen who lived on church lands and were subject to church courts. Indeed, monasteries often resembled independent states in exercising a virtual monopoly of law in their localities. This seems to have persisted rather longer in Eastern Europe, particularly in the Orthodox countries, partly because church and state worked together much more closely, partly because of the greater geographic isolation (which accounts also for the exercise of private law by magnates, and subsequently by serf-owning lords on their estates).

Because the churches strove to eliminate paganism they were natural allies of the state in combating localism and controlling customary law, for customs were often associated with pagan practice.[40] Outside Byzantium, in countries where few laymen received an education, the church was also important in providing literate and learned men to serve the state. The law could hardly be effective without literates to record decisions; and in mediaeval times monarchs normally relied on priests for information on precedents and legal development. In Russia, for example, churchmen provided models for establishing a criminal law and legal procedures, and they were generally responsible for the increasing sophistication of the legal rules and arrangements.[41] This was the case in Catholic states too. In Bohemia, clerics were the first and leading bureaucrats. In time, of course, this situation changed. By the end of the thirteenth century Wenceslas II, who had become interested in the study of law in Paris and Bologna, invited a lay expert, Gozzio of Orvieto, to Prague to advise on the codification of Bohemian law;[42] and Western lay influences were also evident in Hungary under the Angevin Kings.

Clerical or lay, however, a monarch's servants tended to be the butts of much resentment, especially on the part of the nobility. In Bohemia this extended to an hostility to Latin, the chief medium of legal expression; for if they could not understand the law they could not be certain of their ability to defend their interests. And in Transylvania there were to be cases of jealous noblemen murdering bureaucrats who had displaced them as close advisers to the prince. Broader issues than personal jealousy were at stake, for royal power, as expressed by statute and administered by royal courts staffed by non-noble literates, constituted a threat to noble rights.

The process of establishing a uniform legal order was by no means simple, however. It was the custom among Slavs for an edict to lose its force unless it was reaffirmed by successive monarchs. In Tsar Dusan of Serbia's Law Code such a re-affirmation was extended to charters conveying property grants that his predecessors had issued.[43] This fact alone suggests that statute law was potentially unstable. Furthermore, codification was difficult in that customary laws had to be defined before they could be standardized or superceded. As was usual in Orthodox states, Dusan issued his Code together with the country's primate sitting in a joint assembly of synod and lay lords, and the Code began with canon law.

There followed clauses that dealt with property and inheritance, crime, litigation and judicial procedure, mercantile and military law, etc. However, the juxtapositions sometimes reflect a looseness of categorization not commonly associated with law, and, for all its evidence of ethnic and occupational variegation and of the existence of legal clerks (chiefly Greeks presumably) the whole reflects the workings of a basically uncomplicated society. Curiously enough, however, this may help to explain why Dusan was able to produce a codification of laws when monarchs of more advanced, and more permanent, states of the period, despite all their efforts, failed to do so.

Of the three attempts made in Bohemia, the most successful was that of Charles IV in the fourteenth century. It aimed

> not only to strengthen the royal power but also to inculcate in his subjects a higher conception of the state, placing its interests above the selfish aims of the nobles or the mere whim of rulers.

However, it was not a systematic codification and it did not prove acceptable to noble vested interests.[44]

In Poland Casimir the Great attempted to systematize and improve the law, aiming in particular to reconcile the customary law of Great with that of Little Poland. However, the powers of the local courts, which were in the hands of local noblemen, tended to increase during the later fourteenth century, while the activity of the public notaries was confined to canon law. In short, though the law in Poland became more uniform, its administration was characterized by devolution.

German law, which ruled in so many towns and settlements in Hungary, Bohemia and Poland, also represented a devolution of authority, though one which even at the time states usually regarded as beneficial. Autonomy certainly reinforced that sense of confidence which must underpin any business undertaking. On the other hand, it also tended to entrench German culture which was to become a source of alienation in subsequent generations. Nor were a city's rights always respected by the state. In the 1260s, for example, the elected mayor of Buda was replaced by a rector appointed by the king in contravention of the city's charter.[45] The case suggests a capricious or cavalier attitude towards the law at the highest level, which may have contributed towards that lack of trust in, or respect for, the law and legal process which characterized large parts of Eastern Europe in later ages.

There were islands of legal order even then, however. The German Hansa towns on the Baltic and Ragusa (Dubrovnik) constitute examples. The latter's statute book of 1272 set out

> to harmonise the discrepancies [in the law], suppress the superfluities, supply omissions, [and] explain obscurities, so that nothing superfluous, obscure, or captious should remain in them.[46]

This codification was very largely successful. However, port cities on the periphery were hardly typical of cities as a whole. They relied to a great extent on imported German and Italian law. On the other hand the major influence in most of Eastern Europe was Slavonic law, mediated by elements of Byzantine, German or Venetian law according to area. And Slavonic law drew no clear distinctions between law and religion, law and politics, and law and morality. Indeed, the old Russian word for law, *pravda,* also means truth. In the opinion of a distinguished historian of law at the beginning of the century,

> This fact points to an earlier period of development of legal order than in the West. The religious, moral, political, social and economical rules have had no time to differentiate themselves completely.... [So] it is not astonishing that the sources of Slavonic law are not so well developed as those of ... Western Europe.[47]

Legal order therefore constitutes a major source of divergence between the two halves of Europe, but significant differences can also be discerned in institutions and in culture. Together they may help to explain why a 'civil society' failed to emerge in Eastern Europe as it did in the West. One remarks, for example, the marginal effect on Eastern Europe of the feudal system which prevailed in the mediaeval West.

Eastern European historians, drawing on the Marxist canon, have tended to be loose in their use of the words 'feudal' and 'feudalism', using it to denote an historical period, the pre-modern age, or any system of dependency including serfdom. But in the strict sense feudalism denotes a precise set of rules governing social and political relationships, which, though not equal, were reciprocal and demanded duties of all parties. It was a contractual system insofar as it assumed obligations on the part of the lord as well as the duties of fealty on the part of the vassal. In this sense feudalism was almost unknown in Eastern Europe;[48] and outside Byzantium one observes a tendency towards untrammelled lordly power, which evidently derived from the authority of the tribal chief and which was inconsistent with the emergence of a civil society.

A factor vital to the ultimate development of a civil society was the emergence in the mediaeval West, especially in Italy and somewhat later in the Low Countries and elsewhere, of independent cities and an autonomous urban culture. In Eastern Europe, this manifestation was very much weaker and less widespread, while other tendencies, each inimical to social autonomy, were stronger. If the occasional strong monarch could, and sometimes did, ride roughshod over the law, the frequent periods of noble anarchy, when local potentates set out to dominate everything and everyone within their reach, were no less stifling to social autonomy and no less arbitrary. In Western Europe, by contrast, towns had achieved sovereignty by developing 'in the interstices between the sovereignties of rival powers'.[49]

The prevalence of customary laws, which had developed in the isolation of rural life and which were geared to an agrarian economy, was equally inimical to the emergence of an autonomous urban society. In attracting migrants and offering them the rights of German law, some medieval kings recognized their countries' need not only of more people with better skills, but for a humming urban life and a thriving urban culture. Yet Western urban achievements were not to be matched.[50] In part this was due to subsequent restrictions on their legal rights already noted, but sometimes the rights themselves were limited from an early stage. In early fourteenth-century Cracow,[51] for example, the town council had to share authority with the prince's representative; and almost everywhere in the region cities tended to be exotic islands suspended in an alien sea rather than integral parts of their hinterlands as well as of their commercial networks.

Unlike so many cities in East-Central Europe, the populations of mediaeval Russian cities were predominately indigenous. Furthermore, they possessed advantages usually associated with the evolution of autonomous civic structures and a civil society in that they were city states enjoying a participatory governmental institution, the *veche*. This was an urban assembly in which all heads of households seem to have been entitled to participate, and liberal historians have tended to seize on it, as on the Assembly of the Land (see Chapter 7), as proof that the East Slavs had a natural inclination towards democracy. Unfortunately the evidence is insufficient to support the claim. The existence of the *veche* seems not to have diminished the authority of the local prince or bishop, either of whom might chair the meeting rather than the mayor; and in the absence of any system of delegation the 'democratic' element was soon transformed into an oligarchic or plutocratic one in towns of any size.[52]

The Tatar invasions may also have encouraged a tendency for the prince to accrete more power in order to achieve greater military efficiency. However Novgorod the Great, which enjoyed considerable autonomy, lay safely beyond Tatar reach. Princes and their retainers were barred from owning estates within its territories, and as early as 1200 it could be described as a republic, whose citizens elected their own princes, albeit always members of the Riurikid dynasty.[53] But, the prince's retainers played a large part in the administration of justice; and judicial review was reserved to the prince. This suggests that it was the prince rather than the city patricians whose authority was, or became, decisive.[54] In any case Novgorod was unusual, in having an economy based on commerce, in particular the export of furs, rather than on agriculture,[55] and in being open to German influence (the Hansa maintained an important office there). Furthermore, although Novgorod ruled considerable tracts of territory in northern Russia, including other cities, the populations of these dependencies were not enfranchised and enjoyed no autonomy.

Finally certain differences between the churches in Eastern and Western Europe call for comment. The church was of great importance everywhere, of course. It could lend or deny powerful moral and ideological support to princes; it administered vast tracts of land, staffed royal chanceries and contributed knowledge, not least of law, that was essential to the business of government. However, the degree of autonomy the church enjoyed varied significantly between the two halves of Europe, and this had a bearing on institutional development.

The tendency of the Orthodox Church to defer to secular, or at least imperial, authority has already been noted. However the Catholic Church in Eastern Europe was not as in the West. In Western countries, partly because the Popes were temporal as well as spiritual leaders, partly because it enjoyed considerable immunities, the church was institutionally independent of the monarch. In Hungary, Poland, the German marches and even Bohemia it was essentially an extension of the prince's chamber, or else in the power of a nobleman.[56]

Eventually the prelates of Poland gained recognition as a distinct estate, and from 1180 the Polish clergy gained certain privileges and exemptions. Those of Bohemia gained limited freedoms somewhat later. But they did not enjoy the degree of autonomy from the secular authority that they did in the West, and, like their Orthodox counterpart, the Catholic Churches in East-Central Europe did not claim primacy. On the other hand the nobility was rather more succesful in winning guarantees against royal authority. This altered the balance of constitutional forces and restricted the number of competing authorities between which autonomous entities might sprout. The different nature of the Eastern European churches was therefore another factor which helps explain the region's general failure to develop a strong civil society as did the West.

An even more critical factor making for divergence between East and West in the High Middle Ages is not any 'failure' on the part of Eastern Europe, but rather to the idiosyncrasy of the West in generating so much dynamism. The rise of prosperous and powerful cities and the emergence of strong, law-oriented monarchies were among the consequences. Equally important, perhaps, was their ability to work together. No mediaeval political system in the West or the East could be termed democratic, but by 1350 the English and French parliaments were already more representative than their Eastern European counterparts; and the emergence of a certain political pluralism has also been detected that one finds little trace of east of the River Elbe.[57] Finally the West seems to be characterized by a greater willingness to recognize a growing framework of rules, easier access to justice and even, perhaps, by a greater disposition to compromise and by a more pronounced inclination on the part of contesting parties and interests to respect the law.

* * *

Earlier in this chapter we examined the causes of Byzantium's decline, saw how it fell to the Crusaders and how, in the late thirteenth century, it was wrenched away from them. The restoration did not signal much of a recovery, however; and a century and more before the city fell to the Turks contemporaries already recognized that Byzantium was doomed. Theodore Metochites, a scholar and bureaucrat, was philosophical about the prospect.

> People who formerly ruled over others [he wrote] were themselves enslaved in their turn.... Such events occur in cyclical fashion according to the chance of time and fortune. There is nothing constant in

> human affairs; nothing unchangingly eternal. Just as every individual ... suffers birth, growth, decay ... and death, so ... governments and dynasties ... come into being, progress ... and die.[58]

Even so Byzantium's political and military decline was accompanied by a cultural revival. Metochites himself was involved in this as patron of one of its more splendid achievements, the renovated Church of St Saviour in Chora with its wonderful mosaics. The sense of decline from the glories of former ages seems to have imbued the Greeks of the time with an exaggerated awe of the past which inhibited originality. Even so the fourteenth century saw much scholarly activity in which they drew on both Western and Muslim, as well as Byzantine, sources. And although Metochites respected mediaeval tradition and the teachings of the church, he is also considered the 'real father' of secular humanism.[59]

How considerable Byzantine influences were on the rest of Eastern Europe in terms of religion and administration should be obvious by now. But the impact of its political culture on the mentalities of Eastern Europeans was also strong and long-lasting. We have already seen how Orthodox influences promoted a tendency to confuse law with truth, but there are other Eastern European attitudes that Westerners tend to find strange: the tendencies to confuse politics with morality; to seek unanimity rather than decision by majority; and to regard political leaders as sources of salvation rather than arbiters between conflicting interests and fallible promoters of the common good. One looks in vain for the origins of such attitudes in the Communist period (even though the Communist regimes exemplified them) – for they lie, in fact, in an earlier period than any we have so far considered, in the early Middle Ages when Byzantium was in its prime.

Other residual puzzles draw us back to those times too. We have seen how the German element came to be established so strongly in many parts of the region and in many aspects of its life; but we have not examined the earlier stages of the *Drang nach Osten* which helped to give eastern Germany its affinity to Eastern Europe. We have also noticed an ongoing struggle between East and West, exemplified in Hungary in respect of both religion and foreign policy. However, though the causes of the welling hatred between Orthodox and Latins are obvious enough, we have yet to explore the origins of the great schism in what had once been a united universal church; and how the once universal Byzantine Empire came to be challenged by a new empire in the West.

Yet another set of problems which beckons us back to the early Middle Ages derives from the discussion of why some Western institutions failed to prosper in Eastern Europe's soil. In that context we noted a certain instability in political authority, and even greater uncertainty in the matter of law. The preponderance of variegated customary laws was obviously of importance in that context, and in particular the law of the Slavs. But the factors that united the Slavonic peoples in the earlier period have still to be investigated. So has a range of questions concerning their ethnogenesis and those of other Eastern European peoples, including the Albanians and Hungarians. Furthermore, although the great majority of Slavonic peoples acquired literacy through the medium of a standard written language (Old Church Slavonic or Old Slavic), they developed dissimilar languages. That process, which should throw more light on the subsequent development of nationalism (see Chapter 6), also demands consideration.

So, on the last stage of our enquiry, we turn to the later Roman Empire and the barbarian migrations; to the question of how new states were formed in Eastern Europe, and why some survived while others such as Great Moravia, did not; to representative figures like Cyril and Methodius who introduced the Slavs to Christianity and literacy, to the great administrator and missionary St Adalbert and 'Good King' Wenceslas; to the Great Schism in the church, and that awful moment when the Pope pronounced anathema upon the Patriarch of Constantinople and the Patriarch, in retaliation, excommunicated the Pope. Nor should the possible effects of geography on the region's history be neglected. And the question remains: is the fact that the frontiers between Eastern and Western Europe were considered to run along virtually identical lines in Charlemagne's time and Winston Churchill's merely a coincidence? Or not?

REFERENCES

1. I. Banac and F. Sysyn in *Harvard Ukrainian Studies*, 10 (3/4), December 1986, p. 272.
2. The term 'Russian' here is used literally to represent the old Slavonic term *Rus'* which embraced all the East Slavs. There is no evidence that the ancestors of Ukrainians and Belorussians regarded themselves as any different from the ancestors of the Russians at that time.
3. Translation adopted from S.H. Cross (ed.) *The Russian Primary Chronicle* (Cambridge, Mass., 1930) pp. 239–40.
4. For a convenient account of Byzantine-Venetian relations, see D. Nicol, *Byzantium and Venice: A Study In Diplomatic and Cultural Relations* (Cambridge, 1989).
5. See the conflicting accounts of Romanus IV Diogenes by Scylitzes and Psellos, E. Sewter, *Fourteen Byzantine Rulers: the Chronologicon of Michael Psellus* (Harmondsworth, 1982) pp. 350–66.
6. This factor is emphasized by S. Vryonis, *Byzantium and Europe* (London, 1967) pp. 121–6.
7. C. Mango, *Byzantium, the Empire of New Rome* (London, 1980) pp. 52–3; G. Ostrogorsky, *History of the Byzantine Empire* (Oxford, 1980) pp. 321–3 *et seq.* and J. Hussey in *The Cambridge Medieval History* [hereafter *CMed H*], vol. IV, pt. 1 (Cambridge, 1975) pp. 207ff.

8. Nicol, *op. cit.* pp. 55–61.
9. A. Gieysztor in S. Kieniewicz (ed.), *History of Poland*, 2nd. ed. (Warszawa, 1979) pp. 65–71; W. Czaplinski, *et al.*, *Atlas Historyczny* (Warsawa, 1989) pp. 4–5; T. Monteuffel, *The Formation of the Polish State* (Detroit, 1982).
10. G. Vernadsky, *Kievan Russia* (New Haven, 1973) pp. 179–80, see also O. Pritsak, *Harvard Ukrainian Studies*, X (3/4) 1986 [1987], especially pp. 282–3.
11. J. Fine, *The Early Medieval Balkans* (Ann Arbor, Michigan, 1983) pp. 220–6; S. Guldescu, *History of Medieval Croatia* (The Hague, 1964) p. 145.
12. Z. Kosztolnyik, *Five Eleventh Century Hungarian Kings: their Policies and their Relations with Rome* (Boulder, Colorado, 1981) pp. 98ff.
13. Abbot Gilbert of Nogent, adapted from G. Kristo, comp., *Saecula Hungariae 1000–1196* (Budapest, 1985) f.16r-v.
14. Anna Comnena. The translation is based on that of E. Sewter, *The Alexiad of Anna Comnena* (Harmondsworth, 1982) p. 317, n. 37.
15. Gy. Moravcsik, 'Hungary and Byzantium in the Middle Ages', *CMedH*, V, i, *op. cit.*, pp. 566ff., esp. pp. 572–80. Also F. Makk, *The Arpads and the Comneni* (Budapest, 1989) n. 118, pp. 161–2.
16. F. Makk, *op. cit.*, pp. 45–63.
17. The sorry story is recounted in lively fashion by Nicol, *op. cit.*, pp. 74–119.
18. S. Runciman, *A History of the Crusades* (Harmondsworth, 1965)
19. From Geoffroy de Villehardouin's account in M. Shaw, trans., *Chronicles of the Crusades* (Harmondsworth, 1983) pp. 91–2.
20. See Migne, *Patrologia Latina* (Paris, 1844–55) vol. 215, cols 699–702.
21. R.W. Southern, *The Making of the Middle Ages* (London, 1956) p. 61.
22. Peter of Dusberg, *Chronicon Terrae Prussiae*, quoted by H. Schreiber, *Teuton and Slav: The Struggle for Central Europe*, trans. J. Cleugh (London, 1965) p. 76.
23. F. Carsten, *The Origins of Prussia* (Oxford, 1954) pp. 43–51; M. Rady, *Medieval Buda* (Boulder, 1985) pp. 42–3 and 152ff.
24 Matthew Paris, 1243, as rendered by R. Hakluyt, *The Principle Navigations, Voyages, Traffiques and Discoveries of the English Nation*, vol. I (Glasgow, 1903) pp. 50–4.
25. See V. Spinei, *Moldavia in the 11th–14th Centuries* (Bucharest, 1986) pp. 120–2, on the effects the Mongol invasion had on castle-building in Hungary, E. Fugedi, *Castle and Society in Medieval Hungary (1000–1437)* (Studia Historica Academiae Scientiarum Hungaricae, 187), pp. 50ff.
26. C. Halperin, *Russia and the Golden Horde* (London, 1985) pp. 90–4.
27. The term 'oriental despotism' derives from Wittvogel's theory, since discredited, associating great public works with despotic government.
28. See J. Fennel, *The Emergence of Moscow 1304–1359* (London, 1968), p. 47, and *passim* for a painstaking evaluation of the available documentary evidence. For a more accessible treatment of the period 1304–1380 see R. Crummey, *The Formation of Muscovy 1304–1613* (London, 1987), pp. 29–55.
29. See L. Makkai in E. Pamlenyi (ed.), *A History of Hungary* (London, 1975) especially pp. 65–6.
30. On the revival under the Angevin Kings see the still invaluable study by B. Homan, *Gli Angiovini di Napoli in Ungheria* (Rome, 1938) pp. 156–243; for a summation of the social structure, pp. 244ff.
31. Giesztor in Kieniewicz, *op. cit.*, pp. 98–114.
32. F. Dvornik, *The Slavs in European History and Civilization* (New Brunswick, New Jersey, 1962) pp. 120–4.
33. D. Nicol in *The Cambridge Medieval History*, vol. V, pt. 1 (Cambridge, 1966) pp. 295–327; S. Runciman, *The Sicilian Vespers* (Cambridge, 1958).

34. The name 'Wallachia' derives from 'Vlach', a term denoting a Balkan transhumance shepherd, a member of an ethnic group speaking a Latin dialect (or one morphologically related to the Romance group of languages) and is therefore neither Greek, Bulgar, Serb or Albanian. Vlachs populated Moldavia as well as Wallachia, the core of modern Romania; but Vlachs who do not regard themselves as Romanians are still to be found in other parts of the Balkans. Some Romanians may be descended from the Romans and the Dacian tribes who fought against and intermingled with them; whether they populated all the territories of modern Romania continuously since ancient times, as Romanian nationalists assert in support of their territorial claims, is open to question. On the Vlachs and related problems see T. Winnifrith, *The Vlachs* (London, 1987). Also Chapter 11.
35. For the details see J. Fine, *The Later Medieval Balkans* (Ann Arbor, Michigan, 1987) pp. 217–75.
36. The Code survives in several copies. For a translation of the Bistritsa version see M. Begovic (ed.), *Zakonik tsara Stefana Dusana*, kn. 2 (Beograd, 1981) pp. 237–62.
37. Casimir the Great is said to have recorded the Polish common law for Little and Great Poland (Giesztor, *loc. cit.* p. 111). In fact he tried to systematize their customary laws and reconcile them with new ordinances.
38. M. Durham, *Some Tribal Origins, Laws and Customs of the Balkans* (London, 1928) pp. 162–71.
39. Kostolnyik, *op. cit.*, pp. 95–9; Gy. Bonis *et al*, (eds.), *The Laws of Hungary*, I.
40. E.g. laws concerning the family, see M. Kovalevsky, *Modern Customs and Ancient Laws of Russia* (London, 1981) p. 36 *et seq.*.
41. D. Kaiser, *The Growth of the Law in Medieval Russia* (Princeton, New Jersey, 1980) p. 16.
42. The only tangible outcome, however, was the important Mining Code. See Dvornik, *op. cit.*, pp. 125–6.
43. Clause 40 of the Bistritsa version, *Zakonik, op. cit.*, pp. 180–1 and 242.
44. Dvornik, *op. cit.*, p. 126.
45. Rady, *op. cit.*, pp. 24–5 and 161.
46. L. Villari, *The Republic of Ragusa* (London, 1904) pp. 75–8. On the Hansa, J. Schildhauer *et al, Die Hanse* (Berlin, 1985).
47. F. Sigel, *Lectures on Slavonic Law* (London, 1902) p. 151.
48. See M. Bloch, *Feudal Society*, trans. L. Manyon, 2 vols., (London, 1967). On the non-feudal nature of Byzantine lordship see A. Kazhdan and A. Epstein, *Change in Byzantine Culture in the Eleventh and Twelfth Century*, (Berkeley, California, 1990,) p. 61 and 63.
49. See the discussion in J. Szucs, 'The Three Historical Regions of Europe' *Acta Historica Academiae Scientiarum Hungaricae*, 29 (2–4) 1983, p. 137 (from which the phrase is quoted). There are some western equivalents, apparently. Dublin, for example, seems to have developed under 'Bristol law'.
50. This despite B. Krekic's largely unsupported claim that the pace of urban development did not lag far behind that of western Europe: B. Krekic (ed.), *The Urban Society of Eastern Europe in Premodern Times* (Berkeley, California, 1987) p. ix.
51. P Birnbaum, 'Urban Development in Medieval Poland' in Krekic, *op. cit.*, especially pp. 90–2.
52. Vernadsky, *op. cit.*, pp. 185–9.
53. *Ibid.*, pp. 196–201; Fennel, *op. cit.*, pp. 240ff.

54. Kaiser, *op. cit.*, pp. 101, esp. p. 106.
55. M. Malowist, 'The Trade of Eastern Europe in the Later Middle Ages' in M. Postan *et al.* (eds), *The Cambridge Economic History of Europe*, vol. II (Cambridge, 1987) pp. 525–612, esp. 593–9; M. Postan, 'Economic Relations between Eastern and Western Europe' in G. Barraclough (ed.), *Eastern and Western Europe in the Middle Ages* (London, 1970) pp. 125–74, p. 148.
56. F. Seibt, *Hussitenstudien* (Munich, 1987) p. 138, following P. Hilsh, *Die Bischofe von Prag der fruher Staufenzeit* (Munich, 1969); also Seibt in Barraclough, *op. cit.*, pp. 100–3.
57. Szucs, *loc. cit.*, esp. pp. 143 and 150.
58. Metochites, *in lit.*
59. S. Runciman, *The Last Byzantine Renaissance* (Cambridge, 1970) especially Chapter III; J. Meyendorff, *The Byzantine Legacy in the Orthodox Church* (Crestwood, New York, 1982) pp. 133–8. However, Meyendorff is uncomfortable with the term 'humanism' in this context.

11

Beginnings (324–1071)

Every people has different customs, laws and institutions, and should consolidate those things which are proper to it ... for the fusion of its life.

Constantine VII, tenth-century Emperor

The formation of Eastern Europe, the region we recognize today on account of its distinctive mix of characteristics, began after the year 330 when Constantine the Great, unifier of the Roman Empire and the first Emperor to embrace Christianity, inaugurated 'New Rome' (also called Byzantium and Constantinople) as the new imperial capital.

In its early stages the shaping process involved two major constituents: the later Roman Empire itself, which embraced the entire civilized world (so far, at least, as its inhabitants seemed aware); and, beyond its frontier on the River Danube, the inchoate swarms of herdsmen, predators and primitive cultivators, whom the Romans called barbarians. It was largely out of the interaction between classical civilization and the amorphous crowds of humanity, sometimes aggressive, often on the move, that many of the now familiar customs and attitudes, institutions and traditions, and the patchwork of languages and nationalities, was eventually to emerge.

The process was far from simple, however, even in its earliest stages, partly because the principal constituents were themselves undergoing change independently of their impact on each other. The Empire, for example, became progressively less Latin and more Greek, more susceptible to Asiatic influences and, not least, more religious. Then, as Western Europe, overrun by barbarians, began to take on a different, autonomous form, interactions between East and West assumed importance too. A Frankish emperor emerged to rival the Emperor in Byzantium; the Pope was gradually estranged from the other patriarchs of the church until a separation occurred over the use of one vital Latin word, *filioque* ('and the Son'), in the Creed.

Meanwhile, the barbarian tribes had been reacting to each other; and as barbarian super-chiefs laboured to build permanent states out of temporary tribal associations they began to ape emperors, copy their institutions, and to exploit East-West rivalries, both imperial and religious. Chemical agents were added to this brew. One was the invention early in the ninth century of Slavonic script, which allowed the most numerous of all the linguistic groups in the region to keep records as well as to communicate in writing in their own language; another was the missionizing by Greek, Latin and German churches. These catalysts produced significant reactions. And the region's geography, the crucible in which all the complex substances stirred and bubbled, also affected the character and fate of the humanity which it contained.

By the middle of the eleventh century the Roman Empire had been transmogrified into the Byzantine state,[1] and the chaos beyond its European borders had solidified into a much more stable condition. Such changes are easily traced in outline, though they tend to be difficult to reconstruct in detail. This is partly because the period with which we are now concerned includes the 'Dark Ages', from which comparatively little written evidence survives; partly because much of what does survive is imbued with cultural values and assumptions, some of which have long since been abandoned and are therefore difficult for us to fathom. However, scanty documentary evidence can be supplemented with data of other kinds; and the conventional historian who does not trust himself to reconstruct prehistory on his own can lean on the expertise of archaeologists, philologists, numismatists and anthropologists.

Archaeologists, for example, have discovered a great deal about the early Bulgarians and the mysterious Khazars by exploring the remains, and not least the middens, of their old settlements at Pliska and Sarkel.[2] They have reconstructed the lifestyle of the early Slavs by excavating their settlements and burial grounds;[3] shown when and where a particular people changed from herding to agriculture, and used dendrochronology to establish the age of wooden buildings.[4] Philologists have helped establish migration routes and culture contacts by tracing the incidence, types and sources of loan-words that have entered a language;[5] anthropologists can sometimes throw light on pagan practices; numismatists can help reconstruct the directions and the pulse of trade.

Even so, the dangers of misinterpretation loom larger in this period, perhaps, than in any other. This is only partly because of that sense of national pride and national vulnerability that has sometimes led scholars to place loyalty above truth (see Chapter 5) and governments to disseminate half-truths, and even lies, about the past. Churches also distorted the past in order to gain or to solidify a constituency, to obliterate memory of support for a rival creed, pagan or Christian, or, as the forged 'Donation of Constantine' succeeded in doing, to create a basis for a legal claim.[6] Within these limits, however, and mindful of these cautions, we may pursue our investigation.

* * *

In 324 when Constantine decided to build 'New Rome' on a magnificent and easily defensible site above the Golden Horn, he did so for several reasons. It stood at a vital cross-roads between Europe and Asia, and within comparatively easy reach of both the Empire's granary, Egypt, and its two most vulnerable frontiers, Persia and the Danube. Furthermore, the most prosperous of the Empire's provinces were now located in the eastern, not the western, Mediterranean area, and it was convenient for the government to be closer to the chief sources of its revenue.

The city itself, which was subsequently to become Greek and later Turkish, was at first palpably Roman. It was equipped with every appurtenance of Roman civilization: aqueducts and sewage system, elegant palaces, public bath-houses, a stadium, and an orderly system of streets paved with stone and embellished with lively mosaics and marble statuary (much of it brought from Rome in Italy). Many languages were heard in its streets, Greek in particular, but the official language was Latin, and New Rome was the centre of a well-ordered, civilized empire that was ruled by law – though the city was built by the state and with generous use of slave labour. Constantine himself spent comparatively little of his time there and one of his successors, Jovian, never set foot in the place. Even so, by the end of the century New Rome had become a vast metropolis with as many as half a million inhabitants, larger than the former capital.

It was also a Christian centre, though paganism was still tolerated. Constantine had established Christianity as a state religion in 312 but he continued to subscribe to pagan cults, taking care not to offend those devoted to Mithras and Hercules which were popular among the military, and he remained *Pontifex Maximus*. He also raised a great column to Apollo, but substituted his own face for the god's on it. At the same time he had Christian relics gathered into the city, and it was he who called, and presided over, the first ecumenical Council of the Church at Nicaea in 325. In doing so he set a tone calling for ideological conformity which was to echo down to the later twentieth century.

Constantine called the Council to resolve the 'Arian' controversy which had been dividing Christians. The issue, which involved differing views about the Trinity and the divinity of Jesus, need not concern us; the political aspect, and its reverberations down the ages, particularly in Eastern Europe, should. Christianity's value was as a binding force for the very diverse population of an extensive empire. Any divergence on a matter of faith within the Church could legitimize political divergence and foster rebellion. Hence the care taken by subsequent Ecumenical Councils to avert such evil – at Constantinople in 381, which finalized the Creed, established the Patriarchate of Constantinople as second only to the Pope (who as successor of Peter still resided at his church in Rome), and declared Arianism to be heretical; at Ephesus in 431; and Chalcedon in 451, at which Nestorianism and Monophysitism were condemned respectively.

In addressing the fifth Council, held at Constantinople in 553, the Emperor Justinian insisted that

> It has always been the practice of our orthodox and imperial forefathers to counter every heresy as it arose through the instrumentality of the most zealous priests assembled in council and to keep the Holy Church ... in peace by the sincere preaching of the true faith.[7]

However, although an emperor was not entitled to decide a matter of Christian faith or establish a new canon, he had the power to convene church councils and to preside over them. Furthermore, though emperors ceased to identify themselves with any deity, they followed Constantine I in claiming to be the thirteenth apostle; and at the climax of the sixth Council of 681, which condemned Monotheletism (an attempt to explain how Jesus could be both human and divine), those present acclaimed Constantine IV as the Church's protector and the true interpreter of Orthodox Christianity. 'Long live the Emperor [they shouted]. You have revealed the true meaning of the natures of Christ'.[8]

If the Communist Party Congresses of Stalin's time, with their condemnations of deviations to the 'right' or 'left' and their public displays of sycophancy, have a similar resonance it is largely because they were inspired by similar needs. From an historical point of view, therefore, the resemblance is largely coincidental. On the other hand developing notions of Church and State were to have a lasting influence on Eastern Europe's political culture.

The emperor came to be regarded not only as divinely chosen to act as God's vice-regent on earth, but as the guardian of the Orthodox faith and shepherd of the Christian flock. An idea eventually took hold that since fulfilment of his responsibility obliged an emperor to place his soul at risk by shedding blood, he was akin to Christ in taking worldly sins upon himself. But emperors not only presented themselves as Christlike; they simulated divinity in ritual appearances. They surrounded themselves with scarlet pomp and clothed themselves in purple, as well as Christian, majesty.

The consequence was a much wider gap between sovereign and subject than was to characterize the West.[9] Such understandings gave rise to the popular notions (much in evidence in the late 1980s and early 1990s as well as in the 1930s) that spiritual and temporal power are indivisible, that morality, rather than sound policies taken in the interests of the polity, is the litmus test of good government, and that a single flaw or failure is sufficient to prove a regime illegitimate – for legitimate government represents a divine order, as did the rule of the emperors.

This is not to say that the Emperor Justinian did not set out to govern well. His legal code, issued in 534, is a monument to good government;

and he achieved glittering successes besides. The great basilica of St Sophia is his foundation; he reestablished imperial power in both Africa and Italy, which had been overrun by barbarians; and, not least, also his authority over the Pope. After Justinian's death in 565, however, the fortunes of the Empire slumped. There were several causes: epidemic, exhaustion after the effort of re-conquest, and continuing attacks by successive waves of barbarians. But significant change is not limited to geopolitical success and failure, nor to the short term.

Slow but important transformations had been taking place in the realm of culture. Justinian's Code was one of the last major enactments in Latin, and Greek soon became the language of government as well as of a significant proportion of the Empire's subjects. At the same time surviving traces of Rome's earlier oligarchic form of government gradually disappeared. The Senate still existed and some senators were influential, but all trace of republicanism had vanished. Roman law was maintained but some of its expressions became meaningless, or acquired different senses, as the original meanings were forgotten. Communal bathing lost its former popularity.[10] So did the theatre and chariot racing; and the Circus, or Hippodrome, became associated with the sort of display associated with circuses today: juggling and acrobatics. A certain orientalization of fashion also became noticeable; tight-fitting brocade replaced the flowing toga, and most men chose to be bearded rather than clean-shaven. Conventional iconography, symbolic, idealistic and often severe, replaced the freer, cheerful and naturalistic art of former times. Above all, a different, more mystical and much less hedonistic mood came to prevail, especially after the troubles that descended on the Empire following Justinian's death.

Barbarian attacks were a major constituent of the troubles. They were by no means a new phenomenon, of course. The Empire had been assailed by Goths from beyond the Danube as well as Sassanid Persia in the time of Constantine. Later in the fourth century Goths had swarmed over the Balkans and, under their leader Alaric, ravaged their way as far as southern Greece and to the walls of Byzantium itself. The threat had been countered as much by diplomacy as military means. Many of the Goths had been bought off. One group led by a chief called Gainas had even been engaged as an imperial guard, though in 400 he had been slaughtered together with many of his men. Alaric himself had been appointed imperial commander in Illyria, bribed with gold to turn his attentions away from Byzantium. The barbarians swept westwards into Italy. The Vandals sacked Rome in 410. France and Spain were overrun.

Subsequent barbarian attacks had been dealt with in similar fashion. The Huns under Atilla had been calmed by the payment of subsidies and, awed by the impregnability of Byzantium, persuaded to move westwards; Aspar, chief of the Alans, had been co-opted as Gainas had been and suffered the same fate; and in 488 the Ostrogoths under Theodoric had also been deflected westwards. As a result the western half of the Empire collapsed. In this situation Popes had to turn to barbarian chiefs for protection – except when an emperor managed to re-establish a base in Italy, as Justinian did, whereupon Popes generally found it wise to defer to the Emperor's Exarch in Ravenna. However, barbarians not only destroyed the Empire in the West, they severely damaged the Empire in the East as well; and, despite the recovery under Justinian, the barbarian onslaughts continued. The Goths, Alans and Huns were succeeded by Bulgars, Avars and the Slavs.

Why these successive barbarian waves, or tribal migrations, should have occurred and taken the directions they did may still not be perfectly understood, but the outlines, at least, seem to be clear. During the 1930s an American scholar[11] noticed that records of tribal incursions into China were followed at fairly regular intervals of two years or so by reports of trouble on the frontiers of the Roman Empire. The conclusion drawn was that the groups repulsed from China would turn westwards, clash with other tribes and so create a knock-on effect which eventually reached Europe. Furthermore most such groups seem to have been pastoralists whose migrations were set in motion by the need to find sufficient grazing resources for their animals and if necessary to find other means, including plunder, to support the tribe and its associates. The Slavs, however, were different.

They were primitive agriculturalists rather than herdsmen, moved on foot rather than on horses, and lived in rectangular huts sunk into the ground, rather than in round tent-like structures that the pastoralists built for themselves once they settled down. The lifestyle of the Slavs, like their means of livelihood, was different too, and they originated in a different area. The available evidence points to their coming from a zone roughly defined by the middle Dnieper to the east and the upper Vistula to the west;[12] but during the sixth and seventh centuries they moved out in all directions – into what is now Russia proper, into the Balkans, and across the north European plain to the eastern fringes of the Alps, to the River Elbe in what is now Germany, and in places even beyond the Elbe.

Population pressure seems to have been the primary cause of the Slav's expansion; but, unlike most other barbarian groups who moved in large, warlike, parties, the Slavs seem to have extended their areas of settlement gradually, seeping into more and more territory, moving in little groups along the waterways of Eastern Europe, building small, unfortified villages on river banks, and, when need arose, moving into the forests, slashing, burning and growing grain in the resultant clearings. The idea that the Slavs were peaceful, however, is mythical: they wielded a variety of weapons and were adept at ambush and the use of poisoned arrows. But they mingled with, as well as fought, other peoples, and were sometimes dominated by them They constituted a significant portion of the subject population of Atilla the Hun, for example, as they did of the Bulgars.

The Bulgars were Turkic-speaking pastoralists who crossed the lower Danube into Byzantine territory at the end of the fifth century. By the middle of the sixth they had become a menace to Byzantine order in the Balkans and more than once threatened Byzantium itself. To a Byzantine chronicler it seemed that 'these barbarians, having once tasted the wealth of the Romans, never forgot the road that led to it'.[13]

The Bulgars were soon displaced as the major threat by a people called Avars, who had been driven out of Central Asia to the northern Caucasus. In 557 they proposed an alliance with Byzantium. By 570 they dominated central Europe. The fact that a particular tribal grouping occupied an area, of course, does not imply that its former inhabitants had disappeared. In fact the Avars, like the Bulgars, had, as one scholar expresses it, turned from herding animals to herding men.[14] In doing so they had to ensure that their slaves had sufficient to live on. Such may have been the purpose of the Avars in overunning Greece together with the Slavs in the 580s. At least, many Slavs remained after the Avars withdrew.

It should be noted that the dominant group in any tribal mingling did not necessarily impose its language and customs on those they ruled. It was often the conqueror that was absorbed linguistically by the conquered. The language of the Bulgars, for example, became primarily Slavonic rather than Turkic; and the Slavs in Greece adapted themselves not only to mountains and to an economy dominated by the olive and the vine, but to the Greek language and the Christian religion. On the other hand Greek nationalists who to this day insist that the modern Greeks are the genetic descendents of the ancient Greeks, uncontaminated by Slav blood, conveniently overlook the predominance of Slavonic place names in parts of the Pelepponese.[15]

The spurious association of language, territory and genetic inheritance became a particular curse of the region in the nineteenth century (see Chapter 6), and a study of the early mediaeval period reveals many modern nationalist claims to be romantic invention and embroidery. The nationalities of the modern age were to emerge out of a swirl of dialects and cultures. The ancient Greeks and Romans, like the Thracians and Dacians, left their marks. They are to be found, along with the Illyrian legacy, in modern Albanian.[16] At the same time Romanian (for all the work of 'purification' done on it in the nineteenth century) reveals strong traces of Illyrian, Bulgar, and Slavonic as well as Latin.[17] And Dacians, Romans, Gepids, Goths, Bulgars, and Slavs, among others, contributed to the genetic inheritance of the Romanians, as they did in varying proportions to those of other modern nations of the Balkans.

At the same time languages, like peoples, changed and even disappeared. The Russian Primary Chronicle,[18] composed centuries later, was essentially correct in stating that Slavonic was a single language, and that Slavonic and Russian were the same; and this was certainly no less true in the time of the great migrations than it was around 1100 when the Chronicle was composed. In the course of time, however, contacts with different peoples and adaptations to different ways of life in different geographical environments promoted linguistic changes. The West Slavs, including proto-Czechs and proto-Poles, were gradually to draw apart from the East Slavs; and the south Slavs from the others. The arrival in the later ninth century of the Hungarians, who spoke a quite different language, was to accelerate the process because they interposed themselves as a linguistic barrier between the South Slavs and the rest. However, even before this the Slavs did not constitute a homogenous mass geographically. Other linguistic groups, Lithuanians, Prussians and proto-Romanians, constituted barriers of sorts as did the topography of the region: the mountains, the marshlands and the forests.

Later still, differentiations were to occur within each major grouping of Slavs so that Ukrainian, under Polish and Romanian influences, drew apart from Russian, and Serbian from Slovene. At the same time the Slavs in Greece were not the only ones to be assimilated, and no doubt distinctive Slavonic dialects, if not languages, disappeared along with them. It was the extinction in the mid-eighteenth century of Polabian, which had been spoken in an area west of the River Elbe in Germany, and the decline of the Sorbian-speaking communities on the banks of the River Spree that was to move Herder so deeply. But for all the differences between them the Slavonic languages which survived remained closely related. Even today Russians do not find great difficulty in understanding Bulgarians or Slovaks, and there are Macedonians and Croats who will admit that speaking to each other is akin to using a different dialect rather than a different language. In the seventh century, as indeed in the ninth, we may be certain that all Slavs could understand each other.

* * *

Damaging though the Slavs and Avars were, by the early 600s the Byzantine Empire was confronted by an additional menace. In 622 Muhammed made his famous journey from Medina to Mecca and soon the Arabs were on the march, inspired by the new force of Islam. In 638 they captured Jerusalem, in 647 Alexandria. Byzantium lost some of its most populous provinces in the Middle East, including all the wealth of

Egypt. Pressed in and threatened now from all directions, the Empire adapted itself to meet the crisis. The adaptation involved the settlement on deserted land of both tribal invaders and the people they uprooted; and a simplification of the governmental system, devolving much authority to the provincial *theme,* headed by a governor-general (*strategos*) who combined both civil and military powers. How novel the system was and the precise workings of the agrarian system remain matters of dispute, however.[19]

The strategic crisis had been accompanied by a spiritual one, reflected not only in the banning of pagan ritual in 692 but in the continuing theological wranglings over the true nature of Christ already referred to. The loss of so much territory in the East, where, as the mighty surge of support for the new religion of Islam suggests, people inclined towards a more rigid form of monotheism than in the West, might have been expected to have reduced the tensions. In fact it intensified them. Only the focus of disagreement changed. It now centred upon religious images, icons.

Icons had been popular since the fourth century, and from the onset of the crisis in the late sixth century their devotees (iconodules) became ever more numerous and intense. At the same time there was a rising tide of opposition to them. Iconoclasts considered icons to be idolatrous and the very cause of all the Empire's troubles. There had been an icon-breaking riot as early as 641, and in 726 under the Emperor Leo III (the Isaurian) the iconodules, having first been encouraged to speak out, were condemned and purged, and icon-worship banned. The victory proved only temporary, however. John of Damascus constructed a theological defence of icons which gained increasing influence, and the Popes also emerged as doughty iconodules.[20]

The Pope's openness on the subject was related to another sharp change in the strategic position: in 751 the Lombards captured Ravenna. This eliminated the Byzantine military presence in Italy again, although Venice was to remain a Byzantine satellite. No longer was there an imperial Exarch to confirm or deny the election of new Popes, and the present incumbent was freed from imperial pressure. But he was also forced to seek a temporal ally to compensate for the loss of Byzantine protection, and found one in King Pepin of the Franks who ruled the territories that later became West Germany and France, and was a power in Italy. Byzantium had lost Italy before, and she was to reestablish a presence there again. Nevertheless this turn was to prove decisive. Popes now became temporal rulers of what came to be known as the Papal States, an arrogation of sovereignty they attempted to legitimize by means of the 'Donation of Constantine'. Furthermore, until this point about half the Popes had been Greeks or Syrians. Henceforth the papacy was to be a preserve of Westerners.

Under the Emperor Leo IV and his widow Irene, the line on icons was reversed, and in 787 at the seventh Ecumenical Council of the Church (to the consternation of many monks and soldiers) iconoclasm was finally condemned, although the veneration of icons was not to be formally condoned until 853 (an occasion still commemorated in the Festival of Orthodoxy). The Council of 787, however, proved to be the last of an undivided Church. And on Christmas Day in the year 800 at Aachen the Pope crowned Charlemagne, the Frankish ruler, Emperor. For the Byzantines, who believed in one unitary Empire as in a single unitary Church, this smacked of usurpation. A few years later, however, in return for territorial concessions in the northern Adriatic, the Byzantine government was persuaded to grant Charlemagne an imperial title, though not that of Emperor of the Romans. For all its vicissitudes it would not surrender its claim to world supremacy.

This was a reflection of what has been termed Byzantium's 'egocentric phantasy', the notion that, although the Empire had shrunk to a fraction of its former size, it was still the universal Empire, if only in potential, that it remained the centre of the world.[21] There was a rational basis for this ideological illusion. Territory, after all, had been lost and regained before. Byzantium was still a governmental and cultural centre superior to any other within its ken; so was its technology. Its craftsmen could produce the most ingenious devices and inventions: the Emperor had a throne set between metal lions which rolled their eyes and roared at the touch of hidden levers; the organ was a Byzantine invention; so was the deadly secret weapon 'Greek Fire', which helped keep its enemies at bay. And the Byzantine state was still by far the strongest economic power in Europe. Eventually it was to be overtaken, of course, but at the dawn of the ninth century the East was still palpably superior to the West.

Its sense of superiority was enshrined in innumerable ceremonies which claimed to replicate the heavenly order on earth.[22] There were magnificently choreographed occasions that assailed all the senses, processions that took hours to move a hundred yards, forests of guardsmen, rich-robed courtiers, clouds of incense, choirs, as it seemed, of angels, and in their midst an impassive, serene emperor, imitating the heavenly emperor.[23] Such ceremonies purporting to represent a sublime totality awed many a Byzantine subject and many a barbarian envoy.

In the West, however, there was no totality. Church and state might cooperate as the Frankish emperor and the Pope had done, but they remained distinct. As we have seen, the Pope had himself become a secular ruler and, unlike the other patriarchs, he was not governable by any other head of state. On the other hand, he was in no position to exercise full ecclesiastical control over all the states that were emerging in the West. Hence, the German churches were to be almost totally dependent on the secular powers. So no fewer than three modes of Christianity, Greek, Latin and German came to compete for the souls of Eastern Europe's barbarians.

Both Germans and Byzantines came to regard the Christianization of pagans through their churches as a means of furthering their interests; and the papacy, too, recognized the value of building a religious sphere of influence. For their part, the barbarians came to see considerable advantages in embracing Christianity, particularly for purposes of state-building. Not only did Christianization open the road to a higher culture, it presented itself as an antidote to tribal, and hence divisive, paganism.[24] Furthermore, the swearing of oaths was becoming a feature of inter-state relations, and since Christian potentates were disinclined to trust the undertakings of pagans, conversion opened the door to recognition of one's sovereignty. Eastern Europe's religious colouring was to depend in large measure on the relative proximity of the various barbarian groups to the three sources of Christianization; and those within range could play one missionizing centre off against another to their own advantage. But the conversion of Eastern Europe's pagans, like the emergence of states from congeries of tribes with which conversion was associated, is a convoluted story of human ingenuity, heroism and villainy, and it is full of surprises.

Most of the barbarian pagans spoke Slavonic dialects but Slavs tended to be ruled by herding peoples, including the Bulgars, the Croats,[25] and above all the Avars who commanded a large part of East-Central Europe centred in what was later to become Hungary. In the 620s, however, while Bulgars and Croats successfully challenged Avar dominance in the Balkans, the West Slavs under a leader called Samo also rebelled against them and succeeded in creating a political entity of their own. It did not survive its ruler Samo, however, and almost two centuries were to pass before Charlemagne's destruction of the Avar state created room for the emergence of a more viable Slav state in East Central Europe.

In 822 the prince of a new Moravia, Mojmir, acknowledged the Frankish Emperor and allowed Frankish missionaries to enter his domains. Moravia expanded quickly into western Slovakia and southwards to embrace the Slavs of the Dinaric Alps and the Croats beyond. By 855 its ruler, now Rastislav, renounced his allegiance to Louis the Frank and defeated him in battle. He then invited the Pope to send a religious mission to Moravia, and, when the Pope demurred, turned to Byzantium. Rastislav's motives seem to have been primarily political.

The Frankish, or German, priests constituted a subversive presence in his territories and he wanted to be rid of them. Furthermore some Byzantine missionaries were already operating in Moravia and a single form of Christianity was preferable to two. An alliance with Byzantium also commended itself as a help against the Bulgars who threatened

Moravia's southern border. But there was another, more compelling, reason. The administration of a state depended on people who could read and write, and the Church had a virtual monopoly of literates. Yet to employ foreigners as administrators who used a language associated with a rival power (as the Bulgars had once employed renegade Greeks) could pose a threat to state security. A solution would be to find missionaries who could speak Slavonic and, if possible, write in Slavonic too.[26]

This need was supplied by two remarkable sons of a Byzantine officer stationed in Thessalonika, a city in which Slavonic as well as Greek was commonly spoken, the scholarly Constantine (later known as Cyril), and his brother, a former official turned monk, Methodius.[27] Both were to be canonized for their work as missionaries, but their diplomatic and educational work was hardly less important. They invented the first Slavonic alphabet, glagolitic,[28] and their pupils developed another, known as Cyrillic, on which modern Russian and most South Slav scripts are based. However, Cyril and Methodius first came to prominence not as missionaries to Moravia but as diplomatists sent to the Khagan of the Khazars; and their story casts light on a complex set of interlocking circumstances at a critical juncture in Eastern European history.

In 860 Byzantium, which had recently sustained a serious defeat at the hands of the Arabs, was raided by a new enemy, the Russians.[29] They were eventually chased away, but the shock apparently led the imperial government to undertake an important strategic review in which the Patriarch of Constantinople, Photius, was particularly influential. The immediate outcome was the dispatch of an embassy to the court of the Russians' powerful neighbours, the Khazars, a Turkic people who dominated the mouth of the Volga and much of southern Russia and the Caucasus. The Khazars and Byzantium had cooperated before against the Arabs. The aim now was to forge a new alliance directed against the Russians. More significant, however, was the decision to try and convert the Russians, and indeed other pagans, to Christianity – for, as Photius realized, if Byzantium were to be the agency of their conversion, Byzantium, through the Patriarch of Constantinople, would control their churches; and through the church Byzantium might influence them politically. Pending the restoration of the universal empire, Photius had envisaged the foundation of a 'Byzantine Commonwealth'.[30]

Cyril and Methodius were chosen as ambassadors to the Khazar Khan partly, perhaps, because they had a knowledge of Hebrew,[31] for the Khazar elite had recently embraced Judaism. The Khazar empire owed its strength to commerce and presumably wanted good relations with Jewish merchants; and Judaism also served to solidify Khazar solidarity against their Christian, Muslim and pagan neighbours. Having succeeded in their diplomatic purpose, though not in converting many

Khazars, Cyril and Methodius returned to Byzantium in 862. Rather than proceeding to convert the Russians (who were to accept a Byzantine bishop in 867) the brothers were despatched to Moravia in answer to Rastislav's request. They soon ran into trouble.

In 864 Louis forced Rastislav to submit to him again; then the German clergy in Moravia denounced the Byzantine mission to the Pope, alleging that the new Slavonic liturgy was uncanonical. When the Pope sent for Cyril and Methodius they felt obliged to obey for he was primate of the Church. On their arrival in Rome in 868, however, they persuaded him to recognize Slavonic as a canonical language. In fact the Pope, Hadrian II, recognized its potential to gain influence in the vast no-man's-land in Eastern Europe just as the Patriarchal Philaret had done. Only he wanted to use it not only against the Franks, who were too independent, but against the Patriarchate of Constantinople which he regarded as insubordinate. The rising tension between these three parties had been exploited only recently by Boris, ruler of the by now largely Slavicized Bulgars.

Bulgar society had reached a stage at which it needed Christianity, both as a unifying force and as an artery supplying the benefits of a higher culture. But to accept Christianity from neighbouring Byzantium might easily bring political domination in its wake. What Boris needed, if not an independent, autocephalous, church, was one that would not be subject to the Patriarch of Constantinople. He therefore approached the Franks. In 864 a Byzantine offensive forced him to submit. The Emperor stood as godfather at Boris's baptism and he accepted a Byzantine mission to organize a Church. As in many other cases an anti-Christian opposition soon surfaced, led by tribal chiefs who rightly perceived the new religion as a threat to their traditional vested interests. Boris suppressed them but he also seized a suitable moment to break with Byzantium, whereupon he promptly approached the Franks again, and made overtures to the Pope.

The Pope's reply, which answered many of Boris's questions concerning proper Christian practice, throws light on Bulgarian mores of the time and suggests that Boris was seeking a smoother transition from paganism to Christianity. It also confirms that he was seeking to escape Byzantine authority, for Boris had prompted the Pope to contradict the Patriarch on several issues, including his claim to have a monopoly of chrism, the substance needed to anoint a Christian sovereign. So three churches competed over the spiritual fate of the first major independent state to emerge in the Balkans, and Boris exploited the differences between them. Not for long, however. Though the Bishop of Passau had responded to Boris's request by sending him a large group of Frankish missionaries in 867, Boris acceded to the Pope's request to send them packing. Yet the Pope did not profit either. In 870 Byzantium offered Boris a large measure of ecclesiastical authority and recognition of many of his territorial claims. He accepted.[32]

Cyril had died in Rome the year before and Methodius had returned to Moravia as Archbishop of Sirmium and Apostolic delegate to the Slavs.[33] But in 870 Rastislav's nephew, Sviatopluk, rebelled against him and handed Methodius over to the Franks. It took the Pope three years to procure his release. Then Sviatopluk threw off Frankish hegemony and Methodius resumed his work in Moravia. But he was always harried by the German priests. When he died in 885 many of his helpers were hounded out and the Pope withdrew approval of Slavonic, perhaps because he had come to view it as more advantageous to the Patriarch than the Papacy. In any case, by the end of the century Moravia was disintegrating and in 906 it fell a prey to a new invasion from the steppes, by the Hungarians.

The Hungarians, previously associated with the Khazars, were another herding people, who came to dominate almost the entire Danube basin enclosed by the Carpathians.[34] Their arrival might not have been so significant had they been absorbed linguistically by the peoples they conquered, as the Avars, Croats and Bulgars had been, rather than imposing their own language upon them; and their language, Magyar, was outlandish. With its affinities to those of the Turks, Finns and some Baltic and Siberian peoples, it had very little in common with the languages which now surrounded it. In fact Magyar served as a linguistic wedge driven into the heart of Slavonic Europe, and speeded the process of linguistic differentiation among the Slavs. Furthermore, the Hungarians had ensconced themselves at the strategic pivot of both the political and the religious struggles.

The Hungarians only delivered the *coup de grace* to the Moravian state which had already begun to disintegrate; and although the appearance of the Hungarians added to the linguistic difficulties of the missionaries, Greeks and Germans were equally affected. However, the arrival of the pagan Hungarians made communications between Constantinople and the disciples of Cyril and Methodius serving as missionaries among the West Slavs much more difficult; and although the Slavonic rite continued to flourish in large parts of emerging Poland and Bohemia into the eleventh century,[35] its influence would probably have been stronger and lasted longer but for the Hungarians.

Disciples of Cyril and Methodius also established an important new centre of Christian learning and missionizing at Ohrid. This was important both in fending off paganism, which had a brief resurgence among the Bulgarians under Boris's son and successor Vladimir, and in introducing peoples farther to the east, notably the Russians (see *infra*) to

Christianity and Slavonic script. But meanwhile the German church was competing hard for the souls of Eastern Europeans.

* * *

It was during the ninth century that the Germans began their drive eastwards, conquering and recolonizing territory beyond the Elbe. The Saxons began the move, but others were soon involved and churchmen often took the lead. During the tenth century Saxon bishops are said to have harangued their flocks, conjuring up visions of a land of plenty to the east, and referring to its inhabitants in terms no less contemptuous than Byzantine missionaries used of the people to whom they ministered:[36]

> The Slavs are abominable but their land is very rich in meat, honey, grain and birds. Its soil is so fertile that no other can compare with it.... Wherefore, most famous Franks, Saxons, Lotharingians [and] men of Flanders, if ye care to move there ye can both save your souls and acquire the best of land to live in.[37]

Christianization generally was associated with economic and social development, progression to a superior culture and a more sophisticated form of government. But like most processes of 'modernization', it involved much violence. 'Good King Wenceslas', Vaclav I, for example, died in 935, not of exposure on a wintry night as the carol has it, nor martyred by pagans, but murdered by his Christian brother Boleslaw I. Wenceslas's pagan mother, Drahomira, Regent of Bohemia during his minority, had murdered his Christian grandmother who had raised him, and the further one penetrates into the circumstances the more political a figure Wenceslas himself appears The feuding had as much to do with political clientage as religion. Drahomira recognized the Saxon ruler, Henry the Fowler, as overlord; her enemies were backed by the Duke of Bavaria, and it was they who overthrew her and brought Wenceslas to power.

Even Wenceslas's pious foundation of a cathedral church had political implications. It was originally dedicated to St Emmeran, Bavaria's patron saint; but Wenceslas changed the dedication to honour St Vitus. This signalled a change of allegiance to the Saxon king. In any case Boleslav, who succeeded to the throne of Bohemia was not quite the villain that chroniclers chose to represent for propaganda reasons. Boleslav may have disliked German bishops but, so far from being anti-Christian, he applied to the Pope for an independent ecclesiastical organization. Nor, it seems, was the murder itself motivated by religion;[38] and it is ironic that the cult of Wenceslas should have bolstered the Przemyslid dynasty, to which Boleslav also belonged, against the rival Slavniks, whom Boleslav's son Boleslav II was to massacre on St Wenceslas's Day 995.

In due course the cult of St Wenceslas was transmitted to Russia where the story of Christianization was hardly more edifying. The Russians who had raided Byzantium in 860 were the underlings of Viking (or Varangian) trader-venturers who, under their legendary leader Riurik, had penetrated the lands of the East Slavs, and established their base at Novgorod. They had since used the river system to penetrate almost the entire country, leeching up furs, honey, slaves and other marketable commodities, and in the process being linguistically absorbed by the Russians they had come to dominate. They pursued an intermittent war with both Byzantium and its Khazar allies. However by around 930 they had occupied Kiev and, having taken the strategic commercial points they wanted, their wars seemed to be conducted for the purpose of gaining favourable trading privileges rather than territory and plunder. Indeed, as early as 911 they obtained privileged terms for trading in Constantinople for a while.

By this time Slavonic missionaries had penetrated Russia and made some converts, though its rulers continued to cling to their pagan ways until the mid-950s. It was then that the ruling princess, Olga, who is credited with creating a rudimentary administrative and tax collecting system for her domains, accepted baptism and visited Byzantium. The Russians also had trading contacts with Central Europe, and when the time came to set up a state church it was to the Germans that she turned. In 959 she asked the German Emperor Otto I to send a mission headed by a metropolitan bishop. However, when it arrived in 961 the mood changed, apparently because Otto had sent her an ordinary bishop who would be responsible to a superior in Germany. The deal was evidently no better than that on offer from Byzantium. There was a sudden resurgance of enthusiasm for paganism among the Russian elite.[39]

In the middle of the tenth century, under a prince called Sviatoslav, the Russians at last subdued the Khazars and proceeded to establish a commercial base near the mouth of the Danube, where, as he is supposed to have said,

> All the good things converge: gold, precious silks, fruit and wine from Byzantium; silver and horses from Bohemia and Hungary; furs, wax, slaves and honey from Russia.[40]

This imperialistic venture ended with Sviatoslav's death in battle against the Pechenegs (or Patzinaks) in 972, and it was his son, Vladimir, who was eventually responsible for bringing the nascent Russian state into the Christendom. Vladimir was subsequently canonized, but a less likely candidate for sainthood is difficult to imagine.

Vladimir was a pagan who probably presided over ceremonies involving human sacrifices to Perun, the Slavic god of thunder (equivalent to the Vikings' Thor). He is said to have kept over a thousand concubines, though they probably constituted his storehouse of marketable slaves. Even so, Vladimir must have seen some advantage in embracing a higher form of religion. According to the Primary Chronicle he sent out emissaries to the Volga Bulgars who were Muslims, and to both the Greek and German Christians to find out which might be best. The decision was evidently taken on aesthetic grounds.

> There is no joy among the Bulgars [the emissaries reported] but only sorrow and a dreadful stench. Their religion is no good. Then we went to the Germans and saw them celebrating many services in their churches, but we saw no beauty there. Then we went to Byzantium and they took us to the place where they worship.... And we did not know whether we were in heaven or on earth: for on earth there is no such vision or beauty, and we do not know how to describe it; we only know that God dwells there among men.[41]

The source may be accurate in conveying the powerful effect of the liturgy especially as performed in Constantinople, but we may be certain that other factors were involved. In the same year as the conversion, 988, the Russians helped the Emperor Basil II to suppress a rebellion raised by Bardas Phocas, and Basil offered his sister to Vladimir in marriage. She was the first Byzantine princess born in the purple (that is, in the special purple-decorated room of the palace reserved for imperial deliveries) ever to marry a foreigner. So Vladimir was baptized Vasily, the Russian form of Basil, after his godfather, the Emperor; and the idols on the hills of Kiev were duly pulled down. The Russian Church may have been autonomous;[42] but from then on, as we know, Russian history was to be shot through with Byzantine influence.

While the Byzantine church was consolidating its influence among the East and South Slavs, the German church was extending its influence eastwards. A missionary archdiocese had been created at Salzburg as early as 805 and it soon set up advance posts, under suffragan bishops, at Passau and Regensburg. It was priests from these centres who were responsible for the conversion of the Slovenes and some Czechs, but Regensburg also had commercial connections with places farther east and trade routes constituted covenient avenues for missionaries too. Meanwhile the Slavs of central Germany were being subdued.

This process was delayed, however, by the advent of the Hungarians with whom many of them allied themselves. Together they were able to take the initiative; but in 928 a German army crossed the Elbe and conquered a Slavonic tribe known as Hevelians. Very soon the Veletians of the lower Elbe were also forced to submit, as were the Obodrites who lived in what is now Mecklenburg and Schleswig, and the Sorbs of the upper Elbe. Then Slavonic Brandenburg was conquered, and the Emperor Otto consolidated the gains by organizing frontier marches which would also serve as bases from which to launch further offensives to the east.

But, as subsequent uprisings were to show, there was still fight left in many of these Slavs, and conversion was seen as a useful aid in bringing them to heel. Such were the circumstances that led to the establishment of another missionary archdiocese at Magdeburg in 968. Its founder, the Emperor Otto I, who had defeated the Hungarians in 955, envisaged it ministering not only to the Slavs between the Rivers Elbe and Oder but also to the emergent Polish state farther to the east, whose Duke, Mieszko I, had become a Christian in 966.[43] At this point, when the configuration in East-Central Europe north of Hungary had the potential for several different outcomes, a figure emerges to prominence, whose extraordinary qualities and no less extraordinary career were to help fashion the outcome. His name was Adalbert.

He belonged to the ducal Slavnik family of eastern Bohemia, and was educated in Magdeburg under the supervision of its archbishop, who had led the abortive mission to Russia of 961. So Adalbert became familiar with Latin, German and Slavonic. In 983 when he was aged about twenty-six he was invested as Bishop of Prague. Twice, for political reasons, he abandoned his see, going to Italy where he took the vows of a monk in 990. But he remained a bishop in the missionary wing of the German church, and in his subsequent career he exemplified a combination of qualities and functions that seem so much more surprising to the modern than the mediaeval eye, for Adalbert was not only an ascetic, an administrator and diplomatist, but a minister to savages and a friend of rulers. He organized missions in Poland and Hungary, was an intimate of the Emperor Otto III, a friend of Boleslaw the Brave of Poland, and is supposed to have confirmed, if not baptized, Hungary's first Christian King, St Stephen.

In 997, while on a mission to the Baltic Prussians, Adalbert was killed by those he sought to convert. His death made a great impression. The Polish ruler Boleslaw placed a golden cross above his grave at Gniezno, canonization followed, and the tomb became a magnet for pilgrims, including the Emperor who visited it in the year 1000. But there was competition for the saint's remains. In 1038 an invading Czech army exhumed his remains and bore them away triumphantly to Prague.[44] The story symbolized the failure of the West Slavs to combine into a great state. This may have seemed possible in 965 when Mieszko married a

Przemyslid princess from Bohemia; and the fact that their peoples spoke such similar languages would have facilitated their union. But much stronger magnetic forces repelled them.

German influences had entrenched themselves much more deeply in Bohemia than in Poland which was still buffered by the pagan Slavs of what was later to become East Germany. Besides, the Polish leadership was reluctant to accept conversion from the German church which was controlled by the German emperor. This explains the decision by Mieszko, shortly before his death in 992, to place Poland under the protection of the Pope – a political step devoid of the spiritual content with which it was subsequently invested, for its purpose was to obtain sanction for an ecclesiastical organization, headed by its own archbishop, which would be independent of the German hierarchy and hence beyond the control of German secular rulers. In fact the Polish church was to prove the country's chief binding force when, within a few decades, the state broke up into a collection of independent duchies. Adalbert, however, no doubt thought in terms of making East-Central Europe a spiritual rather than a political community; and he certainly contributed towards it. Both as man and saint Adalbert symbolized the eventual victory of the Western church in East-Central Europe.

* * *

In the year 1000, however, the church was still whole. A break between Constantinople and Rome, Greek and Latin, East and West, was looming, but was by no means certain. Hostility to the Slavonic liturgy had not yet developed in Bohemia or Poland; Saint Stephen of Hungary could accept baptism from Passau and recognize the spiritual jurisdiction of Rome, and yet at the same time endow a church in Byzantium and make Greek-speaking Byzantine subjects welcome at his court. And though Andrew, Stephen's nephew, was baptized in Kiev, married a Russian princess and founded a Greek-rite monastery at Tihany on Lake Balaton, his obedience to Rome does not seem to have been questioned.[45] Even so, tensions involving both political and theological differences had been growing between the Eastern and Western Churches; and the mid-ninth century saw a dramatic flaring of hostility between them.

Originally the differences centred on two personalities, the Patriarch Photius, an able layman who, for reasons of state had been ordained and rapidly promoted Patriarch of Constantinople, and Pope Nicholas I who challenged the election. However, the personalities involved in the 'Photian Schism' were less important than the issue of religious supremacy, and a demarcation dispute over whether Rome or Constantinople should have spiritual authority over Syria and Bulgaria, a struggle won, as we have seen, by Constantinople. A theological difference also surfaced and assumed increasing importance with the passage of time. This was the notion, emanating from the West, that the Holy Spirit proceeded from the Son as well as from the Father. The idea, encapsuled in the single Latin word *filioque*, was at variance (at least in the Byzantine view) with the creed established by the second ecumenical Council of 381. Another Church Council called in 867 declared the Pope excommunicate but shortly afterwards a palace coup removed the Emperor and Photius was dethroned.[46]

Within a few years Photius became Patriarch again and this time Rome raised no objections. Yet the controversy had not been stilled. A new emperor, Leo the Wise, dismissed Photius again and installed his own brother as Patriarch; and when the German rulers gained control of the papacy secular interests as well as religious issues became involved on both sides. By 968, when Liutprand, Bishop of Cremona and envoy of Otto I, arrived in Byzantium to propose a dynastic marriage between Otto's son and a Byzantine princess, the stage was set for an unpleasant confrontation.

The Emperor was displeased by the proposal that he should cede his territories in Italy as a dowry, and outraged that the Pope should commend Otto to him as 'Emperor of the Romans', rather than a German king.[47] Liutprand's mendacious claim that emperor (*basileos*) and king (*rex*) meant the same only added fuel to the flames. In his celebrated account of his embassy[48] Liutprand characterized the Greeks as liars. Furthermore they were greedy and effeminate, what with their long hair and flowing robes. Their wine was resinated, their food smothered in evil-smelling garlic and fish sauces; and their emperor resembled a monstrous dwarf. This vituperation reflects a man resentful of his treatment and the failure of his mission, but it also suggests that the longstanding Byzantine disdain for the barbarian West was now fully reciprocated.

Nevertheless in the making of policy interest tends to override sentiment, and as late as the early eleventh century a final breach was far from certain. Relations between the Eastern and Western Emperors had even improved somewhat; a continuing Byzantine presence in southern Italy inclined the Popes to moderation; and for a moment in 1024 it seemed as if both sides might agree to recognize the other as supreme, as 'universal in its sphere'. The arrival of the Normans in Italy and the growth of a reform movement in the Latin Church changed all that.

One factor in the break that followed was the combination of tactlessness and poor timing on the part of the Patriarch Cerularius of Constantinople, who insisted that Latin churches in his sphere follow the Orthodox rites, and who made sure that Rome was informed of his unflattering views of the Western form of communion. The other was the arrogance of the Pope Leo IX's emissary to Constantinople, Cardinal Humbert. The new, reformist, line which he represented was unwelcome in that it envisaged a more powerful, independent papacy, but Humbert's manner was offensive too. The stage was set for an undignified scene at St Sophia in 1054 when the Patriarch's men tried to prevent delivery of the notorious bull of excommunication from a Pope who, it transpired, was already dead.

Whether or not the excommunication was valid the church was now irreparably divided over matters of practice. How far, from the Orthodox viewpoint, the Latins had strayed is suggested by Cerullarius's letter of the same year to the Patriarch of Antioch. Aside from their liturgical deviations, he wrote,

> They eat suffocated animals, shave themselves, celebrate Saturdays [and] eat abominable meats.... They do not observe the first week of Lent nor the Week of Abstinence.... Furthermore, they demand that priests remain celibate.... Their bishops wear rings ... as if they had taken churches to wife ... [and] will go to war and stain their hands with bloo ...[49]

The Great Schism both symbolized and confirmed significant differences between the Eastern and Western Mediterranean regions in the spheres of religion, culture, and, to an extent, institutions. It also had a considerable, negative, influence on the subsequent development of Eastern Europe by driving further wedges between the eastern and the western Slavs, and between the Croats and the Serbs. These wedges were not only religious but cultural in nature, for Orthodoxy and Catholicism were associated with different alphabets and, to an increasing extent as time went by, with different literatures. These factors were conducive to incomprehension and the generation of hatred. Yet the Great Schism was by no means the only source of future difference.

From the time of Charlemagne the new 'Holy Roman Empire' had not only understood itself to constitute 'the West' (*Occidens*) but had arrogated the term 'Europe' to itself. Both the Byzantine Empire and the 'barbarians' beyond the Elbe were excluded from it. In time a more generous definition was given to this European 'West', by including areas farther East, 'from the Elbe to the curve of the Carpathians, from the Baltic to the Adriatic'.[50]

They did not, however, exceed the limits of German colonization and Catholic conversion. The exclusion of the Slavs from Charlemagne's 'Europe' was not merely an expression of prejudice, however. It took implicit account of the fact that the great migrations ceased in the West significantly earlier than they did in Eastern Europe, and that the West enjoyed a start of at least two centuries over the East (Byzantium excepted) in establishing settled society and building viable states. A range of institutional differences flowed from this.

As we have seen, emergent states in Eastern Europe adopted Western as well as Byzantine institutional models, yet in the course of transfer these institutions changed their nature. Thus while some feudal characteristics may be found in mediaeval Eastern Europe one searches in vain among the indigenous peoples there for signs of lateral as well as vertical social ties of obligation, or for any sense of corporate responsibility.[51] A distinguished economic historian was therefore right to remark that

> The divergence between East and West was rooted in the origin of the eastern European states. From their beginnings the princely states of Eastern Europe differed from their Western prototypes.[52]

But if the primary differences were political and cultural, economic differences mattered too. According to the same author, until about 1100, the Baltic areas of Eastern Europe, though linked to Scandinavia, were 'well outside the scope of Western commerce'.[53] Furthermore population densities were lower and the pulses of trade beat slower in Eastern than in Western Europe. It has been estimated that until 1100 Westerners outnumbered the inhabitants of both Central and Eastern Europe by well over two to one; and outside Byzantine territory the region was characterized by an overwhelmingly subsistence economy, that is, one in which the often isolated family household supplied all, or virtually all, of its needs and consumed all, or virtually all of, what it produced.

Coin hoards suggest that the use of money was uncommon, and though furs often served as a currency, and livestock was exported to the West, both towns and markets, like states, tended to be slow to develop and thin on the ground. A division of labour was slow to develop too; and when the pace did begin to quicken in Bohemia, Poland, and Hungary, as it did in the eleventh century, it was often the state that took the initiative in planning the town, promoting the market, and even organizing the division of labour.[54] Thus, circumstances induced even those parts of the region most inclined towards the West to adopt regulatory measures from the very beginning.

The economy of the Byzantine Empire was much more highly developed. Even after its zenith in the ninth century it built ships, produced a wide variety of leather goods and textiles, manufactured soap, candles, and glass, and was noted in particular for its luxury goods, including silks and perfume. The industrial sector constituted a fairly thin layer of icing on a thick agrarian cake, of course. Nevertheless by the standards of the age this was an advanced economy. It was also highly regulated by the government. The state had a monopoly of the profitable silk industry and of mining; owned factories making equipment for the army; controlled the grain trade in order to ensure that bread was available at affordable prices in the cities, and even the guilds. In the judgement of a leading authority,

> the principle object of the guild system was not to serve the interests of the producers and dealers, but ... to facilitate control of economic life by the government in the interests of the state and the consumer.[55]

In governing the trade unions, as in commanding the economy, the Soviet state was by no means original.

It should be added that, although detailed information on the subject is sparse, the churches, both Catholic and Orthodox, played important economic roles in all parts of Eastern Europe; and the monasteries in particular. Some were, or were soon to become, considerable property owners, dominating the economy in particular localities; some, especially of the larger monasteries, also practised a division of labour. Furthermore they engaged in commerce, primitive industry, renting and even usury.

One further matter needs to be addressed, however, briefly, on account of its great importance to the region's economic development: its geography. During the early middle ages Eastern Europe enjoyed certain advantages from its seas and rivers. Until the great Arab advance the Mediterranean was virtually a Byzantine lake. Afterwards the route through the Adriatic was of great importance, costly though it was at times to keep it safe. The Black Sea, also for some time a Byzantine lake, afforded useful access to a route from the Orient, though others also profited from it, sometimes at Byzantium's expense. The Russians enjoyed the advantages of a complex river system which, with the use of portages, linked the Baltic and the Arctic north with the Black Sea and the Caspian. However, it was the Vikings who seem to have taught the Russians its value and given them political coherence.

As we have seen, the Russians also came to appreciate the value of the Danube delta as a commercial centre. On the other hand north-eastern Europe was less well favoured than the south-east in terms of economically valuable communications; and even the great River Danube was not the great commercial asset that the Rhine had become for the West by the later eleventh century. Unlike the Rhine, the Danube was regarded as a frontier to be defended rather than as a potentially profitable commercial route. This was largely due to the continuing migrations of often aggressive peoples westwards and southwards across the Danube; and subsequently to the instability of the political structures that arose beside its banks, and to the comparatively low level of their economic performance.

Parts of Eastern Europe's flatlands had great agricultural potential: the Russian 'Black Earth' belt, Wallachia and the great Hungarian Plain, especially. However, when the tribes were on the move these flatlands tended to be unsafe. Hence, outside the more northerly parts of the region, most of it covered by dense forest, people tended to gather in the mountains, chiefly the Carpathians and the Balkans, whenever danger threatened, leaving the plains to the herdsmen, who were often slow to adapt to their new environment, and to the peoples they enslaved and protected. This may help to explain why animal husbandry played so important an economic role in the plains of the Balkans as well as the highlands. This was not necessarily an uneconomic use of resources given the population levels, though whereas in Western Europe population pressure was arguably to stimulate better farming methods, in Eastern Europe agriculture was long to remain primitive.

It cannot be claimed that Eastern Europe was under-endowed with mineral resources, quite apart from the rich deposits of such under-appreciated substances as oil and coal. Hungary and Bohemia especially were comparatively rich in the silver that was to help them to prosperity in the later Middle Ages. The Baltic countries had valuable amber to exploit; the forests teemed with game and fur-bearing animals, the more open country with aurochs and wild horses, and the rivers were full of fish. Indeed, the early medieval period presents the sharpest of contrasts to the Communist economic system both in its ecological purity and the slackness, if not torpor, of its economic tempo. And these conditions, which in many areas, were to persist virtually unchanged for centuries, may also have left a distinctive imprint on Eastern Europeans.

* * *

Just before the First World War a German scholar wrote the following about the Russians:

> Their character has been influenced not only by a long history of subjugation ... but also by the gloomy forests, the unresponsive soil, and the rigorous climate, and especially by the enforced inactivity of the long winters. In disposition they are melancholy and reserved, clinging obstinately to their traditions....They are easily disciplined ... but have little power of independent thinking or initiation. The normal Great Russian is thus the mainstay of political and economic inertia and reaction. Even the educated Russian gives comparatively little response to the actual demands of life; he is more or less the victim of fancy and temperament, which sometimes lead him to a despondent slackness, sometimes to emotional outbursts. Here we have the explanation of the want of organization, the disorder, and the waste of time which strike the western visitor to Russia.[56]

By no means all of Eastern Europe was covered by dense and gloomy forests of course, and these days it is unfashionable to talk in terms of 'national character' – understandably so in view of what stereotyping can lead to. Yet it is widely accepted that over a period of time human beings may be conditioned, both genetically and behaviourally, by their environments. We need not accept the once popular understanding that Russians love to be beaten, the self-imagery of Hungarians or the national mythery of Serbs and Greeks to recognize that circumstances, as well as genetic inheritance, help to mould people; and that if there is such a thing as national character it is the product of many factors: of geography and environment, of circumstances that have been moulded over time and, not least perhaps, of the aggregate of historical experience.

To accept this, however, is also to accept that common characteristics may define regions as well as nations; and that their history has a strong bearing on their development. But we have yet to review the findings of this enquiry and to reach such conclusions as we may about the fate of Eastern Europe.

REFERENCES

1. See A.H.M. Jones, *The Later Roman Empire*, 2 vols (Oxford, 1964); G. Ostrogorsky, *History of the Byzantine State* (Oxford, 1980); also S. Runciman, *Byzantine Civilization* (London, 1961). A useful introduction is P. Whitting, (ed.) *Byzantium* (Oxford, 1981).
2. On Pliska, R. Browning, *Byzantium & Bulgaria* (London, 1975); on the relevance of the Sarkel digs, A. Bartha, *Hungarian Society in the 9th and 10th Centuries* (Budapest, 1975) pp. 12–15 and n. 50, p. 33.
3. See M. Gimbutas, *The Slavs* (London, 1971) especially pp. 80–97 and 109–30.
4. M.W. Thompson, *Novgorod the Great: Excavations at the Medieval City* (New York, 1967); A. Mongait, *Archaeology in the USSR* (Gloucester, Massachusetts, 1970).
5. E.g., Bartha, *op. cit.*, pp. 49–54; and *infra*, n. 14.
6. See R.W. Southern, *Western Society and the Church in the Middle Ages* (Harmondsworth, 1972) pp. 91–3.
7. F. Dvornik, 'Constantinople and Rome' in J. Hussey (ed.), *The Cambridge Medieval History* [hereafter *CME*], vol. V, pt. 1 (Cambridge, 1975), pp. 437–8.
8. Ostrogorsky, *op. cit.*, pp. 127–8.
9. A. Kazhdan, *People and Power in Byzantium* (Dumbarton Oaks, Washington, DC, 1982) pp. 34–6.
10. A. Kazhdan and A. Epstein, *Change in Byzantine Culture in the Eleventh and Twelfth Centuries* (Berkeley, California, 1990) pp. 6 and 79. Realism was revived to an extent in the later middle ages, however.
11. F. Teggart, *Rome and China: a study of Correlations in Historical Events* (Berkeley, California, 1939).

12. For convenient account of Slav pre-history, see Gimbutas, *op. cit.* See also P. Dolukhanov, *The Early Slavs* (London, 1996), esp. Chapter 8.
13. Procopius, *Secret History*, trans. R. Attwater (Ann Arbor, Mich., 1961), pp. 40–1.
14. Browning, *op. cit.*, p. 126.
15. The notion of the genetic 'purity' of the Greeks was first challenged by J. Fallmerayer who went too far in the other direction. See A. Bon, *Le Pelepponese byzantin jusqu'en 1204* (Paris, 1951) and J. Fine, *The Early Medieval Balkans* (Ann Arbor, Michigan, 1983) pp. 59–64.
16. See A. Buda *et al.*, *Problems of the Formation of the Albanian People, Their Language and Culture* (Tirane, 1984).
17. T. Gartner, *Darstellung der Rumanischer Sprache* (Halle, 1904) pp. 121–35.
18. S. Cross, *The Russian Primary Chronicle* (Cambridge, Massachusetts, 1953).
19. G. Ostrogorsky's views on the *theme* (*The Cambridge Economic History of Europe* [hereafter *CEHE*], vol. I, Cambridge 1966, pp. 207ff.) have been challenged, see P. Lemerle, *The Agrarian History of Byzantium* (Galway, 1979) pp. 58–65.
20. See the treatments in the works mentioned in note 1 *supra*; also R. Jenkins, *Byzantium: the Imperial Centuries 610–1071* (London, 1966) pp. 74–89.
21. For an early formulation of the notion, see Cosmas Indicopleustes, *The Christian Topography*, trans. J. McGrinde (London, 1897).
22. See Constantine VII 'Porphyrogenitus', *Le Livre des Cérémonies*, ed. A. Vogt, Paris 1935, 1939–40.
23. One speculates that this importance attached to appearance may have been related to the practice of mutilating rivals to the throne (particularly relatives) since, if an emperor, as the mirror of heavenly authority, had to be unblemished, mutilation would disqualify him from the throne – though this evidently did not apply in the case of the 'noseless Emperor' Justinian II (685–95 and 705–711). An emperor's deportment and demeanour were certainly important. Perhaps this led to elite insistence on proper bearing and manners.
24. See A. Vlasto, *The Entry of the Slavs into Christendom* (Cambridge, 1970); D. Obolensky, *The Byzantine Commonwealth* (New York, 1971); also Browning, *op. cit.* and *infra*.
25. The origin of the Croats is a subject of contention, but they seem to have been a people of mixed, predominately Iranian-Alan origin: S. Guldescu, *History of Medieval Croatia* (The Hague, 1964) pp. 40ff.
26. Such is the inference to be drawn from Hadrian II's letter of 868–9 to Rastislav and others, approving the use of Slavonic as a fourth liturgical language after Greek, Latin and Hebrew. See F. Dvornik, *Byzantine Missions among the Slavs* (New Brunswick, New Jersey, 1970) pp. 102–3.
27. *Ibid.*, pp. 53ff..
28. On Glagolitic, see *inter alia*, L. Leger in *Grand Larousse*, vol. 18, pp. 1057–9. Glagolitic was to remain popular in Dalmatia for many centuries though elsewhere it was superseded by Cyrillic or, in the case of the West Slavs, Latin script.
29. On the background and the circumstances of the attack, see G. Vernadsky, *Ancient Russia* (New Haven, Connecticut, 1944).
30. The expression was coined by D. Obolensky, *op. cit.*
31. Cyril is said to have learned Hebrew for the mission, but the brothers may already have had some acquaintance of it, coming, as they did, from Thessalonika which had a large Jewish community. In any case Hebrew was a canonical language.

32. Among many accounts see that of Browning, *op. cit.*, who pays attention to the specific problems of state-formation.
33. Dvornik, *Byzantine Missions, op. cit.*, pp. 230ff.
34. See I. Fodor, *In Search of a New Homeland: the Prehistory of the Hungarian People and the Conquest* (Budapest, 1982).
35. Dvornik, *Byzantine Missions, op. cit.*, pp. 194–229.
36. E.g. Theophlact of Ohrid, see D. Obolensky, *Six Byzantine Portraits* (Oxford, 1988) pp. 58–61.
37. Reference mislaid.
38. F. Dvornik, *The Making of Central and Eastern Europe* (London, 1949) pp. 25–30 and *passim*.
39. G. Vernadsky, *Kievan Russia* (New Haven, Connecticut, 1948) pp. 28–46.
40. Cross, *op. cit.*, p. 86.
41. *Ibid.*, p. 111.
42. Vernadsky, *Kievan, op. cit.*, pp. 56–70.
43. On the Polish Church prior to 1000 see H. Lowmianski, 'Baptism and the Early Church Organization' in J. Kloczowski, *The Christian Community of Medieval Poland* (Wroclaw, 1981) pp. 27–56.
44. Dvornik, *Making, op. cit.*, pp. 95–135 *passim*.
45. See Z. Kosztolnyik, *Five Eleventh Century Hungarian Kings* (Boulder, Colorado, 1981) pp. 74–8.
46. For the details see H. Gregoire in *CME*, vol. V, pt. 1, pp. 112–14 and *passim*; and Jenkins, *op. cit.*, pp. 168ff.
47. Dvornik in *CME, loc. cit.*, pp. 457–8; Jenkins, *op. cit.*, pp. 287–8.
48. 'Liutprandi legatio ad imperatorem' in A. Bauer *et al.* (eds.), *Quellen zur Geschichte der Sächsischen Kaiserzeit* (Darmstadt, 1977) pp. 524–89; see also Southern, *op. cit.*, pp. 68–72.
49. Cerularius's epistle to Peter of Antioch, translation adapted from Kazhdan and Epstein, *op. cit.*, Appendix, Ex. 48, p. 260.
50. J. Szucs, 'The Three Historical Regions of Europe', *Acta Historica Academiae Scientiarum Hungaricae*, 29 (2–4) (Budapest, 1983) pp. 132–3.
51. Even the celebrated Russian *mir*, or village assembly, did not arise spontaneously, but in response to the state requiring communal responsibility for taxation – see R.E.F. Smith, *Peasant Farming in Russia* (Cambridge, 1977).
52. M. Postan in J. Barraclough (ed.), *Eastern and Western Europe in the Middle Ages* (London, 1970) p. 170.
53. M. Postan in *CEHE*, vol. II: *Trade and Industry in the Middle Ages* (Cambridge, 1987) p. 228.
54. See A. Gieysztor, 'Trade and Industry in Eastern Europe before 1200', *CEHE*, vol. II, *op. cit.*, pp. 474–524, especially pp. 474, 505 and 511.
55. Ostrogorsky, *op. cit.*, p. 254.
56. Baedeker, *Russia* (Leipzig, 1914) p. xlii.

Conclusion

At the beginning of this book we noted a series of traits which distinguish the countries and peoples of Eastern Europe from those of the West. They included economic backwardness, bureaucratic rigidity, and a range of popular attitudes, among them a disinclination to compromise and tendencies to both utopianism and romantic excess. These qualities contributed to the revolutions of the later 1980s. They also contributed in some measure to the difficulties in adjusting to democratic pluralism and a market economy.

In its earlier stages at least the transition was a painful one, even for the East Germans who had the good fortune to be incorporated into one of the richest economies in the world; and the prospects for the others were not bright.[1] The sudden burgeoning of freedom was accompanied by varying but rising degrees of privation and, especially in the Soviet Union itself, by massive dislocations. In the euphoria of liberation people had thought of what they would gain, rather than of what they might lose. Most had come to take full employment and subsidized housing, food and transportation for granted. As these were cut and people had to learn to fend for themselves, most, especially the older and the less well-educated, found the adjustment difficult.

Many blamed their unhappy situation on their former leaders, and there were understandably strident calls for public vengeance. The new Czech, Hungarian and Polish regimes avoided this pressure, and the former chief of East Germany, Erich Honecker, was placed in protective custody, then spirited away to the Soviet Union. However, his Bulgarian counterpart, Todor Zhivkov, was put on trial, and Nicolae Ceaucescu unceremoniously executed. Even President Gorbachev himself, once regarded by most former dissidents as the genial spirit behind radical reform, was increasingly reviled. Yet most experts in both East and West attributed the difficulties which accompanied liberalization to the legacy of Communism rather than to individuals.

To a large extent they were right. In the economic sphere the old regime had encouraged laziness and inefficiency, rigidity and waste. It had raised expectations beyond its ability to meet them, created confusion as to values, and all but eliminated skills essential to the successful operation of a market economy. As we saw in Chapters 1 and 2 the command economy proved insufficiently supple to cope with the increasingly diversified demands of a new generation. On another level Communist bureaucratism had tended to peripheralize initiative, so that much of it gravitated to the black economy and illegal political activity. Yet, as we noted in Chapters 1 and 2, some of the factors which made the post-revolutionary adjustments so difficult had also contributed to the collapse of the old regime.

It might be argued that after Stalin's death the Communist leaders had themselves undermined the foundations of the system. After 1953, and especially from the mid-1960s, most states of Eastern Europe had become less autarchic and ever more involved with the world economy. In this view the collapse of the later 1980s is attributable to a flirtation with the capitalist West. Nemesis for this sin against the Communist canon came in the form of increased vulnerability to world market forces which eventually led to economic collapse. The regimes had fallen victim to a proverbial 'crisis of capitalism' which began with the oil price revolution of 1973 and deepened thereafter.

This is by no means a sufficient explanation, however. It was the system's inability to provide all that was required quickly and efficiently enough that had encouraged the development of economic relationships with the West in the first place. The attempt to rejuvenate the system and to promote healthy economic development within the Bloc as a whole failed to improve matters sufficiently, partly because of COMECON's clumsy pricing mechanisms (Chapter 2). And little Albania, which had maintained its autarchy much longer than the others, nevertheless found itself in a parlous economic state by the mid-1980s.[2] Yet the economic failure was associated with failures in the social and educational spheres, and all were rooted in a flawed philosophy.

The Communist regimes of Eastern Europe succeeded to a great extent in satisfying the aspirations of those who had experienced World War Two and remembered the hard times that had preceded it. They also raised the expectations of the rising generations. But despite their control of education and propaganda, they found themselves unable to direct their aspirations. In short, they were unable to forecast future demand accurately, still less satisfy it. Yet at the same time they behaved as if the future was foreseeable. Thus, for example, they tended to train the young in narrow, often obsolescent, skills which were expected to serve for a lifetime, rather than encouraging suppleness of mind and adaptability. Similarly their Communist creed encouraged managers to be complacent and workers to think they had a natural right to the basic material comforts of life.

Above all, perhaps, their credo of 'historical inevitability' ran counter to two of history's fundamental lessons: firstly, that, although a knowledge of the past is essential to understand the present and to assess future prospects, not everything is foreseeable. Secondly, that the past not only informs the present, it constrains the possibilities of successful change. So, in their ruthless pursuit of the millennium, the Communists forgot that the young might take what they were given for granted and develop an appetite, not only for more, but for something different; that the inexorable forces of circumstances may thwart the cleverest of schemes, that people tire of idealism, that different generations envisage different utopias. Not until it was too late did Communist leaders appear to have realized that, for all its sophistication and flexibility, Marxism was insufficiently catholic, fundamentally no less reductionist than most other 'isms'.

Yet in the aftermath of World War Two Communism had been much more popular in the region than is commonly admitted. Its doctrinal certainty, its promise to refashion society in favour of the common man, its collectivism, its stress on huge projects, its idealism, even the discipline which the Party represented, were all highly appealing. Nor should the clouds of dust arising from its collapse be allowed to obscure the old regime's achievements any more than its evils and its failures; for the Communist order did succeed in overcoming some serious longstanding problems.

The greater part of the population has been urbanized; and, except in Poland where, as a result of the failure to collectivize agriculture, there are still far too many smallholdings, Eastern Europe's perennial peasant problem has substantially disappeared. Communism proved incapable of sustaining economic development and achieving quality as well as quantity of production, but it industrialized economies which had been overwhelmingly agrarian. It monopolized political life but ensured that everyone was provided with the necessities of life. It exercised an ideological discipline and censorship which were often rigorous and stifling, yet maintained enviably high standards in the performing arts and several branches of learning. It claimed many victims but succeeded for a time in quietening nationalist passions and in maintaining a peaceful order in what had been a notoriously unstable region. In the medium term, at least, most Eastern Europeans who survived World War Two seem to have benefited.

In the longer term, of course, Communism failed. Despite all the efforts to make them prosperous the nations of Eastern Europe remain the poor relations of the Western world. Yet though the old regime proved incapable of solving many of the region's structural problems it had not created them. The region may be desperately short of capital and entrepreneurial skills, but so it was when the Communists took power. Indeed, the very backwardness of most of these countries can be regarded as predisposing them to Stalinist methods of industrial generation (see Chapters 3 and 4). If the majority of its population seems to lack any strong sense of personal autonomy, they did in the pre-Communist era too. The bureaucratism with which Communism was rightly associated appears, in historical perspective, to be no more than a reinforcement of pre-existing trends (see Chapters 4 and 5). Such facts suggest the Communist period may have been less of an aberration from the previous course of the past than is commonly assumed.

A better appreciation of the past also suggests that those who rejoiced in the 'collapse of Communism' and the impending 'triumph of capitalism' in Eastern Europe may have been as incautious in their unbridled optimism as the builders of the old regime had been themselves. After 1989 Eastern Europe faced large-scale unemployment, declining living standards, rising nationalism and political instability – as it had done between the wars (see Chapter 4). It is often said that, had it not been for Stalin's intervention, some, at least, of the countries of the region would have avoided their present predicament. In particular it is argued that if only the Iron Curtain had descended along Hungary's eastern rather than her western frontier in 1945, for example, she would, in time and with help, have become part of the West. Yet the fact that even Hungary had not followed an exclusively 'Western' line of development before the Communists took over casts doubts on the proposition.[3] At the same time, the experience of Greece (Chapter 3) did not suggest that the 'capitalist' way would be an inevitable success in the rest of Eastern Europe.

Since then ancient patterns have been re-emerging, suggesting that the Communist period was but another disappointing interlude in a long, sad history. The economic migrations of Eastern Europeans to the West and in particular of Poles into Germany, Jews to Israel or America and Albanians into Italy, that gained momentum after 1988, for example, replicated long-standing patterns only temporarily interrupted in the mid-twentieth century. The change of policy in regard to travel and migration was widely welcomed, but a high proportion of those leaving consisted of the young, the skilled and the professionally qualified. So the migrations, prompted by poverty, threatened to impoverish the region even farther by depleting the region's store of talent. However, as governments in Eastern Europe allowed greater freedom of migration, most Western countries hastened to erect barriers to keep the migrants out.[4] This, too, replicated a pattern of the past. So had Western governments' exploitation of political émigrés and political opposition movements in order to embarrass or undermine Eastern European regimes.

Napoleon encouraged thousands of Polish émigrés to sacrifice their lives in the interests of France by holding out a prospect of a restored Polish Republic which proved to be a phantom. Britain, France and the United States supported Lajos Kossuth as a means of undermining Austria; and Gladstone fulminated against the Turks on account of the Bulgarian atrocities, ignoring the no less horrible atrocities committed by Bulgarians against Turks (see Chapter 5). In 1918 the Western Powers succeeded in demolishing Austria-Hungary. Yet, as we have seen (Chapter 4) they neglected to secure the new order – with disastrous results. Recent events suggest similar tendencies. For decades the West berated the Soviet bloc for denying political freedom to its subject population. Yet, when those liberties were gained, the West failed to provide the swift assistance necessary to guarantee them – for if freedom and a democratic polity require (among all else) a minimal level of prosperity to endure, most of these countries seemed too poor to sustain it.[5]

For decades the West also gave Eastern Europeans the impression that it was morally superior to Communist regimes – but, again, it was not to live up to its rhetoric. In 1990 the US interfered (unsuccessfully) in Bulgaria's democratic process, evidently because she had suspended payments on her foreign debt,[6] yet in 1991 she was prepared to forgive Poland her foreign debt, even though President Walesa had declared his readiness to use his powers undemocratically. No doubt such inconsistency reflected the pursuit of legitimate national interests, but it also encouraged the values of the free world to be viewed as cynically as the discarded values of the old regime had been.

Cynicism, so often a product of disappointed hopes, was also a common attitude before the Communist era, for Eastern Europe was a region where hopes tended to run unreasonably high. The deep impression the Romantic movement made there (see Chapter 6), as well as the decline of religion, had much to do with this. Ever since, young intellectuals especially have tended to act out Romantic attitudes more intensely than any other Europeans except, perhaps, for the Irish and the Basques. The Romantic legacy includes a preference for grandiose and dramatic political conceptions, the passionate espousal of unrealistic aims, the cult of the righteous victim, even forms of dissent that 'border on insanity'.[7] Such attitudes may have been intensified in response to the hard-line the Communist regime took against its critics. On the other hand, many leading dissenters had once been ardent Communists who shared the millenarian dream and acquired the cynicism of disappointment; and right-wing extremists of the 1930s and 1940s, including intellectuals of the calibre of Mircea Eliade, also reflected something of the spirit of Romanticism. Such tendencies were not confined to Romanians and Russians. They were shared by Czechs and Hungarians. As a former Czech dissident has observed, Marxism (like fascism) was very appealing for 'impatient intellectuals of the impoverished East'.[8]

Communism's messianic promise of a materialistic heaven upon earth may have appealed to the masses, but its attraction for intellectuals lay rather in its potential to improve mankind, as some sort of latter-day 'Enlightened Despotism' (see Chapter 6). There were even dissidents, George Konrad among them, who came to believe that, in its later, more benevolent, guise, Communism might be the best that could be hoped for. Then, suddenly, in 1989, the prospect appeared of something infinitely better: liberty and a fast road to affluence. This delightful vision was soon overshadowed, however, by the spectre of nationalism. Some observers imagined that this bitter product of the Romantic movement, so long confined, would soon be disposed of.[9] It was not. On the contrary, with its convenient way of attributing misfortune to traitors, minorities and neighbours, rather than to nature, ill-fortune and human folly, it gained in popularity. So did populism. A degree of religious bigotry also re-emerged and in some areas local patriotism burgeoned; but above all it was the old nationalism that triumphed, and with it a series of musty but comforting historical myths which sustained collective pride, and suppressed unpalatable truths about the past.

Thus, most Czechs find difficulty in believing that neither the Hussite masters of Prague University nor the Taborites were Czech nationalists;[10] most Poles still reject the notion that it was its own citizens as much as predatory neighbours who undermined the Polish Republic; just as most Hungarians refuse to believe that it was the intransigence of their nobility as much as Habsburg and Turkish domination that hindered their country's development (see Chapters 7 and 8). Both Poland (Chapter 4) and Hungary (Chapter 5) treated their minorities as badly as they themselves were treated when ruled by others; and although most of Russia was overrun by the Mongols in the thirteenth century (see Chapter 10) it was not reducible to 'Western Asia' as Joseph Brodsky once pretended. Indeed for a significant period Russian development was in some respects closer to that of the West than most of the states in between (see Chapter 7); and, as we have noted (Chapters 9, 10 and 11), the considerable influence of the Byzantine legacy on the Orthodox regions of Europe hardly justifies their being classified as oriental.

Nor will Czeslaw Milosz's conclusion, that East-Central Europe was Western in culture but Easternized by force,[11] stand scrutiny. As we have seen (Chapters 8 and 9) the long-term influences of the Renaissance upon the region was slight and the Reformation had little lasting impact upon it either. The Western impression was largely the result of immigration – the direct and indirect influence of Germans, Italians and other foreigners.

Eastern Europe's cultural affinities to the West had at least as much to do with class as nationality, however. By the later eighteenth century Russian aristocrats seemed perfectly at ease in English high society; by the later nineteenth century members of the Romanian elite seemed quite at home in Parisian salons. Neither were obviously less Westernized than their Czech or Hungarian counterparts. But aristocracies and intelligentsias tend to be cosmopolitan. It is in considering people of lower social status, the bulk of the population, that cultural differences between Eastern and Western Europe, in the sense of manners and taste, become obvious. Yet on this level, too, the distinctions between East-Central Europeans, Russians and the Balkan peoples tend to diminish. The Hungarian, Russian, Polish and Romanian peasantries certainly had more in common with each other than with the sober farming stock of Germany and England; and in time these affinities and differences extended to the cities, affecting behaviour at many levels. The reason was also historical.

As was explained in Chapter 8, the imposition of serfdom established a profound difference between Eastern and Western European society. This difference had important cultural and moral dimensions, affecting not only the serfs, whom it degraded, but their owners, many of whom were corrupted by the almost absolute power they wielded over them. As we have seen (Chapter 5), serfdom lasted very much longer in Eastern Europe than in the West, exerting a profound effect both on popular and elite attitudes down to the present day. The modern tendencies towards a disorderliness tempered by servility, and even anarchy, owes much to the heritage of serfdom. The effect of serf-owning is reflected, arguably, in the ready contempt shown for those who hold a different view, the common failure to comprehend pluralistic structures, and the tendency to confuse self-respect with the domination of others.

Not that such traits are the product of serfdom alone. The late date of urbanization in Eastern Europe and its massive scale (see Chapter 5) delayed the absorption of peasants into city life and even 'peasantized' some cities. Civilization, which originated in the prince's palace, is above all the product of the thriving city. Yet, as has already been suggested, cities in Eastern Europe were fewer and on the whole poorer, and urban culture less well developed than in the West.

The Balkans were spared serfdom, of course, though, since the Ottoman Empire was an alien regime, and latterly inefficient in maintaining order, some of the social and cultural consequences were not dissimilar. Since the Sultans also ruled substantial parts of Asia and Africa they are commonly assumed to have orientalized the Balkans. However, this influence should not be exaggerated. Turkish rule certainly had an orientalizing effect on Balkan culture, just as it had a Westernizing effect on its Asian possessions (though it is impossible to gauge with accuracy the extent to which, say, Turkish-Balkan cuisine derives from the Orient, and how far from the Byzantine court and the Mediterranean environment). Furthermore, the Turks borrowed much from the Byzantine Empire (Chapter 9), and though their culture was Islamic they allowed wide autonomy to the Orthodox and other denominations in legal, administrative and cultural, as well as religious matters.

In political terms the Balkans, like Russia, were distinguished from the Habsburg Empire and its successors in their tradition of political absolutism. However, there is another distinguishing feature, which is commonly overlooked: in the Habsburg Empire, as in most of Western Europe, the aristocracy retained political as well as social importance into modern times. By contrast, in Russia and in the Ottoman Empire in its prime those who wielded power under the Tsar and the Sultan were promoted for their abilities.This aligns the Russians and Turks with the Chinese, but also with modern Britain whose governmental service was reformed into a meritocracy on Chinese lines. Furthermore, the aristocratic heritage of East-Central Europe clashes at least as stridently with 'the Western way' as defined by the American Revolution, as it does with Russian absolutism.

Of the three constituent parts which constitute the East of Europe, East-Central Europe is usually considered closest to the West. This affinity is based largely on the predominance of the Catholic religion and on German influences, both on the arts and institutions. Germans were vital from the mediaeval period onwards (Chapter 9) in founding cities and developing urban culture. Yet the influence of this dynamic force was restricted because it was alien; and, with the possible exception of Bohemia after 1627 (Chapter 8), it was unable to sustain the burgher interest in competition with the nobility. If there is a Western European parallel it is surely to be found in Ireland where cities also tended to be strongholds of alien culture. East-Central Europe has some historical coherence insofar as Austria, Hungary, Poland and Bohemia shared similar forms of lordship, a common symbolism and modes of thought since mediaeval times.[12] Yet, as we noticed earlier (Chapter 10) the nature of lordship in this region virtually precluded the independence of the church. This constituted an important difference from the West. It inhibited the development of independent institutions and made for a different balance of social power.

Much has already been made of the adverse effect of an over-powerful nobility on the development of free institutions. In particular, it led to the primacy of the demesne court in the countryside virtually everywhere outside the Ottoman domains. This was tantamount to the privatization of justice. It can be countered, of course, that the English baronage's victory over King John in 1215 constituted a parallel to what happened subsequently in Poland and (to all intents and purposes) in Hungary. However, Edward III managed to recapture much of the ground the crown had lost with the grant of *Magna Carta*. This had no parallel in Eastern Europe. Furthermore, whereas in England and even Ireland from Elizabethan times onwards, state and city shared a common culture, this was not the case in Poland; and even in countries where it was, the crown showed no consistent respect for the autonomous rights of cities (Chapter 9).

Free institutions, personal autonomy and the other elements on which we are assured the Western way of life is founded, are based above all on law and, not least, on legal rights to property. Yet, as was noted in Chapter 10, under Slavonic customary law inheritance was partible and there was no primogeniture. These arrangements were conducive to the maintenance of peace within the family, the village and the clan, but their effectiveness was predicated on a low population and relatively plentiful resources, conditions that were not to last. In the longer term the consequences of these customary understandings were profound and largely adverse; and they took political and cultural, as well as economic, forms.

In the later nineteenth and early twentieth century, in conditions of a demographic explosion, the practice of dividing landholdings among one's offspring resulted in land-hunger and a peasant crisis. At the same time the repartitional commune which prevailed in Russia and some other areas deprived peasants of the incentive to care better for their allotments, which might be reallocated to someone else, and to invest in them. It might be objected that the equal division of land among one's sons *(gavelkind)* was also practised in parts of England, and that it was the custom in Ireland to divide a dead man's property among all the members of his clan. However, in the West such practices were peripheral. In Eastern Europe they were central; and their persistence seems to have promoted a certain clannishness and to have helped entrench a spirit of collectivism at the expense of individualism.

The absence of primogeniture was also conducive to the proliferation of princely titles and, more seriously, to the fragmentation of states and prevalent political uncertainty. Attempts made to counter it were sometimes as dangerous as the disease itself. The Ottoman Turks killed the sibling brothers of a newly-installed Sultan as a precaution against civil war; and in mediaeval Russia the complicated practice by which members of the House of Riurik would come to rule progressively more important cities according to their seniority eventually broke down and, with it, the unity of the state. The tendency of mediaeval Poland to fragment into independent duchies is also attributable, in part, to the lack of primogeniture, as is the instability of early Bulgaria, Serbia and Hungary.

Most German states were similarly disadvantaged, although after 1648 primogeniture became the norm there too; and the Princes of Muscovy also succeeded in breaking convention to introduce a preordained succession (See Chapter 9). This step facilitated the eventual emergence of Russia as a European power. Even so, customary understandings continued to act as a serious long-term obstacle to Russian absolutism. As with the Irish, Slavic custom held that a monarch was not bound by laws enacted by his predecessors. This accounts in part for the tedious repetition of old laws. It also contributed to a general uncertainty about personal rights, including rights to property, and a distrust of the courts which (with the possible exception of the Austrian half of the Austro-Hungarian Empire) prevailed throughout Eastern Europe before the Communist era. This pervasive confusion about the law and distrust of legal process has been conducive both to a sense of insecurity, lack of personal autonomy, and the paucity of free institutions. In these circumstances (as in the 'Wild West' or Hobbes's 'State of Nature') only the strong were autonomous. Furthermore, the influence of ancient customs may help to account for the still pervasive belief in equal shares, which seems to constitute almost as serious a mental obstruction to 'modernization' today as it did before 1914.

Such regional trends and tendencies have coexisted, of course, with others specific to individual areas and nationalities. The distinctive Romanian psyche, for example, is in part a product of the uneasy coexistence between a predominately peasant culture, Turkish influences and an elite drawn to the West; between Eastern Orthodox religion and a language with affinities to French (Chapter 6). For their part the Czechs reflect some ambivalence between Slavonic and German culture, and the burdensome legacy of a past riven by profitless religious quarrels and successive conquests by foreign powers. A case can also be made for the distinctiveness of East Germany with its strong military and musical traditions. It had not, after all, been included in Charlemagne's Empire (Chapter 11); its inheritance was much influenced by clashes and intermingling with Slavs; and, though it provided the political impetus for the first unification of Germany under Bismarck, it had not contained the industrial core which constituted the dynamo of modern Germany.

It can also be argued that in certain periods and in certain limited respects Bohemia and Austria as well as East Germany failed to share in the East European experience. It is progressively more difficult to argue such a case in respect of Slovenia, Croatia, Hungary and all the others. That said, Eastern Europe is not homogenous and never was. Even its geographical monotony, the rolling plains, sometimes taking the form of steppe, sometimes of forests, sometimes of marsh, is interrupted not only by rivers but by the Carpathians, the Eastern Alps and the Bohemian and Balkan highlands. Nevertheless Eastern Europe is an entity, albeit rather a loose one, on account of the powerful Slavic and Byzantine influences upon it, its distinctive social structures, and because of its consistent lateness of development, politically and culturally as well as economically. However, this distinction of 'backwardness' acquires definition only in comparison with the West, and it is at this point that the most substantial problem presents itself, for the West is not homogenous either.

At the time of the Revolution of 1989 there was much talk of Eastern Europe at last embracing the ways of Western democracy and the associated free-market economy through which the West had prospered. Yet there are profound differences between the American, British, French and Italian constitutions. All are democracies but in different ways. Governmental functions are much more centralized in France and Britain than in the United States and Canada. The legal systems and institutional traditions of Britain, Canada and the United States are by no means similar to those of the other Western states, and the 'lobby' representing well-financed, powerful interests has far more influence on the political process in America than in the other democracies. Furthermore, despite the variety of the Western democratic way, none of its forms have proved easy to transplant successfully to other regions of the world.

Similar problems attend the question of the market economy. Some countries of the free West have been very successful economically, though not, for example, those of Central and South America; and Japan with its strong, unashamedly oriental traditions has been more successful than any country in the Western hemisphere. Furthermore, albeit to varying extents and often indirectly, all Western governments interfere in the economy and try to influence the market. Before 1980 Britain's economy included a large state sector and its government spent a major proportion of national income on welfare, yet Britain was considered an integral part of 'the Western world' for all that.

Of course, even pre-Thatcherite Britain was very different from the Soviet system in its prime, in which virtually all economic activity was directed by the state. Nevertheless large-scale governmental involvement in the economy was never confined to 'oriental empires' (the merchant venturer companies of England were guided by the Elizabethan state); the lack of governmental interference (as in the case of early modern Poland) was never a guarantee of economic prosperity; and the economic order associated with the rise of the West dates back only two or three centuries. Economists are still unable to fathom the causes of dramatic fluctuations in the world economy, and there is no particular reason to believe that the Western form of economic order, and the dynamism associated with it, will endure.

Finally it should be recognized that the origins of what is regarded as 'the Western way' are still imperfectly understood. Attempts have been made to explain precisely why the West became prosperous,[13] but they have failed to demonstrate why some Western countries have prospered so much more than others and why economic success is not confined to countries with long traditions of free institutions. It may transpire, after all, that it is not 'the East' but 'the West' which constitutes the aberration; that for all their idiosyncrasies Russia and the other countries of Eastern Europe are rather more 'normal' than we are used to thinking, and that it is those few countries to the West, which embraced democracy comparatively recently and had the good fortune to grow wealthy, which are the oddities.

REFERENCES

1. OECD Report, February 1990.
2. See Ramiz Alia's speeches to the 11th Plenum of the Central Committee of the PLA, 6 and 7 July 1990, Tirana 1990.

3. Jeno Szucs follows Iṣtvan Bibo in identifying 1945 as a point at which Hungary might successfully have joined the West. Yet he also adduces evidence which casts doubt on the proposition: J. Szucs, 'The Three Historical Regions of Europe', *Acta Historica Academiae Scientiarum Hungaricae*, 29 (2–4) 1983 [1984], pp. 131–84.
4. For fears of the consequences of Polish and Czech immigration into German areas in the later nineteenth century, see Z. Zeman, *Pursued by a Bear* (London, 1989) pp. 17–18. By 1991 as many as 2 million Soviet migrants to the west were expected; between January and June 1990, 45,000 Bulgarians who had received higher education failed to return home from visits to the West: *The Financial Times*, 12 February 1991.
5. Barrington Moore's general thesis (*Social Origins of Dictatorship and Democracy* [Harmondsworth, 1969]) seems to have been vindicated even in the case of India, about which he was doubtful.
6. Reported by M. Glenny, *The Rebirth of History* (London, 1990), especially pp. 175–7.
7. V. Havel, *The Power of the Powerless* (London, 1985), p. 192.
8. M. Haraszti, *The Velvet Prison* (London, 1989), pp. 16–17.
9. T. Garton Ash, *The Uses of Adversity* (Cambridge, 1989), p. 288.
10. F. Seibt, *Hussitenstudien* (Munich, 1987), p. 93.
11. Cz. Milosz, 'Central European Attitudes' in *Cross-Currents* (Ann Arbor, Michigan, 1986) pp. 101–8.
12. K. Heilig cited by Seibt, *op. cit.*, p. 148.
13. See, for example, N. Rosenberg and L. Birdzell. *How the West Grew Rich* (London, 1986).

Index